The Lion Led the Way

To Warren & Candace & family,

Thanks so much for your hospitality and your open hearts! Always remember that the Messiah, Jesus, is the real "STAR" of Bethlehem. Keep following the Morning STAR!

Dwight Hutch[illegible]

The Lion Led the Way

Dwight Hutchison

Wise men came from the east saying,
"Where is he who has been born
King of the Jews?"

The Lion Led the Way

ISBN-13: 978-0-9911283-0-3

ISBN-10: 0991128303

LCCN: 2013920854

Published by the author in Somerset, Kentucky, USA.

Book Website:
www.tzedek.info
Email:
contact@tzedek.info
Give feedback concerning the book at:
comments@tzedek.info

Cover and layout by: Victor Henri

The cover image in lower left hand corner shows part of the Cyrus Cylinder containing cuneiform text. Photograph by Mike Peel (www.mikepeel.net).
Permission: Creative Commons CC-BY-SA-2.5
http://commons.wikimedia.org/wiki/File:Cyrus_Cylinder_1.jpg

The Hebrew text on the cover is from Leviticus 23, which describes certain festivals and appointed times established by the God of Israel. The cover image of the zodiac is not intended as an endorsement of either ancient or modern astrology.

Printed in the USA

Table of Contents

Preface

I am greatly indebted to many people who have done studies concerning the wise men and the star of Bethlehem. Many of them have poured hundreds if not thousands of hours into their research. Numerous books, articles, PowerPoint presentations and videos have helped me gain insight into the subject. Many men and women have demonstrated their zeal for God through their public speaking, books, articles and films concerning the Magi and the famous star. Others, unbelieving or unconvinced, have tended to be skeptical, and I have profited equally from their criticisms. The entire subject is fairly complex. There are many aspects of the story which need to be clarified. Some ideas need to be rejected, but other traditions hold keys to bring us greater understanding. I hope that my contribution may be helpful to the larger discussion.

A Little Background:

I have been interested in astronomy since my youth. I am thankful that my parents bought me a telescope toward my 15th year. One of my high school teachers also encouraged me to attend a summer program in astronomy at Berea College in 1976. That month-long course opened up new horizons to me. I will never forget the remarkable meteor which left a glowing trail as it streaked across the western sky on the first evening of observation. That memory stayed with me as my interest in astronomy continued in a quiet way through my university experience and into my working life.

In 2006, during a trip to Cameroon, I saw a television program which described and illustrated certain heavenly events in 7 BC. According to one theory those events could possibly have been associated with the wise men and the famous star. I was intrigued. Researching the subject further, I was not totally satisfied with my results. In 2008, while I was in the Netherlands for a small conference, I stumbled across a National Geographic article about Herod the Great. That same weekend there was a significant conjunction of two planets. Then unexpectedly, at the home of some Dutch friends, I saw the very interesting film called *The Nativity*, which portrays the events surrounding the birth of Jesus while emphasizing Mary and Joseph's unique experience. While I would question many aspects of the film today, I appreciate how it portrayed the difficulties of Mary and Joseph. The explanation it offers concerning the star is probably not tenable.

Returning home after the conference, I decided to do some more research about the birth of Jesus and the famous star. Almost immediately I found a variety of websites, which gave me some new perspectives. Rick Larson's relatively new site and DVD at www.bethlehemstar.net caught my attention. I found many things which intrigued me, but all my questions were not answered. Several authors and teachers had important and helpful insights, but they seemed to stay within a Western perspective. The Magi were from the regions to the east of Judea. To understand them, one needs to know more about the Babylonians, Medes, Persians, Seleucids and Parthians. Each of these peoples had established successive empires in Mesopotamia and Iran. A purely Western perspective and world view lacks many of the ingredients necessary to develop a realistic scenario concerning the star and the wise men.

In January of 2012, I discovered the Hebrew names for several stars and planets, which are perhaps well known to every Hebrew speaking Jewish child, but they were unknown to me. The traditional Hebrew names made a huge difference in my approach to the star of Bethlehem. It became evident that a Jewish perspective was also needed to understand the Magi and the famous star. When Jesus was born, there were hundreds of thousands of Jews living in Mesopotamia and ancient Iran. Their presence in the east has been one of the most seriously neglected keys to understanding the Magi.

Over time I saw, like others before me, that several heavenly events may have been associated with the birth of Jesus. A certain "star" was involved from almost the beginning, and that same star later came to a halt over Bethlehem. The "star" was part of a much larger celestial drama, involving the sun, moon, the planets and several other stars. It became evident that a Jewish perspective on the heavens, united with the Jewish calendar and Jewish ideas concerning the Messiah, all held keys to understanding both the men and the events.

The Good News of the coming of God's Messiah was written in the stars in the years 7 BC through 1 BC. The message is still clear. My general purpose in writing this book is to encourage the worship of the Almighty whose glory is revealed in the heavens. He has "installed His King upon Zion, His holy mountain" (Psalm 1:6). The Messiah's throne shall endure forever as the sun before the God of Abraham, Isaac and Jacob. "It shall be established forever like the moon, And the witness in the sky is faithful." (Psalm 89:36-37)

Dwight Hutchison
Saint Paul-Trois-Châteaux, France
November 2013

Give thanks to the LORD,
for He is good
for His lovingkindness
is everlasting.

To Him who made the
heavens with skill,
for His lovingkindness
is everlasting ...

To Him who made
the great lights,
for His lovingkindness
is everlasting.

The sun to rule by day,
for His lovingkindness
is everlasting,

The moon and stars
to rule by night,
for His lovingkindness
is everlasting.

(Psalm 136:1 and 5-9)

Thanks

I greatly appreciate the significant contributions of several friends who continue to correct and critique my texts. Few people can succeed without the help of friends. Having counsel and encouragement in difficult circumstances greatly lessens one's struggle.

I was involved in several other activities before launching into this research project concerning the Magi and the famous star. Several people graciously released me from my responsibilities to follow my passion and to complete my personal project. I can only say thank you.

Special thanks: I also want to thank the teams of individuals who have produced several high quality astronomy programs: Stellarium, SkySafari and Voyager. Without their passion for astronomy and their attention to detail, a large part of my personal research would have been impossible. The Voyager software was invaluable for establishing the possible dates of the Jewish months, festivals and appointed times. I have used illustrations from the Stellarium application extensively throughout this book, and I am very grateful for the opportunity to use these illustrations. The Calsky site and Alcyone software helped me to verify empirically many celestial events.

www.stellarium.org
www.carinasoft.com
www.southernstars.com
www.calsky.com
www.alcyone.de

Dedication:
For My Beloved Friends
and Family

who have encouraged me to serve
the risen Messiah over the last five decades.

Part 1: Introduction

In the beginning God created the heavens and the earth.... God said, "Let there be lights in the expanse of the heavens to separate the day from the night, and let them be for signs and for seasons and for days and years; and let them be for lights in the expanse of the heavens to give light on the earth, and it was so."

(Genesis 1:14-15)

September 12th

Borsippa, Mesopotamia - Before Dawn at the Nabu Temple Ziggurat

3 BC

The following account is fictional. It depicts, however, events that may have happened in a somewhat similar manner. The astronomical events described in this text actually did happen exactly as described.[1] *(See the note one for further details about this story).*

Ekur-zakir crossed the courtyard on his way to the sanctuary on top of the ziggurat.[2] The event in the heavens was obvious even from the courtyard; the conjunction in the constellation of the lion was taking place as foreseen. Over several days the star, named MUL.BABBAR, had drawn very close to the star LUGAL. In the darkness Ekur-zakir had to be careful, the ziggurat of the main temple complex in the city had fallen into disrepair. After several centuries of relative neglect, even mounting the stairs of the lofty Babylonian pyramid could be dangerous. The deteriorating masonry sometimes cracked under one's feet. Acknowledging the presence of the armed guard at the base of the stairway with a wave of his hand, Ekur-zakir began climbing the stairs toward the top of the ziggurat. A waiting servant helped him by holding a small lamp. Even in the darkness the guards and servants all recognized him as one of the main priests of the god Nabu. Ekur-zakir thought to himself, *It is amazing to see these men awake, they are usually sleeping at this early morning hour despite my comings and goings.*

The sun would soon begin to rise, but at that instant the eastern sky was being dominated by the constellation of the great lion, which was named UR.GU.LA or Aru by the Babylonians, Shir by the Parthians and Persians, Leon by the Greeks and Ari by the Jews. The Jewish name of the constellation came back into Ekur-

Mesopotamia is the land between the two great rivers, the Tigris and the Euphrates. Historically it included lands which were called Assyria and Babylonia. Assyria was located in northern Mesopotamia and Babylonian was in the central and southern regions.

Photo: Some of the partially rebuilt walls of Babylon at a site for tourists in modern Iraq

zakir's thoughts as he stopped briefly on the steps to catch his breath. Looking up again Ekur-zakir saw Ari, the lion, brightly ornamented by the stars MUL.BABBAR and LUGAL.

Climbing the steps again Ekur-zakir thought of the local Jewish community which was very present in Babylonia. The previous evening, across the whole region, the local Jews had sounded their ram's horns following the appearance of the new moon in the west. For the Jews, the beginning of their seventh month was a special holiday, the 1st of Tishrei, the Day of Trumpets, or as they preferred to say "the day of shofars." Several Jewish families had lived in the city of Borsippa in the region of Babylon and the surrounding area for about six centuries. They were well established, a number of families were very prosperous. Thinking of the lion constellation's Jewish name Ekur-zakir also remembered a local Jewish man named Ariel whose name meant, the lion of God. Ariel was a successful farmer with a large date palm plantation on the outskirts of the city. Ekur-zakir appreciated the quality of Ariel's dates and he had instructed his servants to buy dates directly from the plantation. Ariel had come into the city recently on business, by chance they had met in the street. During a few minutes of conversation Ariel had mentioned that his son had left several weeks previously on a pilgrimage to Jerusalem, far to the west, across the Syrian desert. The young man had gone to attend the great fall harvest festival which the Jews called the Feast of Tabernacles. It would begin at the next full moon in 15 days.[4]

Ekur-zakir had seen how many of the Jews were devoted to the God of their fathers, YHWH. Their beliefs were even attractive to some Babylonians.[5] Ekur-zakir's oldest son, Iqisa, had converted to Judaism seven years earlier. Starting in his 25th year the young man had begun to read the Aramaic sections of the books of Daniel and Ezra. His exploration gave him a desire to know more about the God called YHWH. Iqisa eventually asked a few local Jews to teach him the Hebrew language and to give him oral translations of the Torah in Aramaic.[5] As Iqisa continued to study, he discovered the prophets Isaiah, Jeremiah and others. One Jewish man named Zechariah Ben Chokmah had been particularly helpful. His influence had led to Iqisa's conversion. Ekur-zakir was also beginning to entertain serious doubts about the great gods Marduk, Sîn, Ishtar and Nabu. Having recovered from his initial surprise, frustration, irritation and anxiety about his son's conversion, Ekur-zakir wondered if the God known as YHWH might not deserve more of his own attention. Perhaps his son had made a right choice, certainly his behavior and attitudes had improved remarkably.

Ekur-zakir also had plenty of questions. Something profoundly astronomical intensely irritated the aging priest. The god Marduk's star, MUL.BABBAR, and the star of his son Nabu, DUMU.LUGAL, moved in a regular, invariable pattern which the Babylonians had observed, predicted and recorded for hundreds of years. Were the great gods not able to change their path in the sky? Ekur-zakir did not always

MUL.BABBAR and LUGAL together above the Babylonian Ziggurat

MUL is the Sumerian word for any celestial object and especially stars. Planets look like stars to the unaided eye. MUL is written in cuneiform in the manner illustrated below:[6]

like to take the same street to go to the market. Was it impossible for Marduk or Nabu to change their courses? Perhaps the stars were only representative of the gods. But why was there such unending, predictable regularity? In the Jewish texts concerning the original creation of all things, it was mentioned almost in passing that YHWH / Elohim had "made the stars also." It was almost as though the stars of Marduk and Nabu were insignificant for the God of the Jews. Taking a final step onto the second level of the ziggurat, these thoughts bothered the 60 year old priest. Ekur-zakir then turned toward the next flight of stairs.

At first, Iqisa's conversion had been concealed. Then later, when it became known, it was not well accepted by several other priests at the temple. However, in his senior role Ekur-zakir had been able to protect his son's position as an astronomer at the temple ziggurat. Both Ekur-zakir and his son had been able to cite the example of Nebuchadnezzar as a Babylonian who had respected the God of Israel. The ultimate authority, the chief priest, was also not pleased with Iqisa's religious choice, but the young man did excellent work. Knowing that his father could be depended upon to keep Iqisa in line, the chief priest had allowed him to remain in the protected temple complex with his family.

It was evident to all, including the chief priest, that the great god Marduk and his son Nabu, did not have the ascendancy at the moment. Marduk's main temple ziggurat in Babylon had lain largely in ruins for almost 160 years before Alexander had attempted a reconstruction, but his early death had largely stopped the effort. Now three centuries later, much of Marduk's temple complex had been largely leveled; it was being used for garden plots. The conquering peoples -- the Persians, the Greeks and the Parthians -- had maintained some, often limited, financial support for the temple of Nabu in Borsippa and its priesthood. Many astronomers were doing more and more horoscopes in order to supplement their incomes because the official state sponsored astronomy was declining greatly. It was now obvious to all that the Zoroastrians were amassing more and more religious power.

The Zoroastrians were not worshipers of Marduk or Nabu. Their god, Ahura Mazda, apparently appreciated their fascination with the heavens. However, Ahura Mazda had left the Zoroastrians with scant technical knowledge concerning the very stars which they prized so deeply. Zoroastrianism abounded with devotional practices and meditative texts which inspired the Medes, Persians and Parthians. Their religion gave them an interest in the starry heavens. Yet even the origin of their prophet Zoroaster was shrouded in mystery and legend. He was supposedly a great astronomer, but Ekur-zakir had often thought with a bit of irritation that Zoroaster had apparently not succeeded in sharing much of his technical knowledge with his followers. For many generations, Zoroastrian priests with royal support had sought the help of the Babylonians because they needed technical astronomy skills. Every year, several dozen young Zoroastrians were trained at the Borsippa Temple complex and in other astronomical centers in Mesopotamia. Many of them did not enjoy learning to read and write in cuneiform. However, acquiring skills in ancient languages was necessary in order to read the vast libraries of astronomical records spanning hundreds of years.

Ekur-zakir reached the third level of the ziggurat and walked around the side of the tower to the next stairway. There were seven levels to the ziggurat which represented the seven major heavenly bodies: the sun, the moon and the five "wandering stars" that the Greeks called planets. Each level had a separate stairway and on the four upper levels Ekur-zakir took interior stairways covered by vaulted ceilings composed of thousands of mud bricks. Happily, a servant was on each level, helping Ekur-zakir up the stairs.

Reaching the top of the last main flight of stairs, about 60 meters above the courtyard, Ekur-zakir entered the elevated sanctuary. He was very much out of breath and was practically exhausted. The older priest was greeted by one of the four Zoroastrian apprentices on duty that night. Seeing Ekur-zakir's state the young man immediately turned to a side table, poured some water from a pitcher into a small cup and handed it to Ekur-zakir who accepted the precious water gladly. He smiled at the young man who bowed slightly revealing the light of a few dim lamps behind him toward the interior of the high sanctuary. Scrolled documents, wax covered writing boards and cuneiform tablets were lying on several tables. Other documents and tablets were stored in shelves around the walls. Ekur-zakir breathed deeply again and began climbing the last flight of stairs to the roof.

On the flat roof surrounded by a low wall, 230 feet (70 meters) above the courtyard below, a group of ten men looked toward the eastern sky. As Ekur-zakir came out of the stairwell and approached the group in the darkness, they all greeted him respectfully. Then the older priest looked up again toward the heavens himself. The massive lion was still climbing into the sky as a hint of light was beginning to appear in the east. Already for several days, the bright star MUL.BABBAR had been drawing near to LUGAL, the king star, also known as Sharru, in the constellation of the lion. Two of the principal stars in the heavens were meeting together. Every twelve years, the star MUL.BABBAR, meaning the "white star," passed through the constellation of the lion, but it did not always visibly meet the king star. Tonight was different, MUL.BABBAR had moved very close to the king star. Ekur-zakir had seen something similar 24 and 12 years earlier. Ekur-zakir had wondered if there was perhaps another meaning behind those events, because the old omen texts did not satisfy his search for meaning.

Taking his eyes off the conjunction and looking around the group, Ekur-zakir spotted his oldest son, Iqisa, who had also turned toward him, about three meters away. In the dim light, Ekur-zakir could still see the joy on his son's face. Ekur-zakir was certain that they would have a long conversation later in the day. This

MUL.BABBAR in capiltal letters is a modern way of writing one of the names of the star of Marduk. In ancient Sumerian cuneiform script the actual name was written:

The ziggurat at Borsippa had seven levels which represented the sun, moon and the five visible planets. Each level was decorated in various colors. Differing ideas have been proposed concerning the colors and their order. Below is one possibility. The colors are indicated from the top to bottom.

Gold - Sun
Silver - Moon
Light Red - Mercury
Blue - Venus
Dark Red - Mars
Black - Saturn
White - Jupiter

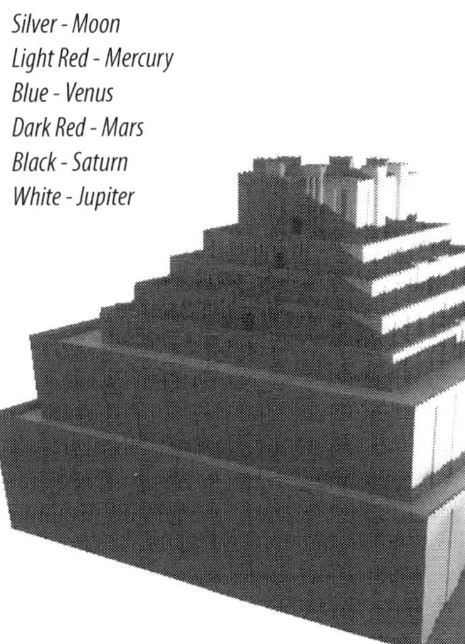

MUL.BABBAR was known by other names as well:

^{MUL}MARDUK (the star of Marduk)
^{MUL}LUGAL (the king star)
$^{MUL\,d}$AMAR.UTU
^{MUL}UD.AL.TAR
$^{d/MUL}$SAG.ME.GAR

In this book Sumerian cuneiform names are written in capitals. Akkadian star names are written in italics. Most people in Mesopotamia actually spoke Aramaic, but the older Sumerian and Akkadian languages were used by professional astronomers.

The name ^{d}ŠUL.PA.E$_3$ above in cuneiform, became an important name for the star of Marduk. It means 'Lord of the Bright Dawn'

was the third time that a conjunction had happened on a significant day in the Jewish calendar in the past six months. Both Passover and Pentecost had been marked by celestial events. LUGAL, the king star, had also been in two other remarkable conjunctions during the summer.

Iqisa was convinced that something important was happening and even to Ekur-zakir it seemed more and more evident. Iqisa had used the Jewish names for the two stars, Melech (king) and Tzedek (righteousness), repeatedly when speaking of LUGAL and MUL.BABBAR in recent days. His son kept talking about an ancient story concerning a legendary righteous king, Melchizedek, who had blessed the Hebrew patriarch, Abraham. It seemed that the celestial events of the past months could be related to the prophesied coming of a descendant of the ancient Jewish king, David, who had reigned over Israel a thousand years previously. Iqisa had cited a text from the prophet Jeremiah several times:

> ***"Behold, the days are coming," declares YHWH, "When I will raise up for David a descendant, a righteous branch. He will reign as king and act wisely and do justice and righteousness in the land. In His days Judah will be saved, And Israel will dwell securely; and this is His name by which He will be called, 'YHWH our righteousness.'"***[7]

Ekur-zakir looked away from the group and back toward the east where the dim red and pale yellow glow of dawn was appearing. The brilliant star of the goddess Ishtar was rising above the horizon. She was usually called ^{MUL}*Dilbat* by the Babylonians. The Greeks associated her with Aphrodite (Venus). In many of the old cuneiform tablets the name ^{d}NIN.AN.NA was used, meaning "divine lady of heaven." Ekur-zakir's son had developed the habit of calling the star by its Jewish name, Nogah, meaning "brightness" or "splendor" and he no longer referred to the star as a goddess. Toward the southeast, the wisps of mist, hugging the ground, were becoming more evident in the growing light. Ariel's date palm plantation was somewhere on the horizon six miles (10 kilometers) away to the southeast. Just outside the city walls to the west, the river Euphrates lay hidden in the mist. A new day was dawning. A few cocks crowed far below in the distance as the stars MUL. BABBAR and LUGAL slowly faded in the growing light.

Ekur-zakir finally suggested to the group that they eat some of the excellent dates waiting in the room below the terrace. He approached his son as they all moved toward the stairs and whispered to him privately, "Perhaps your righteous king is making his appearance. If it is true, it will certainly be confirmed in the coming months. I hope that your ideas are correct, we could certainly use some better government." Iqisa smiled at his father as they reached the steps and the old man smiled back.

After eating in one of the high sanctuary's rooms designated for the astronomical activities, Ekur-zakir sat beside his son's work table while Iqisa spoke to some other men. Glancing at the table Ekur-zakir saw a text written in Aramaic and Hebrew. There was the list of the planets in Hebrew along with several Aramaic phrases and some calculations. Looking closer Ekur-zakir saw a few lines which indicated that the Jewish Feast of Tabernacles in two weeks would begin on the same day as the equinox. The nearly full moon would arise as the sun set at the beginning of the feast on the same day as the solar equinox. The next lines were a passage from the Jewish book of Psalms about David's royal line translated into Aramaic:

> *"His descendants shall endure forever and his throne as the sun before Me. His throne shall be established forever like the moon, and the witness in the sky is faithful."*[8]

Ekur-zakir had never thought of associating the Jewish king with the sun and the moon. According to the calculations and notes before him, on the 22nd of the month Melech, Tzedek and Yareach (the moon) would all be together in the lion constellation on the last day of the Feast of Tabernacles which the Jews called the "Great Day." The older priest shifted in his seat, letting this soak into his heart. The king star, the star of righteousness and the moon were scheduled to be together on the Great Day. Rarely were all of them gathered together on that particular day. Ekur-zakir glanced again at the lines from the Jewish Scriptures and remembered the passage which was often quoted by his son. The sun and the moon were associated with the throne of David and his descendant would be the "Righteous One." The Jewish name Tzedek, --"righteousness"-- seemed important in the story. The Jewish festivals were aligning with events in the heavens which had an apparent messianic emphasis. Such coincidences were remarkable. Astonished and intrigued, Ekur-zakir wondered how long the pattern would continue. He said to himself, *What about the Jewish Day of Atonement coming in 10 days? Had Iqisa also calculated something concerning that? Ekur-zakir's mind started to race, "Would something also happen at Hanukkah and Purim?*

The Traditional Hebrew Names of the Planets:

כוכב חמה
Kochav Chammah
Meaning: sun star

נוגה
Nogah
Meaning: brightness

מאדים
Ma'adim
Meaning: red one / blushing one

צדק
Tzedek
Meaning: righteousness

שבתאי
Shabbatai
Meaning: rest / sabbatical

(The planets will be identified later).

Originally a Magus was a member of a hereditary priestly class among the ancient Medes and Persians. The word Magi is the plural form of the word Magus.

Trying to Understand the Star and the Magi

People have marveled for centuries concerning the visit of the wise men and the unique star which supposedly announced the birth of the Messiah. Old traditions persist concerning three kingly wise men. In France and Quebec a special cake called the "galette des rois" (king's cake) is prepared in January recalling the visit of the wise men to Bethlehem. Christmas cards often show the wise men following a star on their journey to see the King of kings. Films have been produced which also feature the wise men in serious and sometimes comic roles. Below is part of the biblical text concerning their visit (the complete text is in Matthew 2:1-22).

> *Now after Jesus was born in Bethlehem of Judea in the days of Herod the king, magi from the east arrived in Jerusalem, saying, "Where is he who has been born King of the Jews? For we saw his star in the east and have come to worship him" (This could possibly be translated 'to honor him' or to 'pay him homage'). (Matthew 2:1-2)*

Who were these wise men? Why would they come from a far away land to honor a Jewish king? What sort of heavenly event or events could have attracted their attention? In the following pages, we will attempt to answer these questions and many others. We are given very little information concerning the wise men and their famous star, so it may not be possible to have complete and totally satisfying answers for all questions.

Many people have offered explanations concerning the wise men and the star. These explanations include the appearance of a particularly bright angel who shone like a star, a special comet, a supernova and a variety of planetary and stellar conjunctions. Several dates and events have also been suggested including the 12 BC appearance of Halley's comet, three special conjunctions of Jupiter and Saturn in 7 BC, a possible supernova in 5 BC and a series of heavenly events in the period between 3 BC and 1 BC. Thousands of books, articles, video presentations, films, web sites and PowerPoint presentations are available concerning the wise men and the star of Bethlehem. Literally thousands of people have intensely pondered the questions which are raised by Matthew's account concerning the enigmatic Magi and the mysterious star. Some of the theories which have been proposed certainly have more merit than others. Various ideas about the wise men have been developed by devout Christians who are seeking answers. Other propositions have been offered by atheists and people from other religious backgrounds.

The entire account about the wise men and the star has been called into question. Numerous individuals have said: "It does not make sense. How could a star possibly move and come to a halt as indicated in the Bible? How can we possibly believe this?" In the present world, largely dominated by the questioning of the ancient biblical texts, as well as, the rejection of most authority figures this sort of skepticism is understandable. Few people wish to believe seemingly illogical or unreasonable stories if their feasibility and trustworthiness cannot be demonstrated in a rational manner.

Hopefully, believers will find the perspective concerning the Magi and the famous star of Bethlehem presented in this book to be personally refreshing, encouraging and even affirming of their faith. It is the author's hope that the majority of readers will have this experience. Others will find any effort to understand the star and the Magi to be a waste of time, because they have other more pressing concerns. Some skeptics will possibly try to disprove the ideas presented in this book. Still others will find that, despite the author's significant effort this book somehow fails to have a truly biblical perspective concerning the events and the wise men.

The events surrounding the coming of the Messiah, the wise men and the star were certainly unique. Several questions need to be asked in order to better understand what happened. Sometimes the profound questions about the experience of the Magi are simply forgotten; however, to understand the events which took place one must not only ask many questions, but one must also reject several popular misconceptions.

Why is the Story of the Wise Men and the Star Important for Us Today?

The story of the wise men is not specifically centered on the wise men themselves or their wisdom or even the famous incident at Bethlehem involving a star. The message is about the Messiah of Israel. The wise men were determined to find this promised Messiah, the king of the Jews. In their minds, the Messiah was God's designated ruler for the whole world. If Jesus really is the rightful, resurrected, living King of all the earth, then obeying him becomes an important part of daily life. Understanding more about the story of Jesus' birth should lead us to want to know, serve and obey the great King whom the wise men were seeking. According to Christian belief the Messiah was born, lived, suffered, died and was raised from the dead. This risen King is still alive today.

The best reason to study the events surrounding the birth of Jesus is to know God better.

Trying to understand the God of the Bible and appreciating Him are two major reasons that I began my investigations. I wanted to understand what motivated the wise men and how God may have communicated with them through the starry heavens. I have personally grown in my own appreciation of the God of Abraham through discovering more about the star and the wise men. God does work in mysterious ways. While it is possible to discern at least some of God's message in the stars, there may be many things, which we cannot know. However, any truly good study of God's universe will often lead us further than just to a greater accumulation of knowledge. It can lead us to worship. The awesomeness of God should become evident to our hearts and minds. The Apostle Paul wrote in Scripture:

One of the major goals of this book is to lead readers to worship God through discovering more about the famous star and the wise men.

Oh, the depth of the riches both of the wisdom and knowledge of God! How unsearchable are His judgments and unfathomable His ways! (Romans 11:33)

God's ways are well beyond our ways and many of his activities "are past finding out." Even so sometimes he permits us to see some of his manifested wisdom. God is a reasonable being who can be known. He has established a universe which can be examined and appreciated. This reasonable God worked in his creation and human history so that the Magi were able to discern a message in the heavens during the last years of the 1st century BC. God's wisdom and reasonableness are part of his glory. Encountering his glorious presence can transform our lives.

Having increased understanding about the wise men and their star can encourage the faith of some who may doubt. As mentioned previously, many people do question the accuracy of the account of the wise men simply because they do not see a "scientific" explanation for the starry phenomena. Statistically quantifiable answers are not necessary for every question that may arise; however, it is sometimes helpful to use investigative methods to gain further understanding. Hopefully this book will encourage some who may doubt concerning the trustworthiness of the biblical texts. May all gain greater understanding of God's ways, which will help them discover the living Messiah in the world of everyday life. The mysterious child born in Bethlehem is still alive and he can be known.

Astronomy and astrology were historically related, but astrology is not a science and is no longer recognized as having anything to do with astronomy.

What Can We Really Know?

Jesus' birth was heralded by angels, attested by shepherds, prophets and wise men. The events were treasured in the hearts of Mary and Joseph. Even so, we only have a very small source of information concerning the actual story. Anything written about the wise men and the famous star which shown over Bethlehem will be somewhat speculative. This book is no exception. The biblical text concerning the wise men and the events that followed their visit covers 23 verses and possibly 625 words according to the translation, version and language which is used. The wise men themselves are specifically mentioned in 13 verses amounting to about 350 words. As we shall see later, we hardly know anything about the wise men with a great level of certainty. Most everything which can be said, about the birth of Jesus, the wise men and the star will by necessity take the form of hypotheses; however, this does not mean that we must remain completely ignorant. Any person who says that he knows every aspect of what the wise men saw and / or thought, is very possibly deluded or exaggerating.

What exactly were the astronomical phenomena which attracted the attention of the Magi? We can certainly speculate and make educated guesses, but to say that we are totally sure may be presumptuous. While the heavens in the 1st century BC can be recreated with great accuracy using astronomical software, there are still many unknowns. There are difficulties in knowing how astronomical events were interpreted. There are unknowns concerning the weather and the visibility of certain events. There are real difficulties in establishing the dates for many of the events surrounding the birth of Jesus. Even so it does seem to be possible to establish a general timeline and a possible list of events. However, even concerning the timeline there are diverse opinions. Humility is required. This book is presented, not as an absolutely certain case concerning the wise men and the star, but rather as a hypothetical reconstruction of the events. Much care has been taken to make the story plausible and in conformity with what is known about the history and the astronomy of the 1st century BC. However, numerous errors have doubtless been made, and the conclusions will not please all people.

Using a computer to gain a greater understanding of the wise men and heavenly events does not equal "scientific proof" concerning the star of Bethlehem.

Heavenly events can be recreated with a relatively simple astronomy program on a common computer, including some events from the period of Jesus' birth which could have a messianic interpretation. However, using a computer to gain a greater understanding of the heavenly events does not equal *"scientific proof"* concerning the star of Bethlehem. The technology can give us useful insights into the past. Several heavenly events happened exactly as described in this book, but this does not mean that their *possible interpretations* were exactly as written and illustrated in this work. Historical proof and scientific proof function very differently. Scientific proofs are demonstrable by repeatable, completely verifiable experiments. Often experiments are performed in several laboratories to verify the results. History deals with unrepeatable events. Historical proofs rely on the testimonies of good witnesses to establish a correct view of the past. One can also speculate about what may have occurred in history only if one lacks definitive evidence. In the account about the wise men there are simply too many unknowns to claim any absolute certainty about either the men or the events. In this case informed, reasonable speculation is possible and even necessary if one seeks to understand the past. This book presents a reasonable scenario concerning the wise men and the famous star. The author is under no illusions that he can prove everything affirmed in these pages. Even so, we may be able to discover and discern more than one could imagine. Even if one's knowledge is limited, faith can be reasonable. This book is an example of faith seeking greater understanding.

Below: A portion of a model of ancient Jerusalem

Looking at the various scenarios concerning the Magi and at the available cultural, religious, historical and astronomical evidence one must acknowledge that we do not have enough evidence to establish complete certainty about either the men or the events. Even without such absolute certainty, one can still say, "The evidence indicates that something apparently did happen." Much information has been lost concerning the circumstances of the Mesopotamian and Iranian astronomers at the time of Christ. Even so, knowledge concerning the ancient Near East has exploded in the last one hundred years. We know much more now about Babylonian astronomy than at any point during the last 1,500 years. This understanding continues to grow, as thousands of cuneiform texts are being unearthed, carefully translated, interpreted and published.

Any person who says that he knows precisely what the wise men saw and / or thought, is very possibly deluded or exaggerating. The short biblical text in Matthew gives some information but not mounds of data.

Even if we cannot "prove" everything one can still adopt a perspective in which the Bible can be thought of as relating to the "real" world. The ancient biblical text is not simply about spiritual ideas, stories and parables which has no relation to everyday life. The texts were written about real events, real people and profound reality. The messianic hope of Israel is still the best answer for those who deal with the harsh physical and psychological realities of sickness, poverty, death, sin, and oppression. God's messianic hope is solidly anchored in the physical universe where life and death really do matter. The visible, tangibly real, sun, moon, planets and stars carried a divine message two thousand years ago. Today, they are still reminders of that message of hope, centered on the Messiah.

Interpreting the "Star" through Astrology?

Astronomy is the science that deals with the universe beyond the earth. It describes the nature, position, and motion of the stars, planets, and other objects in the skies.[9] Astrology is a study of the heavens that assumes and attempts to interpret the influence of the heavenly bodies on human affairs.[10] Interpretations of heavenly events are typically identified with astrology, soothsaying and omens. Astronomy and astrology were historically related, but astrology as it is defined above is not a science. It is no longer recognized as having much of anything to do with the modern science of astronomy. Some professional astrologers might disagree, insisting that astrology is thoroughly scientific.

Below: A portion of a model of ancient Jerusalem

It is evident from the Bible that God placed lights in the sky for practical purposes: to give light and to establish the seasons, days and years. He also established the heavenly lights for signs. What kind of signs did God desire? Some promote the idea that ancient astrology was the means where by God spoke to the wise men. Others argue that God still speaks through astrology. One can even find astrological charts suggesting proposed dates for the birth of Jesus, indicating specific astronomical information and drawing the appropriate conclusions.

However, there are significant problems. Firstly, it is not so easy to pin down the exact birth date of Jesus. A variety of ideas have been suggested about the date of Jesus' birth, with proposed birth dates ranging over a period of several years, not days or weeks. In order to do any ancient or modern horoscopes, one needs specific dates to establish the positions of the sun, moon and planets at the hour of birth. Being so exact is not always possible or easy, from an earthly perspective the planets can sometimes move very quickly. Venus regularly goes from being an evening star to being a morning star in a period of just eight days. This can make a huge difference when making a birth chart based on the planets. According to the most popular version of the story, the wise men arrived at the time of Jesus' birth. How could they have established his horoscope in order to know his destiny in advance, even before his birth?

A second problem: The famous star was seen while the wise men were in the east. Then it went before them and eventually it stopped moving among the stars over Bethlehem. There is a way that this could have happened which makes sense and can be demonstrated; however, this type of starry behavior is actually very different from anything in either ancient or modern astrology. No horoscope has ever been established based on objects which move in front of an astrologer in such a manner. However, this behavior is a key element of the biblical story concerning the star.

A third problem with connecting ancient astrology to the birth of Jesus is that astrological practice and interpretation are forbidden by the Scriptures. It was also rejected by the early Church Fathers and most churchmen since the early centuries of the Christian era. Astrology teaches that the constellations, sun, moon and the planets all *directly influence* the lives of individuals. However, this is not taught in the Bible. The idea that the heavens might make an announcement concerning the Messiah's birth is radically different from thinking that the Messiah's life would be shaped and directed by the stars. According to the Bible the alignments of heavenly objects and constellations at the moment of one's birth do not shape one's life. The "star" *announced* the Messiah's birth, but it did not mold his life. The Bible allows for signs in the heavens, but it refuses the idea that stellar objects influence the lives and destinies of people. A sign indicating a birth is not the same thing as having one's destiny guided, influenced or shaped by the stars.

Should we try to understand the star of Bethlehem or the Magi through astrology? The answer is plainly no. The God of Abraham, Isaac and Jacob, seems to be solidly opposed to the practice of astrology in both its ancient and modern aspects. In the Bible, God himself uses certain well known constellation names, when he describes the heavens. However, simply using certain names for stars and constellations is not the same thing as seeking guidance and understanding through horoscopes. God is alive; he speaks and acts in this present world. He wants to guide his people himself. It is evident that consulting the stars, but not consulting the Lord, displeases the God of Abraham (See 2 Kings 17:16 and 21:1-9ff, 2 Chronicles 33:1-6, Jeremiah 8:2, Zephaniah 1:4-6 and Acts 7:42). Worshiping heavenly objects or reverently leaning on them for guidance is also forbidden.

> *"And beware not to lift up your eyes to heaven and see the sun and the moon and the stars, all the host of heaven, and be drawn away and worship them and serve them ... (Deuteronomy 4:19) Thus says the LORD, "Do not learn the way of the nations ... And do not be terrified by the signs of the heavens Although the nations are terrified by them. (Jeremiah 10:1-2)*

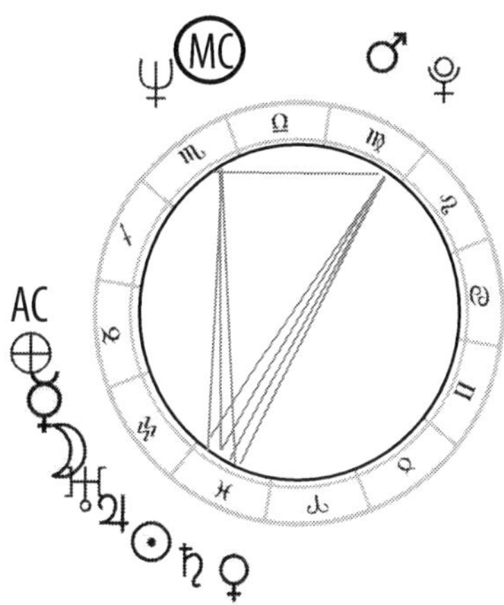

Above: A chart showing the heavenly bodies in relation to the constellations. Such charts can be used to establish horoscopes. Numerous charts, like this hypothetical one concerning the birth of Jesus, can be found on the Internet.

Among the ancient civilisations astronomy and astrology were often related and complementary realms of knowledge. However, in the present time astrology is generally not regarded as a science except by its most advanced practicioners.

A passage in Isaiah 47:1-14 is particular noteworthy because it specifically is addressed to the soothsayers, conjurers and astrologers of Mesopotamia, the Babylonians (Chaldeans):

> *"Come down and sit in the dust, O virgin daughter of Babylon; sit on the ground without a throne, O daughter of the Chaldeans! For you shall no longer be called tender and delicate ... "Your nakedness will be uncovered, your shame also will be exposed ... "You are wearied with your many counsels; Let now the astrologers, those who prophesy by the stars, those who predict by the new moons, stand up and save you from what will come upon you. Behold, they have become like stubble, Fire burns them; They cannot deliver themselves from the power of the flame."*

Despite these very clear texts cited above, some Jewish rabbis still debated about the influence of the stars on the nation of Israel. Epiphanius writes that the Pharisees were heavily interested in astrology in the 1st century BC, despite their zeal for God.[11] Opinions were divided concerning astrological influence on the nation of Israel. The majority of the rabbis quoted in the Babylonian Talmud rejected astrological influences and guidance in the lives of the people of God (See the Babylonian Talmud, Tractate Sabbath 156 parts a and b). In the following quote, we can clearly see that opinions were divided. Some thought that the stars themselves could give wisdom and wealth while others resisted that idea strongly.

> *It was stated that Rabbi Hanina said: The planetary influence gives wisdom, the planetary influence gives wealth, and Israel stands under planetary influence. R. Johanan maintained: Israel is immune from planetary influence. Now, Rabbi Joḥanan is consistent with his view, for Rabbi Johanan said: How do we know that Israel is immune from planetary influence? Because ... (He then quotes Jeremiah 10:2 - cited above). (Tractate Sabbath 156a)*

From the Bible, it appears that God did not intend for men to think of their lives as being either influenced by or guided by the stars. It is clear that God did not make the sun, moon and stars to influence people directly in any astrological sense. God created all the heavenly objects to give light in a very practical way. In the case of the heavenly events surrounding the birth of the Messiah, God used the heavenly bodies as signs to announce the Messiah's birth. They were not the controlling influences which caused his birth or shaped his destiny. Announcing events through the stars and causing something to come to pass through stellar influences are hugely different concepts.

'The Lion Led the Way' Cover Image:

The cover of this book contains an image of the famous clock tower on St. Mark's Square in Venice. Looking at this clock in order to know the hour does not mean that one endorses astrology, in a similar way, this image is not intended as an endorsement of either modern or ancient astrology. The cover simply illustrates the constellations, stars, sun and moon, as well as, time. As mentioned above, God is very aware of the constellations, their names, the stars that are contained in them, their history and their forms. Again, the names of certain constellations and planets are found in the Bible (Job 9:9, 26:13, 38:31-32 and Amos 5:8). However, God does not desire for his people to lean on the stars for guidance and comfort instead of leaning on Him. It is evident from the Bible that the wise men who went to Bethlehem feared God much more than they feared men. We should imitate their example and also live in the respectful fear of God. The God of Abraham opposes the proud, but He gives grace to the humble. May we draw near to God and forsake everything which could lead us away from Him. According to the book of Proverbs, "The fear of the Lord is the beginning of wisdom."

> *"Can you bind the chains of the Pleiades or loose the cords of Orion? Can you lead forth the Mazzaroth (the constellations) in their season, or can you guide the Bear with its children? "Can you lift up your voice to the clouds, that flood of waters may cover you? Can you send forth lightnings, that they may go and say to you, 'Here we are'? Who has put wisdom in the inward parts or given understanding to the mind? (Job 38:31-36, ESV).*

Certainly only the God of Abraham, Isaac and Jacob can do these things.

The Lord took Abram outside and said, "Now look toward the heavens, and count the stars, if you are able to count them." And He said to him, "So shall your descendants be." (Genesis 15:5)

Why would the Magi have thought that any star had something to do with the birth of a Jewish Messiah?

Questioning Christian Traditions

Was the star really spectacular or did something else attract the attention of the wise men?

Questioning popular traditions about the Magi and the famous star might open doors to a better understanding of the people and the events surrounding the Messiah's birth. One does not need to be very intelligent to see that there are problems with the current popular versions of the story. Many of us have never questioned the popular traditions about the incidents surrounding Jesus' birth. However, even 15 minutes of questioning can reveal serious problems with the popular version of the story. As we shall see later, the biblical texts themselves are not necessarily in agreement with the version of the events which is commonly proclaimed.

Christmas cards have beautiful and even very symbolic images, but they may not contain all the truth. In the image above we see the wise men arriving on camels at a town in a desert setting. They see a star in the form of a cross over the town in the distance. The image is especially appealing to Christians because of the cross shape of the star; however, we have no indication from the Bible that the star shone in the form of a cross. The light from the star is shining down indicating the general location of certain buildings. Here again, the Bible does not say that a beam of light shone down onto a certain spot. It simply says that the star stopped moving among the background stars when the wise men arrived in Judea. It also appeared to have stopped above Bethlehem when viewed from Jerusalem. Again, in the image, Bethlehem is in a desert filled with sand dunes and a few palm trees. However, the actual town was an agricultural community in the countryside south of Jerusalem. Many of the hills in the area are still covered with olive groves. Luke tells us there were shepherds who had flocks which certainly ate grass. Near Bethlehem there were very significant springs. Almost one thousand years before the birth of Jesus, King Solomon built an aqueduct which passed beside Bethlehem. This aqueduct brought water to the temple in Jerusalem. It seems that Herod the Great, the Romans and later the Arabs all made their own contributions to this water system. Bethlehem is not in a desert, nor is it a date palm oasis.

At least one of the men in the image above is wearing something similar to a crown. The Bible itself does not mention anything about the wise men being kings. Apparently camels transported goods, but usually dignitaries would ride horses. Is it even certain that the Magi rode on camels? Were the Magi kings or even high officials? The tradition concerning the wise men being kings may only be a popular idea without any real foundation; this will be explored more fully later. Old hymns even repeat this idea of kingship using lyrics which have inspired many generations of people:

> *"We three kings of Orient are bearing gifts we traverse afar, field and fountain, moor and mountain, following yonder star."* [12]

The lyrics of the old hymn "We Three Kings" sounds a bit more like England or New England than the Middle East. Fields and fountains and especially "moors" do not usually come to mind when thinking of the areas well to the east of Jerusalem. Moors, marshes and swamps are related terms. It is true that some of the area around the Jordan River is a bit wet, but it is certainly not a major marsh, moor or swamp. If the wise men came from the general region of Mesopotamia there are many marshes around the Tigris and Euphrates rivers, so maybe that aspect could be at least partially right. However, the phrase "fields, fountains, moors and mountains" has more to do with poetry than a real description of where the wise men traveled. The men presumably crossed the Syrian desert on their way to Jerusalem. They may have returned to Mesopotamia or Iran through the desert in present day Jordan and Saudi Arabia.[13] It is evident that traditions, Christmas cards and hymns all distort the story.

One question that needs a serious answer is the following: "If the star was particularly spectacular and very unusual then why did King Herod not see it?"[14] Why did he have to "call the Magi and determine from them the exact time when the star had appeared"(Matthew 2:7)? Was it not obvious to King Herod and everyone else that there was a special star in the heavens? It would seem that the star may not have had a truly overwhelmingly spectacular appearance. Herod apparently did not notice the star before the wise men arrived in Jerusalem. He could have simply lacked good eyesight, but others would have certainly talked about a truly spectacular heavenly event. Perhaps the star was only seen by the wise men. Paul had a vision on the Damascus road. He saw and heard some things which remained invisible for those who were with him. Perhaps the star was invisible to

If the star was particularly spectacular and extremely bright then why did King Herod not see it?

Why did the king have to call the wise men to his palace secretly to determine from them "the exact time the star appeared." (Mt 2:7)?

Photo: One of the three massive pools built by King Solomon and others to supply water for Jerusalem and the temple complex. Notice the trees, Bethlehem is not in a desert.

If a truly visible light was directed from a star toward a certain spot on the ground, it is probable that hundreds or even thousands of people would have come to see the marvelous light. In reality, only a relatively small group of wise men arrived at Bethlehem.

others, but it would seem unrealistic that the star would "go before" the wise men for approximately two months without being seen by anyone else.

Other questions can be asked: If the star was extremely spectacular and there was a tail extending to the ground then why was not the whole town gathered near the mysterious light? Again, perhaps only the Magi could see the light. If a truly visible light was directed from a star toward a certain spot on the ground, it is probable that hundreds or even thousands of people would have come to see such a marvelous light. In reality, only a relatively small group of wise men arrived at Bethlehem. In addition, the shepherds make no mention of a star, was it not also obvious to them? The shepherds received a verbal message from one angel, who was suddenly joined by a large number of angels. Apparently the shepherds would not have known anything about the special birth except for the message that they received from the angel. Could it be that the incidents involving the shepherds and the wise men do not happen at the same time?

Herod discovered that the wise men had escaped without informing him about the child. He then ordered the execution of all the male children in Bethlehem who were less than two years old. Herod's soldiers themselves would have reasonably preferred to avoid the massacre. The parents of the children and the soldiers would have behaved differently if there had been a beam of light pointing to an exact location where Jesus lay only days before. The spot and the special child would have been well known if a light had shown down from the heavens as in the classic images. The other parents in Bethlehem could have simply led the soldiers to the appropriate location, previously indicated by the light, in order to attempt to save their own children. Why did they not do it if the traditional ideas about a beam of light shining from heaven are correct?

Unfortunately, the star often portrayed on Christmas cards with a long tail pointing to the stable seems to be more a figment of imagination than a real representation of the actual star. The form of a cross is pleasing to Christians and it should be that way. Such images are perhaps honest efforts to portray how the star confirmed the presence of the Messiah, but they are apparently without foundation. The popular version of the story does not seem to answer certain basic questions. We need to go deeper to understand the Magi and the star.

Many More Questions Remain to be Answered:

(1) Who was the expected Messiah supposed to be?

(2) What would he have been like according to the Hebrew Scriptures?

(3) Who were the wise men and what were their origins?

(4) Why would have anyone living in the "east" even have thought that a Messiah might be born in Israel?

(5) Why did the wise men believe that any star indicated something concerning the Messiah of Israel?

(6) Was the star of Bethlehem the brightest star ever seen or do we simply imagine that it was the brightest or a most unusual star in history?

(7) If the star was not exceedingly "spectacular," then how did it attract the attention of the Magi?

(8) Did any heavenly events, which are known to have taken place during the 1st century BC, correspond with the Jewish understanding of the character and destiny of the promised Messiah?

(9) How is it that the Magi saw the star in the east and then they saw it "go before" them as they went to Jerusalem?

(10) Were the Magi accustomed to seeing stars that moved in the heavens?

(11) When the star stopped moving among the other stars over Bethlehem were the Magi surprised ?

(12) How did the wise men find Mary, Joseph and the young child?

(13) Did the Magi and the shepherds actually meet together at a stable?

(14) How is it that Jesus was circumcised (on the eighth day after his birth) and 40 days after his birth he was presented at the temple, supposing that he had to flee to Egypt with his parents immediately following the visit of the Magi?

(15) Is it possible that the wise men were not present in the moments immediately after Jesus' birth?

(16) If the wise men were not present at Jesus' birth, then when did they arrive in Judea?

(17) How long did Joseph keep his family in Bethlehem?

(18) Herod no doubt had a significant network of informers and spies. How were the wise men able to met Jesus and his parents without someone being aware?

(19) Which alternate route did the Magi use to return to their own land? The text says that they returned to their land by different route than the one they had used previously.

(20) How long did Jesus remain with his parents in Egypt?

(21) Did Joseph originally plan to return to Bethlehem from Egypt or did he plan from the start to return to Nazareth?

There are perhaps many more questions which could be proposed. Many unknowns exist and unanswered questions abound.

Above: The countryside around Bethlehem

If the star was extremely spectacular and there was a tail extending to the ground then why was not the whole town gathered near the mysterious light?

Looking at the Biblical Texts

The Birth of Jesus in Matthew and Luke

Luke does not mention any wise men or a star however, he does tell us about the angels, the shepherds, the circumcision of Jesus and events in Jerusalem over 40 days after his birth.

The events surrounding Jesus' birth and events afterwards are outlined in the opening chapters of the Gospels of Matthew and Luke. Luke gives us much more detail concerning how Mary became pregnant, the reason for Mary and Joseph's trip to Bethlehem and the exact events surrounding the birth of Jesus. Luke alone gives us the account concerning the shepherds who were tending their flocks and who were informed of Jesus' birth by a large group of angels. Luke continues with passages about the circumcision of Jesus and his dedication at the temple 40 days after his birth. All of this was carried out according to the Law of Moses outlined in Leviticus 12:1-8. The prophecies given at the moment of Jesus' presentation at the temple amazed his parents, but Luke does not mention any wise men or a star.

Luke's Account:

Now in those days a decree went out from Caesar Augustus, that a census be taken of all the inhabited earth. This was the first census taken while Quirinius was governor of Syria. Everyone was on his way to register for the census, each to his own city. Joseph also went up from Galilee, from the city of Nazareth, to Judea, to the city of David which is called Bethlehem, because he was of the house and family of David, in order to register along with Mary, who was engaged to him, and was with child. While they were there, the days were completed for her to give birth. She gave birth to her firstborn son; and she wrapped Him in cloths, and laid Him in a manger, because there was no room for them in the inn.

In the same region there were some shepherds staying out in the fields and keeping watch over their flock by night. And an angel of the Lord suddenly stood before them, and the glory of the Lord shone around them; and they were terribly frightened. But the angel said to them, "Do not be afraid; for behold, I bring you good news of great joy which will be for all the people; for today in the city of David there has been born for you a Savior, who is Christ the Lord. "This will be a sign for you. You will find a baby wrapped in cloths and lying in a manger." And suddenly there appeared with the angel a multitude of the heavenly host praising God and saying, "Glory to God in the highest, And on earth peace among men with whom He is pleased."

When the angels had gone away from them into heaven, the shepherds began saying to one another, "Let us go straight to Bethlehem then, and see this thing that has happened which the Lord has made known to us." So they came in a hurry and found their way to Mary and Joseph, and the baby as He lay in the manger. When they had seen this, they made known the statement which had been told them

Photos: A model of ancient Jerusalem

about this Child. And all who heard it wondered at the things which were told them by the shepherds. But Mary treasured all these things, pondering them in her heart. The shepherds went back, glorifying and praising God for all that they had heard and seen, just as had been told them.

Matthew's Account:

Matthew gives an extended account of the visit of the wise men and the events which followed, but he does not mention any shepherds. In Matthew's text, the wise men arrive at a house (not at a stable). Joseph, Mary and the baby flee into Egypt because of God's warning concerning Herod's desire to kill the baby. Therefore the wise men must have visited Bethlehem well after the birth of Jesus because Jesus was circumcised and presented at the temple after Mary's purification. According to the ceremonial purity regulations in the Torah a woman who had given birth was not to appear at the tabernacle / temple until at least 40 days after giving birth (Leviticus 12:1-7).

Now the birth of Jesus Christ was as follows: when His mother Mary had been betrothed to Joseph, before they came together she was found to be with child by the Holy Spirit. And Joseph her husband, being a righteous man and not wanting to disgrace her, planned to send her away secretly. But when he had considered this, behold, an angel of the Lord appeared to him in a dream, saying, "Joseph, son of David, do not be afraid to take Mary as your wife; for the Child who has been conceived in her is of the Holy Spirit. "She will bear a Son; and you shall call His name Jesus, for He will save His people from their sins." Now all this took place to fulfill what was spoken by the Lord through the prophet: "BEHOLD, THE VIRGIN SHALL BE WITH CHILD AND SHALL BEAR A SON, AND THEY SHALL CALL HIS NAME IMMANUEL," which translated means, "GOD WITH US." And Joseph awoke from his sleep and did as the angel of the Lord commanded him, and took Mary as his wife, but kept her a virgin until she gave birth to a Son; and he called His name Jesus.

Now after Jesus was born in Bethlehem of Judea in the days of Herod the king, magi from the east arrived in Jerusalem, saying, "Where is He who has been born King of the Jews? For we saw His star in the east and have come to worship Him."

When Herod the king heard this, he was troubled, and all Jerusalem with him. Gathering together all the chief priests and scribes of the people, he inquired of them where the Messiah was to be born. They said to him, "In Bethlehem of Judea; for this is what has been written by the prophet: 'AND YOU, BETHLEHEM, LAND OF JUDAH, ARE BY NO MEANS LEAST AMONG THE LEADERS OF JUDAH; FOR OUT OF YOU SHALL COME FORTH A RULER WHO WILL SHEPHERD MY PEOPLE ISRAEL.'" Then Herod secretly called the magi and determined from them the exact time the star appeared. And he sent them to Bethlehem and said, "Go and search carefully for the Child; and when you have found Him, report to me, so that I too may come and worship Him."

According to Matthew the wise men arrived at a house and not at a stable. No shepherds were mentioned in his text.

Jesus was not a newly born baby when the Magi arrived in Bethlehem.

After hearing the king, they went their way; and the star, which they had seen in the east, went on before them until it came and stood over the place where the Child was. When they saw the star, they rejoiced exceedingly with great joy. After coming into the house they saw the Child with Mary His mother; and they fell to the ground and worshiped Him. Then, opening their treasures, they presented to Him gifts of gold, frankincense, and myrrh. And having been warned by God in a dream not to return to Herod, the magi left for their own country by another way.

Some Observations:

Mathew and Luke wrote about different events. Luke's account is actually at the time of the birth of Jesus. Matthew's account of the Magi takes place many months and even possibly a year later.

Key words are found in Matthew 1:18 and 2:1. The first text tells the story of how Mary came to be pregnant, but it does not give any real details about the circumstances of the actual birth. Matthew 2:1 begins with the words "After the birth of Jesus wise men came ..." It is important to underline the words at the beginning of Matthew's account in chapter two. The word "after" is key.

> *Now after Jesus was born in Bethlehem of Judea in the days of Herod the king, Magi from the east arrived ...*

Despite tens of thousands of Christmas plays, popular songs, books, films and web sites, we can affirm without hesitation that the wise men arrived some time after the birth of Jesus. They did not arrive on the day of his birth. The words "after Jesus was born" say a lot and very little. It is more or less obvious that Luke and Matthew were writing about two different sets of events: Luke tells us about the actual birth of Jesus. Matthew explains the arrival of the wise men later "after Jesus was already born."

One ancient text speaks of Jesus standing beside his mother during the Magi's visit. Babies can usually only walk at one year of age.

Just making a few clarifications gives us a better perspective. The popular idea of nativity scenes with shepherds and wise men together is erroneous. The shepherds saw Jesus as a newborn in a stable. The wise men seem to have arrived many months later, perhaps even a year after Jesus' birth. The wise men saw the Messiah as a young baby, but not as a newborn. One ancient text speaks of Jesus standing beside his mother during the visit of the Magi.[15] If it was a known fact that Jesus was a newborn at the moment of the Magi's arrival, then the idea that he might have been standing beside his mother would have been rejected immediately. Babies can usually only walk at about one year of age. However, we do not know with absolute certainty from the Bible when Jesus was born. Nor do we know the exact day that the wise men made their visit. Some people have pointed out that Luke's account first mentions Jesus as a "brephos" (βρεφος, a newborn, in Greek). Matthew only uses the word "paidion," (παιδιον) to describe the child in his text about the Magi. This word is often used, although not exclusively, for a somewhat older infant. However, Luke also uses the Greek word "paidion," in the passage about the shepherd's visit on the very night of Jesus' birth (Luke 2:17). Therefore, one cannot say that the word "paidion" in Matthew establishes anything about the age of Jesus when he was visited by the Magi.[16]

It is also necessary to give a brief word about the star "going before" the wise men and also how it "stood still." There are at least five schools of thought:

(1) The wise men saw a meaningful stellar event(s) while they were in the east. By some means, before they arrived in Judea, they had understood that the Jewish Messiah *had already been born*. The event(s) was special and it had a particular meaning to the wise men; however, it was not so spectacular that it attracted the attention of vast multitudes. In general only professional or semi-professional astronomers understood the meaning. The Magi prepared themselves and began a journey, which could have lasted at least two months. The star somehow visually moved toward the west during their whole journey, although they did not specifically rely on it for navigation purposes. The geography between Mesopotamia and Judea was well known. The star then seemed to stop over Bethlehem as it was being viewed from Jerusalem. The Magi were joyful because when the star stopped over Bethlehem, its presence over the town confirmed to them that they had rightly understood God's guidance. The star did not point to a specific house or stable. The wise men went to Bethlehem. By making contacts in the town the wise men were able to find the young child and his parents.

The Magi asked, "Where is He who has been born King of the Jews? It would seem that in the minds of the Magi the Messiah had already been born well before their arrival in Judea.

(2) The Magi saw a star while they were in the east which somehow indicated that the Messiah *was to be born*. The wise men began their journey with the star going ahead of them. They relied on it for navigation purposes. However, the star disappeared from view for a period of time after the wise men drew near to Judea. When the wise men arrived in Jerusalem they soon had an interview with the king who encouraged them to go to Bethlehem to look for the young child. Stepping out of the palace the wise men saw the star again. It then led them, perhaps with a brilliant ray of light, directly to the Messiah's location. The wise men were supernaturally guided by a truly supernatural and mysterious star to the exact spot where the young child was with his parents. He had been born only hours before.

(3) There may be combinations of the first two ideas.

(4) There are also various other approaches which have been proposed which vary substantially from the classic ideas presented above. Probably one the most serious of these approaches of how the star "went before" the wise men concerns the Saturn - Jupiter conjunctions in 7 BC, united with a phenomenon called the zodialogical light. This was proposed by Konradin Ferrari D'Occhieppo.[17]

(5) Many authors simply ignore the problem of the stellar movements described by Matthew. Some reject the idea that the star did somehow move from the east toward the west as being inaccurate or false.

This book uses the first explanation.

Some of the Author's Concerns

The Pandora's Box of Speculation

Any author puts himself and his ideas at risk. It is highly possible that some will try to use the information in this book to develop astronomical perspectives concerning the future of Israel and the awaited second appearing of the Messiah. I, myself, strongly discourage such efforts. Very few modern people, myself included, have ever taken the time to examine astronomical events and possible signs in the heavens with as much care and patience as the Bethlehem Magi. We are often much too ready to make great pronouncements about astronomical events and the Bible while having comparatively little knowledge either concerning the Bible, prophecy or astronomy. While God did speak through heavenly events in the past, the material in this book is not intended to encourage speculations about messages in the stars for the present or future. The incidents at the time of the birth of Jesus were not necessarily intended as a model for all that God may do in the heavens in the coming years. It is highly probable that some future celestial events will be so evident to all men that no one will need an interpretation. An enormous amount of time and energy is wasted trying to discern the year and even the day of the Lord's return. The material in this book is not intended to give people more tools in order to do more speculation (See also Appendix 1, page 224).

Secrets and Esoteric Knowledge:

In writing this book, I was not interested in discovering "secrets" or esoteric knowledge. In fact, as will become evident later, most of the interpretive elements in this book are extremely simple and forthright. Esoteric, as well as, ancient and modern astrological interpretations of heavenly events are not endorsed in this study.

"Christian" Perspectives on the Heavens

I have serious reservations concerning the supposedly "Christian" perspective on astronomy called the "Gospel in the Stars." The general idea behind the "Gospel in the Stars" theory appears to have been an effort by well meaning people to make sense of the starry heavens. They desired to give a "Christian perspective on the heavens," but the effort has largely failed to give us a historically based, linguistically accurate, or biblically correct understanding of the heavens. This theory concerning a supposed God given original message in the stars needs to be thoroughly reexamined. It is probable that most of the teaching simply needs to be laid aside. The ideas presented in the "Gospel in the Stars" may even be a hindrance to understanding the heavens from a Christian perspective. Some people have attached so much credence to the theory that it may be painful for them to question it. I do not wish to cause any pain to anyone, but some pain can be beneficial (See Appendix 2, page 225).

Part 2: When was Jesus Born?

"And I will put enmity Between you and the woman, And between your seed and her seed; He shall bruise you on the head, And you shall bruise him on the heel." (Genesis 3:15)

The Lord Himself will give you a sign: Behold, a virgin will be with child and bear a son, and she will call His name Immanuel. (Isaiah 7:14)

For a child will be born to us, a son will be given to us; And the government will rest on His shoulders; And His name will be called Wonderful Counselor, Mighty God, Eternal Father, Prince of Peace. (Isaiah 9: 6)

Dating the Birth of Jesus

Images: Clement of Alexandria and Eusebius of Caesarea

For centuries, there have been problems with specifically dating the birth of Jesus. Even the year of his birth remains a subject of debate. Ancient dates are not easy to calculate. For example, a date involving the Roman calendar often took note of how many years an emperor had been reigning and also mentioned the consuls who were in office during each year. The present calendar terms BC, and AD, were only adopted many centuries after the birth of Jesus. Some errors were made in the date calculation process. Therefore, we now have the odd situation of indicating Christ's birth in the years "BC" instead of in a more logical phrasing "Year of our Lord" (Anno Domini) AD 1.

In the early centuries of the Christian era, many people believed that Jesus was born sometime during 3/2 BC. Christian authors such as, Tertullian, Ireneaus, Origen and Clement of Alexandria indicated that Jesus was born in the 41st or 42nd year of the reign of Augustus Caesar. Octavian, who later became Augustus, was appointed a consul of Rome on August 19th of 43 BC, which is 41 years before the 3/2 BC date. While the Church Fathers may have been sometimes been mistaken, they also deserve some respect. They may have more to offer us than we would expect.

Dates given for the birth of Jesus by several Church Fathers: [1]

AD 130-202	*Ireneaus*	*4/3 BC*
AD 150-215	*Clement of Alexandria*	*3/2 BC*
AD 160-225	*Tertullian*	*3/2 BC*
AD 170-240	*Julius Africanus*	*3/2 BC*
AD 170-236	*Hippolytus of Rome*	*3/2 BC*
AD 185-253	*Origen*	*3/2 BC*
AD 263-339	*Eusebius of Caesarea*	*3/2 BC*

For various reasons which go beyond the scope of this book, many Bibles, commentaries, and godly preachers use a 4 BC date for the death of Herod the Great. This date has been largely accepted and it is the one found in most books and on the majority of websites. There are some very good reasons to take this position. However, few early Christian writers ever placed Jesus' birth or Herod's death in 4 BC or earlier. This type of dating has led many people to search for the famous star in the years preceding 4 BC. Several serious astronomical propositions have been put forward concerning the star in the years from 7 BC to 5 BC. There are significant reasons to support different dates and numerous theories abound. However, a 4 BC date for the birth of Jesus does not solve all the dating problems.

It may actually create several other serious chronological, factual and biblical difficulties.[2]

In more recent times several scholars have again sought to affirm Herod's death in early 1 BC. Jesus would have been born in 3/2 BC, a year or two preceding Herod's death. This book uses the 1 BC date for Herod's death in line with research done by E.W. Filmer, Jack Finegan, Andrew E. Steinmann and several other scholars who have explored all the issues involved.[3] (See also Appendix 11 on pages 242 and 243). Some information will eventually be available on the www.tzedek.info site.

December 25th, the Correct Date?

The December 25th date for the birth of Jesus also has a complicated history. It is often assumed and widely proclaimed that the date was established to replace a pagan celebration; however, on close examination this was most likely not the case. The Roman festival of Saturnalia, celebrating the god Saturn, is often mentioned as a pagan forerunner of Christmas on December 25th. However, the festival of Saturnalia was originally only on December 17th, but later it was extended from the 17th through the 23rd. The festival was never on December 25th, and while it was sometimes associated with the winter solstice it was not the principal aspect of the celebration.[4] The official winter solstice in the Roman Empire during 3/2 BC was on December 25th.

The Roman Emperor Elagabalus, who ruled from AD 218-222, tried to promote his own native Syrian sun god as the main deity in Rome. He was resisted and eventually he was assassinated partially because of his efforts to place the sun at the center of Roman religious life. Elagbalus celebrated his principal sun worship at the time of the summer solstice, not in December. Later the Emperor Aurelian was able to establish some significant sun worship after AD 274, but much evidence is lacking concerning the precise nature of these celebrations. Sun worship supposedly linked to Aurelian's innovations continued through the reign of Constantine (AD 306-337) and afterwards. The Roman worship of the Sol Invictus (the invincible god of the sun) was a fairly late addition to the Roman religious calendar. According to Steven Hijmans the main festivals dedicated to Sol (the sun) were in August and October.[5] Hijmans, in his dissertation about the worship of Sol, Roman art and religions, writes:

> *"There is no evidence that Aurelian instituted a celebration of Sol on that day [December 25]. A feast day for Sol on December 25th is not mentioned until eighty years later, in the Calendar of 354 and, subsequently, in 362 by Julian in his Oration to King Helios"*[6]

When one reflects on Hijman's affirmation that there is no evidence that Aurelian instituted sun worship specifically on December 25th, one is astounded. It should be noted that the mention 80 years later was in a calendar of Roman festivals,

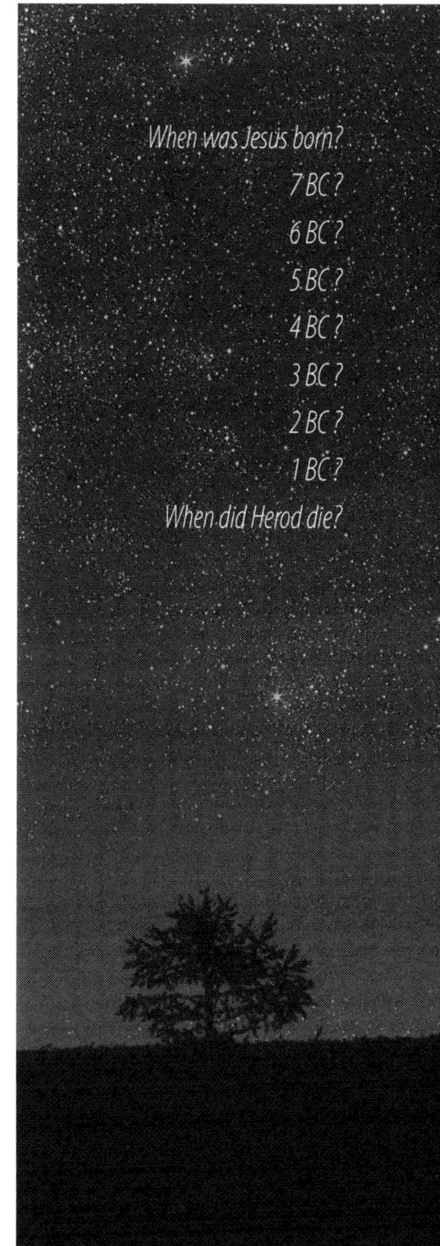

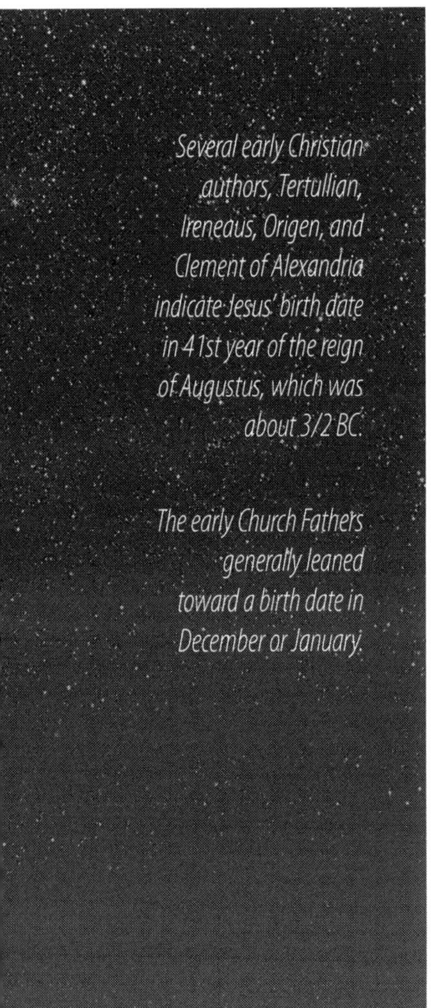

which by that time had incorporated numerous Christian festivals. It is not even absolutely certain that the words "Natalis Invicti" or "Birth of the Unconquered) used in the calendar certainly refer to Sol (the sun). The words used in the calendar inspired at least one person to write:

> *"Natalis Invicti" or "Birth of the Unconquered" was celebrated on December 25, whether that refers to Sol or Jesus is unclear, what is clear is that other feasts of Sol are mentioned by name (for example on August 28) and that the Chronography of 354 AD does say that Jesus was born on Dec. 25 in part 12 [of the document].*[7]

The Emperor Julian the Apostate, who reigned from AD 361-363, insisted on sun worship on December 25th. He did so in part because of his own rejection of Christianity. He promoted sun worship on December 25th out of spite, knowing that the date was a Christian feast day.

It is also widely proclaimed that the god Mithra was associated with sun worship in the Roman Empire. It is safe to say that often this was certainly true. The Roman Emperor Diocletian (AD 284-305) did promote the worship of Mithra in the years before Constantine; however, he did not eliminate or completely marginalize the old Roman gods. Mithranism was a mystery religion in which only men were allowed to participate. With its secretive nature and limited membership Mithranism apparently never had more than one percent of the population of the empire as adherents at any one time. Sun worship became significant, but it did not become the most important aspect of Roman religious experience. The old gods were still adored as they had been for centuries. Christianity already had many more followers than Mithranism when Constantine came to power in AD 306. It is estimated that at that moment, Christians numbered about 10% of the eastern part of the empire. Christians were even in a majority in some villages and smaller towns.[8]

Others contend that December 25th was associated with Babylonian deity Tammuz. However, this deity was principally celebrated in the summer. There seems to be an almost unending series of theories and numerous urban legends concerning the supposedly sinister origins of the festivals of Christmas and Easter. It is also true that pagans often celebrated festivals at the time of the solstices and the equinoxes. However, few would question that Passover always happens near the time of the vernal (spring) equinox. Many activities associated with the modern celebrations of both Easter (Passover) and Christmas are cultural, perhaps pagan and certainly unbliblical, yet it is far from proven that *all aspects* of the celebrations are pagan or have pagan roots. Recognizing the amalgams and rumors may help to correct many errors and perhaps even some bad attitudes. As we shall see later, the links between Passover and the traditional Christmas dates are fairly strong. According to some, the origins of Christmas are supposedly found in the Saturnalia festival, the worship of Tammuz, the worship of Sol Invictus or

Sol Invictus Mithra. It is not possible for all these competing, antagonistic and different religious traditions to be "the source" of the celebration of Christmas on December 25th. An article by Dr Anthony McRoy reproduced in Appendix 4 on page 232 is highly recommended.[9]

The idea that Christians somehow did something incorrect, underhanded or compromising in establishing the date of Christmas on the former date of the winter solstice seems unfounded.

Constantine's Influence on Christian Holy Days and Holidays

Christians were heavily persecuted under the Emperor Diocletian, who ruled from AD 284 to 305. Some persecution continued even after Constantine's rise to power in the west. Constantine only ruled part of the empire for many years. Persecution has a definite tendency to set priorities and greatly purify religious practice. Here is a description of the situation for many Christians from AD 303 to 312:

> *By a decree of February 303, Diocletian ordered all Christian places of worship to be destroyed and their sacred books handed over. Christians were forbidden to assemble and to be denied the protection of the laws. ... A second, more severe decree singled out bishops, priests and deacons for special attention, while later great numbers of Christians from all ranks were seized. They had their eyes and tongue gouged out, their feet sawed off; they died at the stake or in a red-hot chair. Some were thrown to wild beasts to entertain a holiday mob; others were starved to death and thrown into dungeons.*[10]

The influence and favor of the imperial court was arguably not always the best thing for the Church. Even so, in the early AD 300s imperial favor was a welcome relief for most believers. Despite the favorable imperial edicts of AD 311, 312 and 313 it is hard to imagine that people who had been strongly persecuted for their faith only a few years previously would suddenly incorporate pagan practices into their own worship. Imperial favor did not *immediately* bring extreme corruption to the Church or a completely uncontrolled influx of superficial converts. We need to give credit and even honor to people who endured the suffering indicated above.

Many Christians have used the image of the increasing light following the winter solstice to speak of of the "Sun of Righteousness" (the Messiah) who was prophesied.

Constantine favored the Christians in the areas under his control. The Edict of Milan in AD 312, which ended the persecution of Christians in the western part of the empire, protected not only the Christians, but allowed people to worship whichever deity or deities they chose. Later this type of policy was extended to the eastern regions of the empire. Constantine did give Christianity increasing official patronage, but he did not fully make Christian worship and practice mandatory or totally outlaw other religious practices. The old gods were still worshiped, and Christians did not have a state monopoly on religious practice.

There is also a lot of misunderstanding about Constantine's role in establishing Sunday[11] as an official day of rest in the empire. A full exploration of this subject goes beyond the focus of this book. Whatever one's views concerning Sunday worship or Sabbath observance it is evident that at least some Christians were worshiping on Sundays as early as the second century AD, well before Constantine's reign. Justin Martyr writes about Christian worship toward AD 150:

We do not have a definitive, abosolutely proven, date for Jesus birth. but we have many indications that the traditional date may not be far from the true date.

On the day called Sunday, all who live in cities or in the country gather together in one place, and the memoirs of the apostles or the writings of the prophets are read, as long as time permits; then, when the reader has ceased, the president verbally instructs, and exhorts to the imitation of these good things. . . . (Justin Martyr, First Apology 67) [12]

In a similar way, any discussion of the date of the celebration of the Messiah's birth near the winter solstice continues to be dominated by many half truths, rumors, and distortions. A side note in a 12th century manuscript,[13] nearly one thousand years after Constantine, has even been used to say that believers unrighteously and deliberately co-opted a pagan festival. Despite all the very widespread rumors, there is no significant evidence that Christians under Constantine made any deals with the priests of Mithra or others. They did not take over the pagan rituals or include them in Christian worship. However, evidence abounds that Christians in the late Roman Empire made earnest efforts to turn people away from sun worship and refused to mix Christianity with Mithranism or any other religion. The idea that something incorrect, underhanded or compromising of the faith was done in establishing the date of Christmas seems to be unfounded.[14]

Early Christians Usually did not Celebrate Birthdays

Jesus' birthday was not an official Christian celebration during the early centuries of the Church. This may also be the main reason that it has been difficult to fix the exact date of his birth. A number of the early Church Fathers and Jewish leaders did not like the very idea of celebrating birthdays because of the ungodly birthday parties of many unbelievers.

"Not one from all the saints is found to have celebrated a festive day or a great feast on the day of his birth. No one is found to have had joy on the day of the birth of his son or daughter. Only sinners rejoice over this kind of birthday....the saints not only do not celebrate a festival on their birth days, but, filled with the Holy Spirit, they curse the day." - Origen (He lived from about AD 165 to 264).[15]

Unlike the Romans, who celebrated the dies natales of family and friends with gifts and banquets, Christians and Jews seemingly did not recognize birthdays. Josephus remarks that "the law does not permit us to make festivals at the births of our children, and thereby afford occasion of drinking to excess" (Against Apion, II.26). Rather, it was the anniversary of one's death that tended to be observed (cf. Ecclesiastes 7:1, "the day of death [is better] than the day of one's birth").[16]

Certainly it was not necessary to be so strongly against the very idea of being joyful about one's birth. However, it is understandable that many Christians were not in favor of having birthday parties linked with of sexual license and drunkenness. For many early believers, God's incarnation in the Messiah at conception was significantly more important than his actual birth.

Christmas Linked with Passover

Evidence that Jesus was born in December or January is found in the writings of the following Church Fathers: Theophilus (AD 115-181) who was bishop of Caesarea in Judea, Tertullian (AD 160 - 225), Clement of Alexandria (AD 150 - 215), Hippolytus of Rome (AD 170 - 235). Others like Eusebius, Gregory of Nazianzus, Chrysostom, Epiphanius and Augustine, believed it firmly.[17] Christians in the early centuries of the Church often thought that Jesus was conceived in Mary's womb at Passover and that he died on the same day several decades later. In many historic denominations, the Feast of the Annunciation is still celebrated at Easter (Passover), commemorating Gabriel's announcement to Mary that she would give birth to the Messiah.[18]

The traditional December 25th date may not be the actual birth date of Jesus, however, it may not be far from to the correct date.

Passover often falls about the same time as of the spring equinox, and in the early Christian centuries the Roman spring equinox was officially established on March 25th. Perhaps only based on this equinox date, Tertullian and others thought that Jesus had been crucified on March 25th. Their calculations were somehow in error, because March 25th was not a possible date for Passover or the crucifixion in any year from AD 27 to AD 35.[19] Based on these assumptions and calculations about Jesus' conception and death, many thought that the Messiah's birth would have been on the date of the former winter solstice on December 25th, nine months after his conception. Apparently a rough calculation was setting the date although some even tried to designate a specific day and hour.[20] In 3 BC, Passover should have fallen on March 30th and a normal pregnancy is about 38-39 weeks long (40 weeks after the last normal menstrual cycle). This would have placed Jesus' birth on or near the December 25th date. If Jesus was born exactly 40 weeks after Passover, then he would have been born about January 6th of 2 BC. However, Jesus could have been born at 37, 38, 39, 40, 41 or 42 weeks because pregnancies can last from 37-42 weeks depending on various factors.[21]

There seems to be a fairly unaminous opinion among the early Church Fathers that Jesus was born in either December or January.

In the opinion of the author an early January 2 BC birth date seems to fit all the data better than the December 25th date.

The traditional December 25th date may not be the actual birth date of Jesus; however, it may not be far from to the correct date. Many Christians in the early centuries of the Church celebrated Christmas in early January. The Eastern Orthodox Church still celebrates Christmas / Epiphany / Theophany on January 6th. In several denominations, this date is linked to Jesus' birth, the visit of the wise men and his baptism. The two traditional dates in December and January are both possible. The January 6th date may also be extremely close to the actual date of the visit of the wise men. Their visit took place, perhaps one year after Jesus' birth. Events in the heavens in 3/2 BC could lead one to think that the wise men made their visit to Bethlehem at the end of December 2 BC or the beginning of January of 1 BC. This would allow time for Jesus to be circumcised and to be presented at the temple. Much later his family would have fled into Egypt following the visit

If the 24 divisions of priests did an unbroken continous service in the temple (one division after another) then Zachariah's division would have been serving in from the 23rd to 29th of the Jewish month of Elul (September 15-22, 4 BC)

Elisabeth could have easily been in her sixth month in March 3 BC

of the Magi. It seems evident from Matthew's text that Joseph had established his family in Judea instead of Nazareth after the birth of Jesus. Apparently he would have liked to have returned to Bethlehem after fleeing to Egypt, but he was afraid to go there. God gave him instructions in a dream, and he went to Nazareth instead of Bethlehem (Mt 2:22-23). Luke simply skips over the flight to Egypt and any mention of a longer period in Bethlehem. His account underlines how Mary and Joseph and others did things in conformity to the law (Luke 1:5-6, 2:21-30). Matthew seems to underline the fulfillment of prophecy (Mt. 1:22-23, 2:5-6, 2:17-18 and 3:3 are all examples). The goals in the minds of each one of the Gospel writers shaped their manner of writing.

Efforts have often been made to establish the dates of the conception and birth of both John and Jesus by studying the service of the 24 divisions of priests and making a calculation concerning when John's father Zacharias would have been serving in the temple (See Luke 1:8-9 and 23). From these dates, it is supposedly possible to more or less establish when John was born. Jesus' birth should have followed about six months later. Unfortunately, there are problems with knowing exactly when the 24 divisions of the priests began and ended their service. Several authors have dealt with the problems at length.[22] The priests may have used a fixed yearly service schedule starting with the month of Tishrei which varied somewhat according to normal and leap years, but a scheme for a rotating priestly service could have also been possible. We simply do not know in a definitive manner which method was used. According to some estimates, using either method, the division of Abijah (Zachariah's division) could have been serving in the temple in one manner or another in both the late spring and the fall of 4 BC.[23] Zacharias may have even heard the angel's message in the spring and his wife Elisabeth only became pregnant several months later. Zacharias' division may have had ministry responsibilities during one of the major festivals or appointed times like the Day of Atonement or the Feast of Tabernacles.

We do not have a definitive, exact date for either Jesus' conception or his birth. However, one can make educated guesses. As we shall see later there are some other unexpected details which might help establish some reasonably close dates. A profoundly Jewish aspect concerning the timing of the events was always present even in the traditional dates of Christmas (nine months after Passover), but the Hebraic roots were hidden under piles of calendar changes, approximately calculated dates and mounds of Easter eggs.

Modern Messianic Jews and the Birth of Jesus:

Some modern messianic Jews have made efforts to develop a supposedly more Jewish approach to Jesus' birth. They do this by rejecting the traditional dates and proposing that Jesus was born in September during one of the Jewish festivals.[24] Previously I also followed this line of thought. This point of view has helped many of us to reorient our thinking toward the Jewish festivals and appointed times

A Possible Timeline of Events

4 BC

Fall: Elizabeth the wife of Zacharias conceived a son who would become John the Baptist about three decades later.

3 BC

Spring: During the Passover celebration or the Feast of Unleavened Bread (also called Passover), Mary conceived by a miracle of God.

The future John the Baptist was born in the summer of 3 BC.

December 3 BC : Mary and Joseph travelled to Bethlehem in Judea from Nazareth in order to participate in the census ordered by Augustus. Jesus was born at the end of 3 BC or the beginning of 2 BC.

2 BC

January: Jesus was circumcised eight days after his birth.

February: Jesus was presented at the temple in Jerusalem about 40 days after his birth.

Joseph kept his family in Bethlehem during most of 2 BC. He found appropriate housing for his family and he went to work locally in Bethlehem. He may have had family contacts who helped him.

December: The Magi arrived from the Parthian Empire.

1 BC

January 1 BC : The wise men were able to find Jesus and his parents. After leaving their gifts they left the area by a route other than the one they had used initially. Warned by God in a dream about Herod's plot to kill the child, Joseph, Mary and the young child Jesus fled to Egypt.

Herod the Great died in late January and Archelaus took his place.

Joseph was afraid to return to Bethlehem because of Archelaus and after he had received divine direction in a dream he took his family to live in Nazareth.

Passover 3 BC

The first sign announcing the Messiah's arrival took place at Passover in 3 BC. It may have been only many months later, after many other celestial events took place, that wise men understood that the Messiah had been born.

The Jewish historian Josephus specifically mentions a period of over seven months (actually 11-13 months) involving Herod's son Antipater. This long period followed a pledge of allegiance to the emperor which was almost certainly linked to a special census (Josephus, Antiquities of the Jews, Book 17 Ch. 1-7).[25]

The Star

In June 2 BC the wise men saw a specific sign which they later referred to as " His Star."

The Star over Bethlehem

The star visually went before the wise men from Mesopotamia. After the Magi arrived in Jerusalem it stopped moving among the background stars in late December 2 BC.

Eclipse of the Moon

Herod the Great died within weeks of a remarkable eclipse of the moon. (Josephus, Antiquities of the Jews, Book 17, Chapters 6-8)

Can one find a conception date for Jesus that is more profoundly and uniquely Jewish than Passover?

Jesus' profound suffering gives us an example of how we are to love one another even when holding divergent viewpoints.

concerning the birth of Jesus. However, there are good reasons to question this approach. A significant problem is posed because there are no ancient Church traditions linking the fall festivals and appointed times with the birth of Jesus. There is a tradition linking John the Baptist's conception with the fall, but not Jesus' birth. How could heretical texts like the Gospel of Judas and others be preserved but the slightest evidence of Jesus' birth during the Feast of Trumpets or Tabernacles disappeared completely? The idea of a September birth for Jesus appears to be a fairly modern invention. Even so, simply saying that the Church somehow forgot the right date of Jesus' birth may be partly right. As indicated earlier, birthday celebrations were not even desirable for several generations of early Christians. However, it is evident that even if the Church did forget that the actual date of Jesus' birth it was not because of a desire to suppress any Jewish roots linked to his conception and birth. An early Church tradition indicated that Jesus was conceived at Passover. Can one find a conception date for Jesus that is more profoundly and uniquely Jewish than Passover? The Hebraic roots of the traditional birth dates seem to be much deeper than most of us have ever imagined. Most modern Christians including messianic believers have often forgotten that Passover is usually about nine months before Christmas (See Appendix 3 - page 229 for more information).

Some astronomical events could also indicate a more traditional date for Jesus' birth. There was a series of events in the heavens in 3/2 BC that seem to be specifically tied to Jewish festivals and appointed times. These events began with Passover in 3 BC. The partial list on the timeline on the previous page indicates that there were events in the heavens involving the sun, the moon and several stars. One star became a key indicator of the Messiah's appearing in the celestial drama and it finally played the central role over Bethlehem.

It is the author's profound desire to affirm the Jewish roots of the Messiah. It has been a great privilege for him to learn more about his own Jewish roots in the Messiah through his research about the star and the Magi. As a Gentile, he also is one who has been grafted into God's olive tree. May God's olive tree which is composed of a profoundly Jewish root and various branches prosper and bear much fruit.

Dating of the Birth of Jesus with the Best of Attitudes:

While this book does use certain dates for Jesus' birth, there are numerous and varied ideas about his birth, Herod's death and concerning the famous star. Each point of view may have something important to contribute to the discussion. We as believers are called to respect and to love one another whatever one's viewpoints. The Messiah was born, he lived, he ministered, and he finally died and rose again. Jesus' profound suffering gives us an example of how we are to love one another even when holding divergent views. What we have in common in the Messiah through his death and resurrection, is more precious than any opinions we may ever hold.

Part 3: Wise Men from the East

It is written, "I will destroy the wisdom of the wise, and the cleverness of the clever I will set aside."

Where is the wise man? Where is the scribe? Where is the debater of this age? Has not God made foolish the wisdom of the world?

For since in the wisdom of God the world through its wisdom did not come to know God, God was well-pleased through the foolishness of the message preached to save those who believe.

For indeed Jews ask for signs and Greeks search for wisdom; but we preach Christ crucified, to Jews a stumbling block and to Gentiles foolishness, but to those who are the called, both Jews and Greeks, Christ the power of God and the wisdom of God.
(1 Corinthians 1:19-24)

Getting Back to the Past

Above: The Ishtar Gate in the Pergamon Museum in Berlin, Germany. Below: Marduk, the chief god of the Babylonian pantheon, was identified with the planet Jupiter. The god, who was often accompanied by a snake-dragon, was depicted as a human being like other Babylonian, Roman and Greek gods.

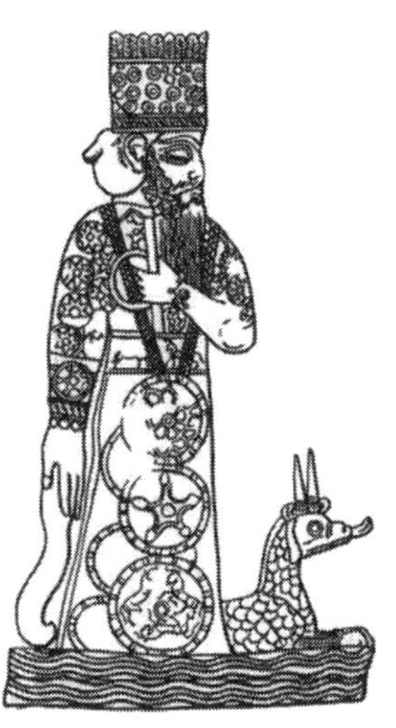

In most discussions of the star of Bethlehem and the Magi much energy is spent in discussing astronomy. However, the lack of any really serious exploration of the world of the Magi may have been one of the greatest obstacles to understanding both the wise men and the famous star which made such an impact on their lives. Getting "back to the past" is an important key to understanding the Magi and their famous star.

In order to get back into the historical context of the Magi, it will be necessary to explore, at least briefly, some largely unknown historical, cultural and religious territory. The Magi, who eventually arrived in Bethlehem, had apparently lived most of their lives between the great rivers Tigris and Euphrates, in what would later become modern Iraq. Some Magi associated with Zoroastrianism may have come from the mountains and high plains of present day Iran. Mesopotamia and Iran have been the home of some of the earth's most ancient civilizations. However, even the present inhabitants of Iraq and Iran are usually quite uninformed about the civilizations which preceded Islamic rule in the region. Relatively few outsiders have visited these regions in recent years except for the purpose of combat in wars. Even now, little tourism is taking place in either Iran or Iraq. The ancient Mesopotamian world remains largely foreign and unfamiliar to most modern people. The Sumerians, Assyrians, Syrians, Elamites, Babylonians, Medes, Persians, Seleucids and Parthians are often briefly studied in school, in most countries around the world. Even so, the actual history, culture and world view of the ancient Middle East remains very far removed from the vast majority of us. The principal group of people that were living in Mesopotamia when Jesus was born were the Babylonians (also known as the Chaldeans). This group and other peoples including the ancient Sumerians and Assyrians had lived in the region of modern Iraq for millennia.

Simply briefly hearing about Zoroaster, Nebuchadnezzar, Marduk, and the hanging gardens of Babylon and really understanding what happened in Mesopotamia or Iran in the ancient past are two different things. Who were the famous men who lived in that period? Why were they recognized as "history makers?" Where were the great cities of Babylon, Ur, Uruk, Sippar, Nineveh, Persepolis, Ctesiphon, Seleucia on the Tigris, Susa or Ecbatana? What were they like? How does one know anything about such places or the people who lived there? What was happening in Mesopotamia when Jesus was born? These questions go well beyond the main subject matter of this book; however, some familiarity with Mesopotamian history and geography can give insights into the lives of the Magi. Being uninformed can never provide the same insights as answering the type of questions listed above.

The fictional story situated at the ziggurat of the temple of Nabu in Borsippa, at the beginning of this book, brings to light some of the realities of ancient Mesopotamia. The unfamiliar, strange sounding Mesopotamian names in the opening story actually were the names of one family associated with Babylonian astronomy and astrology. This is known from cuneiform texts from the Mesopotamian city of Uruk. The city of Borsippa was chosen for the opening story because of its proximity to the ancient city of Babylon. Large numbers of Jews lived in the general area of Babylon and Borsippa. The imposing ziggurat of Borsippa was damaged in a revolt against the Persian Emperor Xerxes in 484 BC. It largely survived the ensuing war and retributions of the emperor while most of the city of Babylon and its massive ziggurat eventually fell into total ruin. By the time of Jesus' birth, the city of Babylon was already largely abandoned by most of its inhabitants.

Above: A model of the Ishtar Gate

Life in Mesopotamia

The word Mesopotamia means "the land between two rivers." The Tigris and the Euphrates rivers have been shaping Iraq's landscape and watering its crops for thousands of years. Both rivers start their course to the sea in southern and eastern Turkey and they arrive in the Persian / Arabian Gulf after many months. Flowing by some of the greatest cities of the ancient world, both rivers have regularly deposited so much alluvium in their combined delta that the sea is now over 125 miles away from where it was during the life of Abraham. The Hebrew patriarch was born in Ur which was originally closer to the mouth of the Euphrates River.

Even in Abraham's day the region was warm and rainfall was somewhat limited, although there may have been more rainfall than today. However, a massive network of canals and an extensive irrigation system based on the two great rivers supplied water and assured good crops. Innumerable fields of barley and wheat were cultivated by the various peoples who occupied the region. Other vegetables and grains supplemented the Babylonian diet including onions, chick peas, lentils, broad beans, sesame and millet. Vast plantations of date palms provided dates, which are still the pride of some regions of Iraq.[1] The Jews in Babylonia became merchants, farmers and workers. Some became exceedingly prosperous. Iran and Central Iraq were important transportation hubs on the silk routes.[2] A good number of Jews were apparently involved in the silk trade, having been a link between the producers of silk in the Far East and the markets in the Mediterranean region.

By the time of Jesus' birth Aramaic had already been the main language of communication in Mesopotamia for several centuries

Jacob / Israel, the grandson son of Abraham, is referred to in the Bible as a wandering Aramean (Deut. 26:5). The Arameans settled in the region over a period of several hundred years; Eventually, the Aramaic language became the most prominent language in the Mesopotamia. By the time of Jesus' birth, it had already been the main language of communication in the region for several centuries. Present day Hebrew Bibles are written with the square Aramaic script. For many people living in Babylonia, it would not have been difficult to have learned some of the

English	Babylonian Names are indicated in SUMERIAN and Akkadian (As well as the gods associated with each heavenly body)		Greek	Roman	Zoroastrian
Sun	UTU / *Šamaš (Son of the moon god Sîn)*	Samas	Helios / Apollo	Sôl	Mithra
Moon	^{MUL}GAL / ^{d}*Sîn (Father of Marduk and Ishtar)*	Sîn	Selenê / Artemis	Luna	?
Mercury	DUMU.LUGAL / ^{MUL}*Na-bu-*u_2 *(Son of Marduk)*	Nabû	Apollo / Hermes	Mercurius	?
Mars	^{d}GIR^{3}.UNU.GAL / *Salbatânu*	Nergal	Ares	Mars	?
Jupiter	MUL.BABBAR / *kakkab šarri*	Marduk	Zeus (Dias)	Iuppiter	?
Venus	^{d}NIN.AN.NA / *Dilbat (Daughter of Sîn or Anu)*	Ishtar	Aphrodite	Venus	Anahita ?
Saturn	^{MUL}SAG.UŠ / *Kajjamanu*	Ninurta	Kronos	Saturnus	?

Table 2.1 Above: The gods associated with the sun, moon and the planets from Babylonian, Roman, Greek and Zoroastrian backgrounds.

There were an impressive number of ancient Mesopotamian names for the celestial bodies. This table only cites a small number of the names used by the Babylonian astronomers.

biblical Hebrew which is linguistically related to Aramaic. This familiarity with Aramaic would have made it relatively easy for a good number of Babylonian and Zoroastrian priests to have read some portions of the biblical texts.

According to the Gospel writer Matthew, the wise men came from the east, so it is perhaps best to simply disregard most interpretations of heavenly events, which are strongly linked to Roman or purely Hellenistic perspectives. While some very influential Greeks did live in Mesopotamia we do not have any records of highly influential Greek astronomers among the Mesopotamian wise men. Even so, the English names of the planets are all linked to names associated with Greek and Roman gods. We have difficulties in referring to the planets without some shadows of the ancient Roman gods continuing to lurk in the background. Linking our understanding of the Magi to Western deities and Western astrological traditions, may have been one reason that we have had difficulties in understanding the star and the Magi. This subject will be explored later in greater detail.

The Babylonian gods were somewhat similar to and partially equivalent to the Greek and Roman gods, but not entirely so; there were some profound differences. The chief Babylonian god in the years preceding the birth of Jesus, named Marduk, had overcome the primeval ruling sea-monster goddess, Tiamat, to become chief of the Mesopotamian gods. Marduk was also identified with the planet Jupiter, which was known in Babylonia as MUL.BABBAR, "the white star," but the planet also had several other names. Marduk's father was the sun god UTU/Shamash and his grandfather was the moon god Sîn. Both the sun and the moon were masculine in the Babylonian world view. The planet Venus was associated with the

Babylonian goddess of sex and fertility, named Ishtar, who was a daughter of the moon god Sîn. Venus was often called *Dilbat* among the Babylonians. Some other gods were Nabu, Nergal and Ninurta. The gods were especially celebrated during the Babylonian New Year, in the spring, at the time of the barley harvest. This was marked by a large religious festival called the Atiku, which celebrated the victory of the Babylonian god Marduk over the sea goddess Tiamat. In a special ceremony during the Atiku festival, the Babylonian king's divine mandat was renewed, or a new king was crowned. We do not have any record that the Parthian emperors ever participated in these ceremonies although at least some of the Persian and Greek kings apparently did so.[3]

The wise men came from the east so it is perhaps best to simply disregard most interpretations of heavenly events which are strongly linked to Roman or Greek perspectives.

A General Timeline of Mesopotamian History

Dates	Empires
3000+ BC - 1400 BC	The Sumerians, Elamites, Akkadians, Babylonians, Kassites, Hurrians and Hittites and other groups dominated Mesopotamia.
1400 BC - 605 BC	**Assyrian Empire** There were two stages: (1) the Old Assyrian Empire and (2) the Neo-Assyrian Empire that was overthrown by the rise of the Neo-Babylonian Empire.
620 BC - 539 BC	**Neo-Babylonian Empire** Nebuchadnezzar was the most famous king of the Empire. The greatest domination of the Neo-Babylonian Empire was from 609 BC to 539 BC.
539 BC - 330 BC	**Persian Empire** Cyrus, Darius and Xerxes are the better known emperors.
334 BC - 323 BC	**Conquests of Alexander the Great** Upon Alexander's death the Empire was divided into four parts. The Seleucid Greeks reigned over Mesopotamia.
312 BC - 63 BC	**Seleucid Empire** Seleucus "Nicator" and Antiochus VI (Epiphanes) are the best known among the Seleucid kings.
247 BC - AD 224	**Parthian Empire** The Parthians were an Iranian people from Central Asia, they were not Persians. Over time they became more and more favorable to Zoroastrianism.

Below: A small portion of cuneiform text of the Cyrus Cylinder in the British Museum. Photograph by Mike Peel

Who Were the Wise Men?

The terms Magus and Magi were used for wise men and astronomers / astrologers from many backgrounds. in the 1st Century BC.

Most Christians and the majority of people from whatever background may find it difficult to understand the Magi. We often cannot point out more than three constellations in the heavens, most of us may not be able to tell the difference between a star and a planet in the night sky. For the most part we have no idea concerning what ancient wise men knew or how they thought. Relatively few people have ever given any profound reflection to questions concerning the ethnic or religious origins of the wise men who arrived in Bethlehem.

The words used in the Roman world for wise men from the east were Magus (singular) and Magi (plural). It appears that the term "Magus" was in use for the wise men of Babylon even before the victory of the Medes and Persians and their occupation of Babylon in 539 BC. We read in Jeremiah 39:3 that Nergal-sar-ezer, the Rab-mag (chief Babylonian wise man), was present at the fall of Jerusalem in 597 BC. We know few other details about his specific ethnic or religious background. He had apparently married Nebuchadnezzar's daughter and he eventually seized the Babylonian throne after murdering Nebuchadnezzar's son Evil-merodach. His name, Nergal, refers to the Babylonian deity associated with the planet Mars. The word Rab means "chief," and Mag is related to the word Magus.

A multitude of ideas exist concerning the ethnic origins, roles and activities of the ancient Middle Eastern wise men in general. We do not know the exact ethnic or religious background of the Bethlehem Magi. The Parthian Empire, the dominant power in the east, was populated by Parthians, Persians, Medes, Armenians, Greeks, Babylonians (Chaldeans), Jews and other ethnic groups. It may be that the group that arrived in Bethlehem could have had a mixed ethnic and religious background. Even the traditional three, Melchior, Gaspar and Balthazar, often mentioned in the Western traditions concerning the wise men, all had different ethnic origins.

The Parthian Empire, the dominant power in the east, was populated by Parthians, Persians, Medes, Armenians, Greeks, Babylonians (Chaldeans), Jews and other ethnic groups.

Zoroastrian Priests, Babylonian Priests, Others?

It is often assumed that the Magi mentioned in Matthew's Gospel were Zoroastrian priests, who originally came from the land of the Medes in present day Northwestern Iran. We read in the Bible about how the Medes and the Persians came to power in Mesopotamia during the life of Daniel. This happened immediately following Daniel's interpretation of the famous "handwriting on the wall." It is certain that the Median priests were called Magi at the time of Daniel (6th century BC). While some of the wise men at Bethlehem in the 1st century BC may have been Zoroastrians, it is far from proven that they were all Zoroastrian priests. Herodotus (484-425 BC) mentions the role of the Median Magi in his book *Histories (I. 107, 120 and VII.19),* during the Persian period, well after the time of

Daniel, who most likely died about 530 BC. According to Herodotus, the Median Magi were very skilled in interpreting dreams, he did not mention anything about them concerning astronomy or astrology. The Median Magi apparently had a major role in naming the new Persian kings and in giving them counsel. However, following the Greek invasion under Alexander (334 BC to 323 BC), other forces came to power. The Greek domination was followed by Parthian rule in the whole region. Although the Parthians were ethnically Iranian, they were not Medes or Persians. In their early reign they were not known to be extremely religious followers of Zoroaster. That prophet's religion played a greater role toward the end of the Parthian Empire (AD 100 - 200), and its influence grew considerably during the Sassanid Era that followed. The once strong influence of the original Median Magi apparently declined in the Greek period and at least part of the Parthian period.

The Roman writer Pliny the Elder, who died at Pompei in AD 79, used the term "Magus" when referring to Moses!

At the time of Christ men from other ethnic, cultural and religious backgrounds played a major role in the Parthian court. A very large and influential Greek community arose in ancient Syria, Mesopotamia and Iran following the conquests of Alexander the Great. The Greek community in Mesopotamia was still highly influential when Jesus was born. Greek scholars in the region usually would not have been specifically identified as Magi although there may have been some possible exceptions. We do know that the Greek cultural influence was truly pronounced in the Parthian court. For example, in 53 BC the Roman general Crassus was defeated by the Parthians and killed at the battle of Carrhae. Crassus' decapitated head was used in a Greek play *The Bacchae* which the Parthian emperor was watching during the marriage celebrations of his son, the crown prince. The play was a celebration of the Greek god Dionysus. This, and other evidence suggests that the

Left: The Magi - A painting by James Tissot: Most people traveling from Mesopotamia to Judea would have walked or rode horses. Dromadairies were mainly used for transporting commercial goods. The wise men may have used camels (dromadairies) if they travelled through the deserts of Saudi Arabia and Jordan, possibly on their return trip to Mesopotamia.

Philo, the Jewish philosopher, who lived in Alexandria (20 BC - AD 50) referred to Balaam, the as a "magus"

Parthian monarchs were not strongly aligned with their ancestral religious practices. Zealous practitioners of the Zoroastrian religion would have most likely been reluctant to include a Greek play in the events surrounding the marriage of the crown prince. The early Parthian leaders seem to have been extremely tolerant of the various religious expressions which existed under their rule.

Many Different People Were Known as Magi

Some ethnically and religiously Babylonian wise men were also known as Magi. The Babylonian astronomers had technical abilities and remarkable mathematical skills. They had observed the skies for hundreds of years, keeping extensive records of their careful observations. Among the peoples in the Parthian Empire the Babylonians had most of the technical knowledge concerning the heavens. The 1st Century BC Greek writer Diodorus Siculus gives a highly relevant perspective concerning the Babylonian (Chaldean) astronomers in his book *Bibliotheca Historica*. Portions of this book are reproduced in Appendix 10, pages 240-241. In the coming pages more and more will be revealed about their astronomical knowledge, methods, culture and religion. The Zoroastrians of the 1st century BC apparently did not have the same skills or the extensive astronomical records found among their Babylonian counterparts. Some concepts related to Babylonian astronomy seem to be linked to the celestial events surrounding Jesus' birth.

By the 1st century AD, the word Magi had come to be used for many different "wise men." In the Roman world, the words Magi and Magus were not reserved uniquely for the Median Magi. Over the centuries, the words no longer referred exclusively to the Median priestly tribe. Apparently the terms Magus and Magi came to be used as a general term for wise men in the Persian, Seleucid, Parthian and Roman Empires. Some would have held a specifically priestly function and others who would not have had such a role. From ancient sources and the Bible, we discover that several Jewish people were also referred to as Magi.[4] The Roman writer Pliny the Elder, who died at Pompeii in AD 79, used the term "Magus" when referring to Moses. From Pliny's perspective, Moses was an ancient eastern "wise man." Philo the Jewish philosopher, who lived in Alexandria (20 BC - AD 50), referred to Balaam, as a "Magus" (see Numbers 22-24). Balaam lived toward the middle of the second millennium BC. In the Bible, we find references to two men who were spoken of as practitioners of magic and prophecy. The same root word for "Magus / Magi" was used for both men. The first was Simon, a Samaritan magician, who is mentioned in Acts 8:9-25. Bar-Jesus, also called "Elymas," was a second "Magus" (magician) mentioned later in the book of Acts. As a *Jewish* false prophet, he opposed Paul's missionary efforts (see Acts 13:4-12).

Matthew, the first century Jew, who lived most of his life in Judea and Galilee, may have had other ideas about the wise men than the modern tendency to immediately identify them as Zoroastrian priests. We do not know who gave Matthew any

Ziggurats were used in Mesopotamia for religious and possibly for astronomical purposes. The upper platforms of a ziggurat could have given any astronmer a good vantage point to observe the sky.

of the details about the coming of the wise men. Matthew himself was possibly born at about the same time as Jesus. It is unlikely that he was an eye witness to any of the events surrounding the coming of the Magi. It is also doubtful that the event was overly remarkable. Traditionally it is thought that Mary gave Luke information about the events concerning the birth of Jesus and the shepherds. Matthew may have received information directly from Mary. He could have also met many other people who were eye witnesses.

In the Parthian Empire various men from different ethnic and religious groups would have been qualified to be counselors, administrators and "wise men" by their ethnic and priestly origins, their studies, their recognized professional abilities and their family ties. Some "wise men" could have been from a Median or Babylonian background, a Syrian or Mesopotamian Greek background. In addition, there may have been Arabs and visiting Indians or others among the Magi. In various traditions, the wise men have been described as coming from different ethnic backgrounds; however, few people have ever suggested that there may have been an explicitly Jewish ethnic link with the Bethlehem wise men. This is not illogical or impossible. Jewish wise men would have been interested in the Messiah of Israel. Before exploring some possible Jewish connections to the wise men, we will briefly explore some subjects concerning the followers of Zoroaster.

The Zoroastrians

Who was Zoroaster?

It seems that the original Median Magi became followers of the prophet Zarathustra (Zoroaster) who supposedly came from Central Asia. The Median priests had already been Zoroastrians for possibly a few centuries when Babylon was overrun by the Medio-Persian army in 539 BC. We know very little about the beginnings of the Zoroastrian religion, even the dating of the life of Zoroaster is very uncertain. Most scholars believe that Zoroaster lived sometime between the 15th and the 6th century BC. Plutarch, writing in about AD 100, indicated that Zoroaster should be dated at about 6000 BC. It can be safely affirmed that no one is able to establish the dates of Zoroaster's life with any assurance.

Median Magi and the Jewish Messiah

The Zoroastrian Magi left little written material. This happened either through their own choice or because their texts were destroyed during various wars and religious persecution following the rise of Islam in the seven and eighth centuries AD. Relatively little is known about their specific teachings and activities during the Parthian period (247 BC - AD 224). Despite their reputation of having been great astronomers and astrologers, at present, we do not even know what names

Above: Bactrian camels from Central Asia

the Magi gave to the "wandering stars," the planets. It is actually remarkable how little we know about Zoroastrian Magian astronomy / astrology before about AD 300. More than one author has pointed out the lack of information.

> *In fact, virtually nothing is known of the astronomy and astrology of pre-Sansaian Iran. There was indeed a Greek astrological text of the second century BC ascribed to Zoroaster of which the fragments are preserved by Proclus and the Geoponica, the material with which it deals is overwhelmingly Babylonian ... However, trustworthy knowledge of Iranian astronomy and astrology is non-existant before the reign of Sâpûr I (240-270 AD).* [5]

Despite the very widespread claims concerning Persian astronomy, which one can find in popular literature and on the Internet, there is absolutely no evidence that the Persians had any developed system of astronomy, stellar divination or astrology in 3,000 BC or even in 500 BC. The so called "royal stars of the Persians" seem to be an invention / interpretation of a few Frenchmen in the 18th century (see Appendix 6 on page 236). As mentioned previously, Herodotus, writing in about 440 BC, indicates that the Magi were well known interpreters of dreams, but he does not mention anything concerning their astronomical skills.

Were the Bethlehem Magi actually Zoroastrian priests? Perhaps, perhaps not. One cannot be totally certain.

The greatest, well-attested period of Persian / Zoroastrian astronomy and astrology was during the Sassanid period well after the birth of Christ. The Zoroastrians apparently inherited much of their astronomical knowledge from the Babylonians. Later the conquering Arabs learned from the Persian astronomers and highly praised them. This plausibly accounts for at least part of the immense astronomical reputation of the Persian Magi. The lack of solid detailed information has caused speculation to abound concerning the beliefs and practices of the Magi. The original Median Magi and many of their successors remain fairly mysterious and unknowable figures to this day. Some Magi may have practiced a Zoroastrian faith akin to that which existed later under the Sassanids (AD 224 - 651). Others supposedly turned more and more toward magic and some became true charlatans. Modern Zoroastrians largely reject one such "heretical" group called the Magussaeans.

Zoroastrian Beliefs

The main Zoroastrian religious texts, called the Avesta, were largely compiled in their present written form well after the birth of Jesus, during the Persian cultural revival which started in about AD 200 and continued through AD 1200. The original Avestian language used in the texts still survives among very small isolated groups in Iran and India. Translations of the ancient religious texts have been widely circulated in recent decades. Presently there are about 2.5 to 3 million Zoroastrians from many ethnic backgrounds worldwide. Devoted Zoroastrians have a very important presence on the Internet. Some Westerners and others have found modern interpretations of Zoroastrian thought to be attractive.

Above: The somewhat angelic "faravahar" is one of the best known symbols of the Zoroastrian religion. Zoroastrians had well developed ideas of individual guardian angels who would help and protect each person.

Ahura Mazda is an ancient name for the chief divinity of Zoroastrianism. The word Ahura means "light" and "mazda" means wisdom. Zoroastrian thought was and remains largely dualistic. Ahura Mazda was believed to have been the creator and upholder of truth who was opposed by Angra Mainyu, a wicked demon spirit who will ultimately be vanquished. Human beings were called to resist the forces of evil in thought, word and deed. Ahura Mazda also created a number of godlike spirits who help him reign over creation. These beings called "Amesha Spentas" and "Yazatas" have been compared to archangels and angels. However, in Zoroastrian circles worship of these godlike spirits was also encouraged. This is a significant difference between Zoroastrian thought and Judaic ideas concerning angels.

While many scholars believe that Zoroastrian thought influenced Judaism and Christianity, in reality the religion is only superficially similar to both Judaism and Christianity. One can see the profound differences and superficial similarities when one explores the topic of the so called Zoroastrian "world saviors" (messiahs). It is not at all clear why Median Zoroastrian priests would have been interested in a Jewish Messiah. Typical Zoroastrian priests from the period simply lacked any direct connection with the hopes of the people of Israel, whose messianic aspirations were centered on the royal line of king David. The Zoroastrians had no link to David in their theology, their general culture or their world view.

In the form in which it has come down to us the Zoroastrian idea of "world saviors" speaks of three different Messiah figures. Each one was supposed to be born at the end of the three different one thousand year periods that make up the last 3,000 years of world history. The last savior, called the Saoshyant, will be victorious in the final battle against all evil. The Zoroastrian saviors were supposed to be born of three separate virgins who would become pregnant while bathing in lake Kasaoya (Hamun) in present day Eastern Iran at the border of Afghanistan. Zoroaster's "seed" (his actual semen) was supposedly miraculously preserved in

Central Asia, where Zoroaster was supposed to have lived, is a region of great contrasts. Above one sees a desert sand dune beside a marsh.

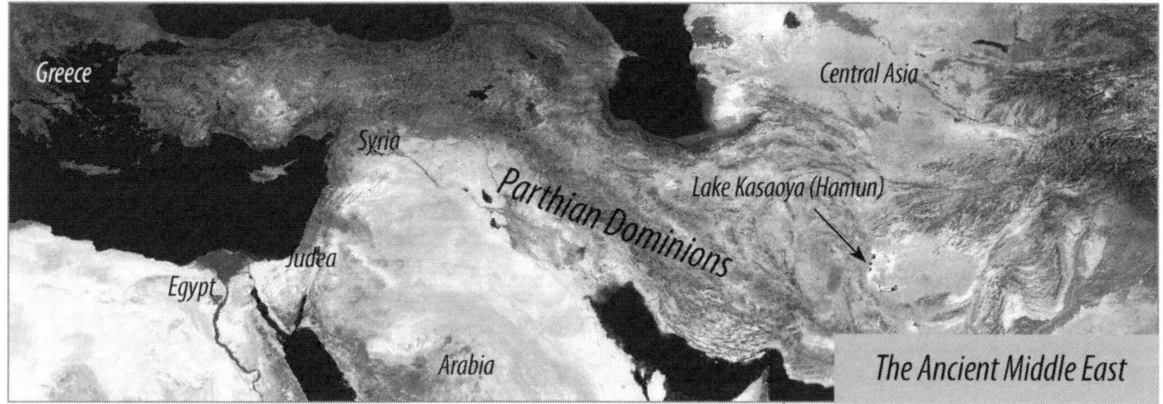

It is not at all clear why Median Zoroastrian priests would have been interested in a Jewish Messiah.

the lake awaiting the time when it would impregnate the virgins one by one over a period of millennia (see Appendix 7, page 237). If the Bethlehem Magi were seeking one of the three Zoroastrian saviors, logically they would have traveled to the east, toward Afghanistan, looking for one of their awaited saviors, and not toward Judea. One might even ask if the Zoroastrian ideas of the world saviors, most of which were only written down well after the birth of Christ, might not have been at least partially influenced by Greek and Roman thought, Judaism or even Christianity.[6] It would seem reasonable to at least ask the question.[7]

While some aspects of Zoroastrian thought concerning the final world deliverers might be somewhat similar to biblical ideas, the differences are also extremely profound. The impregnation of the virgins by Zoroaster's seed is not at all the same thing as the miraculous conception of Jesus in Mary's womb. Mary's pregnancy did not involve either semen or its miraculous preservation. According to the biblical account Mary conceived based on a sovereign decision of the God, who said, "The seed of the woman will crush the serpent's head (Genesis 3:15).

The Exile / Daniel Connection:

Few people have suggested that there could have been a firm Jewish connection with the wise men; however, this may be the most logical manner of understanding the Magi.

Matthew's Gospel explicitly says that the wise men came seeking the "King of the Jews." It would be reasonable to explore possible Jewish links with the Magi as well, instead of simply assuming that they were Zoroastrian priests, Babylonians, Indians, Arabs or Greeks who had no direct connection with the Jewish messianic hope. Men from many backgrounds may have been attracted to the Jewish hope centered on the Messiah. If the Magi were from other ethnic and religious backgrounds, they almost certainly had some contact with Jewish people and / or the Jewish Scriptures in Mesopotamia and Iran. The ancient world did not have large numbers of people who were agnostics or religiously neutral. Whatever their background, the Magi must have had a favorable view of the Jewish people and the God of Abraham. They no doubt obtained at least some of their information about the Jewish Messiah from Jewish sources. This was certainly possible because ancient Mesopotamia and Iran had substantial Jewish populations.

Daniel and Jewish Links to the Persians, Greeks and Parthians

It would not have even been impossible for one or more of the wise men to have been ethnically Jewish. Hundreds of years before the birth of Jesus, Daniel had been the head of all the wise men in Babylon (Daniel 2:46-49). Having been born in the land of Judah about 625 BC, Daniel went into exile to Babylon in 605 BC. He died in Mesopotamia or Iran in about 535 to 530 BC. It is still possible to visit his supposed tomb located in the ruins of ancient Susa, which was one of the imperial cities of the Persians and later of the Parthians. As a young man, Daniel distinguished himself and God gave him great favor. He eventually became a high official in the Babylonian administration. Through Daniel's position and influence, several Jews were introduced into important roles in the Babylonian royal court (think of Shadrach, Meshach and Abed-nego). In later governments Mordechai, Esther and Nehemiah had significant influence in the Persian court.

After some Jews returned to their homeland, other Jews continued to live in ancient Iran and Iraq under the Persians. They continued to live there after the defeat of the Persians by Alexander the Great. A small Jewish minority remained in Iraq till the 20th century AD and a very small number still live in Iran. There may have been several hundred thousand Jews living under Parthian rule. It has been estimated that there were up to one million Jews in Babylonia and elsewhere in the Parthian realm. Certain towns and cities had a majority Jewish population. Altogether they numbered perhaps 5-10% of the population of the Parthian Empire.

The Jewish community in Babylonia had, since ancient times, consisted of 'countless myriads of which none can know the number' (Josephus, Jewish Antiquities

Whatever their ethnic origins, the Magi sought a specifically Jewish Messiah.

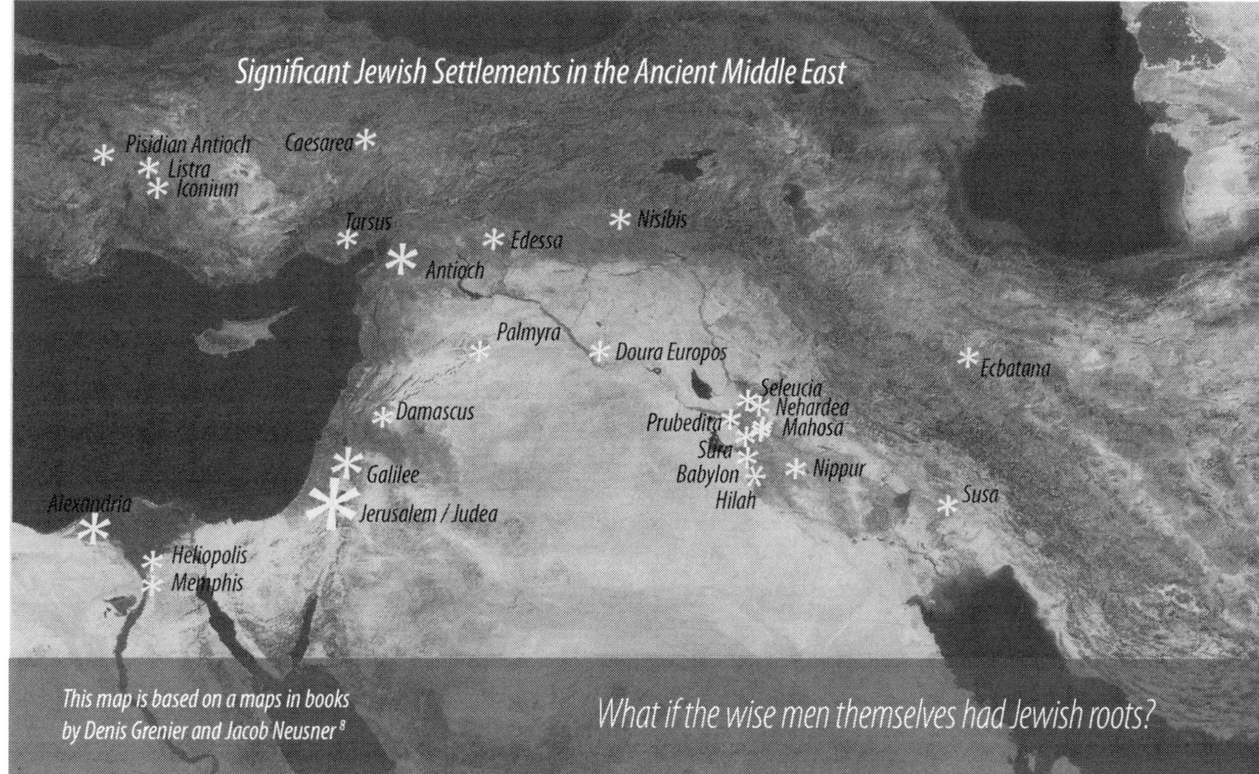

This map is based on a maps in books by Denis Grenier and Jacob Neusner[8]

Above: A wall mural depicting a scene from the Book of Esther at the Dura-Europos synagogue which is located on the Euphrates River in present day Iraq, dated AD 245.

11.133). Some of Babylonia's greatest cities, such as Nehardea, Nisibis, Mahoza and others were entirely, or almost entirely, populated, maintained and garrisoned by Jews. ... The Jews of Babylonia regarded themselves as the faithful guardians of Jewish tradition and lineage, in the sense that they had not intermarried with proselytes whose conversion was suspect, with foreign slaves who had not been fully emancipated, ... Where lineage was concerned the Babylonian Jews felt superior even to their brethren in the Land of Israel ...

Not all the wide area of Babylonia was closely settled by Jews, and not all Jews were considered to be of good lineage; this attribute was reserved for those who lived in the section of land between the Tigris and the Euphrates where the two rivers were connected by the main canals ... [9]

Some of the Bethlehem Magi may have had their origins in such families. If one or more of them came from a Jewish aristocratic or priestly background that could explain how they were interested in the Jewish Messiah. It also might help explain their possible interpretations of heavenly events. A good number of Jews presumably entered into royal service during the 6th and 5th centuries BC through the influence of Daniel, Mordechai, Esther, Nehemiah, their followers or their descendants. The events linked with Esther would have opened doors of opportunity for the Jews in the Persian Empire. However, under the Seleucid Greeks at certain moments possibly very few Jews, or even none at all, were in royal service. The actions of Greek leaders like Antiochus IV Epiphanes (175-164 BC) in Judea led to the Jewish Maccabean revolt, but we do not know exactly how Jews in Mesopotamia experienced it. Later the Jews in the Parthian domains were largely in favor with the Parthian government. Early during his reign, Herod appointed a Babylonian Jew as high priest in Jerusalem. He did this in order to calm opposition to his own reign and to win the favor of the Jews in the Parthian Empire.

The famous Jewish religious leader, Hillel the Elder, apparently came from Babylonia and settled in Judea only in the later part of his long life. Born about 100 years before the birth of Christ, he lived until AD 10. Hillel moved to Jerusalem in about 30 BC and remained there till his death. Some have even speculated that Jesus may have met the famous man in the temple during his 12th year (Luke 2:39-52). It was Hillel's grandson, Gamaliel, who taught the Apostle Paul (Acts 22:3). The debates between the "School of Hillel" and the "School of Shammai" and their respective founders are well known in Judaism. It is said that Hillel's attitude was more acceptable to God, and his patience and kind temperament are legendary in Talmudic literature.[10] Babylonian Jews have certainly influenced their brethren all over the world for over two millennia through men like Hillel. Written works like the massive 9,000 pages of rabbinic commentaries called the Babylonian Talmud continue to influence Jewish faith and practice worldwide, 1,500 years after they were compiled.

While we do not know the names of any Jewish astronomers from Babylonia, there is evidence that some Jews were well versed in astronomy during the period surrounding Jesus' birth. Johanan ben Zakkai, who lived in the land of Israel from AD 30 to AD 90, had a very good knowledge of the solstices and the calendar. He had the ability to compute the course of the sun and the moon (Tractate Sukkot 28a). Following the disastrous revolt from AD 66-73, Johanan ben Zakkai was the founder of the Jewish academy at Yavne. This institution was a key element in the survival and redefining of Judaism after the fall of Jerusalem. If such a key figure as Johanan ben Zakkai had significant astronomical knowledge, is it not possible that some Jews in Mesopotamia could have been equally well versed in the subject?

The Magi were apparently influenced by the Jewish people, their theology, and their Scriptures.

A Jewish Link?

The descendants of Abraham were entrusted with knowledge about the God YHWH, and his ways. Over generations, this knowledge had been handed down both in oral traditions and through written texts. In the 8th, 7th and 6th centuries BC the Jews were exiled to Mesopotamia and hundreds of thousands of Jews still lived in the area until the 1st century BC and afterwards. Could certain signs in the heavens related to the promised Messiah have been properly interpreted by these Mesopotamian Jews? The wise men came seeking a Jewish Messiah. Could the Magi have had specific links to the Jews who were living in 1st century Mesopotamia and Iran? Were at least one or more of the Magi ethnically Jewish?

Whether great or small, there was almost certainly some kind of Jewish connection with the Magi. However, there are other questions that also need to be asked. A whole range of ideas about the star and the Magi need to be explored before we can try to understand a possible Jewish perspective concerning the men and events.

High and even middle level Parthian officials and kings would have most likely ridden on horseback even in the desert. Below is a modern day example of Omani horsemen.

Were the Wise Men Kings?

> *Let the kings of Tarshish and of the islands bring presents; The kings of Sheba and Seba offer gifts. And let all kings bow down before him, All nations serve him. (Psalm 72:10-11)*
>
> *The wealth of the nations will come to you. A multitude of camels will cover you, The young camels of Midian and Ephah; All those from Sheba will come; They will bring gold and frankincense, And will bear good news of the praises of the LORD. (Isaiah 60:5-6)*

Do these two texts refer specifically to the wise men?

Despite the commonly accepted idea, Matthew's account does not tell us that the wise men were kings. It is fairly doubtful that they were actual kings. In the ancient world and even today, a king or a group of kings, visiting a far away country, would be housed and fed for the duration of their visit by the local monarch. A state visit would have obliged Herod to extend hospitality to any visiting royalty even as it would be necessary today. In Matthew's account, the wise men were Herod's guests only when they were secretly called to come to the palace. Apparently the wise men were not kings on a state visit.

It is certainly possible that the wise men were Parthian court officials (coming directly from Ctesiphon, Ecbatana or Susa). They certainly may have been chief astrologers and astronomers. However, it is somewhat doubtful that they would have been the highest court officials or possibly even the highest ranking astronomers because they would have had significant responsibilities, forbidding their absence. Higher officials might have been older, and they would have been less apt for the journey. However, there could have been very high ranking wise men in the group. They obviously had ties to wealth. Their gifts make it clear that they were not poor men, and they certainly had enough means to travel.

There is some evidence from the biblical text that the Magi did not make great efforts to be known during their visit. While their presence did become well known in Jerusalem fairly quickly, the Magi's first stop was apparently not at Herod's palace. The wise men may have even desired to avoid meeting Herod. They only went to see the king when they were summoned. At that point they were obliged to meet him. It is doubtful that the Magi actually wanted the goal of their visit to be known to the king. Herod had executed his own heirs and other immediate family members who seemed to pose a threat to his rule and his royal line. Being aware of this fact, the wise men were most likely discreet, seeking to avoid attention. However, the real reason for their arrival in Judea soon became well known. The news of their coming may have come even to the ears of Joseph in Bethlehem.

Herod almost certainly had a network of informers and secret police to keep watch on anyone who could have been a threat to his government. When Herod heard about the wise men and their questions concerning a newborn king he first called his own religious advisors together without the Magi. Then he later invited the wise men privately to ask them precise questions about the Messiah and the star.

Even Herod himself handled the entire situation with discretion. Herod summoned the wise men secretly, not necessarily wanting anyone to know that he was in contact with them personally. It would appear that Herod's own advisors were not present during the king's private discussions with the wise men. Herod almost certainly saw the general object of the Magi's visit as a threat to his throne and his royal line. He may have preferred not to draw any more attention to the wise men than necessary. He did not want to encourage others to seek them out.

Why were the Magi thought to have been kings?

Some believers in the centuries following the death and resurrection of Jesus came to believe that the wise men were kings because of texts in Isaiah 60:1-7 and Psalm 72:8-15. In Psalm 72:10-11 there are also references to kings and others bringing gold and other gifts to the king of Israel.

Psalm 72 was written by Solomon and it is commonly seen as being prophetically messianic. However many of the things mentioned in the text were also experiences which were accomplished in the life of David's son. King Solomon did reign over a vast area up to the river Euphrates but not to the ends of the earth. The Queen of Sheba and others did come to him bringing gifts and tribute of spices, gold and precious stones (See 1 Kings 10:1-29). There are some aspects of the psalm which are beyond Solomon's experience, but many things were certainly part of his own personal life and reign.

The Isaiah 60 passage cited on the previous page is concerning God's people in general. The passage is not about the Messiah in particular. According to the text the gifts mentioned (including gold and frankincense) come from the nations and kings and go toward God's people and Jerusalem. It is important to read the text in its context starting in Isaiah 59:15b and go on through 60:7. While the Messiah is representative of God's people it seems that this text is really about God's people specifically.

Note: The author lives and works in France. Each year he is delighted to eat the "Galette des Rois" (king's cake) during the holidays and the month of January. Of course the cake takes its name from the "kingly" Magi (Les rois mages). In order not to offend his French friends the author suggests that the king's cake become the cake of KING Jesus. One might still call it "the cake of the Magi" as well. It would still be possible to still sing, "We wise men of Orient are ..." or "We Magi of Orient..." We can adjust to the truth, but we should not adjust the truth to fit our ideas.

The Names of the Wise Men

Below are examples of the names of the wise men from several ethnic and cultural backgrounds.

Caspar
Balthasar
Melchior
Larvandad
Gushnasaph
Hormisdas
Hor
Karsudan
Basanater
Kagpha
Badadakharida
Badadilma
Apellius
Galgalat
Amerius
Malgalat
Yazdegerd
Damascus
Sarachin
Perozadh
Karsudan
Gushynasaph

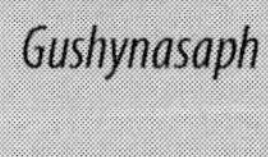

Gold, frankincense (light) and myrrh (dark)were the three gifts of the wise men.

Other Questions That Should be Answered

How many wise men were there?

We do not know how many wise men came to Bethlehem. We do know that they brought three gifts; however, the biblical text does not specify the number of wise men. Western traditions concerning three wise men can be dated to about AD 500-600. At least one ancient document mentions twelve or more wise men going to Bethlehem to seek the Jewish Messiah. Arriving in Jerusalem with a very large group might have been ill advised and even dangerous. Again, Herod's paranoia concerning his throne and his succession were well known.

What were the names and ethnic origins of the wise men?

The names of the wise men are also unknown. According to one's cultural and ethnic traditions there are a variety of names and titles given for the Magi. Western traditions often speak of an Arabian, a Persian, and an Indian being in the group. In addition, sometimes a European, an African (possibly Ethiopian) and an Asian are cited. The suggested ethnic origins of the wise men vary greatly depending upon the sources and the preferred perspective of various authors and ethnic / cultural traditions. The list on page 59 contains several names, which have been used in various cultural backgrounds for the biblical Magi.

Questions concerning the gifts:

The wise men may have been inspired by Psalm 72 and Isaiah 60 to bring their gifts of gold and frankincense. However, we do know that the gifts brought by the wise men were valuable items and certainly appropriate gifts for a king. Myrrh was sometimes used as a perfume and as medicine. While some have speculated that the gift of myrrh was specifically given for Jesus' burial, we do not actually know if this was in the minds of the wise men. Myrrh was not always used for embalming. It also had value medicinally and as a perfume. Jesus was embalmed with a mix of myrrh and aloes. However, the spices came from Nicodemus, they did not come from Mary or anyone from Jesus' family. The large quantity of myrrh used for embalming Jesus' body was well beyond what Mary and Joseph could have carried with them to Egypt (John 19:39-40). It is not certain that the wise men envisioned the death of the Messiah at all. God's wisdom revealed in the cross and resurrection was hidden even from his own disciples until after the events had taken place. We do not know if the wise men linked their gifts to Jesus' death and resurrection. The gifts did provide abundant finances for the trip to Egypt. Without doubt this helped Joseph to move forward with much confidence knowing that he had the resources to provide for his family during the journey.

The Technical Abilities of the Magi

It is often assumed and it is probable that the Zoroastrian priests had extensive knowledge of the stars. However, in reality we have very little or no actual documentation concerning their astronomical expertise in a tangible, mathematical or truly analytical form. As mentioned previously, we do not even know what names the Zoroastrians used for the planets or most stars. However, the astronomers from the Old Babylonian Empire and the Assyrians kept extensive records and omen catalogs based the observation of the heavens. For example, cuneiform tablets dating from about 1700 BC have been discovered, which describe the eight year cycle of Venus. This indicates clearly that the Babylonians were astronomically well informed even at that comparatively early date.

In the last one hundred years, it has become clear that the Neo-Babylonian Empire (626-539 BC) and its successors had a significant concentration of astronomers /astrologers who made important contributions to the science of astronomy. Technical, observational and mathematical astronomy was strongly developed by the Babylonians. It is probable that the analytical and technical ability of wise men who traveled to Bethlehem may have been profound. The wise men may have been some of the best minds in the east and not merely some wild-eyed stargazers interested only in novel and esoteric knowledge. The astronomers / astrologers of Mesopotamia had a vast stock of records which allowed them to see patterns and develop theories concerning the heavenly bodies. The influence and ideas of Babylonian astronomy continued to be developed under the domination of the Persians, the Seleucids (Greeks) and the Parthians. The Greek writer Strabo mentions several of these astronomers in his book *Geography* (published about AD 20). Such famous men would have certainly been known to the Magi.

> ***... The astronomers are divided into different groups, which hold to various different dogmas about the same subjects. And the mathematicians make mention of some of these men; as, for example, Cidenas (Kidinnu), Naburianus (Nabû-rîmannu), Sudines and Seleukos (Seleucus of Seleucia).*** *(Strabo, Geography 16.5-6)*

Gnomon - The gnomon is the part of a sundial that casts the shadow. The name is related to an ancient Greek word meaning "indicator", "one who discerns," or "that which reveals."

Kidinnu (4th century BC), mentioned in Strabo's text, may have been involved in developing a fairly precise manner for calculating the position and orbit of the moon. Seleucus of Seleucia on the Tigris (2nd century BC) is credited with being one of the first persons to attribute the tides to the interaction of the earth with the moon. He also further developed the idea of a sun centered solar system, which had been proposed by the Greek astronomer Aristarchus. Seleucus has the same Greek name as the one of Alexander's generals, Seleucus Nicator, who founded the Seleucid dynasty. Seleucus may have had strong Greek influences in his life because he championed Aristarchus' theory. He certainly does not seem to be an

It is thought that the Greek astronomer Hipparchus may have invented the astrolabe and the armillary sphere during the second century BC. The pictured instrument above is from much later. It is very possible that the wise men may have used similar instruments. From what we know of Babylonian astronomy some fairly precise measurements could be made.

It would not be surprising that many of the Magi could understand and read Sumerian and Akkadian cuneiform, Persian, Aramaic, Hebrew (related to Aramaic) and also Greek. Some Babylonian wise men may have had ability to read Latin as well.

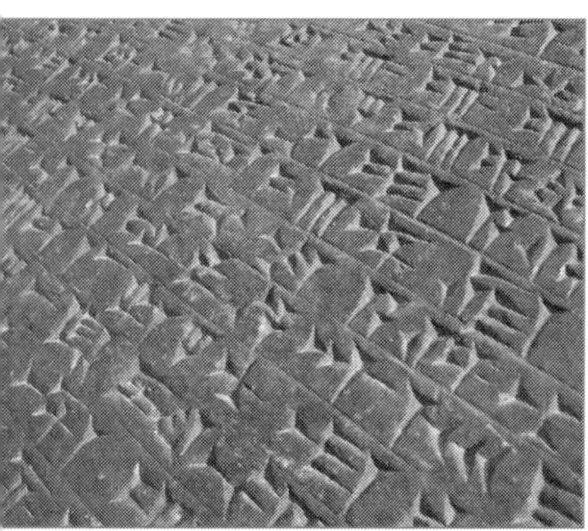

isolated relatively unknown Babylonian living in the ruins of Babylon. Even his name is connected to a large city with a significant Greek population.

The Greek astronomer Hipparchus, who lived from about 190 to 120 BC, was reputed to have been the greatest astronomer of the age. He was born in Nicaea and died on the Island of Rhodes. He was a contemporary of the Babylonian (Chaldean) astronomer Seleucus of Seleucia. It is very possible that Seleucus and other Chaldean / Zoroastrian astronomers may have met Hipparchus or that they would have had some knowledge of his work. Hipparchus was heavily influenced by the Chaldeans. Although we do not know how Hipparchus obtained his information, it appears certain that Babylonian data was helpful to Hipparchus in his research and discoveries. He may have easily traveled to Mesopotamia because the area was under Seleucid (Greek) control for most of his life. No other region of Europe, Africa or the Middle East at that time could boast of so many astronomers or such extensive astronomical records. Some Greek translations of Mesopotamian cuneiform tablets have even been found in Egypt.

The first trigonometric table was compiled by Hipparchus, who is now known as "the father of trigonometry." He discovered the precession of the equinoxes in about 127 BC and also apparently invented several astronomical instruments. He tried to estimate the distances of the sun and moon and did extensive work on predicting eclipses. Hipparchus made some efforts to develop a model of the planets centered on the sun, but he finally opted for an earth centered system because he found that the orbits of the planets and the moon were not perfectly round (There is an exception; the orbit of Venus is almost perfectly round). Hipparchus' influence is evident in Ptolemy's famous book, *The Almagest*, written in the 2nd century AD. However, there is no evidence of any knowledge of precession or trigonometry in the Mesopotamian cuneiform tablets so far recovered and translated. Part of the story of the interactions of Mesopotamian and Greek astronomers may still be hidden in the sands of Iraq.

Pliny the Elder published his book, *A Natural History*, sometime between AD 77 and 79, and dedicated it to the Roman Emperor Vespasian. In Chapter II, called "Concerning the Figure of the World," Pliny writes the following lines: "The form of the world is round, in the figure of a perfect globe, its name in the first place, and ... all men agreeing call it in Latin 'orbis' (a globe)."[11] These statements are an amazing contrast to modern tendencies to classify the ancients as "flat earthers." Whatever their perspective on the position of the earth and the sun in the solar system, few, if any, of the ancient astronomers in the Middle East or the Mediterranean world in the 1st century BC were "flat earthers." The Latin educated churchmen, all throughout the Middle Ages, were in agreement with Pliny. This is even reflected in the papal blessing "Urbi et Orbi." Officially, the ritual of the papal blessing "Urbi et Orbi" (to the city and to the world / globe) developed in the 13th century under Pope Gregory X, who was Pope from AD 1271-1276.[12] This was during the high Middle Ages, well before the lives of Galileo, Kepler and Copernicus. In the 1st century BC basically all the astronomers, along with large parts of the general population in Rome, believed that the earth was round. Pliny assumes this is the case in most of the "known" world as he writes, "all men agreeing call it in Latin 'orbis' (a globe)."

The surviving, incomplete series of cuneiform tablets from Mesopotamia do not indicate any significant speculations about the physical shape of the earth or the solar system, but not all cuneiform tablets did survive; many documents were destroyed and others simply deteriorated. While most of the ancients did think that the earth was at the center of all things and that the sun, moon and the planets revolved around the earth, it would be surprising if any Babylonian Magi had promoted "flat earth" ideas knowing that one of their own, Seleucus of Seleucia, had insisted on a sun centered solar system.

Some sophisticated scientific devices also existed in the 1st century BC. In about 1901 the so-called "Antikythera mechanism" was discovered in a ship wreck in the Aegean Sea. It has been demonstrated that the device was designed to calculate astronomical positions for the sun, moon and the planets relative to the stars. Several such devices may have existed because it is doubtful that marine archeology has recovered the only example which was ever made. Of the known artifacts from the ancient world, the complexity of this early 1st century BC device was not equaled again until the 14th century AD when some mechanical astronomical clocks were built. Considering the present state of knowledge about Babylonian observation instruments John Steele, an expert on Babylonian astronomy writes:

> *Nowhere ... is there any mention of an observing instrument. From other sources we know that water clocks were used to measure time, but no examples have been found in the excavations of the Babylonian cities. It is quite possible that the only observing instruments used were the water clock, the naked eye and possibly something like a graduated stick held at arms' length to measure distances in the heavens.*[13]

We do not know all the types of instruments that Magi may have used. However, complicated instruments were not necessary to understand the message written in the heavens from 7 BC to 1 BC. In the scenario presented in this book, most everything could have been observed and understood with the unaided eye or by using longstanding, well known, mathematical and calendar methods familiar to the Babylonians.

The Technical Capabilities of the Babylonian Magi:

The Mesopotamians knew how to calculate by different means and with some precision the movements of the sun and moon, as well as, the five visible planets. They developed a purely mathematical astronomical theory. This allowed them

Year BC	Astronomical Diaries	Goal Year Texts	Normal Star Almanacs	General Almanacs
-142	X	X		
-141	X	X		
-140			X	
-139			X	
-138	X			
-137	X	X	X	X
-136	X			
-135	X	X	X	
-134	X		X	X
-133	X			X
-132	X			
-131	X	X		
-130	X	X		
-129		X	X	X
-128		X	X	
-127	X	X		X
-126	X	X		X
-125	X	X	X	
-124	X	X	X	
...				
-12				X
-11				X
-10				
-9				X
-8				
-7				X
-6				
-5				
-4				
-3				
-2				
-1				

Table 2.1 This is a sampling of the still existing cuneiform astronomical records and predictive texts according to their dates. Some of the documents exist in multiple copies such as the almanac for the Seleucid Era Year 305 which straddles the years 7 BC to 6 BC. It is unfortuante that no known documents still exist from 6 BC to 1 BC.[14]

to place seven months at regular intervals during 19 years, in order to keep the lunar months and the solar year aligned. The Greeks gave this same manner of calibrating the months, seasons and years the name of the cycle of Menton.

A method of counting was born in Mesopotamia, based on the number 60 which served as the basis of the present system of 360 degrees. This was later developed into minutes and seconds.[15] The ancient inhabitants of modern Iraq developed an idea of constellations which is still largely present with us today although there were some modifications. Systems of heavenly constellations were recognized in the very ancient past in several cultures.[16] Originally in Mesopotamia there were about 17 or 18 constellations in the zodiac. That group of constellations was arranged in a circle of animals, objects and human figures spread across the sky. The Mesopotamians called the zodiac the "path of the moon." Toward the 5th century BC, a Babylonian zodiac of 12 constellations was finally firmly established and it became a referencing tool. Each constellation was attributed about 30° of the sky. However, even as late as the 1st century BC, the Babylonian, Greek and Roman ideas of the signs sometimes differed.

Babylonian cuneiform records still exist concerning the stars, sun, moon and planets over many hundreds of years. Ptolemy, writing in the years following AD 150, indicated that Babylonian astronomical records dating back to about 747 BC were available in his time (a span of 900 years). While the Babylonian astronomers were quite technically capable, 750 years before the birth of Christ, their competence grew significantly in the last 300 years before the end of the 1st millennium BC. They developed a profoundly scientific and mathematical approach to their astronomy. This included documents, which are now called Astronomical Diaries. In addition there were "Goal Year Texts," "Normal Star Almanacs," procedure texts (technical guides for making calculations) and predictive almanacs. The earliest "Goal Year Text" dates from 256 BC, while the first known predictive stellar / planetary almanac was compiled for 282 BC.[17] Many astronomical records and predictive documents dating from about 300 BC to 60 BC still survive even until our day. After 56 BC, the number of surviving cuneiform documents such as diaries, goal year texts and almanacs drops off in a precipitous manner. There are no surviving records or almanacs from 55 BC to 31 BC. Only some almanacs have survived in later periods. These are dated in the following years: 30, 29, 21, 15, 12, 11, 9 and 7 BC. Small numbers of almanacs have also survived from the years following the birth of Christ: AD 31, 36, 44, 61 and 74.[18]

Babylonian Almanac Predictions for theYear 7/6 BC

Year	Month	Day	Lunar M	Date	Planet	Constellation	Phenomena
7 BC	April	1	I	1	NA	NA	Year Begins
7 BC	April	3	I	3	Saturn	Pisces	Heliacal rising
7 BC	April	22	I	21	Mars	Virgo	1st Stationary Point
7 BC	April	29	I	29	Sun/Moon	Taurus	Partial Eclipse Sun
7 BC	May	4	II	5	Mercury	Gemini	Heliacal Rising
7 BC	May	20	II	21	Venus	Cancer	Enters Constellation
7 BC	May	25	II	26	Mercury	Cancer	Enters Constellation
7 BC	June	11	III	12	Mercury	Cancer	Heliacal Setting
7 BC	July	12	IV	14	Venus	Virgo	Enters Constellation
7 BC	July	20	IV	22	Jupiter	Pisces	1st Stationary Point
7 BC	July	27	IV	29	Saturn	Pisces	1st Stationary Point
7 BC	August	13	V	16	Mars	Scorpio	Enters Constellation
7 BC	Sept	7	VI	12	Venus	Scorpio	Enters Constellation
7 BC	Sept	16	VI	21	Jupiter	Pisces	Opposition
7 BC	Sept	16	VI	21	Saturn	Pisces	Opposition
7 BC	Oct	29	VIII	5	Venus	Scorpio	Heliacal Setting
7 BC	Nov	6	VIII	13	Venus	Scorpio	Heliacal Rising
7 BC	Nov	12	VIII	19	Jupiter	Pisces	2nd Stationary Point
7 BC	Nov	14	VIII	21	Saturn	Pisces	2nd Stationary Point
7 BC	Dec	9	IX	16	Mars	Aquarius	Enters Constellation
6 BC	Jan	1	X	10	Venus	Sagittarius	Enters Constellation
6 BC	Jan	17	X	26	Mars	Pisces	Enter Constellation
6 BC	Feb	26	XII	7	Mars	Aries	Enters Constellation
6 BC	Feb	28	XII	9	Saturn	Pisces	Heliacal Setting
6 BC	March	22	XII^2	1	Jupiter	Aries	Heliacal Setting
6 BC	April	18	XII^2	28	Saturn	Aries	Heliacal Rising
6 BC	April	19	XII^2	29	NA	NA	Year Ends

Table 2.2

This table shows selected planetary data from actual Babylonian astronomical predictions for the Seleucid Era Year 305 which corresponds to April 1st, 7 BC to April 19th, 6 BC. A second month of Adar was added to the calendar in the winter / spring of 6 BC, listed as XII^2 in the chart. More material could be added. The terms in the "phenomena" column are explored in greater detail in part seven (page 119).[19]

The Babylonians could calculate the dates of solar eclipses. They could even forecast the specific time of day when the eclipse would take place (see the text below). Below: The partial solar eclipse on April 29th 7 BC

An Example Of The Almanac Entry For The First Month Of The Year 7/6 BC

Month I (Nisanu / Nisan), The 1st of which will follow the 30th(?) of the previous month. Jupiter will be in Pisces, Venus in Taurus, Mars in Virgo. On the 3rd, Saturn will be visible for the first time in Pisces. On the 13th, there will be a lunar eclipse, five months after the previous eclipse possibility, but it will not be visible. On the 15th, moonset after sunrise. On the 21st, Mars will reach its (first) stationary point in Virgo. On the 25th, Venus will reach Gemini. On the 28th will be the last lunar visibility before sunrise. On the 29th, three hours before sunset, a solar eclipse is to be watched for.[19]

The phrase, "The stars of the path of the moon" was the expression used by the Assyrians and Babylonians to designate the zodiacal constellations.

A typical Astronomical Diary covered six or seven months, recording on a nightly basis, the astronomical events such the positions of the sun, moon, and the five visible planets. Passages of the moon and the planets by so called "Normal Stars," (a type of "marker stars") were noted. Other important moments of planetary and lunar cycles were included, as well as, the observed eclipses, the dates of possible eclipses, the dates of solstices and equinoxes, and the dates of the rising and setting of the bright star Sirius.[20]

> *When a lunar or solar eclipse took place, its date, time, and duration were noted along with the planets visible, the star that was culminating, and the prevailing wind at the time of the eclipse.*[21]

The diaries regularly give the dates of solstices (šamãšGUB) and equinoxes (LÁL-tim, Akkadian šitqultu). ... The dates were often not the result of observations, which is evident from the remark "I did not watch" in many of the texts. The dates were apparently established by some form of computation.[22] Also in the diaries one finds ...

> *Other, less common, astronomical events such as comets, the weather, particularly when it was bad enough to prevent observing, or in the case of an ominous event such as a rainbow. At the beginning of each month is a statement of whether the previous month had 29 or 30 days, and at the end of each month is a summary of the planets' positions during the month and a section summarizing non-astronomical events. In later Diaries (infrequently from -453 onwards, and regularly from -266) the planetary summary would also contain the dates of planets' first and last appearances ... From -212 onwards the summaries also generally contained the dates on which a planet moved to the next zodiacal sign. ... In the non-astronomical section would typically be found prices of staple goods in Babylon's market during the month, measurements of the river level and how it changed during the month; and a report of news which had reached the Diary compilers' attention, either events occurring in the city of Babylon or news from elsewhere.*[23]

The full moon setting with Jupiter and Saturn before dawn on September 9th 7 BC.

Below are some examples of diary entries, which even contain calculated or estimated "ideal" dates for the first appearances of Venus and Mercury. These appearances apparently had been delayed by clouds or atmospheric dust:

> *On the 14th of the month, Mercury's first appearance in the west in Virgo, it stood 2 ½ cubits (5°) behind Venus to the west; it was bright and high, 16° separated the sunset from the setting of Mercury; The ideal first appearance of Mercury should have been on the 12th.*[24]

> *On the 18th of the month, Venus' first appearance in the east in the end of Taurus; it was bright and high, from the rising of Venus to sunrise there was 9°30'; The ideal first appearance should have been on the 16th.*[25]

The list of "normal," (marker) stars below, in Table 2.3, well illustrates how much we are removed from the world of the Babylonians. The terms used even for the transliterations seem very strange. Without translation, we would not recognize any of them. Some of the "normal stars" do not correspond to modern constellation designations. For the Babylonians, Beta Virginis, also called Zavijava, was in Leo. Instead of being in the Virgin, it was the rear foot of the lion. In Babylonia the constellation Virgo was called the Furrow, as in a furrow for planting. The constellation's main star, Spica, was named the "bright star of the Furrow."

Celestial Divination and Astrology

While we do not have many details about the wise men who arrived at Bethlehem, apparently they were not intellectual or technical lightweights, neither were they easily influenced mystics. Their scholarly and technical capacities may have been particularly great. However, the Mesopotamian astronomers did embrace some concepts which are often unacceptable to the majority of modern scientists. Originally Mesopotamian astronomy was used in state sponsored celestial divination. Apparently that state sponsored astronomy declined over the centuries. The conquering Persian, Greek and Parthian kings may have consulted the astronomers in Babylon, Sippar, Borsippa and Uruk, but they were much less dependant upon them than the Assyrian or Babylonian kings.

Divination is not exactly the same thing as astrology. Although related, they use very different approaches to interpreting celestial events. Originally divination in

Table 2.3 A partial list of "normal or marker stars" used to indicate positions in the sky.[26]

Sumerian names*	The English Meaning	English name	Astronomical name
MÚL MÚL	The Bristle	Pleiades	Eta Tauri
MÚL SAG A	The Head of the Lion	Ras El Asad A.	Epsilon Leonis
MÚL LUGAL	The King	Regulus	Alpha Leonis
GÍR EGIR-tum šá A	The Rear Foot of the Lion	Zavijava	Beta Virginis
DELE šá IGI ABSIN	Front Star of the Furrow	Porrima	Gamma Virginis
SA_4 šá ABSIN	Bright Star of the Furrow	Spica	Alpha Virginis
RÍN šá ULÙ	Southern Star of the Scales	Zubenelgenubi	Alpha Librae
RÍN šá SI	Northern Star of the Scales	Zubeneshschamali	Beta Librae
MÚL e šá SAG GÍRTAB	Upper Head Star - Scorpion	Graffias	Beta Scorpii
SI_4	The god Lisi	Antares	Alpha Scorpii

** The Sumerian names were used by the Babylonians. The English names have Greek, Latin and Arabic roots.*

Among the Babylonian astronmers / astrologers a halo around the moon was often thought to have significance.

Heavenly signs announce and confirm things which God himself has decided to bring to pass. The signs do not make events happen, they announce and accompany God's activities.

Mesopotamia sought to discern the will, thoughts and messages of the gods. Royal, military and economic interests dominated the interpretations of events in the heavens.

> *In the immense sky of Mesopotamia it was not the destiny of just anybody which one was interpreting, it was the destiny of nations and kings. Astronomical observation was put into the service of the state and became a truly political instrument. At the court the royal astronomer had a major influence, he was both a scientific expert and a political counselor. In the Neo-Assyrian Empire the king was the head of a network of astronomer / astrologers who regularly sent him reports. Through their observations one could foresee defeats, famines, floods as well as the good and bad harvests.*[27]

For centuries the Babylonian Magi used an extensive catalog of omens which described various heavenly events, as well as, their possible meanings. Methods were also devised to try to change the course of events through special techniques and ceremonies, as well as, supplications and sacrifices addressed to various deities. The Mesopotamians believed that the omens were not definitive, unchangeable signs about the future, but that the will of the gods could be influenced.

At some point, the Magi seem to have recycled their knowledge about the heavens into predicting the future of individuals based on their birth dates. This was the beginning of the astrology which we know today. The first known horoscope is a Babylonian document dated in 409 BC[28] although they were probably being done much earlier. Babylonian horoscopes were being developed over several centuries. Some astronomers / astrologers did use their knowledge to make horoscopes for individuals, yet, according to Strabo (64 BC - AD 24) many Chaldean astronomers resisted and even rejected such practices at least till the 1st century AD. Strabo's text may possibly demonstrate his own prejudices against natal horoscopes or his own lack of more detailed knowledge.

> *In Babylon an area was set apart for the native philosophers called Chaldeans, who are chiefly devoted to the study of astronomy. Some, who are not approved of by the rest, profess to understand the casting of horoscopes. .... There are several classes of the Chaldean astronomers. Some have the name of Orcheni, some Borsippeni, and many others, as if divided into sects, who disseminate different tenets on the same subjects. (Strabo, Geography 16.5-6).*

About 30 or so short Babylonian horoscope documents spanning several centuries are known to have survived until today.[29] Of these texts, only five have predictive texts associated with them. Some experts believe that the predictions may have been given orally, instead of in a written form. Such limited texts are in great contrast to the extensive writings of the Greek, Egyptian and Roman astrologers such as, Manilius, Valens, Ptolemy, Firmicus and others.

John Steele, in his book *A Brief Introduction To Astronomy in The Middle East,* indicates that there is a significant gap in our knowledge concerning the activities of the Babylonian astronomers / astrologers. As Steele indicates, we really do not know why they devoted so much energy to their calculations. Were they being paid as government functionaries? Were they simply interested in making discoveries? We do not know. Even for experts on Mesopotamian astronomy many profound questions remain about the astronomers / astrologers of ancient history. Our knowledge is limited.

> *One curious fact concerning Babylonian numerical astronomy continues to puzzle historians: we have almost no evidence to show whether any of it was used for anything. Many ... calculated phenomena are known, but this calculated data is not the source of the predictions found in the Diaries and Almanacs ... Why go to all the trouble of formulating these extremely complicated numerical methods if they were not to be used? This question exposes a fundamental gap in our understanding of Late Babylonian astronomy.*[30]

At least some information may have been used in producing horoscopes. Again according to Steele a tablet in the collection of the Oriental Institute of Chicago may give a partial answer. The tablet, which belonged to a man named Anu-bel-Sunu, contains calculated astronomical information from a period more than 50 years previous to the date of the tablet's composition. In Steele's words:

> *Why did Anu-bel-Sunu calculate planetary and lunar phenomena for more than fifty years earlier? It may have been to provide data for constructing horoscopes. By a remarkable chance, Anu-bel-Sunu's horoscope survives and places his date of birth in year 63 of the Seleucid Era (249 BC). Did Anu-bel-Sunu make this text to allow himself to cast his own horoscope?*[31]

Michael Molnar, a retired astronomy and physics professor at Rutgers University, argues that Babylonian astrology had developed into a more Western form of Hellenistic astrology by the end of the 1st century BC. This implies a shift to Hellenistic style natal horoscopes along with their complicated system of trines, squares, sextiles and oppositions. Prof. Molnar writes that any links with the older system of astronomy involving observations from ziggurats and the interpretation of omens was more or less completely outdated by the end of the 1st century BC.[32]

However, Professor Molnar may go too far in almost completely discounting the old system of astronomical omens in favor of Western style natal horoscopes. The writer Strabo (64 BC - AD 24), cited above, does not agree with him. Francesca Rochberg, in her book on the Babylonian horoscopes, states that the Babylonian and Greek horoscopes reflect substantially different ways of doing date of birth astrology. There was little similarity between their underlying world views.[33] It is certain that Babylonian astrology underwent significant changes over time, however, we are lacking information to make very precise statements about the state and

Astrology teaches that one's destiny is linked to the heavenly bodies. The placement of the sun, moon, planets and stars at one's birth was thought to shape all aspects one's life. In the Greco-Roman world astrology had links to fate, fatalism and gnosticism.

Jesus is the Lord over all creation. If the stars had dictated his destiny, role, power and abilities he would not be the Lord over the heavens, but rather he would have been in subjection to the heavenly lights.

Divination in Mesopotamia sought to discern the will, thoughts and messages of the gods. Heavenly omens were viewed as the communication of the gods concerning possible events.

Methods were developed to counter any evil which was foreseen or announced in celestial omens. Mesopotamian divination was not fatalistic. The future could be changed. It depended on the interaction of the gods and men.

content of Babylonian astronomy and horoscopy at the time of the birth of Christ. The imperial archives of the Parthians and the Sassanids were largely destroyed by the invading armies in various wars. Other information may still be buried in the sands of Iraq or it may remain untranslated in cuneiform text collections in museums around the world.

The Babylonian system of astral knowledge extended greatly beyond making horoscopes. Babylonian astronomer / scribes also practiced a type of exorcism and were involved in astral medicine. Records show that many also functioned as notaries. Their stellar knowledge and societal role touched several aspects of daily life. The old temples of Marduk, Nabu, Ishtar and other Babylonian gods were still functioning in Sippar, Borsippa, Uruk and to some degree in the ruins of Babylon in the 1st century BC.[34] Several ziggurats were still in a reasonably good state and could have been used for astronomical purposes. The traditional Astronomical Dairies, Almanacs and "Goal Year" texts were compiled and used in the century before to the birth of Jesus although the number of surviving copies is limited. Perhaps these documents were used for other purposes, but their form and content remained unchanged from the previous centuries. Some astronomers still identified themselves as *scribes of the Enuma Anu Enlil* (the vast omen catalogue) as late as 119 BC, but records are lacking for later dates.[35]

It is certain that the roles of the Babylonian priests of Marduk, Nabu and Ishtar had changed in a significant manner by the late 1st century BC. In the 8th through the 6th century BC the astronomers had maintained substantial correspondence with the Assyrian and Babylonian kings. They were constantly reporting to their masters, and indicating means of avoiding the possible outcomes of ominous celestial events. In the succeeding centuries the Persian, Seleucid and Parthian governments did not have the same profound connections with the Babylonian gods or with their temple astronomers and priests. However, many of the kings did at least give ceremonial respect to the old Babylonian gods. In addition they sometimes did continue to finance the temples, including their reconstruction, maintenance and daily functioning.

In the 1st century BC both Western and Eastern civilizations were still largely influenced by omens on a variety of levels. From the common laborer to the highest ranks of society, omens were taken seriously. Sometimes the principal Roman augurs, who were often politically astute senators, invented reports of ominous events for their own purposes. For example, reports of thunder during a sacrifice could have been an "inauspicious" indicator concerning political debate. The spectacular appearance of a comet in July 44 BC played a decisive role in the exalting of Julius Caesar to godhood. Heavenly events like the setting of the planet MUL.BABBAR (Jupiter) with the new crescent moon in June of 3 BC would have still looked ominous to many Babylonians, as well as, the Greek speaking inhabitants of Mesopotamia and the Parthian Iranians. The two occultations of the star LUGAL / Sharru (Regulus, the king star) by the moon in November 3 BC and January of 2 BC may still have sparked some interest and solicited interpretations by the non-astronomers in the Parthian court. Striking, highly visible and well known planetary conjunctions like the ones in 7 BC, 3 BC and 2 BC would have most likely still have prompted more traditional interpretations by astronomers / astrologers in the service of the Parthian royal court. The societal role of omens in divination and prediction remained strong in both Rome and in the Parthian Empire. We have no proof that the state sponsored "omen related astronomy" in Babylonia had completely ceased in the 1st century BC, nor do we have proof of its existence.[36] One can imagine that royal favor and patronage would have followed the sharing of useful insights with the authorities. This alone may have inspired an exceedingly large amount of astronomical research, as well as, the interpretations of countless heavenly events.

The Wisdom of God

Like Daniel before them, the Magi who went to Bethlehem probably did not obtain their wisdom from astrology or omen catalogues.

Astrology teaches that one's destiny is linked to the heavenly bodies. Among astrologers, the placement of the sun, moon, planets and stars at one's birth was and is thought to shape all aspects one's life and future existence. In the Greco-Roman world astrology had links to fate, fatalism and gnosticism. The system of celestial omens developed by the Mesopotamians signaled possible events such as famines, insurrections and wars. Measures were proposed to counter these evils. It would appear that the men who came to Bethlehem may have had a totally different experience than what might have been expected through astrology or divination.

Jesus is the Lord over all creation. If the stars had dictated his destiny, role, power and abilities he would not be the Lord over the heavens, but rather he would have been in subjection to the heavenly lights. Believers have been united with the Messiah so that they are now "in Christ." Just as the Messiah is not in subjection to the heavenly bodies, neither are believers in subjection to them in the present. Nor are believers at the mercy of many possible events only foreseen by celestial omens. The destiny of those who believe in the Messiah is to become like the one who was sent into the world to save mankind (to be conformed to the image of Christ, as described in Romans 8:29-30).

Like Daniel before them, the Magi who went to Bethlehem probably did not get their wisdom from astrology or omen catalogues. They had apparently encountered someone who was infinitely more mysterious and wise than any human being. The Holy One of Israel, YHWH, may not have used any of the traditional means to speak to the wise men. He has his own means and methods. Heavenly signs announce and confirm things which God himself has decided to bring to

The fear of YHWH is the beginning of wisdom; A good understanding have all those who do His commandments; His praise endures forever. (Psalm 111:10)

pass. The signs do not make events happen, nor do they simply indicate possible future events. Divinely inspired heavenly signs announce and accompany God's own resolutely determined activities.

The wise men remain enigmatic. Who were they really? Were they Zoroastrians, Babylonian priests or Jewish wise men? What motivated them? How did they think? Other questions concerning their astronomical knowledge and reasoning will be explored later. However, it should be remembered that Jewish people would not have named just any scholar a "wise person." While they would have recognized the position, role, learning and activities of the Zoroastrian or Babylonian Magi, the Jews would not have been in agreement that everything done, said or thought by the scholars and priests of Mesopotamia was indeed wise. Matthew would have certainly have hesitated to call just any scholar a "wise man."

There were many different types of Jewish thought and practice in the 1st century BC, but the majority of committed practicing Jews were centered on the application of knowledge in the fear of God. The accumulation of knowledge without specific daily application of right principles was not greatly valued. Truly devout Jewish people living in Babylonia, Judea and Galilee, would not have been terribly impressed by any scholar, who was not in submission to the God of Israel. It seems that the Magi in Matthew's text were at least "God fearing." They would not have been men who took the Jewish religious law lightly. They would have been well informed about the Hebrew perspective on the sun, moon and stars, as well as the creation in general. The opposition of the God of Israel to astrology and typical Babylonian divinatory methods would not have been unknown to such men. If the wise men were seeking the Jewish Messiah, they must have appreciated the thoughts of King Solomon, who said that the fear of the Lord is the beginning of wisdom.

A Text from Solomon, King of Israel, Concerning His Own Book of Proverbs :

> *To know wisdom and instruction, to discern the sayings of understanding, to receive instruction in wise behavior, righteousness, justice and equity; to give prudence to the naive, to the youth knowledge and discretion,*
>
> *A wise man will hear and increase in learning, and a man of understanding will acquire wise counsel, to understand a proverb and a figure, the words of the wise and their riddles.*
>
> *The fear of YHWH is the beginning of knowledge; Fools despise wisdom and instruction. (Proverbs 1:1-7)*

Ultimately to understand the wise men one also needs to know something about the historical context of the Roman Empire and the ancient Middle East in the 1st century BC. That is the subject of part four.

Part 4: The Kings of the Earth

The Rulers of the Mediterreanean and the Middle East in the Late 1st Century BC

There was a specific historical context concerning the birth of Christ. While it might be possible to explore celestial phenomenon and neglect the context of the events surrounding the birth of Jesus, it is not the best manner to understand the Magi or the star. The modern perspective is very far removed from the world view of the 1st century BC. We all read texts from the Bible with preconceptions. We often do not see the profound implications of the arrival of the Messiah in the ancient world. The following pages will attempt to highlight some aspects of the historical, cultural and religious circumstances in the period from about 7 BC to 1 BC.

God is not impressed by the great ones of the earth:

> *Because the foolishness of God is wiser than men, and the weakness of God is stronger than men. For consider your calling, brethren, that there were not many wise according to the flesh, not many mighty, not many noble; but God has chosen the foolish things of the world to shame the wise, and God has chosen the weak things of the world to shame the things which are strong, and the base things of the world and the despised God has chosen, the things that are not, so that He may nullify the things that are, so that no man may boast before God. (1 Corinthians 1:25-29)*

Rome

Augustus Rules the Mediterranean World

Above: A coin bearing Augustus' image with a reference to the "divine Julius" (Divus Iulius) on the back. The image illustrates the famous comet of 44 BC.

(Used by permission: www.cngcoins.com)

Caesar Augustus, formerly called Octavian, was emperor when Jesus was born. Octavian was the nephew of Julius Caesar and his adopted son. At Caesar's death, he inherited the great bulk of Caesar's immense fortune. After several years of political maneuvering, hard negotiating, as well as, difficult and bloody conflict, Octavian defeated Mark Anthony and Cleopatra in a contest for supreme power. As a result of the Battle of Actium in 31 BC, Octavian became the undisputed ruler of the Roman world. In January of 27 BC Octavian formally returned power to the Roman Senate but in return the Senate gave him the titles of "Augustus" (the revered one) and later "Princeps" (First Citizen). This created the principate, which was the core of the Roman imperial system in which "Princeps" was the official title of the Roman emperors. Augustus maintained the outward forms of the Roman Republic including the Senate and many elected offices, but in reality he held most of the political and military authority. In the following years, Augustus was greatly appreciated as the one who had brought peace, security, justice and freedom to the Roman world. After many decades of internal strife and civil war Augustus' stable administration was a welcome change. The external conflicts with rival powers were few. Augustus knew how to negotiate and solve some problems without war. In 4 BC, the 750th anniversary of the founding of the city of Rome was celebrated. Augustus was the head of an empire that was peaceful, stable and powerful. All seemed to be well.

As head of state, Augustus had some other honorific titles of great importance. Following the appearance of a remarkable comet in the summer of 44 BC, Julius Caesar had been acclaimed as a god. This event had happened during games held in his honor. The Roman Senate affirmed the divinity of Julius Caesar, in 42 BC, two years after his death. In 29 BC, a temple was dedicated to the divine Julius on the Forum in Rome. A few years later Augustus received the title "son of the divine Julius" which essentially made him the "son of a god." The phrase "son of the divine Julius" was written on Augustus' imperial coinage. As the high priest of the Roman religion (Pontifex Maximus) Augustus was essentially fulfilling the role of a priest king. Augustus remained on the throne till his death in AD 14 when he was succeeded by Tiberius. Two days after Augustus' death the Roman Senate decreed that the dead emperor had also gone to be among the gods. However, the true Son of God had been born in humble circumstances about 16 years previously in Judea.

Why Was there a Census at the Time of Jesus' Birth?

In 3 BC, apparently at least some members of the Roman Senate indicated their desire to give Augustus the honorary title "Father of the Country" (Pater Patriae). This was designed to happen near the date of Augustus' 25th anniversary of assuming his official role as Princeps. Crowds were already acclaiming the emperor by the title "Pater Patriae," which was only given to the greatest of the Romans. Only four other Romans had received the title before Augustus received it in 2 BC. However, the politically astute Augustus apparently decided to link his reception of the title and the projected public celebrations of his reign in 2 BC with a general census and inventory of the empire.[1] According to Tacitus, the census / inventory covered a general description of the resources of the State, including the number of citizens and allies under arms, the fleets, subject kingdoms, provinces, taxes, and expenses.[2] This inventory served as propaganda, putting the the resources and strengths of the Roman imperial system on display. A summary of the results of the census was published in 2 BC under the title: *Breviarium Totius Imperii.*[3] In the following years the statistics were updated from time to time. It seems that Josephus and certainly Augustus later used some of the information in written texts.[4] The Romans and the subjected peoples from across the empire were also called upon to swear an oath of allegiance to the emperor as a major aspect of the census.[5] The census and pledge probably took place sometime between October 3 BC and January 2 BC.[6] It was during this period that Mary and Joseph traveled from Galilee to Judea and that Jesus was born.

All the peoples of the great nations took an oath, and at the same time, through the participation in the census, they were made part of one society.

The 5th century AD historian Orosius connected this particular census / registration to Jesus' birth. While Orosius was not always accurate, he does command some respect because of his extensive writings which tried to give a Christian interpretation of history. His historical accounts were some of the most widely read texts during the Middle Ages. Here is his text concerning the census associated with Jesus' birth:

> *Augustus ... ordered that a census betaken of each province everywhere and that all men be enrolled. So at that time, Christ was born and was entered on the Roman census list as soon as he was born. This is the earliest and most famous public acknowledgment which marked Caesar as the first of all men and the Romans as lords of the world ... Since in this one name of Caesar all the peoples of the great nations took an oath (of allegiance), and at the same time, through the participation in the census, were made part of one society.*[7]

Orosius understood very well that the census had a political purpose; it was not primarily about taxation (the Greek text of Luke says nothing about taxes). This particular census was an instrument of uniting the empire behind Augustus. On February 5th in 2 BC, perhaps within weeks of finishing the census, Augustus received the title "Pater Patraie" (translated either "Father of the Fatherland" or Father of the country). This is what Orosius means when he writes that Augustus

Below: The Pantheon in Rome

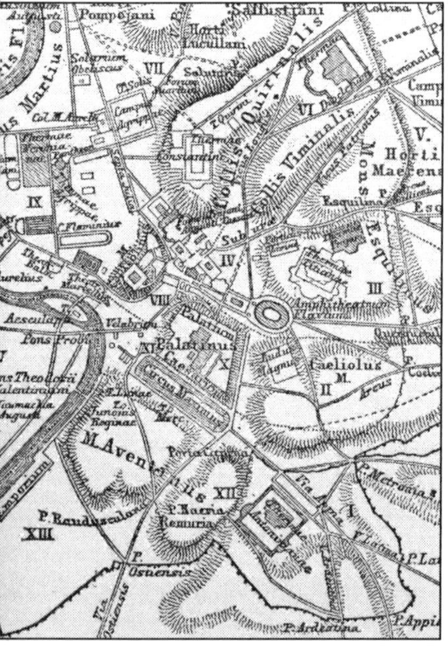

Marcus Licinius Crassus

had become the "first of all men." In a sense, Augustus had become the Ruler and "Father" of the whole Roman world. Josephus writes about an incident which involved swearing allegiance to king Herod and the emperor possibly about one year before Herod's death.[8] He seems to be writing about the same census / registration. About 6,000 Pharisees in Judea refused to swear allegiance to either Augustus or Herod. The refusal of this large group of Pharisees to swear allegiance eventually led to a whole series of events which reversed the fortunes of several people in Herod's court. The events affected Herod's own health, perhaps even shortening his life. We will explore some of these events later.

In Judea, it would not have been practical to have such a registration during the harvest times. In addition, major Jewish festivals like Passover, Pentecost and Tabernacles could have hindered and complicated the process of having a census. In October and November the fall rains came, and the first plantings of crops usually took place. It appears that a Jewish Sabbatical year may have begun in September of 3 BC, and therefore, no planting would have taken place in that agricultural year. The winter season could have been a practical time to do a census in a largely agricultural country with a mild climate. *The land of Israel is not known for severe winters.* Sheep, shepherds and travelers would not have suffered from the mild temperatures. Abraham always lived in tents and had vast flocks. The current average temperatures are: 14°C (57°F) as a high in December, with lows of 7°C (45°F). In January, the average temperatures are even better: highs of 22°C (71°F) and lows of 12°C (53°F).[9]

Roman and Parthian Relations

In the year 3 BC, Jerusalem was at the far edge of the Roman Empire, but the region, including Egypt was vital to Roman interests. The grain supply, much of which came from Egypt, was key to the survival of the city of Rome and the empire. Ensuring the supply of grain for Rome's population of about 1,000,000 people was a constant challenge. The Romans kept a close watch on the affairs of Syria and Judea because of their proximity with Egypt.

In 53 BC, a significant Roman army of about 45,000 men under the command of Marcus Licinius Crassus had mounted an invasion of the Parthian Empire from Syria. Crassus and the whole army were motivated by gold and glory. Parthian Mesopotamia had not seen war for about 75 years. Its great cities like Seleucia on the Tigris were wealthy and prosperous. The prize seemed fairly easy to acquire, so Crassus launched his campaign. The Romans did not go very far into Parthian territory before being soundly defeated by Parthian mounted archers in a battle lasting several days. Near the town of Carrhae (Harran) most of the Roman forces in the east were destroyed. Later in dealing with the Parthians Augustus followed a policy of peaceful coexistence, negotiation and even collaboration. This policy proved to be the wisest approach, and the Parthians were generally happy with the arrangement.

Parthia

The "King of kings" in the East

When Jesus was born most of the vast region to the east of Judea beyond the Syrian Desert, was under the domination of the Parthians. Their empire endured from about 247 BC to AD 224 in present day Syria, Turkey, Iran, Iraq, Pakistan and Turkmenistan. The Parthians had managed to become the most important power brokers east of Rome during the 2nd century before Christ, supplanting the Greek Seleucids. Originally nomads, the Parthians came from Central Asia. Many generations earlier they had settled in a region of present day Turkmenistan and northwestern Iran near the Caspian Sea. Their empire was ruled by a feudalistic military elite, which was well known for their formidable mounted archers. Loosely organized through a chain of authority based on local lords the whole empire was subject to the Parthian emperor, called the Shahanshah, "the King of kings."

The Parthian emperor was known as the "Shahanshah" which means "King of kings"

Over several generations, the Parthians were able to conquer the possessions of the Seleucid (Greek) successors of Alexander the Great. The Seleucids had been ruling over much of present day Iran, Mesopotamia and Syria. A variety of peoples including, Parthians, Persians, Elamites, Medes, Chaldeans, Armenians, Greeks and Jews made up the empire. All these peoples had their own cultural and religious preferences. The Parthians were not strong ethnic or religious zealots at the time of Jesus' birth. Large numbers of Greeks had moved to Syria, Mesopotamia and

Above: A coin with the image and the incription of Praates IV King of Kings and "Lover of the Greeks." (Photo: Courtesy of Pars Coins)[10]

present day Iran after Alexander's conquest of the Persian Empire in 330 BC. These Greeks were involved in business affairs and the administration of the Seleucid Empire, which had developed following the death of Alexander. The Greeks were still a very dominate class in many of the larger cities even under the Parthians. Jews were also present in significant numbers in the region of Babylonia, Northern Mesopotamia, Seleucia on the Tigris and the imperial capitals of Ctesiphon, Susa and Ecbatana.

The rulers of the empire had a reputation for being "lovers of Greek culture." The Parthian emperors had a phrase written on their coins, which shows that they recognized, embraced and even politically promoted the diverse nature of their empire. The Emperor Phraates IV, who reigned from 38 to 2 BC, followed the general tendency. On his coins, the phrase was written: "Phraates IV, King of kings, lover of the Greeks." The Persian Empire, which had been destroyed by Alexander the Great, would certainly not have minted coins with the words "lover of the Greeks." This underlines the mixed nature of the empire and the various factions, whom all had a share in power.

Jewish influence in the Parthian administration was also known during certain periods. Josephus tells us that some Jews held significant power in the province of Babylonia in the AD 20s and 30s. The rejection of the Jewish influence and rule by the Greek and Chaldean ethnic groups was accompanied by deadly riots. About 50,000 Jews died in the riots in the city of Seleucia on the Tigris in AD 37. The Jews in the city numbered about ten percent of the population. Even after the riots and massacres in AD 37, large numbers of Jews continued to live in Mesopotamia and Iran for hundreds of years.

The Parthian emperors were constantly shifting their royal residence among three imperial capitals. The court spent the winters in the relatively warm regions around Ctesiphon in Babylonia or Susa in southwestern Iran. The emperors spent their summers on the high plateaus and in the cooler mountainous areas around Ecbatana, Rhagae and Hecatompylus. If some of the Bethlehem Magi had been associated with the imperial court, they might have lived in various cities for several months each year.

Phraates IV was on the Parthian throne in 3 BC. Having reigned since 38 BC, it is probable that he was emperor when Jesus was born. When Phraates had seized power, he had put to death his own father and 30 of his brothers in an effort to secure the throne. The Emperor Phraates IV was murdered by his wife Musa and his son Phraataces in 2 BC. However, the exact date of his assassination is not known. Later, the mother and her son were legally married and ruled together until they were both deposed in AD 4. It is probable that Phraataces and Musa were reigning when the wise men made their visit to Judea. Musa had originally been a slave, who had been offered as a gift from Augustus to Phraates IV. She was extremely beautiful, ambitious and gifted. She quickly rose to become queen. Later Musa maintained her position and influence by marrying her own son. She was possibly slightly less than 40 years old, and her son may have been 20 years old in 3/2 BC.[11] Knowing this historical background it would not be surprising that biblically minded men in Parthia would have aspired to have a more righteous government. The Jews, who knew the promises of a coming Messiah from the royal line of David, would have even had greater reasons to desire the rise of God's anointed ruler, who was to reign over all the earth.

Above: Phraataces and his mother Musa[12]

The Romans and the Parthians are often spoken of as mortal enemies. At the time of Jesus' birth, the two great powers had fought several wars, and they would do so again in the following years. However, at the end of the 1st century BC both Rome and Parthia were in a largely peaceful period, having fairly good relations with each other. Further positive negotiations and exchanges took place between the two empires in the period immediately following Jesus' birth. At that time, it was relatively easy for people from the Parthian Empire to travel to regions under Roman control. The Magi would not have been rejected at the "passport control desk." Thousands of Jews and proselytes traveled from Parthian controlled areas to the religious festivals in Jerusalem every year. The yearly Pentecost celebration is a good example. An exceedingly unique Pentecost celebration is described in the book of Acts, but the regular festival was celebrated each year as it had been for well over a thousand years.

The Magi were most likely Parthian subjects, who longed for God's kingdom to become a reality. They went to Judea seeking the promised Messiah, who was destined to reign in righteousness over all the nations. They had certainly experienced unrighteousness through the behavior of their monarchs. The true, righteous, King of kings would eventually arise.

Left: The date palms of Mesopotamia are still a very important source of food.

Judea

The Last Days of Herod the Great

After Jesus was born in Bethlehem of Judea in the days of Herod the king, Magi from the east arrived in Jerusalem. (Matthew 2:1)

The Kingdom of Judea was being ruled by Herod the Great at the time of Jesus' birth. Herod was actually an Idumean, a foreigner, he was not ethnically Jewish. Idumea was south and east of Judea and was formerly called Edom. Herod was born in about 72 BC. At the age of 25, he was named governor of Galilee by his father, who was then in a position of power in Judea. Within a few short years Herod's father was assassinated. In the years 40 BC to 37 BC, the Parthians extended their power into Judea and placed a king of their own choice on the throne in Jerusalem, forcing the young Herod to flee. He appealed to the Roman Senate for help and they decided to make him king of Judea if he could recuperate the throne. After several years of fighting Herod came to power with Roman help by overcoming Antigonus, the Parthian supported Judean king.

Herod was a capable leader and he knew how to survive. Herod lived through the Roman civil war in the 40s and 30s BC. He saw the defeat of Mark Anthony and Cleopatra and the ultimate full domination of Octavian (Augustus). Being thoroughly submitted to Rome was a central part of Herod's survival strategy. He owed practically everything to Roman might, and he sought to honor the emperor and the imperial family on many occasions. Caesarea, on the coast, was founded by Herod and named in honor of Augustus Caesar. The ruins of this city are still a major tourist attraction in Israel today. Known as a great builder, Herod restored the Jerusalem temple to its former splendor in about 20 to 18 BC. The building was completely rebuilt from the foundations all the way to the roof. Herod spend a fortune on the work, it is one reason that he later became known as Herod, "the Great." Herod built an impressive palace on the heights west of the lower city of Jerusalem. He also built many other palaces and fortresses in various parts of the country including the fortress / palace of Masada which was on the plateau in the photo above.

Below: The Jerusalem temple and the fortress of Antonia

It is very probable that the appearance of the wise men in Judea would have been extremely disturbing to Herod. The Bible says that the king was greatly troubled. He was coming to the end of a particularly long reign, being about 70 years old. Profound difficulties had surfaced in working out his own succession. Several years before the end of his reign Herod had two of his possible heirs put to death on the charge of treason. According to Josephus the charges against the two heirs were at least partly trumped up by Herod's son Antipater, who wanted to secure the throne for himself by removing his brothers. The execution of two of the heirs to the throne was not well received by the general public in Herod's dominions.

Josephus gives us significant insights into the court of Herod concerning palace intrigues, attempted coups, building projects and wars. However, Josephus does not give us much insight into how the daily governmental affairs were actually conducted. This is especially important when one considers the death of Herod and the subsequent reigns of his sons. It would appear that in the years preceding Jesus' birth, Herod's chief heir, Antipater, was actually sharing power with his father in some manner. Josephus writes plainly on at least two occasions that Antipater "governed the nation jointly with his father, being indeed no other than a king already; and he was for that very reason trusted, and the more firmly depended upon ..." (Antiquities of the Jews, Book 17, Chapter 1:1-3).[13] Even so, Antipater's responsibilities did not prevent him from taking a extended trip to Rome over a period of more than seven months in the year preceding Herod's death.

Herod owed practically everything to Roman might, and he sought to honor the Emperor and the imperial family on many occasions.

Much of the trouble dating the end of Herod's life and the beginning of the reigns of his sons Archelaus, Antipas and Philip stem from unknowns concerning the last years of Antipater and Herod. The situation became extremely complicated. During the last two months of Herod's life, Antipater was in prison, having been accused of plotting to murder his own father and to seize power. From Josephus' writings it appears that the crown prince was guilty. He was executed five days before Herod's own death. The three young men who eventually did succeed Herod and governed parts of the kingdom may have backdated their reigns by three years because it seems clear that their official "reign" was dated from 4 BC. The backdating would have taken into account the fact that Antipater had been the legally appointed successor to their father for several years. This type of "backdating of a reign" was not uncommon. It was often used if there were any legal questions or if there was any lack of clarity in a succession. It is also possible that they had roles of leadership in the kingdom, which we are not informed about. As mentioned above, we are actually ignorant of many things concerning the day to day governance of Herod's realm. See Appendix 11: "Dating The Death of Herod," on pages 242 and 243, which gives a detailed argument for dating his death in 1 BC.

Photo: A model of Herod's palace

Herod's son Archelaus, who is mentioned in Matthew 2:22, did succeed his father as his principal heir upon Herod's death, with reduced powers. Augustus named him an ethnarch, which is lower in rank than a king. The post might be more or less the equivalent to a prince. After fleeing to Egypt, Joseph feared to return to Bethlehem, because Archelaus reigned in the place of his father. Another one of Herod's sons, Herod Antipas, inherited the rule of the regions of Perea and Galilee, which was about one fourth of the kingdom. Herod Antipas was still reigning many years later when Jesus was crucified and raised from the dead (See Matthew 14:1-12, Mark 8:15, Luke 13:31-32, 23:7-11).

Some of Herod's court astrologers / astronomers may have been aware of many of the heavenly events described later in this book. However, they could have been wary of giving any significant information to the king. They knew the king was extremely worried about his own security, his throne and his succession. Any truly pious Jew would have tried to hide information about the actual birth of the Messiah from a dangerous man like Herod. It is more probable that the court astronomers / astrologers were committed to pagan perspectives concerning the heavens, causing them to miss God's signs. If this was the case then they would have been as surprised as anyone else concerning the arrival of the Magi.

A Possible Timeline of Events in Herod's Court from 4 BC to 2 BC

4 BC

Two of Herod the Great's sons were executed because of rumors that they were trying to overthrow their father in a coup. Some of these rumors may have been started by Herod's son Antipater in order to supplant his brothers and secure his place as Herod's principal heir. At this time Herod made his son Antipater his principal heir and allowed him to share some power over the kingdom.

Summer / Fall 3 BC

Augustus issued a decree concerning a census of all the empire perhaps sometime during the late summer or early fall of 3 BC. The census was actually carried out months later in the land of Israel after a period of communication and organization. It possibly began in Herod's realm after Hanukkah (December 5th-13th in 3 BC). At this time Joseph took Mary to Bethlehem from Nazareth. Jesus was born possibly in December of 3 BC or early January of 2 BC. Joseph apparently decided to settle in Bethlehem for a longer period and found some work and more appropriate housing (Matthew mentions them being in a house).

Winter / Spring 2 BC

About 6,000 Pharisees refused to pledge an oath of allegiance to Augustus and King Herod during the census. They were fined for their refusal. The wife of Herod's brother, Pheroras, the tetrarch of Perea and Galilee, became involved in an effort to pay the fine because the Pharisees were favorable to her husband. The Pharisees even desired that Pheroras replace Herod. This caused a major crisis between Herod and his brother. As the crisis developed Antipater arranged for himself to be sent to Rome away from his father. Antipater went to Rome in early March of 2 BC.

The rest of the story will be told later along with the incidents surrounding the visit of the Magi.

Part 5: God's Chosen King

The Promised Messiah

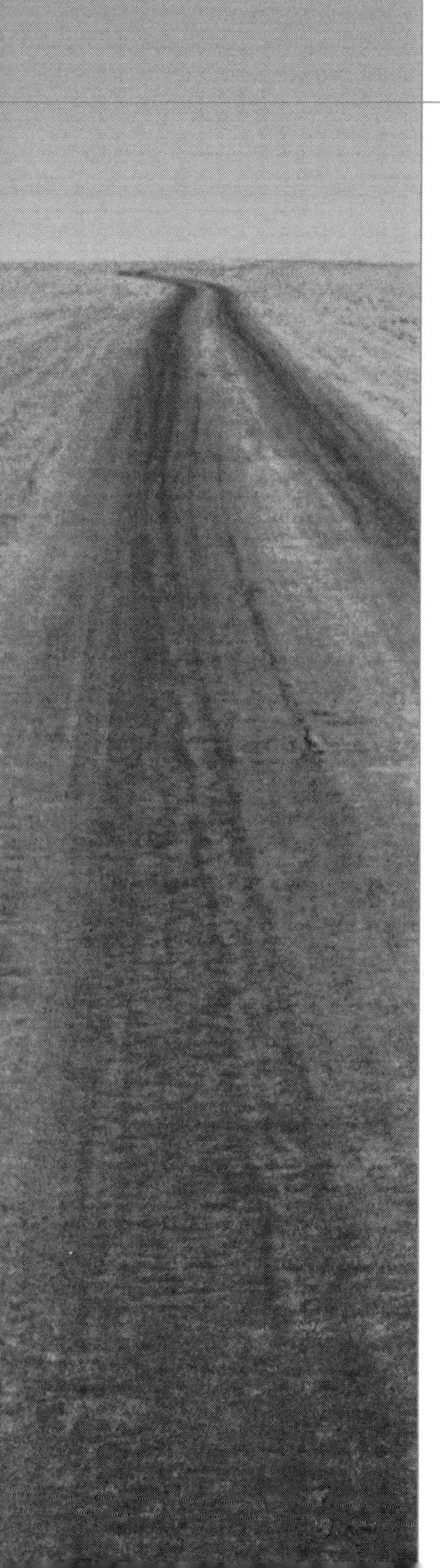

Focus and Perpsective Concerning the Prophecies of the Messiah

It is impossible to understand the star of Bethlehem or the Magi without understanding the expectations of the Jewish people concerning their Messiah. The descendants of Abraham, Isaac and Jacob at the time of the birth of the Jesus were looking to God to send a righteous world ruler who would vanquish corrupt rulers and oppressing empires, as well as, paganism and idolatry. This Messiah was expected to bring God's rule of peace and justice over all the earth. It was understood that the Israelites who walked in faithfulness to YHWH would be delivered from their enemies and that God would rule over all the nations from Jerusalem. God's promises concerning the Messiah came to the Jewish people through prophecies given by a variety of individuals over hundreds of years.

The Suffering Servant

Among the many biblical prophecies about the Jewish Messiah, several speak of the Messiah as someone who might suffer in his battle against evil. Jews have called the Messiah indicated by these prophecies as the Messiah Ben Joseph. Even one of the very earliest prophecies of a coming deliverer has an aspect of this suffering Messiah mentioned in it.

> *The LORD God said to the serpent, "Because you have done this, Cursed are you more than all cattle, And more than every beast of the field; On your belly you will go, And dust you will eat All the days of your life; And I will put enmity Between you and the woman, And between your seed and her seed; He shall bruise you on the head, And you shall bruise him on the heel."* *(Genesis 3:14-15)*

This ancient prophecy speaks of the victory of the "seed of the woman" over evil. Even at the dawn of human experience, mankind was led to think of an ultimate future victory over evil. As will be indicated later, one star named Spica/Zerah, the seed, could be associated with this prophecy. Although it was not the "star of Bethlehem" this heavenly light did play a significant role in the celestial drama which ends with a star over Bethlehem.

There are other texts concerning God's prophesied salvation in the Messiah. He is the suffering servant who would justify the many and who would bear their iniquities. He would pour out his soul to death and be numbered among the transgressors (Isaiah 53:11-12). These are wonderful key aspects of the Messiah's victory over evil, and they are central to the message of the cross.

The Messianic King

The wise men came seeking the King of the Jews. We do not know all of their thoughts concerning this king, perhaps their perspective included ideas about the suffering servant. It would seem that they thought of this king as someone who would bring in a reign of righteousness on the earth.

Many of us have become so accustomed to thinking of the Messiah's kingdom as being somewhere in the heavens. This is to misunderstand passages like John 18:36. When Jesus said, *"My kingdom is not of this world,"* he is actually saying "My kingdom does not come from here below (from this world), and neither does it use the methods of this world." His kingdom comes from above, but it is for this world. Therefore, we pray as Jesus taught us, *"Thy kingdom come, and thy will be done on earth as it is in heaven."* Certainly for those who die in the faith there is a time in the presence of God in heaven. However, the apostles and the early believers were looking for *"new heavens and a new earth in which righteousness dwells"* (2 Peter 3:13). This was a central part of the Jewish messianic hope before the birth of Jesus. The wise men were looking specifically for the king of the Jews. Whatever their ethnic or religious origins, they were looking for Israel's Messiah.

We can only understand the true nature of the messianic king and his kingdom by looking at the Jewish Scriptures. The Magi would have received most of their own perspective about the Messiah through Jewish people, the Hebrew Scriptures and possibly through texts like the Book of Enoch. These documents were readily available to the large Babylonian Jewish community living in the Parthian Empire. It is the author's conviction that the Tanakh (the Old Testament) and the New Testament Scriptures are important and reliable key texts. They give us a greater understanding concerning the Jewish messianic hope, as well as, the famous star and the Magi who traveled to Bethlehem. The author accepts the historicity of Abraham, Moses, David, Isaiah, Daniel and the others. He is well aware that many reject Daniel as a historic prophet. He recognizes that there are many debates about the historicity and dating of the biblical characters and texts.

The next section explores some of the prophecies from the Old Testament that the wise men could have been familiar with and which they may have even known by heart. Jesus is the real Sovereign Lord of the world now. He is the promised King who would be like a Son to his Heavenly Father (2 Samuel 7:14 and Psalm 89:26-27). The suffering servant of Isaiah chapter 53 has been raised from the dead. While the wise men did not understand all things concerning the Messiah in advance, this king is the one whom the wise men were seeking.

> *He has been declared the Son of God with power by his resurrection from the dead (Romans 1:1-4).*
>
> *All power has been given to him in heaven and on earth. (Mt. 28:18-20).*

For a child will be born to us, a son will be given to us; And the government will rest on His shoulders; And His name will be called Wonderful Counselor, Mighty God, Eternal Father, Prince of Peace. (Isaiah 9:6)

The Lion Leads the Way

The Blessing Given by Jacob to Judah in Egypt About 1900 BC

The ancient prophecies of the Messiah include a passage from the book of Genesis. In Egypt, about two thousand years before the birth of the Messiah, the Patriarch Jacob announced the future concerning his son, Judah, who was referred to as a young lion. In the prophecy, a person named the "Shiloh" is mentioned. The "Shiloh" refers to the "person who has the right to the ruler's staff" (ruler's scepter). A scepter signifies dominion, power, and authority. This person would have the role and responsibility of being the leader of the Jewish people. It is also mentioned that his rule would concern the obedience of various peoples. This is the earliest prophecy dealing with a specifically kingly role for an individual who would later be recognized as the Messiah. This book derives its name from this prophecy which becomes a key element in interpreting the heavenly events in 7 BC to 1 BC.

> *"Judah, your brothers shall praise you; Your hand shall be on the neck of your enemies; Your father's sons shall bow down to you. "Judah is a lion's whelp; From the prey, my son, you have gone up. He couches, he lies down as a lion, and as a lion, who dares rouse him up?" The scepter shall not depart from Judah, nor the ruler's staff from between his feet, until the Shiloh comes, and to him shall be the obedience of the peoples. Genesis 49:8-10 (NASB)*

If one examines the entire section starting at verse one, it becomes evident that three other brothers were disqualified to be the leader of the Jewish people. Reuben, Jacob's firstborn, was disqualified because he had defiled his father's bed by having sexual relations with his father's concubine Bilhah (Rachel's servant). See Gen. 35:22; 49:4; I Chron. 5:1. Simeon and Levi had used significant violence in avenging the rape of their sister Dinah. This had displeased Jacob / Israel and he made it clear to them (Gen. 34:25-31 and 49:5-7). So the leadership of the Jewish people ultimately fell to Judah.[1]

Lion **Shiloh** **scepter**

Moses and the Prophet to Come

15th Century BC

Jesus was certainly more than a prophet according to the New Testament. However, he was also a prophet according to the Apostles. (See Acts 3:22 and 7:37)

> *"The LORD your God will raise up for you a prophet like me from among you, from your countrymen, you shall listen to him. This is according to all that you asked of the LORD your God in Horeb on the day of the assembly, saying, 'Let me not hear again the voice of the LORD my God, let me not see this great fire anymore, or I will die.' "The LORD said to me, 'They have spoken well. 'I will raise up a prophet from among their countrymen like you, and I will put My words in his mouth, and he shall speak to them all that I command him. 'It shall come about that whoever will not listen to My words which he shall speak in My name, I Myself will require it of him. (Deuteronomy 18:15-19)*

Balaam's Prophecy of a Star

About 1400 BC

Balaam was a prophet, who was called by the king of Moab, Balak, to curse the Israelites as they were moving slowly toward the promised land under Moses' leadership. According to the story, Balaam could only bless Israel as he prophesied, he was not able to pronounce a curse. Part of Balaam's prophecy is a famous passage about a "star that would come forth from Jacob." This passage is often cited by Christians as referring to the Messiah and a specific star. However, one should pay more attention to what the "star" does in this prophecy. Here, the "star" refers to an individual who wages war against several peoples. It is evident that Jesus did none of those things. The "star" is not a natural star at all; it is an individual. The text says that the "star" (a person in this case) *will come forth from Jacob*, from the people of Israel. This "star" is symbolic; it was not to appear in the heavens.

Balaam on his donkey.

> *Balaam took up his discourse and said, "The oracle of Balaam the son of Beor, And the oracle of the man whose eye is opened, The oracle of him who hears the words of God, And knows the knowledge of the Most High ... "I see him, but not now; I behold him, but not near; A star shall come forth from Jacob. A scepter shall rise from Israel, and shall crush through the forehead of Moab, and tear down all the sons of Seth. Edom shall be a possession, Seir, its enemies, also will be a possession, while Israel performs valiantly. One from Jacob shall have dominion, and will destroy the remnant from the cities." And he looked at Amalek and took up his discourse and said, "Amalek was the first of the nations, But his end shall be destruction..." (Numbers 24:15-19 NASB)*

Balaam receives the messengers of Balak.

Balaam's prophecy was about a military leader. David, the king, is the most logical person to connect with the prophecy; he actually did all the things listed in the text. The prophecy was fulfilled through David, the bright one, "the star," who arose out of Jacob and waged war against Moab, Edom and other sons of Seth. The symbolism of being a bright, remarkable, shining "leader" is clear. The book of Second Samuel spells this out in detail:

> *David defeated the Philistines and subdued them; and David took control of the chief city of the Philistines. He defeated Moab... and the Moabites became servants to David, bringing tribute. ... David put garrisons among the Arameans of Damascus, and the Arameans became servants to David, ... So David made a name for himself when he returned from killing 18,000 Arameans in the Valley of Salt ... In all Edom he put garrisons, and all the Edomites became servants to David. And the LORD helped David wherever he went. So David reigned over all Israel; and David administered justice and righteousness for all his people. (2 Samuel 8:1-15)*

It is also obvious that the star in the prophecy cannot be speaking specifically of the ultimate Messiah directly because God said to David, 'You shall not build a house for My name because you are a man of war and have shed blood' (1 Chron. 22:8). The ultimate Messiah would build the true house of the Lord.

> *He will judge between the nations, And will render decisions for many peoples; And they will hammer their swords into plowshares and their spears into pruning hooks. Nation will not lift up sword against nation, And never again will they learn war. (Isaiah 2:4 and Micah 4:1-7)*

Jesus himself made it clear that war was not his way of liberating Israel. His vision and methods were different from those of David. Historically many Jews did believe that Balaam's prophecy referred to David and also to the ultimate Messiah. They expected the Son of David to win military victories over all the Gentiles (symbolized by Edom). In the Dead Sea scrolls the prophecy is often cited concerning the awaited Messiah, who would win military victories and do justice and righteousness. This type of messianic hope, linked to violence, ultimately led to the destruction of the nation of Israel in AD 67-73 and again in AD 132-135. The Rabbi Akiva in about AD 132 used the prophecy in reference to Simon ben Kosiba whom he renamed Simon Bar Kokhba "the son of the star." Simon Bar Kokbah led the Jewish revolt against Rome. For Akiva,the prophecy of a star did not refer to a physical, visible object in the heavens, but to a person.

In the days before the birth of Jesus, no one used the prophecy to indicate that God would place an actual star in the heavens as a sign concerning the coming of the Messiah. They all knew that the prophecy was symbolically speaking of a person and not a physical star. Matthew repeatedly uses Scripture to underline Jesus' messianic mandate. It is very noteworthy that Matthew himself does not make the association of Balaam's prophecy with the physical star of the Magi.

If the Balaam's prophecy had anything to do with a physical "star" then Matthew would have probably cited it in support of Jesus' messianic role, however, he did not make the association. Balaam's prophecy was fulfilled through David and in a very indirect manner perhaps it still speaks of God's ultimate Messiah.

The Morning Star, The Son of David

Administering justice and righteousness were significant aspects of David's reign. He was God's anointed leader, and his kingdom gave a foretaste of the coming kingdom of God's future Messiah. There is no doubt that Jesus was from the royal line, he was a descendant of David. In the book of the Revelation, Chapter 22:16, we read: *"I, Jesus ... I am the root and the descendant of David, the bright morning star."* This is related to texts in Isaiah 11:1 and 10: *"Then a shoot will spring from the stem of Jesse (David's father), and a branch from his roots will bear fruit. ... Then in that day The nations will resort to the root of Jesse, who will stand as a signal for the peoples; and His resting place will be glorious.* Jesus is a true "Son of the Star," He is the descendant of David. Jesus is the bright and remarkable ruler which the world needs. His presence signals the dawn of God's new creation.

God's Promises to David

About 1000 BC

Son of God

Priest

Melchizedek

King

> *The word of the LORD came to Nathan concerning David, the king, saying, "When your days are complete and you lie down with your fathers, I will raise up your descendant after you, who will come forth from you, and I will establish his kingdom. He shall build a house for My name, and I will establish the throne of his kingdom forever. I will be a father to him and he will be a son to Me; when he commits iniquity, I will correct him with the rod of men and the strokes of the sons of men, but My lovingkindness shall not depart from him, as I took it away from Saul, whom I removed from before you. Your house and your kingdom shall endure before Me forever; your throne shall be established forever." (2 Samuel 7: 4, 12-16 NASB)*

> *The LORD says to my Lord: "Sit at My right hand until I make your enemies a footstool for your feet." The LORD will stretch forth your strong scepter from Zion, saying, "Rule in the midst of your enemies. ... The LORD has sworn and will not change His mind, "You are a priest forever according to the order of Melchizedek." (Ps. 110:1 A Psalm of David NASB)*

The name Melchizedek, or Malki Tzedek, should be translated as "my king is righteous." David captured the city of Melchizedek and established his government in Jerusalem. Melchizedek had lived there at the time of Abraham about 1,000 years previously. The worshiping priest king, Melchizedek, became a model both for David and for the Messiah, who like David, was to be from the tribe of Judah.

David's throne will endure forever

Other Promises to David

10th Century BC

Psalm 89 was written by Ethan the Ezrahite. Ethan's father was a singer who was involved in temple worship during the lifetime of King David. Ethan remembers the promises given by God to David.

> *I have made a covenant with My chosen; I have sworn to David My servant, I will establish your seed forever and build up your throne to all generations." ... I have found David My servant; with My holy oil I have anointed him," ...*
>
> *"My faithfulness and My lovingkindness will be with him, ... He will cry to Me, 'You are my Father, My God, and the rock of my salvation.' I also shall make him My firstborn, The highest of the kings of the earth. My lovingkindness I will keep for him forever, And My covenant shall be confirmed to him. So I will establish his descendants forever And his throne as the days of heaven."*
>
> *... His descendants shall endure forever and his throne as the sun before Me. It shall be established forever like the moon, and the witness in the sky is faithful."*

The whole text of Psalm 89:1-37 contains extremely important verses about the Messiah's throne being established forever. The two principal heavenly lights are witnesses to the enduring reign of the Messiah.

In Psalm 132 we can also see how the psalmist speaks of God's promises concerning David's descendants. The crown of David will shine but his enemies will be clothed with shame.

> *For the sake of David Your servant, do not turn away the face of Your anointed. The LORD has sworn to David a truth from which He will not turn back: "Of the fruit of your body I will set upon your throne. If your sons will keep My covenant And My testimony which I will teach them, Their sons also shall sit upon your throne forever. For the LORD has chosen Zion; He has desired it for His habitation. This is My resting place forever; Here I will dwell, for I have desired it. I will abundantly bless her provision; I will satisfy her needy with bread. Her priests also I will clothe with salvation, And her godly ones will sing aloud for joy. There I will cause the horn of David to spring forth; I have prepared a lamp for Mine anointed. His enemies I will clothe with shame, But upon himself his crown shall shine." (Psalm 132:1-18)*

A Psalm of Solomon

10th Century BC

The texts below speak of Solomon's own reign as David's son, but the passage is also often thought to be messianic. In his early years, King Solomon's reign exemplified a reign of justice and righteousness. In the minds of the Israelites, the glory of Solomon's reign was a foretaste of the messianic kingdom. Unfortunately, in his later years, Solomon turned away from the Lord. The Jewish hope of a godly and righteous ruler is well illustrated in Psalm 72:1-17. Also the description given by the Queen of Sheba concerning Solomon contains the themes of doing justice and righteousness.

> *"Give the king your judgments, O God, and your righteousness to the king's son. May he judge your people with righteousness and your afflicted with justice. Let the mountains bring peace to the people, and the hills, in righteousness. May he vindicate the afflicted of the people, save the children of the needy and crush the oppressor. Let them fear you while the sun endures, and as long as the moon, throughout all generations. May he come down like rain upon the mown grass, Like showers that water the earth. In his days may the righteous flourish, and abundance of peace till the moon is no more.*
>
> *May he also rule from sea to sea and from the river (Euphrates) to the ends of the earth. Let the nomads of the desert bow before him, and his enemies lick the dust. Let the kings of Tarshish and of the islands bring presents; The kings of Sheba and Seba offer gifts. Let all kings bow down before him, may all nations serve him.*
>
> *For he will deliver the needy when he cries for help, The afflicted also, and him who has no helper. He will have compassion on the poor and needy, And the lives of the needy he will save. He will rescue their life from oppression and violence, And their blood will be precious in his sight; So may he live, and may the gold of Sheba be given to him; And let them pray for him continually ... May his name endure forever; May his name increase as long as the sun shines; And let men bless themselves by him; Let all nations call him blessed.*

The Words of the Queen of Sheba:

> *Blessed be the LORD your God who delighted in you to set you on the throne of Israel; because the LORD loved Israel forever, therefore He made you king, to do justice and righteousness." (1Kings 10:9) ... therefore He made you king over them, to do justice and righteousness." (2 Chronicles 9:8)*

Justice

Righteousness

He shall rule ... even to the ends of the earth.

Isaiah: The New Heavens New Earth

8th Century BC

"In that day shall the branch of YHWH be beautiful and glorious."
Isaiah 4:2

"There will be no end to the increase of His government or of peace."
Isaiah 9:7

Peace

שלום

The entire book of Isaiah gives a grand vision of God establishing his kingdom in new heavens and a new earth in which righteousness dwells. God's Servant, the descendant of David, will reign in this new creation where the lion lies down with the lamb (certainly figuratively and possibly literally). Isaiah speaks of the image of a tree with a shoot coming from the root of Jesse (Jesse was David's father). A branch coming from David's roots will bear fruit. This theme is later repeated by Jeremiah about 100 years later. Peace and righteousness are major themes of the kingdom of the Messiah. They were a major focus of the Jewish messianic hope.

> *The Lord Himself will give you a sign: Behold, a virgin will be with child and bear a son, and she will call His name Immanuel. (Isaiah 7:14)*

> *For a child will be born to us, a son will be given to us; and the government will rest on His shoulders; and His name will be called Wonderful Counselor, Mighty God, Eternal Father, Prince of Peace. There will be no end to the increase of His government or of peace, on the throne of David and over his kingdom, to establish it and to uphold it with justice and righteousness from then on and forevermore. The zeal of the LORD of hosts will accomplish this. (Isaiah 9:6-7)*

> *Then a shoot will spring from the stem of Jesse, and a branch from his roots will bear fruit. The Spirit of the LORD will rest on Him, the spirit of wisdom and understanding, the spirit of counsel and strength, the spirit of knowledge and the fear of the LORD. And He will delight in the fear of the LORD, And He will not judge by what His eyes see, nor make a decision by what His ears hear; But with righteousness He will judge the poor, and decide with fairness for the afflicted of the earth; and He will strike the earth with the rod of His mouth, and with the breath of His lips He will slay the wicked. Also righteousness will be the belt about His loins, and faithfulness the belt about His waist.*

> *And the wolf will dwell with the lamb, And the leopard will lie down with the young goat, and the calf and the young lion and the fatling together; and a little boy will lead them. .... They will not hurt or destroy in all My holy mountain, for the earth will be full of the knowledge of the LORD As the waters cover the sea. Then in that day the nations will resort to the root of Jesse, who will stand as a signal for the peoples; and His resting place will be glorious. (Isaiah 11:1-6, 9-10)*

Behold, My Servant, whom I uphold; My chosen one in whom My soul delights. I have put My Spirit upon Him; He will bring forth justice to the nations. He will not cry out or raise His voice, Nor make His voice heard in the street. A bruised reed He will not break And a dimly burning wick He will not extinguish; He will faithfully bring forth justice. He will not be disheartened or crushed Until He has established justice in the earth; And the coastlands will wait expectantly for His law."

Thus says God the LORD, "Who created the heavens and stretched them out, Who spread out the earth and its offspring, Who gives breath to the people on it And spirit to those who walk in it, I am the LORD, I have called you in righteousness, I will also hold you by the hand and watch over you, And I will appoint you as a covenant to the people, As a light to the nations, To open blind eyes, To bring out prisoners from the dungeon And those who dwell in darkness from the prison. (Isaiah 42:1-7)

You should be My Servant To raise up the tribes of Jacob and to restore the preserved ones of Israel; I will also make You a light of the nations So that My salvation may reach to the end of the earth." (Isaiah 49:6)

The following references indicate important passages concerning the Messiah in the book of Isaiah: 49:1-9, 50:4-10, 52:13 - 53:12, Chapters 60-62 and others. The very well known text concerning the suffering servant in Isaiah 52 and 53 did become a key passage in Jesus' own experience. That text is among the most precious in the Law and the Prophets. The messianic claims to kingship and a reign of righteousness and justice were central to Jewish messianic hope. Jesus did become king. Very few people, if any, expected his exaltation to be through suffering, death and resurrection.

Righteousness

Amos

8th Century BC

Looking ahead, the 8th century shepherd prophet Amos, announced many judgments throughout his prophecies. He spoke of a time when God "would raise up the fallen booth of David, ... and would also raise up its ruins and rebuild it as in the days of old ..." Judgment would not endure forever. A day would come when the exiles would be gathered again: "I will restore the captivity of My people Israel, and they will rebuild the ruined cities and live in them; They will also plant vineyards and drink their wine, and make gardens and eat their fruit."
(See Amos 9:1-15)

Justice

משפח

Micah Speaks of Bethlehem

8th Century BC

Photo above: A view of present day Bethlehem. It is possible that the angels appeared to the shepherds near one of the nearby hills in the photo. We do not know all the details about exactly where the events took place.

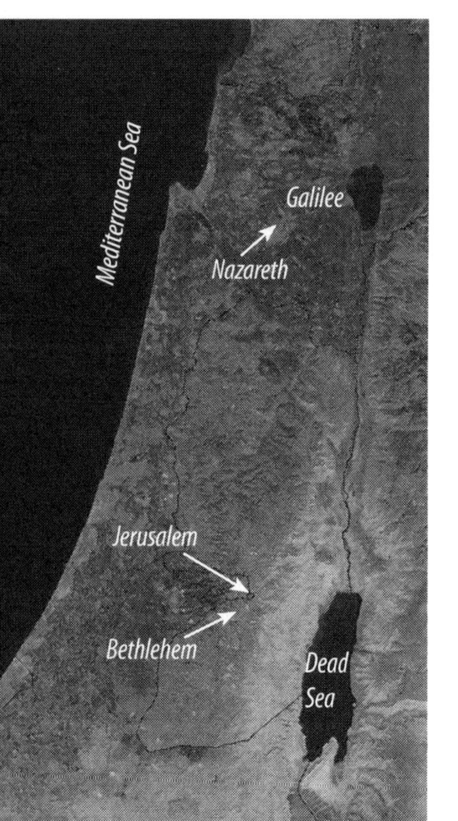

In the life of Jesus, Bethlehem, Nazareth and Jerusalem are key locations. When Jesus was born, the town or village of Bethlehem was most likely not inhabited by more than about 1,000 people. The wise men may have gone to Jerusalem thinking that the Messiah would be found there. Psalm 132:13-17 says: *For the LORD has chosen Zion (Jerusalem) ... "There I will cause the horn of David to spring forth; I have prepared a lamp for Mine anointed.* However, the Messiah was not to be found in the great city. God has often chosen the foolish and weak things of the world to shame the things which are strong (1 Corinthians 1:27-29). From this perspective it is entirely reasonable that Jesus would be born in a small town and even in a stable.

The following prophecy was given by Micah concerning the birth of the Messiah. The wise men may have also already been aware of this prophecy before arriving in Judea, but of course they first went to the capital. Herod was the one who asked the religious authorities where the Messiah was supposed to be born. He then consulted secretly with the Magi and sent them to Bethlehem. It is possible that wise men may have already thought of visiting Bethlehem before being summoned by Herod. However, after their visit to the king, they were obliged to go to Bethlehem.

> *"But you, Bethlehem Ephrathah, though you are little among the thousands of Judah, yet out of you shall come forth to Me the One to be Ruler in Israel, whose goings forth are from of old, from everlasting. Therefore He shall give them up, until the time that she who is in labor has given birth; then the remnant of His brethren shall return to the children of Israel. And He shall stand and feed His flock in the strength of the LORD, In the majesty of the name of the LORD His God; and they shall abide, For now He shall be great to the ends of the earth; And this One shall be peace. (Micah 5:2-5 NKJV)*

Jeremiah

7th and 6th Century BC

The Righteous Branch of David

Unlike his contemporaries Daniel and Ezekiel, Jeremiah never went to Babylon. His life ended in Egypt where he was taken against his will. Jeremiah's prophecies about the coming Messiah are key aspects of a Jewish perspective on the Messiah. In Jeremiah's prophecies the "branch of David" (Hebrew: tsemach) is referring to a descendant of David, similar to using the word "offspring" when speaking of one's descendants.

> *"Behold, the days are coming," declares the LORD, "When I will raise up for David a righteous Branch; And He will reign as king and act wisely and do justice and righteousness in the land. In His days Judah will be saved, And Israel will dwell securely; And this is His name by which He will be called, 'The LORD our righteousness.' (Jeremiah 23:5-6)*
>
> *'Behold, days are coming,' declares the LORD, 'when I will fulfill the good word which I have spoken concerning the house of Israel and the house of Judah. In those days and at that time I will cause a righteous Branch of David to spring forth; and He shall execute justice and righteousness on the earth. 'In those days Judah will be saved and Jerusalem will dwell in safety; and this is the name by which she will be called: the LORD is our righteousness.'*
>
> *For thus says the LORD, "David shall never lack a man to sit on the throne of the house of Israel; ... 'As the host of heaven cannot be counted and the sand of the sea cannot be measured, so I will multiply the descendants of David My servant and the Levites who minister to Me. ... If My covenant for day and night stand not, and the fixed patterns of heaven and earth I have not established, then I would reject the descendants of Jacob and David My servant, not taking from his descendants rulers over the descendants of Abraham, Isaac and Jacob. But I will restore their fortunes and will have mercy on them." (Jeremiah 33:14-17, 22, 25-26)*

Tzedek / Tzedakah - Justice and Righteousness

By ensuring justice, one does what is required by the law. By doing righteousness one goes beyond the simple rule of law. One actually accomplishes all the good attitudes and actions which God has always desired. If one does what is right, it is a manifestation of what God would do himself. He would save, and he would do good toward the poor and needy. The Jewish messianic hope was concentrated on God's Chosen One who was to reign doing justice and righteousness.

Daniel

The Prophet Lived from Possibly 625 BC to about 530 BC

Daniel's interpretation of one of Nebuchadnezzar's dreams concerning world empires is well known. As a young man, Daniel distinguished himself. God gave him such favor that he became a high official in the Babylonian governmental administration. He became the head of all the wise men of Babylon (Daniel 2:46-49). Through Daniel's position and influence, several Jews were introduced into significant realms of influence in the Babylonian royal court. One thinks of Shadrach, Meshach and Abed-nego. Later, Mordechai, Esther and Nehemiah had significant influence in the Persian court.

Daniel is a key figure in the prophecies concerning the Messiah. His prophecies are cited in the New Testament concerning Jesus. The "Son of Man" passage in Daniel 7:13-14 was a key text in Jesus' condemnation by the Jewish elders during his trial before his crucifixion. Jesus, himself, quotes part of the following passage to the high priest before his condemnation:

> *""I kept looking in the night visions, and behold, with the clouds of heaven One like a Son of Man was coming, and He came up to the Ancient of Days and was presented before Him. To Him was given dominion, glory and a kingdom, that all the peoples, nations and men of every language might serve Him. His dominion is an everlasting dominion which will not pass away; and His kingdom is one which will not be destroyed." (Daniel 7:13-14)*

Early in the book of Daniel, a vision of a magnificent statue illustrates several world empires including one which will eventually fill all the earth. Daniel interprets the "head of gold at the beginning of the vision as being king Nebuchadnezzar. The great mountain at the end of the vision is certainly referring to the Messiah's kingdom:

A Kingdom which shall endure forever

Everlasting righteousness

> *You, O king, were looking and behold, there was a single great statue; that statue, which was large and of extraordinary splendor, was standing in front of you, and its appearance was awesome. The head of that statue was made of fine gold, its breast and its arms of silver, its belly and its thighs of bronze, its legs of iron, its feet partly of iron and partly of clay. You continued looking until a stone was cut out without hands, and it struck the statue on its feet of iron and clay and crushed them. Then the iron, the clay, the bronze, the silver and the gold were crushed all at the same time and became like chaff from the summer threshing floors; and the wind carried them away so that not a trace of them was found. But the stone that struck the statue became a great mountain and filled the whole earth. (Daniel 2:31-35)*

The interpretation of the vision is given by Daniel in chapter 2:36-45:

> *You, O king, are the king of kings, to whom the God of heaven has given the kingdom, the power, the strength and the glory; .... After you there will arise another kingdom inferior to you, then another third kingdom of bronze, which will rule over all the earth. ... Then there will be a fourth kingdom ... In the days of those kings the God of heaven will set up a kingdom which will never be destroyed, and that kingdom will not be left for another people; it will crush and put an end to all these kingdoms, but it will itself endure forever.*

Prophecy of 70 "Sevens" for the People of Israel and the Holy City

> *Seventy "sevens" have been decreed for your people and your holy city, to finish the transgression, to make an end of sin, to make atonement for iniquity, to bring in everlasting righteousness, to seal up vision and prophecy and to anoint the most holy place (some put the most Holy One - the Messiah). So you are to know and discern that from the issuing of a decree to restore and rebuild Jerusalem until Messiah the Prince there will be seven "sevens" and sixty-two "sevens"; it will be built again, with plaza and moat, even in times of distress. (Daniel 9:24-26)*

It was perhaps in late 539 or 538 BC that Daniel received this well known revelation about the 70 "sevens," which is divided into 7 "sevens," 62 "sevens" and one "seven." These numbers are usually interpreted as 70 "weeks of years," making a total of 490 years (See Daniel 9:24-27). Daniel presents a coming messianic kingdom and he even mentions everlasting righteousness in the prophecy. It should not be surprising that the character of the Messiah would be profoundly marked by righteousness. This is in line with many of the other prophecies of a kingdom of righteousness ruled by "the Messiah, the Son of the Blessed One" (Mark 14:61).

The prophecy in Daniel 9:24-27 is specifically concerning the Messiah, the Jews and Jerusalem. The Messiah is destined to come at the culmination of the 7 + 62 "sevens," but before the 70th "seven." As some prophetic calculations were done during the 1st century BC, some groups apparently thought that the time for the Messiah's appearing was near. A well known more recent calculation was done by Sir Robert Anderson[2] and later Harold W. Hoehner modified it.[3] Professor Hoehner's dating of the prophecy starts in 444 BC and ends in March 33 BC. The end point was taken to be Jesus' entry into Jerusalem at the end of 69 weeks of years (7 x 7 and 62 x 7 = 483 years). Some scholars and authors have made objections to Anderson's and Hoehner's calculations because they are based on supposedly "prophetic years" of 360 days. There may even be several other possibilities to understand the prophecy. The next three pages outline another possible interpretation.

Above: The incident of the handwriting on the wall recorded in Daniel 5:1-31.

Atonement

Seventy weeks

Son of Man ...

dominion, glory and a kingdom

Above: A small portion of a larger extract from the Cyrus Cylinder (lines 15–21), giving the genealogy of Cyrus and an account of his capture of Babylon in 539 BC. Another portion of the text contains the Babylonian version of Cyrus' declaration allowing Jews and other peoples to return to their homelands.

(Image and text: Wikipedia)

70 Sevens

Sabbath Years, Jubilees and Daniel's Seventy Sevens

In writing this book the author avoided almost anything to do with the prophecy in Daniel 9:20-27 for well over a year. The prophecy is widely acknowledged as being incredibly difficult. At first it appeared that making a direct link with the prophecy was not necessary in order to establish a scenario concerning the Magi and birth of Jesus. There were several meaningful messianic events in the heavens in the last years of the 1st century BC. However, eventually it became evident that Daniel's prophecy was probably an integral part of the Magi's experience. The prophecy is mysterious. God's wisdom and glory are hidden in it. One should be careful in making great pronouncements about it.

In Daniel's prophecy the word that is often translated as "weeks" in many Bibles should actually be translated as "sevens." Surprisingly, the time element of the prophecy has several layers. The prophecy actually is linked to "sevens" of days, weeks, months and years. Almost everyone who has ever written about Daniel 9:20-27 has concentrated on the role of the years. However, some other aspects of the prophecy will shine, as we explore the events near the birth of Jesus. For the author it was only through some collaboration and sharing over a period of months, that a possible solution to the enigma of the prophecy finally took form.[4]

The Jewish system of Sabbatical years and Jubilees seems to play a central role in explaining the enigma of the "sevens." One of the significant reasons for the exile was linked to the Sabbath years and Jubilees. Since the Israelites had not practiced these God appointed periods of rest, God imposed a Sabbath rest of 70 years. This also had implications for Daniel's 70 "sevens" prophecy (See 2 Chronicles 36:20-21). In a second century AD rabbinic text called the *Seder Olam,* in the passage about Daniel's prophecy, the term "sabbatical periods" is used to describe the "sevens." Even so the rabbinic interpretation presented concerning the prophecy was profoundly erroneous. The rabbis used a timeline of events which was divorced from historical reality, reducing the timeline of the Persian kings from more than 200 years (539 to 330 BC), to no more than 34 years. However, if one uses a timeline based on real history, as well as, the Jewish calendar and the Sabbatical year system, a partial solution to Daniel's 70 "sevens" prophecy does become evident.

Daniel's prophecy follows the sequence of 7 "sevens," 62 "sevens" and one "seven," designating them all as separate periods. The complete series of "sevens" begins with Cyrus' declaration to restore and rebuild Jerusalem in the first year of his reign over Babylonia. The Persian king's declaration may have taken place sometime in 539 or 538 BC. A large number of Jews did return to Jerusalem fairly soon after Cyrus' declaration, as outlined in the book of Ezra (Ch. 1-2), while others remained in Mesopotamia and Iran. The restoration and reconstruction of

Jerusalem took place over a long period of almost 100 years lasting from Cyrus' decree until 445 or 444 BC. The temple, the city of Jerusalem itself and its walls were finally completed after many unexpected delays and the interventions of numerous kings and officials. Darius I and Artaxerxes I, both Persian kings, also made decrees which eventually brought about the completion of the restoration and rebuilding of the city.

... from the issuing of a decree to restore and rebuild Jerusalem until Messiah, the Prince, there will be seven "sevens" and sixty-two "sevens."

The counting of the Hebrew years for the religious festivals and dating the reigns of kings began in the month of Nisan in (March / April) and continued to the end of the month of Adar (February - March). However, Jewish Sabbatical years followed the agricultural cycle which was linked to the planting season in the fall. According to studies done by Samuel Zuckermann and Donald Blosser concerning the Sabbatical year system,[4] the year from the fall of 535 BC to the late summer of 534 BC (535/534 BC) was probably a agricultural Sabbatical year. This would have been the first Sabbatical year following Cyrus' declaration. Therefore, the first year of a new series of seven years could have begun on the 1st of Nisan in 534 BC. The 7 "sevens" of years in Daniel's prophecy would have taken place from 534/533 BC to 486/485 BC, representing one period of 49 years (7 X 7 = 49 years). Normally this period should have ended with a Jubilee year. However, the Jubilee years were not celebrated after the exile and apparently they were never celebrated regularly before the exile.

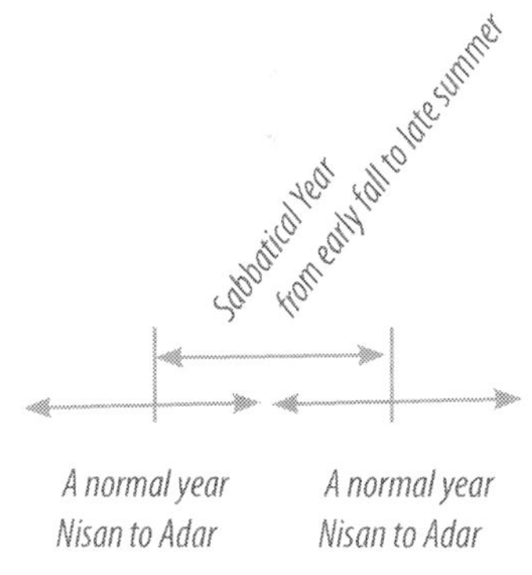

A normal year for dating and for the religious festivals was from the 1st of Nisan in the spring to the end of Adar at the end of winter.

Afterwards, there was apparently a break from 485/484 BC until 437/436 BC. It appears that the 49 years in between 485 and 436 BC represented a skipped period of what would have normally been one Jubilee period. There has been much debate about the starting points of both the 7 "sevens" and the 62 "sevens," as well as, the separation period between the groups of "sevens." Skipping either one sabbatical period of seven years or a Jubilee period of 49 years between the groups of "sevens," could have been a logical and appropriate separation period. Otherwise, one would need to justify why there would be two "sevens," three "sevens," or possibly more than 7 "sevens" separating the time periods indicated in the prophecy.

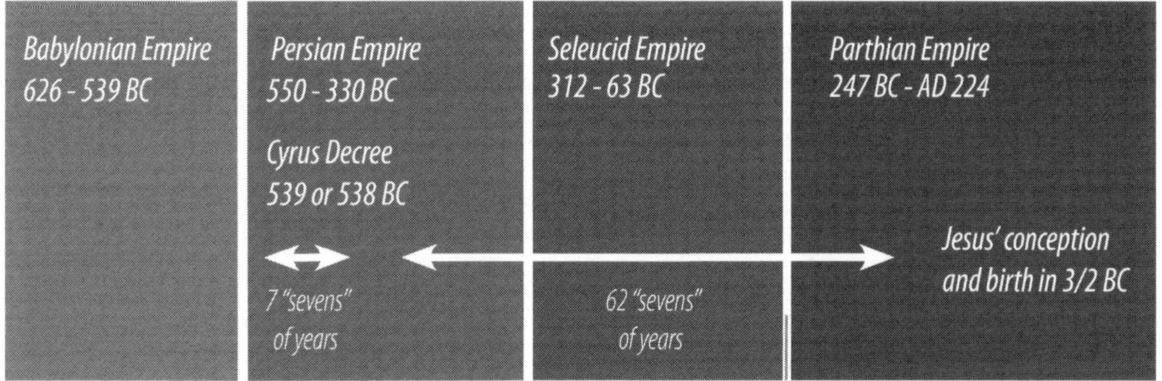

Making atonement for iniquity, bringing in everlasting righteousness, and anointing the the most Holy One, the Messiah, are part of the 70th "seven" of years.

The year 436/435 seems to have been the beginning point for the count of the 62 "sevens" (62 x 7 = 434 years). The prophecy says that there will be 7 "sevens" and 62 "sevens" ***until*** the coming of the Messiah. The culmination of the 62 "sevens" falls in the year starting with the 1st of Nisan in 3 BC, which continues into 2 BC. Many of the astronomical events concerning Jesus' birth fall within this particular year and its associated Sabbatical year.

The actual 70th "seven" stands apart from the 7 "sevens" and the 62 "sevens." Apparently Jesus' ministry may have taken up about one half of the last "seven." There are many debates about the last "seven," but investigating the 70th "seven" is well beyond the scope of this book.

The wisdom of God is often multifaceted. The prophecy in Daniel 9:20-27 appears to be much simpler and also much more complex than one might even dream. There are apparently several levels of meaning in the prophecy concerning the "sevens" linked to days, weeks, months and years. We will explore the different layers of meaning in the coming chapters.

The Cyrus Cylinder in the British Museum

Timeline of the 70 "Sevens" of Years

539/538 BC ? : Cyrus the Great's Decree

537 BC and following: Many Jews returned to Jerusalem and Judea.

535/534 BC : Sabbatical Year

7 "Sevens" of Years

534 BC : 1st Nisan - The beginning of the 7 "sevens" of years

485 BC : 29th of Adar - The end of the 7 "sevens" of years

485 - 436 BC : A skipped period of 49 years

62 "Sevens" of Years

436 BC : 1st Nisan - The beginning of the 62 "sevens" of years

3 BC : 1st of Nisan - The last year of the 62 "sevens" of years

3/2 BC : Jesus' conception and birth were during the last year of the 62 "sevens."

2 BC : 29th day of 2 Adar - The end of the 62 "sevens" of years

1 "Seven" of Years

This was partially fulfilled during Jesus life, ministry, death and resurrection.

Haggai

Late 6th Century BC

> *'I will shake all the nations; and they will come with the wealth of all nations, and I will fill this house with glory,' says the LORD of hosts. 'The silver is Mine and the gold is Mine,' declares the LORD of hosts. 'The latter glory of this house will be greater than the former,' says the LORD of hosts, 'and in this place I will give peace,' declares the LORD of hosts." (Haggai 2:7-9)*

The first line in the passage above is often translated: "the desire of all nations shall come," instead of "they will come with the wealth of all nations." The "desired (one) of all nations" has been taken to mean the Messiah. Complete theories of the Bethlehem star have been developed around this text and the constellation of Coma, "the desired one," near Virgo. This author does not share this idea for two reasons:

(1) It is not obvious that "all nations desire" the Messiah. The Bible makes the case that mankind in general is not seeking the Lord, His kingdom or His righteousness. "There is none righteous, not even one; There is none who understands, there is none who seeks for God. (Rom. 2:10-11). However, happily, God is seeking man. Jesus came seeking and to save that which was lost.

(2) The text can simply be translated as the "wealth of all nations" which makes more sense in the context (the next line refers to silver and gold). The text may certainly refer to the messianic age to come (see also Isaiah 60). Herod did greatly transform the temple and the glory of God was manifest there in Jesus (Malachi 3:1-4). The book of Revelation indicates that the ultimate manifestation of God's glory will come when the glory and honor of the nations will be brought into the heavenly city where there is no temple. However, even so there is still a temple, "for the Lord God Almighty and the Lamb are its temple."

> *And the city has no need of the sun or of the moon to shine on it, for the glory of God has illumined it, and its lamp is the Lamb. The nations will walk by its light, and the kings of the earth will bring their glory into it. In the daytime (for there will be no night there) its gates will never be closed; and they will bring the glory and the honor of the nations into it; (Revelation 21:23-26)*

The text of Haggai certainly makes one think of the glory to be manifest during the Messiah's reign. Even so, it is a doubtful exercise to establish a whole theory of the star of Bethlehem based on this text and a relatively obscure constellation beside Virgo. The nations are not now specifically desiring the Messiah and another translation of the text concords with many other passages of Scripture.

The Prophet Haggai in a Russian icon from first quarter of 18th century, Kizhi monastery, Russia

Ezekiel, Zechariah and Malachi

6th and 5th Centuries BC

The sun of righteousness shall arise with healing

Branch

My servant David

Shepherd

Ezekiel was taken into exile in Babylon at the same time as Daniel. It is possible although it is not certain that they may have met. Ezekiel also speaks of the Lord's servant from David's family line who would reign forever:

> *"Then I will set over them one shepherd, My servant David, and he will feed them; he will feed them himself and be their shepherd. And I, the Lord, will be their God, and My servant David will be prince among them; I the Lord have spoken.*
>
> *"My servant David will be king over them, and they will all have one shepherd; and they will walk in My ordinances and keep My statutes and observe them. They will live on the land that I gave to Jacob My servant, in which your fathers lived; and they will live on it, they, and their sons and their sons' sons, forever; and David My servant will be their prince forever. (Ezekiel 34:23-24 and 37:24-25)*

Zechariah uses language similar to Jeremiah concerning the "Branch." Note here that there is a priest on the throne of David.

> *Then say to him, 'Thus says the LORD of hosts, "Behold, a man whose name is Branch, for He will branch out from where He is; and He will build the temple of the LORD. "Yes, it is He who will build the temple of the LORD, and He who will bear the honor and sit and rule on His throne. Thus, He will be a priest on His throne, and the counsel of peace will be between the two offices. (Zech. 6:12-13, see also Zech. 3:8)*

Later toward 400 BC Malachi also specks of the Messiah:

> *But for you who fear My name, the sun of righteousness will rise with healing in its wings; and you will go forth and skip about like calves from the stall. (Malachi 4:2)*

Malachi's "sun of righteousness," is thought to have referred to the Messiah. Notice the emphasis on righteousness. The Hebrew word "wings" in Malachi's text can also refer to the borders or corners of an ancient Jewish garment. This is probably the background scripture concerning the healing incident in Matthew 9:21-22. The woman in the story may have had the prophecy in mind when she tried to touch the hem of Jesus' garment. She apparently exercised faith in Jesus as a healer based on this text.

The Book of Enoch

Portions of this book may be very ancient. Otherwise 3rd - 2nd Century BC

The non-biblical book of Enoch was well known in the period before the birth of Jesus and it could have been a significant book for any Magi who were interested in the Jewish Messiah. The book was certainly widely available. Many scholars date most portions of the book from about 160 BC to 100 BC. Historically, some portions of the book have been attributed to Enoch, the biblical figure, who lived before the flood. Several early Church Fathers defended the book, and even urged that it become part of the recognized, canonical Scriptures. Enoch is mentioned and quoted in the biblical book of Jude; however, the book was finally not officially accepted as part of the Jewish or Christian Scriptures. Some portions of the Book of Enoch could be very ancient, but this is far from proven.

Above: Enoch ascending into heaven when the Lord "took him" in Genesis 5:24.

The angel Uriel, who is referred to as the commander of the heavenly lights, supposedly revealed much astronomical knowledge to Enoch. In chapters 72-82 of the book, there is a significant astronomical component especially concerning the sun and the moon. Some scholars have thought that the passage could indicate a familiarity with Babylonian lunar theory although many aspects of the Book of Enoch are in error concerning astronomy.

> *Thus the signs, the durations of time, the years were shown to me by the angel Uriel, whom the Lord, God of eternal glory, has appointed over all the luminaries of heaven, – both in heaven and in the world – in order that they – the sun, moon, and stars, and all the created objects which make their revolution in all the chariots of the heaven – that they should rule on the face of the heaven and be seen on the earth, to be guides for the day and the night. (1 Enoch 75:3)*

The book does not contain anything which would be helpful to identify a physical star with the expected messianic king. However, there are many passages in the book of Enoch (especially in chapters 37-71), which speak of thc Messiah in terms which are well known to readers with a biblical background. These titles include: "The Righteous One, the Elect One, the Anointed One and the Son of Man." See the following references: 38:2, 39:6-7, 45:1-6, 46:1-8, 48:1-10, 49:2-4, 51:1-5, 52:1-9, 53:3-7, 61:5-13, 62:1-15, 63:10-12, 63:26-29, 70:1- 4, 71:1-16. These texts would have certainly attracted the attention of any people interested in God's Messiah. The emphasis on righteousness is very strong throughout the book and the hope of a new world in which righteousness dwells is a major theme. Below are some examples of the text:

The Elect One

Righteous One

Anointed One

> *And all the children of men shall become righteous, and all nations shall offer adoration and shall praise Me, and all shall worship Me. And the earth shall be*

Above: One of the caves where the Dead Sea Scrolls were discovered and an example of one of the documents.

cleansed from all defilement, and from all sin, and from all punishment, and from all torment, and I will never again send (them) upon it from generation to generation and for ever. (Enoch 10:21b-22)

In those days a whirlwind carried me off from the earth, and set me down at the end of the heavens. And there I saw another vision, the dwelling-places of the holy, And the resting-places of the righteous. ... In that place my eyes saw the Anointed One of righteousness and of faith, and I saw his dwelling-place under the wings of the Lord of Hosts. Righteousness shall prevail in his days. The righteous and elect shall be without number before Him for ever and ever. All the righteous and elect before Him shall be strong as fiery lights, their mouth shall be full of blessing, their lips extol the name of the Lord of Hosts and righteousness before Him shall never fail ... (1st Book of Enoch Chapter 39: 6-7)

The Essenes, who certainly used the book of Enoch, had a dating system which indicated the moment of the coming of the Messiah (or Messiahs) based on Jubilee years. After the exile, the Essenes were the only Jews who were still actively seeking to practice the Jubilee year. Using a view of time dominated by Jubilee years, the Essenes thought the history of the world was going to be completed over a period of 100 Jubilees (4900 years). This supposedly began at creation. Traces of this scheme are found both in the book of Enoch and the book of Jubilees. According to the Essene reckoning, the end of the 10th Jubilee (490 years) since the exile was a key moment when God would intervene in history (this corresponded with the end of the 7th decade of Jubilees). Their calculations placed this date somewhere between 3 BC and AD 2.[5] Even so, it was not exactly as they expected. The Essenes believed that there would be two messianic leaders: (1) a kingly leader and (2) a priestly leader. Both of them were supposed to work together to bring about the establishment of God's reign. According to the Essenes, only after a period of two other decades of Jubilees (490 years x 2 = 980 years), would all of mankind be converted. At that point, the new age of righteousness would be complete.[6]

The Messiah was not Zoroastrian

As indicated previously, it is often assumed by some modern scholars that Zoroastrian concepts and beliefs influenced the Jewish ideas and hopes concerning their Messiah. It is practically impossible to do any serious research about the Magi without finding this assumption at almost at every turn. However, the supposed similarity and influence of Zoroastrian thought to Jewish thought seems more superficial than real. Zoroastrian thought does include three world saviors and three virgin births. Even so, we know almost nothing concerning the real origins of Zoroastrian messianic thought.

Things are much different concerning the Jewish messianic hope. Its prophecies of the kingly Messiah date to Jacob's lengthy stay in Egypt, 4,000 years ago. Moses mentions the coming Messiah as a prophet similar to himself. David receives several promises concerning the enduring nature of his royal house. The reigns of David and Solomon became models for the coming messianic age. All these men existed centuries before the Assyrian deportation, the exile in Babylon and the rise of the Medes and the Persians. The Zoroastrian religion was most likely relatively unknown to the Jewish people until the beginning of the exile of the northern kingdom of Israel some decades before 700 BC. However, it is not even sure that those first exiled Israelites met many Zoroastrians.

Passages from the books of Isaiah and Jeremiah are extremely important concerning the Davidic Messiah. Neither of these men ever traveled to Babylon, nor did they have any known significant contact with the Medes or the Persians.

Passages from the books of Isaiah (written before 680 BC) and Jeremiah (before 580 BC) are extremely important concerning the Davidic Messiah. Neither of these Hebrew prophets ever travelled to Babylon, nor did they have any known significant contact with the Medes or the Persians. Neither prophet could not have been influenced by Zoroastrian thought concerning the Messiah. Even though Isaiah prophesied a virgin birth linked to the coming of the Messiah, this unusual birth does not seem to have been a strong focus of Jewish messianic hope. Their hope was more centered on the coming government of peace and righteousness than on the means of the messianic birth.

While both Ezekiel and Daniel lived in exile in Babylon, all of Ezekiel's prophecies and several of Daniel's prophecies were given before the actual conquest of Babylon by the Persians. Zoroastrianism is not known to have been very important in the ancient Middle East before 600 BC. It was certainly important during the Persian administration from 539 BC onward. However, the Median Magi were out of favor for a period following an attempted coup d'état against Cyrus' successor by a Magian leader in 522 BC.

When one takes all these factors into account, it would seem that the Jewish messianic hope drew its inspiration from Hebrew roots, and not from Zoroastrian ideas. In addition as written earlier the Zoroastrian concept of multiple Messiahs separated by thousands of years does not correspond to Jewish thought. Neither does the proposed method of conception of the Zoroastrian Messiahs.

The promises given to David are key aspects of the Jewish messianic hope. There would have been no reason for the Jewish people to seek inspiration or messianic insights from the Zoroastrians. The Magi certainly could have been from among the Medes, Persians, Parthians, Chaldeans, Greeks, Ethiopians, Arabs, Jews or perhaps from other ethnic groups. The most obvious reason for the wise men's focus on a Jewish Messiah was because they were somehow influenced by Jewish people and / or the Jewish Scriptures. In the coming sections of this book, the Jewish links become evident as one considers the Jewish ideas about the heavens, the Jewish calendar and the heavenly events which took place in from 7 BC to 1 BC.

A Key Point

There was no biblical prophecy of a physical star that would appear in the heavens at the time of the Messiah's birth. This means that the wise men were almost certainly <u>not waiting</u> for any stellar manifestation to accompany the Messiah's appearing. *One needs to discover why they might have believed that any star might have had something to do with the birth of the Messiah.* The lack of a specific prophecy about a star is also a strong objection to the manifestation of a purely "miraculous" star. Without a prophecy of a star, one no longer has no any explanation for associating *any star* with the coming of the Messiah.

Essentially there is no biblical prophecy of a physical star that would appear in the heavens at the time of the Messiah's birth.

The Babylonian and Zoroastrian wise men often counseled kings, and they often interpreted stellar, lunar and solar signs concerning the king of Babylon / Parthia. Why would they have linked the heavens with something to do with the Messiah of Israel? Daniel and his friends were trained in all the wisdom and literature of the Chaldeans. God gave them further insights, well beyond what is possible to learn with books (Daniel 1:4 and 17). The wise men may have been specifically informed in advance concerning a star through some type of revelation, possibly involving a dream, a vision or an angelic visitation. Were some of Daniel's insights linked with the star? We do not know. It will become evident in the coming pages that there was more than enough evidence in the heavens in 7 BC to 1 BC to convince the wise men that the Messiah of Israel was making his appearance.

The wise men may have calculated the year of Jesus' birth before they ever saw anything concerning a star. They had some major advantages over the later interpreters of Daniel because they actually lived in Mesopotamia. During their lifetimes, it was still possible to do historical research about the reigns of the various kings. The archives recording the history of the Babylonian, Persian, Seleucid and Parthian Empires were still available in cuneiform and Aramaic. The men could have determined the dates of Cyrus' decree and the dates of the Sabbatical years with greater accuracy than we can today. The early Church soon lost many of its Jewish roots and was largely cut off from the archives of the Mesopotamian Empires. The loss of the Jewish roots and the lack of reliable records hindered others from understanding the prophecy for hundreds of years.

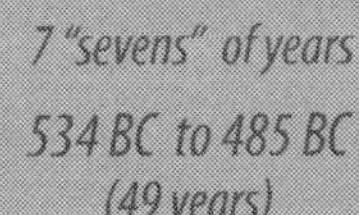

69 "Sevens" of Years

7 "sevens" of years
534 BC to 485 BC
(49 years)

62 "sevens" of years
436 BC to 2 BC
(434 years)

Spring of 3 BC:
Conception of Jesus in the last year of the 62 "sevens"

The Righteous One

The God of our fathers has appointed you to know His will and to see the Righteous One and to hear an utterance from His mouth. (Acts 22:14)

God's own faithfulness, lovingkindness, justice and righteousness are major themes in the Bible. It is appropriate that they would be significant aspects of the Messiah's character and be manifest in his reign.

> *The word of the LORD is upright, and all His work is done in faithfulness. He loves righteousness and justice; The earth is full of the lovingkindness of the LORD. (Psalm 33:5)*

The moral virtue of doing what is right, which is called righteousness or "tzedakah" in Hebrew, is exemplified in the text of Deuteronomy 24:12-13:

> *"If he is a poor man, you shall not sleep with his pledge. When the sun goes down you shall surely return the pledge to him, that he may sleep in his cloak and bless you; and it will be righteousness for you before the LORD your God.*
>
> *"If you lend money to My people, to the poor among you. You are not to act as a creditor to him; you shall not charge him interest. If you ever take your neighbor's cloak as a pledge, you are to return it to him before the sun sets, for that is his only covering; it is his cloak for his body. What else shall he sleep in? And it shall come about that when he cries out to Me, I will hear him, for I am gracious.*

Here, righteousness is linked to God's own compassionate character. If one does what is good, it is a manifestation of what God would do himself. He would save; he would do good toward the needy.[7] The Jewish messianic hope was concentrated on Israel being released from bondage through God's Chosen One. He was to reign doing justice and righteousness in the land.

One of the messianic titles, which is used in the book of Acts, refers specifically to this quality of God's own character and actions which would be manifest in the Messiah. Several times the Messiah is referred to as the "Righteous One." This descriptive title evokes the entire vision of a "new heavens and a new earth in which righteousness dwells."

> *Which one of the prophets did your fathers not persecute? They killed those who had previously announced the coming of **<u>the Righteous One</u>**, whose betrayers and murderers you have now become ... (Acts 7:52)*
>
> *But you disowned **the <u>Holy and Righteous One</u>** and asked for a murderer to be granted to you ... (Acts 3:14)*
>
> *"A certain Ananias, a man who was devout by the standard of the Law, and well spoken of by all the Jews who lived there, came to me, and standing near said to*

Ruler in Israel
Son of God
Shiloh
Scepter
Righteousness
Everlasting
Melchizedek
Lion
The Righteous One
Peace
Shepherd
Son of Man
Glory
King
Branch
Atonement
My Servant David
Chosen One
Justice
The Righteous One
Healer
A Kingdom

> *me, 'Brother Saul, receive your sight!' And at that very time I looked up at him. And he (Ananias) said, 'The God of our fathers has appointed you to know His will and to see **the Righteous One** and to hear an utterance from His mouth. (Acts 22:14)*

Most Christians today do not refer to the Messiah, Jesus, as "the Righteous One." Even so, the title was significant to the early believers. This is echoed in Daniel's 70 "sevens" prophecy. Bringing in "everlasting righteousness" is one aspect of the events listed during the 70 "sevens. In addition "anointing the most holy" plays a role. Some translations read "anointing the most holy place," but most of the early commentators thought that it should be translated "anointing the Most Holy One," the Messiah.

> *"Seventy sevens have been decreed for your people and your holy city, to finish the transgression, to make an end of sin, to make atonement for iniquity, to bring in everlasting righteousness, to seal up vision and prophecy and to anoint the most Holy One. (Daniel 9:24)*

A Summary of the Prophecies

The word "righteousness" is repeated in the prophecies. This is often combined with the word "justice." The Hebrew word "tzedek," (righteousness), becomes a key concept for understanding the wise men. It is also actually the name of a certain "star" in Hebrew. The enduring nature of the Messiah's kingdom is underlined several times in the prophecies. According to the texts, the Messiah would restore the world to its original owner. The priest / king Melchizedek of the city of Salem (later Jerusalem) became a model of the Messiah. According to the prophecies God would rule the world from Jerusalem. His reign would extend to the ends of the earth and all nations and peoples would serve God's chosen king. The apostle Peter tells us that the hope of the early Christians was centered on the ultimate victory of God and the transformation of the world.

> *"According to His promise we are looking for new heavens and a new earth, in which righteousness dwells." (2 Peter 3:13)*

Isaiah speaks of God's ideas concerning kingship:

> *A throne will even be established in lovingkindness, and a judge will sit on it in faithfulness in the tent of David; Moreover, he will seek justice and be prompt in righteousness. (Isaiah 16:5)*

Part 6: God's Appointed Time

But when the fullness of the time came, God sent forth His Son, born of a woman, born under the Law, so that He might redeem those who were under the Law, that we might receive the adoption as sons.
(Galatians 4:4-5)

Jesus came into Galilee, preaching the gospel of God, and saying, "The time is fulfilled, and the kingdom of God is at hand; repent and believe in the gospel."
(Mark 1:14-15)

The Hebrew Calendar

"Let there be lights in the expanse of the heavens ..."

The Jewish mixed lunar / solar calendar seems to contain significant keys for understanding the wise men that went to Bethlehem. A basic understanding of both the Hebrew calendar and the Lord's appointed times and festivals is necessary in order to see the significance of many of the heavenly events from 7 BC to 1 BC.

A Hebrew Day:

Hebrew days always began in the evening and continued on through to the next evening. This manner of thinking goes back to the first chapter of Genesis where we read that there was darkness before the creation of light. ***"There was evening and morning, the first day."*** For the Hebrews a new "day" began at nightfall; it continued through the dawn, and then into the daylight hours until the next evening. Traditional Jewish dates always begin in the evening.[1]

The Hebrew Days of the Week:

The Hebrew names for the days of the week contrast very sharply with the names actually used in many countries. The days of the week in English, French, German, Spanish and many other languages are all related to pagan gods. They often take their names from the celestial objects or gods and goddesses: the Sun, Moon, Mars, Mercury, Jupiter, Venus, Saturn. Usually we do not associate days of the week with pagan gods because the former pagan meaning focusing on these deities is no longer the common meaning. Saturday does not invoke ideas of the god Saturn for most people. Nor does Friday imply worship of the old English goddess Frige / Frigg, the goddess of fertility (Venus for the Latins). The Hebrew names for the days of the week were different. Below they are listed in numeric order. the days followed the sequence: evening, night, dawn, daytime, then evening ...

Yom Rishon = "first day" = Sunday
Yom Sheni - = "second day" = Monday
Yom Shlishi = "third day" = Tuesday
Yom Revi'i = "fourth day" = Wednesday
Yom Chamishi = "fifth day" = Thursday
Yom Shishi = "sixth day" = Friday
Yom Shabbat = "Sabbath day (Rest day)" = Saturday

The Hebrew Month:

The Hebrew month began with the first sighting of the crescent moon in the western sky at sunset. The moon's illuminated surface increases until the 15th day of the month when it rises as a full moon in the east at sunset. From the 15th day to the 28th or 29th of the month the light of the moon wanes, becoming a crescent moon, only visible in the east just before sunrise. On the 29th and 30th days the moon is invisible in the solar glare. Each lunar month varies slightly from 29 to 30 days depending on several factors (It actually lasts an average of 29.53 days).

At the present time, the so called "new moon" in modern calendars is equated with the period when the moon is invisible in the solar glare. However, for the Jews and many ancient civilizations the new moon was the first crescent moon visible at sunset in the west after the moon's passage near the sun. The Hebrew name for the new moon is "Rosh Chodesh" (the head of the month).

There were also some rules in place to determine the beginning of the month if there was a period of prolonged cloudy weather, which would make the observation of the new moon impossible. The lengths of the months were generally known through experience, some months usually had 29 rather than 30 days. Over hundreds of years, the Jews were exposed to and used the Babylonian calendar which had been well refined. The influence of this calendar is obvious in the Hebrew calendar. Over a long period, even the original Hebrew names for the months fell into disuse, and were largely forgotten, being replaced by the Babylonian names. We do not actually know all the names of the months which may have been used by Moses, David and others. Some Messianic Jews today refuse to use the generally accepted names of the months because they have links with Babylonian polytheism. For example, the month of Tammuz draws its name directly from a Babylonian deity. Everything that is "Jewish" does not necessarily come directly from heaven. The Jews have interacted with many people over their long history.

Names of the Jewish Months
Spring
1. Nisan (also called Aviv)
2. Iyyar (formerly called Ziv)
3. Sivan
Summer:
4. Tammuz
5. Av
6. Elul
Fall:
7. Tishri (formerly called Ethanim)
8. Marheshvan (formerly called Bul)
9. Kislev
Winter
10. Tevet
11. Shebat
12. Adar 1
13. Adar 2 (in leap years only)

The Hebrew Year:

Since a lunar year is only 354 days long, it can quickly fall out of synchronization with the seasons of the solar year of 365.25 days. However, at some point a method was devised to solve this problem. The Hebrew calendar was adjusted regularly by adding a 13th month to keep it in line with the seasons. While it is often said that the Hebrew calendar is lunar, in reality it is a mixed lunar / solar calendar. It is actually much more accurate than some might be led to believe. The additional 13th month was dictated by the ripening of the barley harvest. If the harvest was not ripe in the spring of the year, then a 13th month would be added. This allowed time for the crop to mature allowing the "First Fruits Offering" to be presented at the temple on the second day of the Feast of Unleavened Bread. The Passover sacrifice was on the 14th, Unleavened Bread began on the 15th and the First Fruits Offering was presented on the 16th of the month of Nisan (Aviv). If the barley

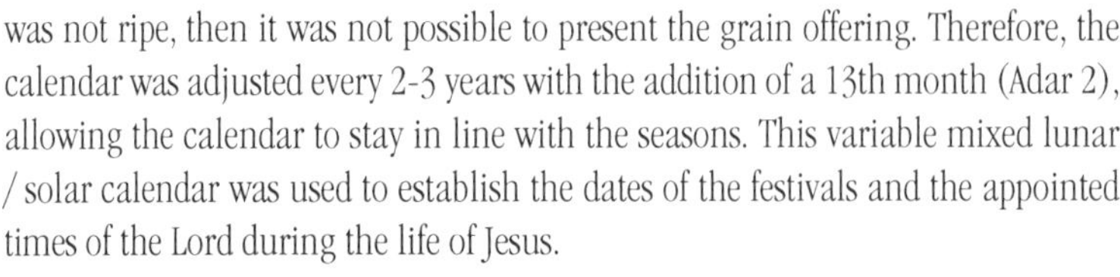

was not ripe, then it was not possible to present the grain offering. Therefore, the calendar was adjusted every 2-3 years with the addition of a 13th month (Adar 2), allowing the calendar to stay in line with the seasons. This variable mixed lunar / solar calendar was used to establish the dates of the festivals and the appointed times of the Lord during the life of Jesus.

A brief summary of the Jewish year from an agricultural perspective is found in the "Genesis (Bereshith) Rabba." The six periods of the year overlap modern months, therefore some months can be found in two categories:

> ***(September - December):*** *The period covering the second half of Tishrei, the whole of Marheshvan, and the first half of Kislev is the season for sowing.*
> ***(November - January):*** *The second half of Kislev, the whole of Tevet, and first half of Shevat is winter.*
> ***(February - April):*** *The second half of Shevat, the whole of Adar, and first half of Nisan is spring.*
> ***(April - June):*** *The second half of Nisan, the whole of Iyyar, and first half of Sivan is harvest-time, according to the climate.*
> ***(May - July):*** *The second half of Sivan, the whole of Tammuz, and first half of Av is summer, and*
> ***(July - September)****: the second half of Av, the whole of Elul, and first half of Tishrei is autumn.*[2]

The grain crop was sown in the ground in the autumn months. Therefore, it did have some possibility of growing even during the winter, and it was harvested in the early spring. The grain harvest began in earnest immediately after the Feast of Unleavened Bread (the 15th - 21st of Nisan in March and April). The festival was generally not far removed from the vernal equinox. The barley harvest was already happening in Israel and Babylonia when the spring months were just beginning in northern Europe. Winters were comparatively mild in Israel and Babylonia, making this type of farming practice possible.

The Equinoxes and Passover:

The vernal (spring) equinox has become a key element in the calculation of Jewish and even Christian calendars. However, this was not always the case. The spring and fall equinox dates were not the most important aspect of establishing the Jewish calendar in the 1st century BC. Decisions were taken each year concerning the calendar. If the barley was not ripe enough to be presented as the "First Fruits" Wave Offering during the Feast of Unleavened Bread, then an additional month was added to the calendar. Below is an example of this type of decision in a letter written to Jews by the Rabbi Gamaliel II in the 1st century AD.

> *May your peace be great forever! We beg to inform you that the turtledoves are still tender and the lambs too thin and that the first-ripe grain has not yet appeared.*

It seems advisable to me and my colleagues to add thirty days to this year (They added one month - Adar 2).[3]

Roger Beckwith comments on this passage in his book on calendars and chronologies: "***The lambs would of course be needed for the Passover itself, the turtledoves would be needed to purify the unclean before they partook of the Passover (Lev. 18:8; 14:22, 30; 15:14,29; Num. 6:10); while the first-ripe grain would be needed for the offering of the Sheaf (Firstfruits Wave Offering), during the festival of Unleavened Bread.***"[4] In the 1st century AD, the date of Passover only depended upon sighting the new moon, the ripening of the barley and the condition of the lambs for sacrifice. Religious priorities were more important than the fixed date of the equinox. It is evident that after three years in a row without adding a leap year the calendar would have fallen out of line with the seasons rather quickly. Some decisions concerning the calendar were no doubt taken well in advance. By simple calculation, it would have been evident that a 13th month would be added to certain years because some dates for the month of Nisan would be much too early for the barley harvest. In other cases if winter lasted longer than foreseen as sometimes happens, the month of Nisan could also be delayed to allow the barley crop to ripen. The actual date of the 1st of Nisan was still fixed by the sighting the new moon.

In AD 359, a purely mathematical calendar was finally adopted by the majority of the Jews. This mainly happened because the Jews were widely scattered after the two destructions of the Jewish nation in AD 70 and AD 135. Without the central point of reference which had formerly been at Jerusalem it became impossible to fix the dates for everyone in a simple manner. A similar thing happened as Christians tried to set universal dates for their own celebrations. Although some Jews still insisted on observing the moon in order to establish the months and the dates of the festivals, over several centuries the vast majority of Jews switched to their present calculated dating system. To simplify the dating system a rule was adopted that the Passover could never fall before the spring equinox. However, in previous times it is possible that the Jewish Passover did sometimes take place before the spring equinox. The text below, from the Apostolic Canons, was probably written in the second or third century AD. It gave instructions to Christian religious authorities concerning the celebration of Passover:

If any bishop, presbyter or deacon shall celebrate the holy day of the Pascha (Passover/Easter) before the spring equinox, with the Jews, let him be deposed (Apostolic Canon 7).[5]

Some Jews were certainly celebrating the Passover before the equinox from time to time otherwise it would have not been necessary to give this instruction to Church leaders. The threat of deposing someone from office was in place to keep Church unity concerning the dates of Passover/Easter, not to suppress any Jewish influences. Note that the more Jewish term "Pascha" is being used for the Passover.

Table 6:1 The Babylonian and Jewish calendar names are practically the same and the two calendars were often in agreement.

Babylonian Month	Hebrew Month
Nisannu	Nisan
Ayyaru	Iyar
Simannu	Sivan
Du'uzu	Tammuz
Abu	Ab
Ululu	Elul
Tasritu	Tishri
Arahsarnna	Marhesshvan
Kisilimu	Kislev
Tebetu	Tebet
Sabatu	Shevat
Addaru	Adar

The Jewish Calendar and its Relation to the Babylonian Calendar

For the vast majority of Jewish dates in the ancient past we do not have any absolute certainty concerning exactly when a 13th "leap year" month was added. Almost all dates in Jewish history are a bit tentative. However, this does not mean that it is completely impossible to know anything about the historical Jewish dates. Using astronomy and calendar software it is still possible to have some idea of the dates. Some hypothetical dates are clearly too late, and others are certainly too early. However, one will not obtain correct dates by simply punching numbers into one or more date conversion or astronomy programs. One must take into account the actual possible sightings of the new moon. Software does not always calculate the days when it is visually impossible to see the moon in the solar glare.[6] There are many aspects of the Babylonian lunar / solar calendar which are similar to the Jewish calendar. Even so, the two calendars are not essentially identical.

> *The Hebrew calendar, following the period of the Babylonian Captivity (597-539 BCE), was closely related with the Babylonian calendar, ... the rules for inserting an intercalary month in the Babylonian calendar and in the Hebrew calendar were probably different, so, although similarly named, the months in both calendars did not necessarily correspond with each other.*[7]

If the barley was not ripe enough for the First Fruits Wave Offering, then an extra month would be added to the Jewish calendar. The Babylonian calendar did not have the same specific association with the barley harvest. The two calendars were often in agreement again after a year or two despite being out of synchronization during some years. The First Fruits Offering determined much of the rest of the calendar. This "natural" link actually kept the calendar in line with the seasons and set the Jewish calendar apart from the Babylonian calendar. Through the ripening of the crops, God had control of the Jewish calendar.

In the Babylonian calendar the 1st of Nisan (the first month of the year) always began on or after the equinox. During the entire 500 year period before the birth of Christ, *the beginning of the Babylonian month of Nisan always took place on or after the equinox (See page 238).* During the whole period after the Babylonian exile until now the Jewish calendar has often deviated from the Babylonian calendar. If the two calendars had been completely the same it would have rendered any debate about Passover being after the equinox completely meaningless. Passover would have always fallen well after the equinox in the Babylonian scheme without exception. However, there have been significant efforts and debates in Jewish and Christian circles to keep the Passover / Easter from falling before the equinox (especially after the fall of Jerusalem in AD 70). If the Jews had been following a Babylonian model faithfully there would have never been any discussion at all. In reality, the Jews never were using a calendar completely subservient to the Babylonian model while the temple services were taking place.

Dating in this Book

The dates used in this book were originally linked to the Voyager astronomy software, but they were later reworked to fit a more feasible scenario which took into account Parker and Dubberstein's Babylonian calendar dates,[8] as well as, other factors. An application on the www.torahcalendar.com website was used to establish lunar visibility each month.[9] The calendar dates cited in 3/2 BC involve Passover celebrations on March 30th in 3 BC and on April 18th in 2 BC. Both these dates were at the first full moon after the spring equinox. The Jewish leap years near Jesus' birth date are listed below according to the dating system used in this book (See Appendix 8 page 238 for more information).

4 BC = leap year (add a 13th month resulting in Adar 1 and Adar 2)
3 BC, not a leap year
2 BC = leap year (add a 13th month resulting in Adar 1 and Adar 2)
1 BC, not a leap year

Originally another dating scheme was used which gave interesting timelines, but the resulting scenario was far less compelling than this intercalation scheme.

The Jewish Festivals and Appointed Times

The religious, social and economic life of the ancient Israelites functioned through a system of festivals and appointed times described in chapters 23 and 25 of the book of Leviticus. The festivals and appointed times were also very much linked to the celestial events at the time of the Messiah's birth. This linking of the heavenly and earthly must have been a key indicator that the prophecies concerning the Jewish Messiah were coming to their fulfillment. The following is a short summary of the festivals and appointed times.

The Sabbath — Weekly Day of Rest

(See Exodus 20:9-10, 23:12 and Leviticus 23:1-3) The Sabbath was specially set aside each week for rest and communion with God and others. This helped set priorities for the people as well, so they were not consumed with work and material success.

Rosh Chodesh — Monthly New Moon

(See Numbers 10:10 and 28:11-15) This was not formally an appointed time for all the people, but certain sacrifices were to be presented to God at the beginning of each month. Marking each month was important to maintain the whole calendar, but it was only in the seventh month that there was anything exceptional attached to the first day of the month (this was the Day of Trumpets).

Many Christians do not realize that the Feasts of Passover, Pentecost and Tabernacles were celebrated every year among the Jews since the time of Moses. It was only in AD 33 that something totally unexpected happened during the Feast of Pentecost, when the Holy Spirit was poured out on the disciples.

Spring Appointed Times:

Pesach — Passover — Feast of Unleavened Bread — First Fruits — Nisan

The Hebrew year originally began in the month of Nisan, also called Aviv, in the spring (March / April). Passover and the Feast of Unleavened Bread were reminders of the Hebrew bondage and their liberation from the Egyptians by God's power. The sacrifice of a lamb from each household on the 14th of Nisan was followed by the Feast of Unleavened Bread on the 15th which lasted seven days. On the second day of the feast,[10] a special "first fruits of grain" offering involving a sheaf of barley was "waved before the Lord" in thankfulness in a unique ceremony. This event was also the signal for the beginning of the barley harvest which would follow the feast. The first of a whole series of events in the heavens recorded in this book happened at Passover in 3 BC. As mentioned previously, many early Christians believed that the Messiah was conceived at Passover.

Shavuot — Feast of Weeks — Pentecost — 6th of Sivan

(See Leviticus 23:15-22 and Deuteronomy 16:9-12) This yearly festival was in May or June.[11] The festival takes its name from the seven weeks which preceded it. The exact day for the festival was established by counting seven weeks (49 days) after the grain offering during the feast of unleavened bread. This process of counting the 49 days was called "Counting the Omer," referring to a measure of grain, an omer. The 50th day after the First Fruits Offering was the date for the Shavuot festival, which was related to the wheat harvest (following the barley harvest). The Pharisees and the Sadducees differed strongly in their manner of calculating the 49 days from the First Fruits Offering, giving them differing dates for Pentecost.

> *The Pharisees held, that the time between Passover and Pentecost should be counted from the second day of the feast; the Sadducees insisted that it should commence with the literal "Sabbath" after the festive day. But despite argument, the Sadducees had to join when the solemn procession went on the afternoon of the feast to cut down the "first sheaf," and to reckon Pentecost as did their opponents.*[12]

While there is still some debate, it seems clear that the Pharisaic method was the method used at the time of Jesus' birth. The High Priesthood was in the hands of the Sadducees, however, they were a minority group which had to bend to the will of the more numerous Pharisees. Today, the Sadducees are largely rejected by a majority of Christians. It is true that they did not believe in the resurrection of the dead or the ministry of angels. However, all their ideas may not be worthy of rejection. The Kairites, a Jewish group that recognizes only the Old Testament and rejects the traditional Oral Law of the Pharisees, embraces some ideas closer to the Sadducean perspective. Notably, they hold to the Sadducean convictions concerning the First Fruits Offering and Pentecost. The Essenes and the Samaritans, like the Sadducees, also believed that the First Fruits Offering should have been on the day after the weekly Sabbath during the Feast of Unleavened Bread. Today, many Pharisaic ideas are also rejected by practicing Christians such as the tradition of the Oral Law which was supposedly also given at Sinai. According to the rabbis, the Oral Law was said to have as much authority as the the Bible. This book does not seek to defend the ideas of either the Sadducees or the Pharisees. Amazingly there were significant signs linked to both the Sadducean and Pharisaic dates for Pentecost in 3 BC and 2 BC.

The Pharisaic and Sadducean First Fruits Offerings probably fell on the same day in AD 33, the year of Jesus' probable death and resurrection. This happened because the 15th of Nisan was also the weekly Sabbath. Both the Pharisees and the Sadducees would have been in agreement about the date for Pentecost in AD 33. The dates would have happened as follows:

- *April 2nd in the late afternoon / evening - 14th Nisan - The lambs were slaughtered. Jesus and his disciples ate the traditional Passover meal, which would have lasted into the night. At some point the whole group went to the Garden of Gethsemene.*
- *April 3rd, before dawn - still the 14th of Nisan - Jesus and his disciples were met by the temple guards and Judas. Jesus was arrested, then there was a trial.*
- *April 3rd, after dawn - still the 14th of Nisan - Jesus was taken before Pilate and Herod Antipas. Jesus was crucified starting from about 9 AM. After 12 Noon the sky became dark until about 3 PM.*
- *April 3rd, late afternoon - still the 14th of Nisan - Jesus was buried.*
- *April 3rd, after sunset - the 15th of Nisan began the Feast of Unleavened Bread. It was also the weekly Sabbath.*
- *April 4th, after sunset - the 16th of Nisan began.*
- *April 5th, morning - 16th of Nisan, Jesus was raised from the dead. The First Fruits Offering was presented by the High Priest. Both the Sadducees and the Pharisees acknowledged this day as the correct date for the First Fruits Offering.*
- *Pentecost would have taken place on May 23rd/24th.*

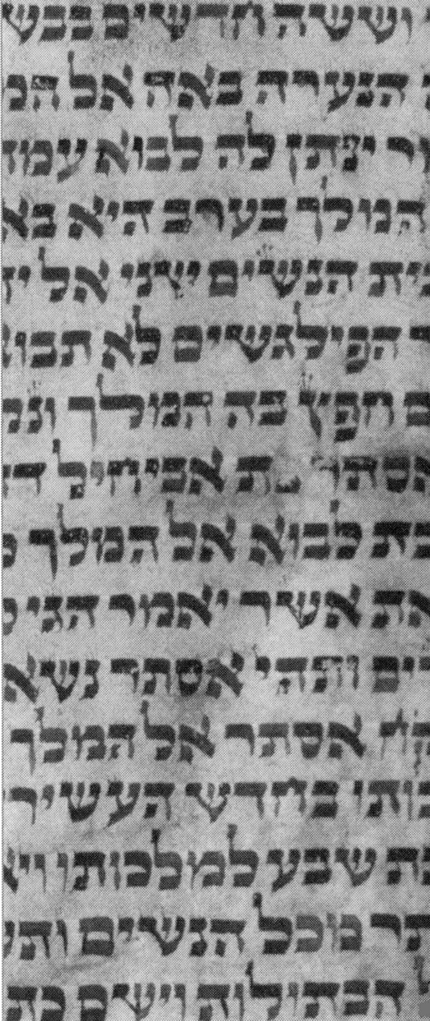

Above: Hebrew text from the book of Esther

Autumn Appointed Times:

Yom Teruah — Day of Trumpets (shofars) — Ist of Tishrei

(See Leviticus 23:23-25 and Numbers 29:1-6) This appointed time, celebrated in September and October, was a reminder of the trumpet that sounded at Sinai at the moment of the giving of the Law (Exodus 19:10-25). Other events were also associated with it. Yom Teruah was / is seen as the beginning of preparations for the Day of Atonement. This day also began the Jewish civil year, and became known as Rosh Hoshanna, partly replacing the original "head of the year" date in Nisan.

Yom Kippur — Day of Atonement — 10th of Tishrei

(See Leviticus 23:26-32 and Numbers 29:7-11) The 10 days between the Day of Trumpets and the Day of Atonement were used for personal self-examination and

The festivals and appointed times of the Lord seem to be a major key to understanding the thinking of the wise men.

This becomes evident when one looks at the heavenly events from 7 BC to 1 BC.

repentance. The Day of Atonement was a day of fasting which was accompanied by sacrifices and ceremonies in the temple. Passover was a reminder of God's deliverance of his people from slavery and all their enemies, the Day of Atonement spoke of God's spiritual provision for communion with his people through their purification.

Sukkot — Feast of Tabernacles (or Booths) — Begins 15th of Tishrei

(See Leviticus 23:33-44 and Numbers 29:12-40) This festival in September or October reenacts the people of Israel living in the desert with Moses. Temporary shelters were, and continue to be, constructed as a reminder of God's people being in the desert and how God had provided for them. This feast was also associated with the last part of the general harvest. There were special ceremonies which included pouring water out before the Lord and asking him for good rains for the coming season of planting and sowing. The eighth day, on the last day of the feast there was a great assembly. This day has been referred to as the "Great Day of the Feast."

Other Festivals and Appointed Times:

Hanukkah — Festival of Lights — Begins 25th Kislev

This festival commemorates a unique miracle of light in the newly consecrated temple after the victory of the Jews over the Seleucid Empire in 165 BC. The festival is usually celebrated in November or December.

Purim — Festival of Lots — 13th and 14th of Adar

This festival, celebrated in February or March, commemorates God's deliverance of the Jewish people through Esther, the Queen of Persia. Risking her own life Esther had intervened on behalf of her people before the king in order to save the Jews from certain death.

The Sabbatical Year and the Year of Jubilee

Every seventh year the Jews were supposed to leave their cropland fallow, relying on their provisions and what grew naturally to see them through to the next year. Every 49 years (seven times seven sabbatical years) a year of release was proclaimed. A special Jubilee year was supposed to happen at the end of seven sabbatical periods (every 49 years). Apparently God designed this system as a means of regulating the Israelite economy. Debts were to be forgiven, ancestral lands were recuperated, and slaves were to be freed. The canceling of debts and renewed freedom for indebted people would have rejuvenated the Israelite economy. It seems that the period of the fall 3 BC through the summer of 2 BC was a Sabbatical year. The Essenes still practiced the Jubilee in which all men were freed from their debts and servitude. Some calculations have shown that they may have done this sometime during the period of 3 BC to AD 2 however, we do not know which year. The Sabbatical years seem to be a key element in understanding Daniel's 70 "sevens" prophecy (Daniel 9:24-27).

Part 7: Looking to the Heavens

It is He who made the earth by His power, Who established the world by His wisdom; And by His understanding He has stretched out the heavens. Thus says the LORD, who gives the sun for light by day And the fixed order of the moon and the stars for light by night, Who stirs up the sea so that its waves roar; The LORD of hosts is His name: "If this fixed order departs from before Me," declares the LORD, "Then the offspring of Israel also will cease From being a nation before Me forever." (Jeremiah 10:12, 31:35-36)

The Jewish Heavens

"Let there be lights in the expanse of the heavens ..."

The Lord by wisdom founded the earth, By understanding He established the heavens. (Proverbs 5:19)

If the Magi were ethnically Jewish or if they were greatly influenced by religious Jews then one could expect that Hebrew ideas may have also shaped their perspective concerning the sun, moon and stars. The Hebrew Scriptures celebrate God's creation of the heavens. All functioned well at creation, God saw all that he had made and said that it was "good." The essence of this goodness was that the sun, moon and stars fulfilled their role, they did what they were designed to do. While the Hebrews may have been very appreciative of the beauty of the starry heavens, much of the Hebraic vision of the heavens was essentially functional. The great lights were created to give light on the earth. They were also supposed to indicate the times and seasons and serve as signs. The Hebrew calendar was linked to the monthly sighting of the new moon. Their festivals were related to the agricultural cycle which was itself tied to the Hebrew mixed lunar / solar year. The cycle of evenings and mornings (sunset and sunrise) established limits for the activities of men and the Sabbath ensured rest for all.

The Hebrews, in contrast to their many neighbors, did not normally think of the stars in association with various gods and goddesses. At least that was the case when they were obeying the God of Abraham. Religiously practicing Jews did not normally direct their worship to the heavenly bodies and this was exceptional in the ancient world. According to God's law and the message of the prophets, the Hebrews were not supposed to worship the sun, the moon, the stars or anything in the heavens. God's wrath came upon the Jews in the days of Isaiah and Jeremiah, in part, because the people were involved in worshiping the "Queen of Heaven," (Ishtar / Astarte), the planet Venus. (2 Kings 17:16 and 21:3)

> *"Beware not to lift up your eyes to heaven and see the sun and the moon and the stars, all the host of heaven, and be drawn away and worship them and serve them ..." (Deuteronomy 4:19, see also Deut. 17:3 and 2 Kings 23:5)*
>
> *"The houses of Jerusalem and the houses of the kings of Judah will be defiled like the place Topheth, because of all the houses on whose rooftops they burned sacrifices to all the heavenly host and poured out drink offerings to other gods." (Jeremiah 19:13)*
>
> *... they were prostrating themselves eastward toward the sun." (Ezekiel 8:16)*
>
> *"You also carried along Sikkuth your king and Kiyyun (Saturn), your images, the star of your gods which you made for yourselves." (Amos 5:26)*

The Origin and Function of the Heavenly Bodies

The Hebrew Scriptures are very clear about the origin, nature and function of the heavenly bodies. The following texts show the perspective of practicing Jews and perhaps that of the wise men, who eventually went to Bethlehem. The creator was to be worshiped in Judaism, not the creation itself.

> *In the beginning God created the heavens and the earth.... God said, "Let there be lights in the expanse of the heavens to separate the day from the night, and let them be for signs and for seasons and for days and years; and let them be for lights in the expanse of the heavens to give light on the earth"; and it was so. God made the two great lights, the greater light to govern the day, and the lesser light to govern the night; He made the stars also. God placed them in the expanse of the heavens to give light on the earth, and to govern the day and the night, and to separate the light from the darkness; and God saw that it was good. There was evening and there was morning, a fourth day. (Genesis 1:1 and verses 14-19)*

> *Thus says God the LORD, Who created the heavens and stretched them out, Who spread out the earth and its offspring, Who gives breath to the people on it and spirit to those who walk in it ... "It is I who made the earth, and created man upon it. I stretched out the heavens with My hands and I ordained all their host. (Isaiah 42:5, 45:12)*

> *The heavens are telling of the glory of God; And their expanse is declaring the work of His hands. (Ps. 19:1)*

> *Thus says the Lord, who gives the sun for light by day and the fixed order of the moon and the stars for light by night, who stirs up the sea so that its waves roar - the Lord of hosts is his name. "If this fixed order departs from before me, declares the Lord, then shall the offspring of Israel cease from being a nation before me forever." (Jeremiah 31:35-36)*

The heavens were and remain a major part of the revelation of God's power and glory in nature. He is the maker of the heavens and the earth. The pagan gods and goddesses who were worshiped by the ancient peoples were very small and almost powerless by comparison. While the Babylonian Marduk (Jupiter) supposedly reigned over the gods, only one visible star / planet was identified specifically with him. It was similar for Ishtar (Venus), Nergal (Mars), Nabu (Mercury) and Ninurta (Saturn). These gods were supposedly "great ones" but they were represented by a single star / planet. The outstanding greatness of the God of Abraham, Isaac and Jacob could not be matched. In the book of Genesis, it is mentioned almost in passing that "God made the stars also." Who among the ancient gods is like the God of Isaiah who thinks of the nations, "like a drop from a bucket, and regards them as a speck of dust on the scales" (Isaiah 40:15). Unfortunately, the Jews were often unfaithful to the God of their fathers and as the Scriptures say "They went

Below: In Hebrew the Milky Way is now called the "Fire-Stream," a name which was apparently borrowed from Daniel 7:10 where a scene before the throne of God is described.

"A river of fire was flowing and coming out from before Him; Thousands upon thousands were attending Him, and myriads upon myriads were standing before Him; The court sat, and the books were opened."

The Traditional Hebrew Names of the Planets:

כוכב חמה
Kochav Chammah
Meaning: sun star
(Mercury)

נוגה
Nogah
Meaning: brightness
(Venus)

מאדים
Ma'adim
Meaning: red one / blushing one
(Mars)

צדק
Tzedek
Meaning: righteousness
(Jupiter)

שבתאי
Shabbatei
Meaning: rest / sabbatical
(Saturn)

The word Kochav (star) can be added to any of these names.

after other gods." Yet God's faithfulness to his people is well illustrated through the fixed order of the heavens as cited above in Jeremiah Chapter 31.

The Jewish Names for Certain Heavenly Bodies

There are seven heavenly bodies near the earth, which can be seen with the unaided human eye: the Sun, Moon, Mercury, Venus, Mars, Jupiter and Saturn. In the following paragraphs, the traditional names for the planets are listed in Hebrew. We do not know when all these names were first used. They may have been first used during the Babylonian exile as an alternative to the pagan names for the planets. Some of the names may also have been used much earlier in Jewish history, including the eras of Abraham, Moses and David. One or two of the names may have only been used after the birth of Christ and the destruction Jerusalem.

The traditional Hebrew planet names are the following: Kochav Chammah (Mercury), Kochav Nogah (Venus), Ma'adim (Mars), Tzedek (Jupiter) and Shabbatei (Saturn). One finds these names in the Babylonian Talmud (AD 200-500), which summarizes Jewish teaching from much earlier periods. Another list of planet names used by the Pharisees before the birth of Christ contains some of these names and / or their equivalents.[1] These traditional names are still the names of the planets in the Hebrew language today. In the rest of this book, we will assume that the traditional names were in use in Babylonia during the 1st century BC. This is a significant assumption, but it seems evident that at least one or two of the names may also have a specifically Babylonian origin. These traditional names may partly explain the profound confidence of the wise men concerning the birth of the Messiah. *In the remaining chapters, the Hebrew names for the stars and planets will often be used instead of the usual English names. This is done in order to give a deeper appreciation of the heavens and the events related to the birth of the Messiah from a Jewish perspective.*

Where Should One Look in the Heavens?

The prophecies in the Old Testament refer to a seed, a lion, a righteous king and a branch (a descendant) of David born of a young woman / virgin. Signs announcing or confirming the accomplishment of the prophecies should have been found in a region of the sky which has objects related to the prophecies. Such an area does exist in the constellations of Ari (Leo) and Bethula (Virgo). Each year the constellations of Ari (Leo) and Bethula (Virgo) are visible for about 10 months. During the other two months, they pass behind the sun, and they are lost in the solar glare. During the summer of 3 BC Ari was mostly hidden behind the sun in late July and much of August and Bethula was hidden in August and September. At the present time, the two constellations are visible about a month later than they were at the time of Christ because the earth because of a phenomenon called the procession of the equinoxes. This is the slightly earlier occurrence of the equinoxes each year due to the slow continuous westward shift of the equinox points.

The Sun, Moon and Stars:

Shemesh or Chammah: The Hebrew names for the sun, Shemesh and Chammah / Khamma mean "light, brilliance, heat" and "the hot one." The ancient Sumerians, the Assyrians and the Babylonians also used the same or a similar word, Shamash, for the sun (In Hebrew / Aramaic script the words look the same, the vowels were only added later). The oldest documents in the Bible, the book of Job and the five books of Moses, all use the very ancient word "Shemesh" for the sun. The word Shamash was sometimes used as a word for a servant in Hebrew. This may indicate that the Hebrews thought of the sun as a servant for man and not as an object for worship, but this idea is not completely proven. Such a concept would be in stark contrast to the world view of other ancient Near Eastern peoples who thought of the sun, moon and even some stars and planets as deities and objects of worship.

Shemesh or Chammah
Shamash
Sun

Yareach or Levanah: Both these words are the Hebrew names for the moon. In Hebrew Yareach means "paleness," and Levanah means "white." According to the scenario presented in this book, the moon plays a significant part in the heavenly events concerning the Messiah's birth. It was repeatedly involved with the famous star and other objects as well. The text already cited in Psalm 89:36-37 seems to be significant in the whole celestial story in 3/1 BC.

"His descendants shall endure forever and his throne as the sun before Me. His throne shall be established forever like the moon, and the witness in the sky is faithful."

Yareach or Levanah
MUL Sîn
Moon

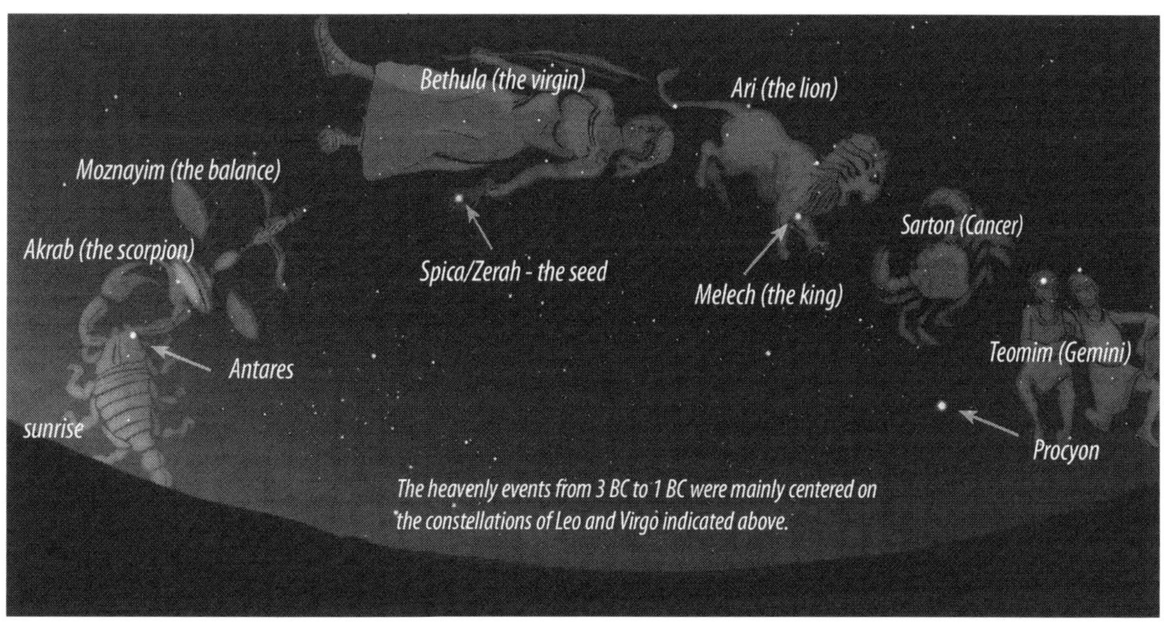

The heavenly events from 3 BC to 1 BC were mainly centered on the constellations of Leo and Virgo indicated above.

Kokab, Kowkab or Kohav
Kakkab
Stars

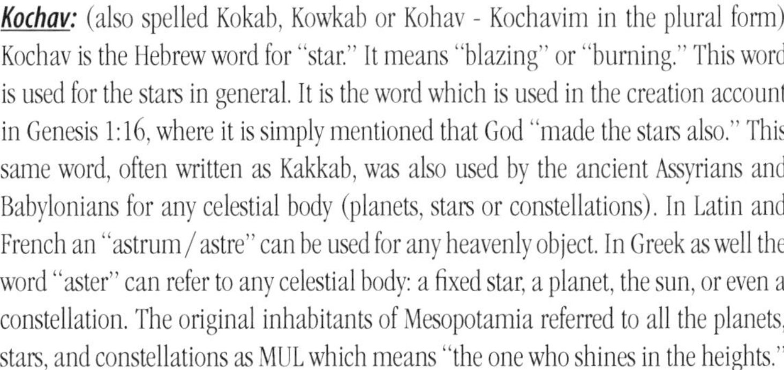

Kochav: (also spelled Kokab, Kowkab or Kohav - Kochavim in the plural form) Kochav is the Hebrew word for "star." It means "blazing" or "burning." This word is used for the stars in general. It is the word which is used in the creation account in Genesis 1:16, where it is simply mentioned that God "made the stars also." This same word, often written as Kakkab, was also used by the ancient Assyrians and Babylonians for any celestial body (planets, stars or constellations). In Latin and French an "astrum / astre" can be used for any heavenly object. In Greek as well the word "aster" can refer to any celestial body: a fixed star, a planet, the sun, or even a constellation. The original inhabitants of Mesopotamia referred to all the planets, stars, and constellations as MUL which means "the one who shines in the heights."

The word "kochav" has also been used with the names of each of the five visible planets, simply because they look like stars when seen with the unaided eye. The ancients definitely saw the marked difference between the stable "fixed" stars and the dynamic planets, but they had no idea concerning their real nature. No one actually saw the planets close up until the invention of the telescope in the Renaissance period about 1,500 years after the birth of Jesus. The planets move, they disappear and they reappear. They also vary in brightness. The Babylonians, Greeks and Romans often called the planets "walking stars" or "wandering stars." The word Kochav is still often used with the planet names Kochav Chammah and Kochav Nogah.

The Planets Near the Sun:

The planets closest to the sun are never visible all night, but only during the hours following sunrise and sunset.

Kochav Chammah
Phainon
Mercury

Kochav Chammah: The Hebrew meaning of this name is "sun star." Appropriately the name indicates that the planet is always very close to the sun. The Jews also thought of Kochav Chammah as the sun's scribe or attendant which was a similar role to the Babylonian understanding of this planet. The Babylonians identified it with Marduk's son Nabu (Nebo), who was spoken of as a scribe. Another source lists it as Kochav Chochmah, the star of wisdom. In Greek this star was originally called "Phainon," meaning the "gleamer," but it was also identified with the Greek god Hermes (the Roman - Mercury) and Apollo.[2] For the Greeks and Latins Hermes / Mercury was not a scribe but a messenger god. Both gods were thought of as gods of wisdom along with Apollo. The Babylonian origins of the idea of the planet Kochav Chammah being the sun's "scribe" are evident.

Kochav Nogah: The Hebrew meaning of Nogah is "brightness, brilliance, radiance, splendor." This "wandering star" is the brightest object in the morning or evening sky. It is never visible for more than about four hours any night except at very high latitudes. In Greek, this star was originally called "Phosphorus," meaning the "light bringer" until it became more identified with the Greek goddess Aphrodite (the Roman - Venus). The Babylonians identified the planet with the goddess Ishtar. Kochav Nogah seems to play a significant role in the events surrounding the Messiah's birth. Another word, Zerouah / Zerva, associated with the Aramaic word "light" was also used by the Jews for Nogah in the 1st century BC. We know this from the writings of a 4th century AD Christian writer Epiphanius.[3]

Nogah
Phosphorus
Dilbat
Venus

The Outer Planets:

As seen from the earth, the outer planets move through the heavens along the general path of the sun and the moon. Depending on several factors, these outer planets can be visible much of the night.

Kochav Ma'adim: The Hebrew word Ma'adim means to blush or to redden making Ma'adim the blushing, reddening star. This "wandering star" is orange / red. The Babylonians simply called the planet the "red star" or the "strange star." In Greek, this planet was originally called "Pyroëis," meaning the "fiery one" until it became more identified with the Greek god Ares (the Roman - Mars). The Jews were known to have also used the name Kochav Okbol for the planet, however, the meaning of the name is unknown. Astrology and Babylonian omens link this planet with war and death, making it a malefic planet. The author finds no reason to believe that God designated some planets as malefic and others as beneficial. This planet does seem to play a minor role in the events surrounding Jesus' birth.

Ma'adim
Mars

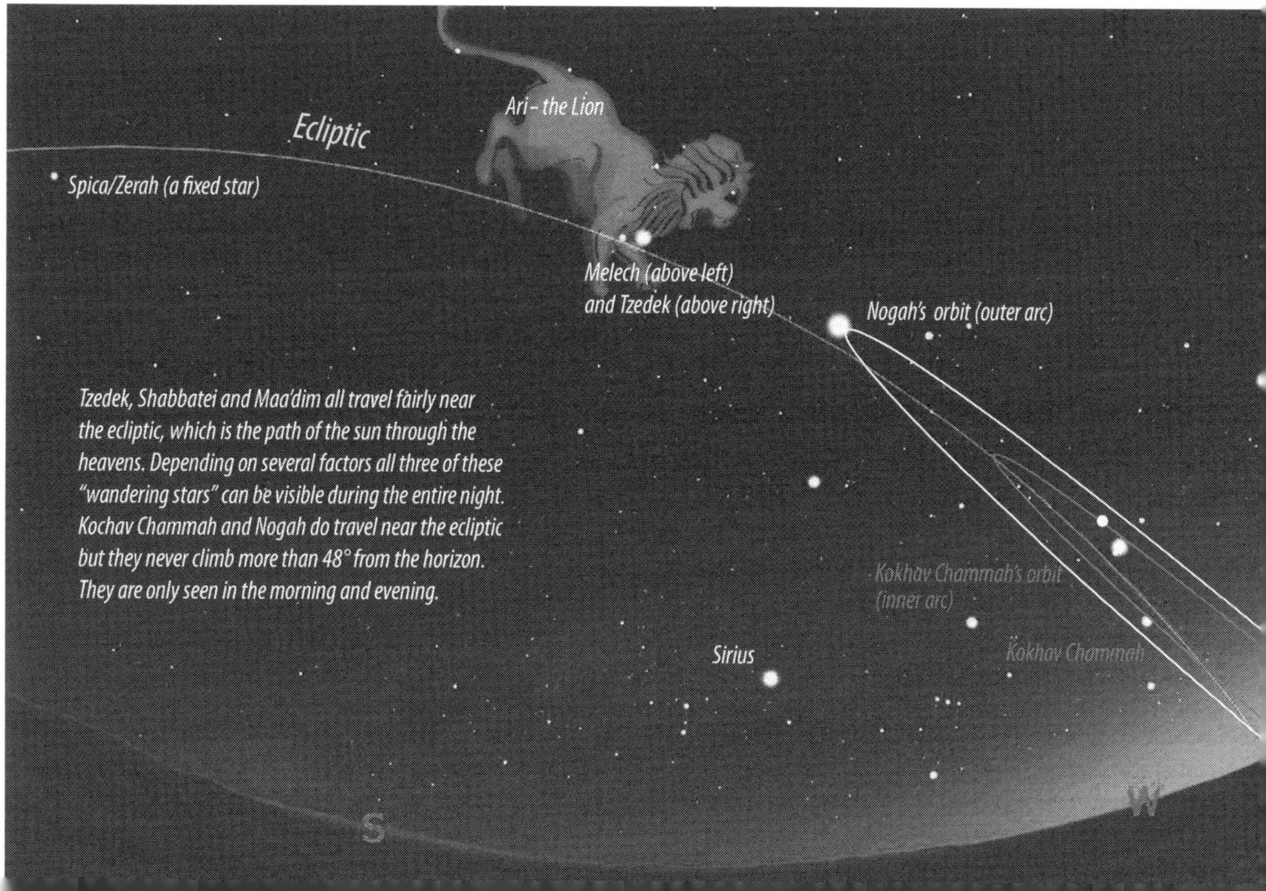

Ecliptic
Ari - the Lion
Spica/Zerah (a fixed star)
Melech (above left) and Tzedek (above right)
Nogah's orbit (outer arc)
Kokhav Chammah's orbit (inner arc)
Kokhav Chammah
Sirius
S
W

Tzedek, Shabbatei and Maa'dim all travel fairly near the ecliptic, which is the path of the sun through the heavens. Depending on several factors all three of these "wandering stars" can be visible during the entire night. Kochav Chammah and Nogah do travel near the ecliptic but they never climb more than 48° from the horizon. They are only seen in the morning and evening.

Tzedek
Phaëthon
MUL.BABBAR
MUL Marduk
Jupiter

Kochav Tzedek: This is also spelled Tsedeq, Sedeq and Zedek. The Hebrew meaning of Tzedek is "righteousness or justice." Kochav Tzedek means "the star of righteousness." The God of the Bible is righteous, he does what is good and right to all. He is dependable and faithful in keeping his covenant. God's righteous character conveys a sense of deliverance and salvation (See Isaiah 41:10, 45:21, 46:13). The meaning behind the name Tzedek is very positive.

Tzedek is the brightest of the outer planets. It takes about 12 years for Tzedek to complete its orbit around the sun. Planets like Nogah and Kochav Chammah are only visible in the morning and evening sky. This "wandering star" can be visible during the whole night. In most ancient cultures Tzedek, under various names, ruled among the planets and was even referred to as the "king planet." Being the brightest planet which traveled across the whole sky it had special honor. The Greeks and Romans associated this star / planet with the god Zeus / Jupiter. The planet's Greek name was originally "Phaëthon," meaning the "bright one." The planet was called MUL.BABBAR, meaning the "white star," by the Babylonians although they also had several other names for it.[4] In this book, Tzedek plays a central role in the events surrounding the Messiah's birth.

According to Epiphanius the planet was also called Kochav Baal by the Judean Pharisees in the 1st century BC. If they were referring to the truly ancient Canaanite deity, Baal, the name would seem very negative. It would identify the planet specifically with Jupiter / Marduk, who was also known as Bel. However, the word "baal" has several positive senses in Hebrew. It is a typical word used for a husband and also an owner, "a master," which is its most essential meaning. The word is used in the Orthodox Jewish Bible for "husband" in Matthew 1:16 and elsewhere. The Talmudic term "baal teshuva," literally means "a master of repentance," referring to someone who has left significant sin in order to follow God, (See the Orthodox Jewish Bible, Luke 15:17). According to Epiphanius in the 1st century BC the Pharisees were very interested in astrology. Having strong ties to astrology it would seem illogical if they retained only a truly negative meaning for the name of a principal planet. The Pharisees may simply have referred positively to the planet as Kochav Baal, the "master star / planet." They could have also thought of it in a very negative way, but in an illogical manner. It is possible that Epiphanius simply left out the name Tzedek in his text in order to paint a truly negative picture of the Pharisees. As he develops his arguments against the Pharisees and others it is obvious that he wants to "paint the kettle black." It is certain that the positive name Tzedek would have complicated his arguments.

In most ancient societies, Jupiter was known as the "king planet." This contains a very similar idea to the name "master star." In this book, we will retain the positive name Kochav Tzedek, meaning "star of righteousness." Even so, using the phrase "master or king planet" might not make much difference in several key interpretations of events from 7 BC to 1 BC. However, the interpretations are much clearer using the name Tzedek. Some Judean Jews may have used the name Kochav Baal while others in Babylonia used the name Kochav Tzedek. The name Kochav Tzedek is found in the Babylonian Talmud. It is certain that the planet was called Tzedek by about AD 200 (about 200 years before Epiphanius' writings).[5] It would seem strange if the planet only began to be called Tzedek in the 2nd century AD, but it is possible. The other planets had some truly positive Hebrew names. Perhaps the Pharisees saw the name Kochav Baal partly in the positive manner mentioned above. We simply do not know exactly how, when or why the Jewish name Tzedek came to be attached to this planet.

Kochav Shabbatei: The Hebrew meaning of this name is "rest" or "sabbatical." It is related to the word Sabbath. This is the slowest of the visible planets, taking 29 years to complete its orbit around the sun. The slowness, the resting nature, and stability of this planet gave rise to the name Kiyyun / Kayun / Kiwan mentioned in Amos 5:26: "You also carried along Sikkuth your king and Kiyyun, your images, the star of your gods which you made for yourselves." The Akkadian word, 'Kajjamanu' means 'the steady one', which is similar to the Hebrew (qayam or Kiyyum) – 'exists', or the Arabic (kawn) – 'existence.' The present Hebrew name seems to have its origins in the Jewish community in Babylonia. In Greek, this star was originally called "Phainon," meaning the "shiner." It became identified with the Greek god Chronos (the Roman Saturn). The planet Shabbatei does have a crucial role in the celestial events surrounding the Messiah's birth in 7 BC to 1 BC. It was also very present in other significant events in 26 BC. Epiphanius indicates that the Pharisees definitely used the word Shabbatei for Saturn before the birth of Christ. The text from the Book of Amos above demonstrates that the planet was possibly only named Shabbatei after about 700-600 BC.

Shabbatei
Kajjamanu
Phainon

Some Observations:

The name Tzedek may have been a Jewish response to the identification of the principal Babylonian god, Marduk, with the planet Jupiter. Daniel or other exiled Jews may have been involved in establishing all the traditional planetary names. The prophet Daniel seems to have been one of the few people who could have had enough influence to suggest, proclaim or perhaps even impose planetary names in Jewish history, although there may have been several others. The exile was a good moment for the Jews to focus on God's righteousness and faithfulness following their own unfaithfulness as a nation. Daniel's prayer, in chapter nine of his book, indicates that God had been righteous in all that he had done. Daniel also invokes God's own righteousness when referring to the end of the exile. The planetary name Tzedek would have reminded the Jews of God's own righteousness. In Psalm 97:6 we read "The heavens declare His righteousness, and all the peoples have seen His glory." Could this text have been in mind when the star was named or was the text inspired by the name of the planet? We do not know. Did Daniel invent the Hebrew names of some stars and planets? We have no certain proof of how, when or where the traditional Hebrew names of the planets originated.

Some Fixed Stars:

LUGAL
Sharru
Melech
Regulus
Βασιλίσκος

Melech: The name Melech, an ancient Hebrew word for a king, was apparently the Hebrew name of the brightest star in the constellation of Ari, the lion (Leo). One finds the word as part of the roots of the names Melchizedek and Abimelech. The Babylonians named this star LUGAL in Sumerian cuneiform, while "Sharru" was the Aramaic name meaning "king." It seems almost certain that Jewish people would have referred to the star as Melech (the Hebrew word for king). Unfortunately there are no ancient documents which definitively demonstrate this with all certainty. It was referred to in Greek as "Basiliskos" by Ptolemy. The Greek word Basilískos, "little king," was translated into Latin as Regulus meaning "little king." In English and modern Hebrew it is now called Regulus. Melech seems to play a major role in announcing the birth of the Messiah. However, the astronomer Konradin Ferrari D'Occhleppo has pointed out:

> *One important remark is necessary here: in Babylonian astrology, the fixed star Regulus in the constellation of the Lion was always related to the King of Babylonia, never to any foreign ruler. Hence, whatever happened in that constellation about the beginning of the Christian era, would have been understood as an omen relative to the then Parthian rulers of Babylon, but not to Herod or to the expected Messiah.*[6]

From a Babylonian perspective, it would not have been habitual to use this star to indicate anything about a Jewish Messiah. However, from a Jewish perspective it is very possible that connections with a Messiah could have been drawn. The true identity of the wise men remains unknown, however, men seeking a Jewish Messiah must have had either a Jewish background or some Jewish influence in their lives. In unusual circumstances, such men could have interpreted events surrounding Melech as concerning the Jewish Messiah.

Zerah
SA_4 sa ABSIN
Spica

Spica/Zerah: The constellation of Bethula (Virgo) contains the bright star Spica which, in the past, was possibly called Zerah, the Hebrew word for "seed." It does not seem to be possible to prove decisively that this star was known by the name of Zerah among the Jews in the 1st century BC. Even so, it has been popular to use this name in some Christian circles. The present name "Spica" means an "ear of grain," referring to the part of a cereal plant, such as wheat or barley, that contains the seeds, grains, or kernels. The Greek name for the star, "Stachys," has a similar meaning of "seed." This is also the meaning of the modern Hebrew name of the star, "Shibboleth." In French it is l'Epi, meaning "the ear of grain" and it is similar in other languages.

We will assume that the name Zerah (seed) is at least a name which could be rightly associated with this fixed star, Spica (a spike - head of grain). The Hebrew word zerah was used in several significant passages in the Bible (Genesis 3:15, 12:7, 13:15, 15:13 and 18). These passages speak of the promise that the "seed of the woman" would crush the serpent's head (Satan's head). It is certain that the

Jews referred to Virgo as Bethula, a virgin, in the 1st century BC. The word zerah is used as well concerning the posterity (seed) of Abraham which would inherit the land and be a source of blessing for all the families of the earth.

Spica/Zerah was known among the Mesopotamian astronomers as SA_4 sa ABSIN meaning the "bright star in the furrow." In the earliest of times, the constellation of the virgin was linked to Shala, (the consort of Adad, the storm god), a goddess of grain. Later the constellation was also identified with the Babylonian goddess Ishtar. The constellation and the star Spica rose in the early morning sky in the autumn months when the Babylonians and the Hebrews did their planting. That explains the name ABSIN, "the Furrow," which was given to the constellation in the Babylonian astronomical texts:

> *... from 440 BC onward Spica is SA_4 sa ABSIN, "the bright star of ABSIN." The Sumerian ABSIN means "furrow," and the constellation name is generally so translated. Note, however, Sachs ... and Thureau-Dangin ... , preferred the translation "Barley-stalk" (French épi) for ABSIN. The picture of the lady holding an ear of barley (Spica?), ... may reflect the later influence of Greek ideas.*[7]

So historically the Babylonians called the constellation Virgo "the Furrow" and Spica/Zerah was apparently the seed which was sown in the furrow.

Some Bible teachers have said that the star Spica was called "Tsemach" by the Jews. The present Arabic name for Spica, Al Zimach or Al-Simak al-A'zal has a similar spelling. The word "tsemach" is used in Jeremiah 23:5-6 and 33:14-17 concerning the righteous branch (descendant) of David as we have already seen. However, the word "tsemach" (branch) is most likely not the right name for Spica. The Arabic name for the star, actually does not mean "a branch." It means an "unprotected, undefended guardian." The same Arabic name "Al-Simak" is used for the nearby star Arcturus where the word is joined to the term "ramih" meaning "arrow." These two neighboring stars seem to form a pair whose names mean, "the guardian with an arrow" and "the defenseless guardian." The star Gamma Virginis, also called Porrima, has been indicated on some old star maps as Al Zimach as well.[8] This would seem to be a more logical place to have a "branch"(tsemach) because a barley "stalk" could be in the area of Porrima. However, seed grain has always been identified with Spica.

Spica/Zerah was exceedingly important during the period near the birth of Jesus. For about 100 years before and after the birth of the Messiah, Spica/Zerah was rising and setting less than one degree from true east and true west when seen from Central Mesopotamia.

Spica/Zerah was exceedingly important during the period near the birth of Jesus. For about 100 years before and after the birth of the Messiah, Spica/Zerah was rising and setting less than one degree from true east and true west when seen from Central Mesopotamia. This made Spica a very helpful indicator for astronomers and navigators. In our present time, Spica/Zerah does not indicate due east or due west. Today the star rises about 13° south of due east when it is observed from Central Iraq. In about 130 BC, Hipparchus, while studying the position of Spica/Zerah, was able to understand that the equinox points seemed to move over time in relation to the stars. This "procession of the equinoxes" is a very important concept in astronomy even today. Spica/Zerah did play a significant role in announcing the Messiah's birth, however, it was not the star of Bethlehem.

Antares
Bilu-sha-ziri
Kak-shisa
Dar Lugal
Masu Sar
Kakkab Bir

Antares: The star Antares seems to be somewhat involved in the events surrounding Jesus' birth. It has historically been associated with the angel Uriel whose name means "God is light." Uriel had a significant role explaining various astronomical concepts to the man Enoch, according to the Book of Enoch. However, it is not known how, why or when Uriel came to be associated with Antares. In ancient Mesopotamia, Antares was known by the following names: *Urbat* (unknown meaning), *Bilu-sha-ziri* ("the Lord of the Seed"), *Kak-shisa* ("the Creator of Prosperity"), *Dar Lugal* ("The King"), *Masu Sar* ("the Hero and the King"), and *Kakkab Bir* ("the Vermilion Star" - because of its reddish color).[9] The present name has Greek origins. It means "anti Aries" (in opposition to Aries / Mars). The reddish color of the star is similar to the reddish color of the planet Ma'adim (Mars). The original Hebrew name is unknown. We do not know how the Jews would have referred to this star in the 1st century BC.

The Constellations and the Months

Among the Jews Virgo was called Bethulah and was associated with the idea of abundance in harvest. It was assigned by the rabbis to the tribe of Asher, because Jacob had declared "his bread shall be fat."[10]

Table 6: 1 Constellations

Each Israeli tribe was historically linked to a constellation. Judah was usually linked to Leo, the lion. The order of the months corresponds with the period when the constellation is lost in the sun's glare.

Constellation	Hebrew Name	Month
Aries	Taleh	Nisan
Taurus	Shor	Iyar
Gemini	Teomim	Sivan
Cancer	Sarton	Tammuz
Leo	Ari	Av
Virgo	Betulah	Elul
Libra	Moznayim	Tishrei
Scorpio	Akrab	Cheshvan
Sagittarius	Kasshat	Kislev
Capricorn	Gedi	Tevet
Aquarius	D'li	Shevat
Pisces	Dagim	Adar

Think Like A Magus - Part 1

The Magi were probably not men who would be easily impressed with astronomical events. Any idea that the wise men were impressionable, wild-eyed mystics should be banished from our minds. The wise men would not have necessarily been elated with emotion simply because they saw a bright star, having already observed a multitude of astronomical phenomena. They were most likely men who had their feet firmly planted on the ground. The wise men would have been harder to impress than most people. Modern research concerning the Assyrian, Neo-Babylonian / Chaldean astronomers during the seven hundred years preceding the birth of Jesus indicate that the men were generally fairly scientific in their approach. They recorded many events over hundreds of years, without fanfare or exaggeration. They did also consult divinatory omen texts concerning the interpretations of events and made astrological predictions. However, their approach to the heavens was based on mathematically verifiable data.

Ancient astronomers often concentrated their stargazing in the fairly dynamic period of hours preceding sunrise and following sunset. In Babylonian astronomical records the morning and evening observations are very prominent. Conjunctions involving the principal stars, planets, sun and the moon would also have interested the wise men. We will see that there were an abundance of conjunctions, which could have had a messianic interpretation during the years 7 BC to 1 BC.

The Chaldeans divided the day into twelve hours, one for each sign of the zodiac each equaling about 30 degrees (360° for the whole circle). Herodotus tells us that the Greeks anciently borrowed the same system from them, saying: "The sun clock and the sundial, and the twelve divisions of the day, came to Hellas not from Egypt but from Babylonia."[11] At night it was possible for the ancients to see the progression of time by watching the rising and setting of the constellations. In this way the Babylonians and others could estimate the time even at night. Whereas in the daylight hours a sundial would have marked the hours.[12]

Regular Cycles:

Some celestial events happen in a cyclical fashion. Just looking at Tzedek's (Jupiter's) position a Magus could have generally predicted the planet's position for several years in advance. He would have known that the planet goes through the whole zodiac in slightly less than 12 years. A Magus would have known that Tzedek would repeat the same pattern of movements about 71 and 83 years in the future. The ancient Mesopotamian astronomers were well aware of the first appearances and last appearances of certain stars and planets. Planets also have stopping points, where they visually seem to stop moving among the background stars from an earthly viewpoint. A heliacal rising is the first visibility of a planet or

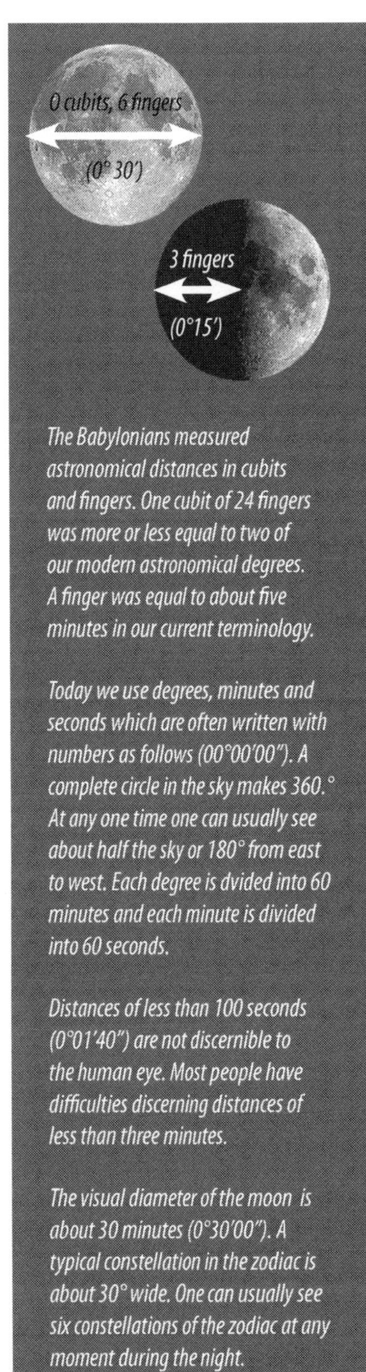

The Babylonians measured astronomical distances in cubits and fingers. One cubit of 24 fingers was more or less equal to two of our modern astronomical degrees. A finger was equal to about five minutes in our current terminology.

Today we use degrees, minutes and seconds which are often written with numbers as follows (00°00'00"). A complete circle in the sky makes 360.° At any one time one can usually see about half the sky or 180° from east to west. Each degree is dvided into 60 minutes and each minute is divided into 60 seconds.

Distances of less than 100 seconds (0°01'40") are not discernible to the human eye. Most people have difficulties discerning distances of less than three minutes.

The visual diameter of the moon is about 30 minutes (0°30'00"). A typical constellation in the zodiac is about 30° wide. One can usually see six constellations of the zodiac at any moment during the night.

Every 24 years Tzedek and Nogah are together in the constellation of the lion. Their presence together in Leo in 3/2 BC may have been significant in the story of the birth of the Messiah.

star at dawn before sunrise, after it has not been visible for a period of time because its apparent nearness to the sun. The inner planets Kochav Chammah and Nogah can also have a heliacal rising in the evening after sunset. This is not possible for the outer planets. A heliacal setting is the last opportunity to observe an object in the evening after sunset (last visibility), before it gets lost in the glare of the setting sun. For the inner planets, Kochav Chammah and Nogah, a heliacal setting can also happen just before dawn. Through their observations and calculations it was possible for the Babylonian astronomers to predict with a significant level of accuracy when a stellar or planetary rising or setting would visibly take place, although they could often be "off the mark" by one or two days because of atmospheric conditions. Each year any given constellation will be hidden in the solar glare for about six weeks. For example, the heliacal rising of Spica/Zerah (the seed) took place in October which was also the beginning of the planting season.

Stars rise in the east four minutes earlier each day. This means that they will be about one degree higher in the sky each day. On the other side of the horizon in the west, stars set about four minutes earlier each day. Planets are similar, but they also have their own independent movements.

Babylonian astronomers would have been familiar with the following cycle lasting about 399 days for the planet Tzedek (Jupiter / Babylonian: MUL.BABBAR or MUL*Marduk*).[13] This involves a heliacal rising and setting as well as two stationary points and an opposition. Understanding this cycle allowed the Babylonians to predict events well in advance.

A typical series of heavenly events for Jupiter:

1. Heliacal rising to 1st stationary point = about 125 days
(1st visibility of Jupiter in the east in the morning to the place where it first stops moving among the background stars).

2. 1st stationary point to opposition = about 60 days
(The moment when Jupiter rises in the east at sunset)

3. Opposition to 2nd stationary point = about 60 days
(From rising in the east at sunset to the second place where it stops moving among the background stars).

4. 2nd Stationary point to heliacal setting = about 125 days
(From the second place where Jupiter stops moving among the background stars to its last visibility in the evening sky).

5. Heliacal setting to the new heliacal rising = about 30 days
(Last visibility in the evening sky to its first visibility in the morning sky).

The cycle then repeats.

Each year the planet Jupiter makes its first yearly appearance in the east (heliacal rising) about 30+ days later than the previous year.

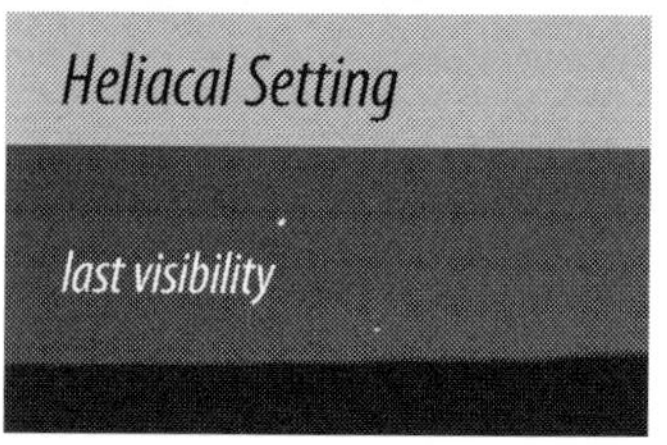

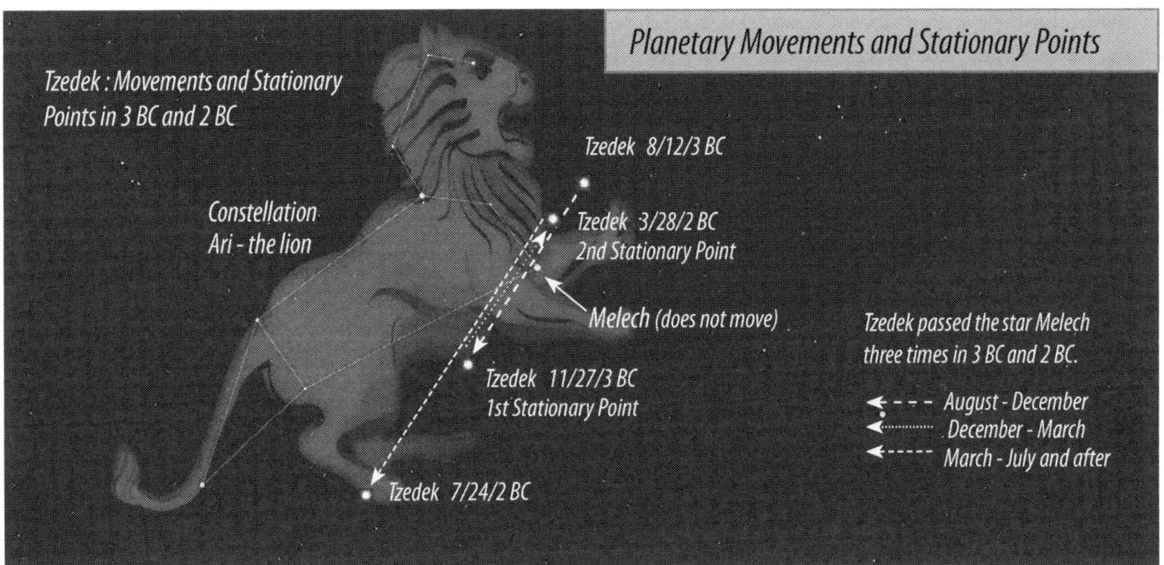

The planet Tzedek regularly, visually stops twice as it is going through this approximately 399-day cycle. The fact that Tzedek's cycle is about 34 days longer than a normal solar year causes it to shift through the whole zodiac in about twelve years. The Magi were accustomed to "wandering stars" (planets) that visually move among the stars and also appear to stop. They were expecting those events, calculating them well in advance and noting their actual occurrences. A "star / planet," which stopped among the background stars above Bethlehem, would not have been unusual for the Magi. However, the timing and location would have certainly been significant to them. A 50-year-old Babylonian astronomer, who had worked for 30 years, would have seen about 60 stationary points of the planet Tzedek (MUL.BABBAR / Jupiter). He would have seen Shabbatei (Saturn) stop about an equal number of times, as well as other stationary points for Ma'adim and the inner planets. Many people, this author included, have often wondered how a "star" could have possibly moved and then stopped as Matthew's text seems to indicate. The probable answer is that planets look like stars to an unaided eye, and these type of events are normal for planets.

A number of Christian teachers have claimed that Matthew was using technical astronomical language for a heliacal rising when he wrote, "For we saw His star in the east and have come to worship Him." Some have thought that this text speaks of the star rising in the east. It probably only means that the wise men saw the star while they were in the east. Matthew was not using technical astronomical language even though there were some incidents of heliacal risings and settings which seem to be linked to Jesus' birth (See Appendix 5 on page 235).

Table 6:2 The synodic period of a heavenly body is the time that it takes for a planet, the sun or the moon to start repeating its movements. For example: Shabbatei visually rises as a morning star every 378 days. Therefore the synodic period is 378 days. The moon's synodic period is the time between successive recurrences of the same phase. For example: The time between one new moon to the next is about 29.5 days.

Heavenly Body	Synodic period (Days)
K. Chammah	116
Nogah	584
Ma'adim	780
Tzedek	399
Shabbatei	378
Moon	29.53

Just looking at the planet Nogah (Dilibat / Venus) an ancient Babylonian astronomer would have understood exactly where the planet would be exactly eight years into the future.

The www.caeno.org website is a good source of information about Babylonian astronomy.

The Inner Planets

The inner planets, Kochav Chammah (Mercury) and Kochav Nogah (Venus), behave a bit differently from the outer planets. The sequence of planetary events noted by the Babylonian astronomers over hundreds of years for the inner planets was as follows: (1) evening rising (first visibility in the west after sunset), (2) first stationary point (in the evening, in the west after sunset), (3) evening setting (last visibility in the west after sunset), (4) morning rising (first visibility in the east before sunrise), (5) second stationary point (visually stopped in the east before sunrise), (6) morning setting (last visibility in the east before sunrise) and then the cycle repeated itself. This entire cycle, called a synodic period, takes 584 days for Nogah (Venus) and 116 days for Kochav Chammah (Mercury). When Nogah finishes five of these cycles, equal to almost exactly eight years, it returns to the same spot in the sky when viewed from the earth. If one sees Nogah as an evening star, one can be sure that in exactly eight years, the planet will return to the same spot among the stars when viewed from the earth and it will appear at about the same moment in time. Just looking at the planet Nogah (*Dilibat* / Venus) an ancient Babylonian astronomer would have understood exactly where the planet would be eight years into the future and he could have calculated all the intermediate positions of the planet from one fixed date to the next. Documents exist which demonstrate that the Babylonians already understood this cycle in about 1700 BC.

The Magi would have been aware of many of these cyclical and periodic events involving all the heavenly bodies. They would not necessarily have been overly impressed by conjunctions or other phenomena simply because some things were repeated in the heavens on a regular basis. However, the events at the time of Jesus' birth were unique because of their relative rarity, number, timing and meaning. Through their extensive record keeping, the Magi would have been well aware of the rarity of some of the events.

The Babylonian constellations were not exactly in the same boundaries as modern outlines. From the research done by several people it has been possible to establish the western and eastern boundaries of Leo. These begin with Subra (Omicron Leonis) and Ras Elased Australis (Epsilon Leonis) and end with Zavijava (Beta Virginis). In the illustration below, Ras Elased Australis is the eye of the lion. Zavijava was supposed to be the end of one of the lion's hind feet. These boundries do not fit the modern outlines of the constellation. Babylonian categories have Cancer encroaching on Leo, and the lion encroaches on the present outline of Virgo. It is similar for many other constellations. Leo (Ari) is specifically indicated below because of its significance in the story of the wise men.

The Babylonian constellations were not exactly in the same boundaries as their modern outlines.

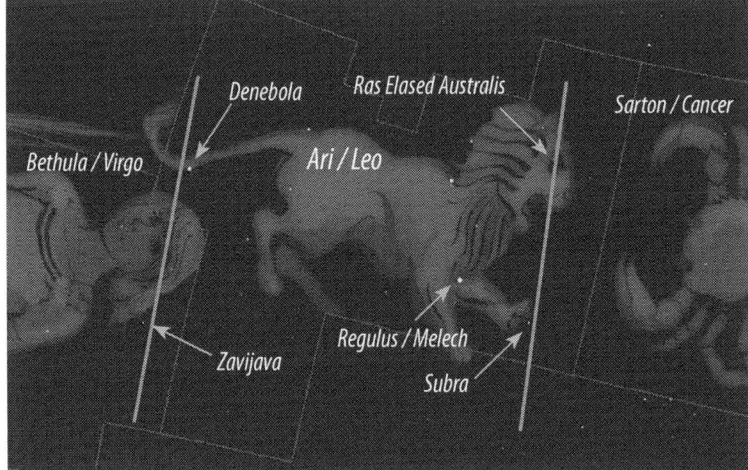

Below: Venus makes morning appearances in the east for a period of about eight months. Afterwards Venus disappears for a bit over two months, then it reappears in the west for about eight months. Finally Venus disappears into the solar glare again only to reappear about eight days later in the morning sky. Then the cycle repeats. The whole cycle takes 584 days.

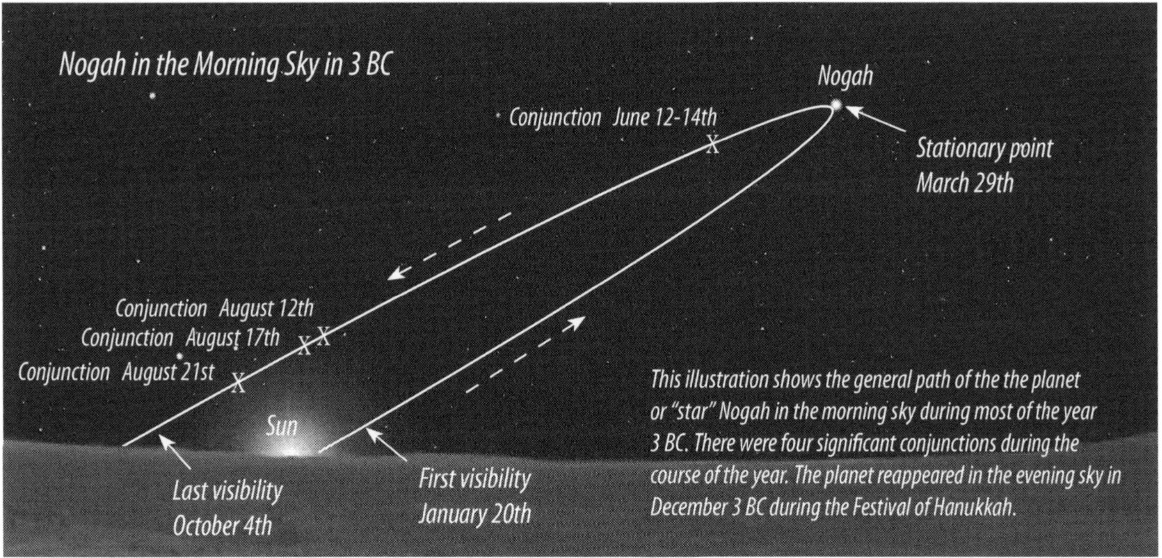

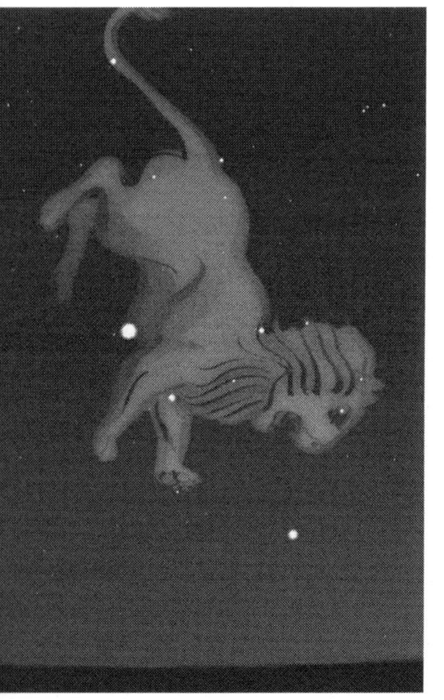

Think Like A Magus - Part 2

Modern and Ancient Interpretations

Conjunctions, eclipses and occultations involving planets, stars and the sun and the moon have often inspired and mystified people around the world. In astronomy, a conjunction happens when two or more heavenly bodies appear to meet or draw close to one another. Each year there are a variety of conjunctions. An eclipse is defined as the total or partial obscuring of one celestial body by another. An occultation is similar to an eclipse, but the term is mainly used when the moon passes in front of a star or planet. In what circumstances could this have been considered special? Why would any of the events described above be considered unique and even meaningful?

As indicated earlier in this book, there are several theories / ideas about the star of Bethlehem. In the last 40 years, one scenario concerning a number of significant conjunctions involving several planets and stars in 3/2 BC has been heralded as a possible explanation of the star of the Magi. This series of events may explain why the wise men really did think that the Messiah of Israel was making his appearing. Attention was first drawn to these events when the astronomer Roger Sinnott wrote an article which appeared in December 1968 Sky and Telescope magazine. In the article, Mr. Sinnott proposed the particularly impressive conjunction of Jupiter and Venus in Leo on June 17th 2 BC as a possible explanation of the Messiah's star. Until 1968, no one had suggested this particular conjunction as a possible candidate as the "star of Bethlehem." The event seems to have been unknown or forgotten during most of history. Through modern computer technology it is now possible to recreate some aspects of past events which have been lost to us. Over the last four decades, the theory linking this particular June 2 BC conjunction to the "star of Bethlehem" has been developed by several people. It has become fairly popular among Christians, especially in North America. A major DVD was produced in 2007 which explores the conjunction in some detail, as well as other events in the period. A multitude of articles and a few books have been published on the subject. This conjunction theory does has some explanatory merit, but in its normal presentation it has some interpretive problems.

A practical exercise of interpreting heavenly events can give some perspective. The reality of modern misconceptions concerning the ancient peoples becomes clear by exploring how the conjunction in June 2 BC has been interpreted by some modern Christians. Their interpretation is remarkably different from what the Babylonians themselves would have understood. If the Magi were Zoroastrians, we are left with several serious unknowns. For example, we do not even know their names for the planets. Nor do we know much about how they would have interpreted such a conjunction. We simply cannot make absolute pronouncements about their perspectives. However, learning about one proposed interpretation of the June 2 BC event should help us to understand the Babylonian Magi much better.

Through modern computer technology and data bases it is now possible to recreate some aspects of past events which have been lost to us.

The June 17th 2 BC Conjunction

During the late spring of 2 BC, the brilliantly illuminated planets Jupiter and Venus approached each other for several weeks. Finally, on the evening of June 17th 2 BC they were so close together in the constellation of the lion (Leo) that it was impossible to distinguish them visually one from the other. The two planets traveled together for almost two hours like a single star until they set in the west. As they were shining together, the full moon rose in the east facing them. It was as though the moon was adding its voice to the display. The next day, the two planets were close to each other, but no longer unified. In the following days, they moved quickly apart. The conjunction seems to have been the brightest event of its kind which has ever been recorded. It is certainly the longest lasting and most brilliant conjunction known, although it was not the brightest star which has ever been seen (We shall explore this unique event in much greater detail). It does seem to have something to do with the whole story of the wise men and the famous star. However, it is first necessary to explore in detail a proposed interpretation of the 2 BC conjunction.

Identity Really Does Matter

In many ancient civilizations, the more important gods were identified with the wandering stars, as well as, the sun and the moon. The chief, ruling god among the Greeks and the Romans, known as Zeus / Jupiter lent his name to the planet which still dominates the night sky. In mythology Jupiter reigned over a whole pantheon of other gods, human beings and other creatures. Mars, the god of war, often associated with blood, was symbolized by the "red planet." Venus the goddess of love, fertility and war shone forth as the evening and morning star. Saturn was recognized as a slowly moving planet / star. Mercury, the messenger god, never left the general area of the sun.

The god Jupiter's character, and that of the other gods, left plenty to be desired. The "king of the gods" was far from being a great example of righteousness, in stark contrast to the righteous acts and the faithful character of the God of Israel. For example, Jupiter, in a conspiracy with his mother, overthrew his father Chronos (Saturn) to take the leadership of the gods. It is true that Chronos was not very upright himself and without doubt he needed to be overthrown. However, the whole scenario of a scheming mother aiding her son to overthrow his father does not reflect the best of family values. Although Jupiter was married to a goddess, he found himself sexually involved with various other goddesses, human women and nymphs. He fathered over 20 descendants through various consented and non-consented relationships, which included rape. Jupiter's faithfulness and goodness to any person, god, goddess or various peoples could be debated.

Above: Jupiter / Zeus, the chief of the Roman / Greek gods.

Above: Dates on the tree
Below: A picture of the Tigris River and a forest of date palms

Interpretations of the June 17th 2 BC Conjunction:

Some, often very well meaning Christian speakers and authors, have tried to interpret the close conjunction of the two planets in June 2 BC in a way which symbolically ties the event specifically to the actual birth of Jesus. Lacking any real knowledge of the ancient perceptions of heavenly events, some believers developed a possible interpretation of the conjunction. The explanation has not been very attractive even for some of its chief promoters because of its association with pagan gods.

The proposed, problematic, interpretation of the June 17th 2 BC conjunction usually goes as follows: The unique close union of the two planets supposedly was a visual demonstration of a father god figure (Jupiter) and a mother goddess (Venus), coming together. Their union in the constellation of Leo astrologically announced the birth of a Jewish child king. According to some, this idea inspired the wise men.[14] But does such an explanation really give us any needed answers? Is this explanation even feasible from a Christian perspective? Does it match ancient ideas concerning astrology, omens, mythology or signs in the heavens?

While there are some associations of Venus with motherhood, she was *worshiped* as a goddess of love, sex and fertility. Any Christian interpretation of heavenly events which invokes such a goddess would seem to be misplaced. This is especially true when one of the principal characters in the story of the Messiah's birth was his virgin mother. While the God of the Bible did create sexuality, and he understands it better than any man or woman, he did not create perversions of sex. The God of Abraham did not create sex goddesses or approve of their worship. In addition, from a Christian perspective Jupiter was certainly not a righteous "father figure," so how could he possibly be symbolically involved in the birth of God's Messiah? The proposed interpretation actually incorporates ideas which are in opposition to the biblical revelation of the character and ways of God. This interpretative idea of the June 17th 2 BC conjunction has often been proposed by well-meaning Christians. Unfortunately they did not make efforts to place themselves in the ancient context in order to discover the historical, religious and cultural aspects of the events.

A Hypothetical Babylonian Interpretation of the June 17th 2 BC Event

Let us return to the previous example concerning Jupiter and Venus and assume that the wise men may have been Babylonian (Chaldean) astronomers / astrologers. We might again speculate from our modern perspective about the conjunction. A hypothetical Babylonian interpretation of a conjunction of the planets Venus *(Dilbat)* and Jupiter (MUL.BABBAR) might also involve the uniting of Marduk and Ishtar, like the Greek / Roman example above. However, such a conjunction of planets would involve relations between a divine nephew and his divine aunt. Marduk was the grandson of the moon god Sîn through his son

UTU /Shamash, the sun god. INANNA/Ishtar was the daughter of Sîn and the sister of UTU/Shamash. Again such an interpretation does not rhyme well with the ways of the God of Israel, who forbid sexual relations and marriage between a nephew and his aunt from the time of Moses in the 2nd millennium BC till now (Leviticus 18:12). The Babylonian Ishtar, a sex and fertility goddess, was also one who may have been worshiped through sacred prostitution. Is there any possible interpretation involving this goddess which could be the equivalent of the virgin Mary conceiving or giving birth to the Messiah of Israel? The answer is certainly no. However, the difficulties of interpretation are even more serious. Ishtar was thought of as having a dual of role, being female and at least somewhat male. In the evening sky, the Babylonians thought of Ishtar as a "bearded" male deity, a god of war. Ishtar was only thought of as a uniquely female being in the morning sky, making the proposed interpretation of a "mother planet" meeting a "father planet" in the evening sky completely untenable.[15]

We now know, at least in part, what Babylonian wise men during the 1st millennium BC could have thought about the conjunctions of planets and incidents involving the sun, the moon and the stars.

Are the categories of "mother planets" and father planets" really the way that the Babylonian astronomer priests would have also interpreted a special conjunction of Jupiter (MUL.BABBAR) and Venus (*Dilbat*)? The answer is clearly, no. Historically, it can be affirmed with assurance that no Greek, Roman, Assyrian or Babylonian would have developed an interpretation of the conjunction of Venus and Jupiter in 2 BC corresponding to the "modern" hypothetical examples above.

The Babylonian Omen Catalogs

The Mesopotamians had their own complete and well developed systems of interpretation. It is now possible to know, at least in part, what Babylonian wise men at the end of the 1st millennium BC could have thought about the conjunctions of planets and incidents involving the sun, the moon and the stars. There is still some uncertainty about their interpretations as indicated on pages 69-70. However, the ancient cuneiform texts are clear about how the Babylonians interpreted celestial omens. Many of these texts have been discovered and translated in the last 150 years. They give significant insights into the world view of the Babylonian wise men. The original inhabitants of Mesopotamia, the Sumerians, Akkadians, Assyrians and Babylonians, developed an extensive collection of omens, which was arranged in the form of a vast catalog, covering a multitude of subjects.

Below: The Mušuuššu, the snake dragon, which was associated with Marduk. This artwork in brick is part of the Ishtar Gate exposition in Berlin.

As mentioned previously, the omen catalogs were mostly oriented toward predicting the future. They were centered on the king, military affairs, internal and international politics, the weather and the economy. If they did have an official divinatory role in the 1st century BC, the Babylonian priests would have mainly sought interpretations of heavenly events for the affairs of the king, but there is evidence that the priests did not limit their role only to such activities. Making horoscopes probably consumed plenty of their energy and became a significant source of revenue for at least some Magi. However, foretelling or announcing the birth of a world

Above: Ishtar, the goddess of sex and fertility. The goddess was also represented by the eight pointed star above which symbolizes the planet Venus (DILBAT).

ruler, forecasting famines, economic crises or wars did not generally fall in the category of making horoscopes. Such activities would have been more connected to a divinatory role.

Some translations of Babylonian cuneiform tablets containing material about conjunctions of the planets like Venus and Jupiter were first published in English in 1870. Knowledge of these texts has grown significantly in recent years. Scholars such as Noel Swerdlow, Francesca Rochberg and Erica Reiner have made huge contributions to understanding the ancient Mesopotamian world view. Below are some examples of the interpretations of conjunctions concerning the planets *Dilbat* and MUL.BABBAR (Venus and Jupiter) adapted from Erica Reiner's book about Babylonian planetary omens. These examples spell out how the Babylonians themselves might have interpreted the Venus / Jupiter conjunction in June 2 BC using their omen catalogue.

> *If Venus reaches Jupiter (or in a variant text "comes near Jupiter and stops,") then a flood will carry off the land, high water will come.*
>
> *If Venus reaches Jupiter and they follow upon each other, then high water will carry off the land.*
>
> *If Venus reaches Jupiter and passes it, a mighty flood will come.*
>
> *If Venus and Jupiter come close, then there will be a reign of destruction (concerning) the king of Amurru.*
>
> *If Venus comes near Jupiter : in the land altogether - brother will become hostile to his brother.*
>
> *If Venus enters Jupiter, then the king of Akkad will die, the dynasty will change, either a soldier will go out or the enemy will send a message to the land (asking for peace).*
>
> *If Venus and Jupiter are side by side and the moon stands between them: the furrow will diminish its yield. (The harvest will be diminished).*
>
> *If Venus rises in the east, (or in a variant text "in the west") and Jupiter passes (her): there will be famine in the land.*
>
> *If Venus and Jupiter are side by side and meet: This indicates the end of the dynasty of the king of Amurru.*[16]

Normal Babylonian interpretations of the Jupiter and Venus conjunction in 2 BC would not have led a single Babylonian wise man to Bethlehem.

The actual interpretations developed by the Babylonians themselves concerning the interactions between these two planets could have been interesting to the Parthian emperor. The interpretations are very different from what we might have assumed from a modern perspective. There are no discussions of relations between "mother or father planets," sex or marriage between the gods, or the birth of a Jewish baby. The normal Babylonian understanding of the MUL.BABBAR / Dilbat (Jupiter and Venus) conjunction in June 2 BC would not have led a single Babylonian wise man to Bethlehem.

One can also examine other Babylonian omen texts about the sun and the moon, the other planets and their associated gods, some stars and even the constellations to see if a messianic meaning could be found from a Babylonian perspective. However, the results would be similar for the other heavenly objects and the other deities. Any interpretation of a celestial event relating it to a Jewish Messiah would have been radically different from anything which the Babylonian astronomers would have understood using their authoritative omen texts. They would not have varied from their classic interpretations unless they had some very good reasons to understand the events differently. Other interpretations were also possible based on a more Hellenistic astrological approach, but they do not match well with the ways of the God of Israel.

Christians have generally always refused to worship, to invoke or to use other gods as means to interpret events in the heavens. In the example cited above some believers developed possible interpretations of events based more on their own lack of understanding rather than a serious comprehension of the ancient world view. From a Christian perspective, one could question any approach that adopts a traditional astrological interpretation or uses the ancient gods to communicate a message. One simply does not find the Jewish God using traditional astrology or other gods to help men understand his plans or greater purposes. The effort to make the June 2 BC conjunction into a symbolic announcement of the *actual birth* of Jesus does not succeed. However, there may be another way of interpreting the conjunction which would make sense and which could tie the event to an announcement concerning the arrival of God's chosen Messiah.

Interpretive Approaches Which Please the God of Abraham?

Another system of interpretation is needed to understand why the men from the east came seeking the Jewish Messiah. The Hebrew planet names Tzedek and Nogah (Jupiter and Venus) carry meanings which are certainly more useful in interpreting events from a biblical perspective. For practicing Jewish monotheists there would have been no compromise concerning the Messiah in relation to other gods. The attitudes toward the gods in the ancient world as compared with a Jewish perspective is summarized below:

> *"Almost everybody took the gods mildly seriously; hardly anybody took them very seriously. In the world Paul had come from, however, there was only one God. He was the creator of the world; he was also the God of Israel. And almost everybody took him very seriously indeed."* [17]

The Jews in Babylonia and ancient Iran would have had several reasons to take the God of their fathers seriously. One major reason was that even their geographic location reflected God's choice to send them into exile. Their actual physical surroundings reminded them of the reality of God's previous judgment.

The Babylonians were familiar with the repeating cycles of the planets. Each planet repeats its behavior in the sky at regular intervals. However, many of the cycles span generations and even hundreds of years. Having such an understanding of the planetary cycles required hundreds of years of observation.

The repetition of planetary cycles in years: [18]

Mercury: 6, 13, 46, 60, 125, 355

Venus: 8, 16, 48, 56, 64, 6400

Mars: 15, 32, 47, 64, 79, 126, 284

Jupiter: 12, 71, 72, 83, 95, 166, 261, 344, 427

Saturn: 30, 59, 147, 265, 560

One simply does not find the Jewish God using traditional astrology or the gods of other religions to send messages or to help men to gain understanding about his plans or greater purposes.

The God of the Bible had his own thoughts concerning the other gods.

> *"Watch yourself that you make no covenant with the inhabitants of the land into which you are going, or it will become a snare in your midst. But rather, you are to tear down their altars and smash their sacred pillars and cut down their Asherim --for you shall not worship any other god, for the LORD, whose name is Jealous, is a jealous God-- otherwise you might make a covenant with the inhabitants of the land and they would play the harlot with their gods and sacrifice to their gods, and someone might invite you to eat of his sacrifice, and you might take some of his daughters for your sons, and his daughters might play the harlot with their gods and cause your sons also to play the harlot with their gods." (Exodus 34:12-16)*

We in the modern, post modern and post / post modern world think that everyone should be as tolerant as we supposedly are ourselves. We are often shocked by stark, firm statements which we may find intolerant. The God of the Bible has been criticized on this basis, however, many of us do not realize that even in our criticisms we are often being very intolerant. It is obvious from the passage above and other similar ones that any interpretations of celestial events which invoke pagan gods as explanatory agents would not be pleasing to the God of Abraham, Isaac and Jacob.

The God of the Israelites was in opposition to the other gods and they were in opposition to Him. Very little middle ground was accepted, and religious tolerance was not one of the primary values of the ancient world. Sometimes there were situations where various religious groups lived in relative harmony for generations, but often one group or another tried to get the upper hand. The relative tolerance of the Parthian rulers concerning the Greek gods and even Judaism did not endure throughout Parthian history. As mentioned on page 78, the Babylonian and Greek inhabitants of Seleucia on the Tigris massacred 50,000 Mesopotamian Jews in AD 37. Later Zoroastrianism became increasingly important in the Parthian court. Under the Persian Sassanids, who succeeded the Parthians as the rulers of Mesopotamia, Iran and parts of Central Asia, the trend favoring Zoroastrianism increased.

The next several sections of this book are devoted to examining the celestial events from 7 BC to 1 BC in some detail. The perspective which will be presented has substantial links to Judaism. It may offer an interpretive framework, which could have been much more acceptable to the God of Abraham. It also may help us to understand the Magi and their experience with the star.

Part 8: Introduction: Events in the Heavens

For My thoughts are not your thoughts, nor are your ways My ways," declares the LORD. For as the heavens are higher than the earth, so are My ways higher than your ways and My thoughts than your thoughts. (Isaiah 55: 7-9)

Apparently God made it evident to the Magi in a most unexpected manner that the Messiah was being or had been born. God's thoughts really are higher than our thoughts and his ways are higher than our ways. As we have seen there was no prophecy concerning a physical star, which would supposedly mark the Messiah's birth; however, God did use the heavens to announce the coming of the Messiah.

Heavenly Events: Meaningful or Spectacular?

"I, wisdom, dwell with prudence, and I find knowledge and discretion." (Proverbs 8:12)

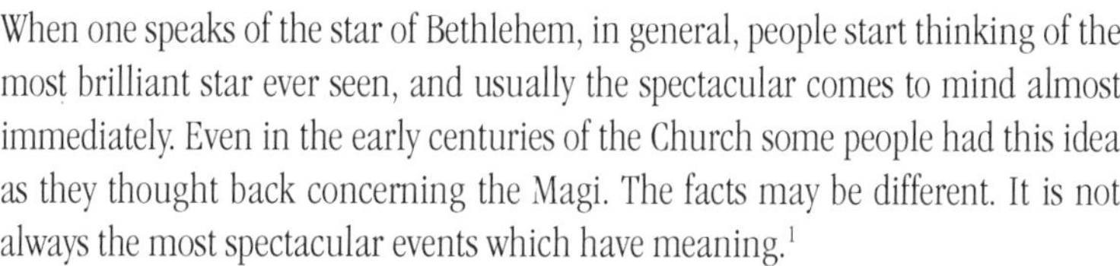

When one speaks of the star of Bethlehem, in general, people start thinking of the most brilliant star ever seen, and usually the spectacular comes to mind almost immediately. Even in the early centuries of the Church some people had this idea as they thought back concerning the Magi. The facts may be different. It is not always the most spectacular events which have meaning.[1]

When one looks at explanations of the "star of Bethlehem," what usually lacks is a reasonable explanation of why the Magi would have thought that <u>any</u> star would have had anything to do with the birth of a Jewish Messiah. Why would any supernova, comet or planetary conjunction have given a message concerning the Messiah of Israel? Among all the prophecies about the Messiah, there was no known prophecy concerning a physical star which was destined to appear to proclaim the coming of the Messiah.[2] The Magi had a unique experience for which there was no precedent in the Bible. As far as we know, no one ever thought that there would be a sign in the heavens concerning the Messiah before it actually happened. God may have revealed mysteries to Daniel or to other prophets about a messianic sign in the heavens, but it is far from certain that there was such a revelation. Some people may have made calculations, which would have led them to believe that the Messiah's appearing was imminent. However, we have no record that anyone was waiting for star or a series of heavenly events.

Meaningful events must be the key to understanding the experience of the wise men. There had to be significant *reasons* why they came to think that any star had something to do with the Jewish Messiah.

What Makes the Heavenly Events from 7 BC to 1 BC Special?

Most of us only think of one star mentioned in the Bible when thinking of the Magi. However, if we examine the time period of the Messiah's birth in detail, we find there was a whole series of heavenly events, which could have been interpreted as heralding the arrival of God's anointed king. The Bible mentions a single star, and certainly there was a key star involved. However, it may be that one star only became important in the context of events involving other stars, several planets, as well as, the sun and the moon.

Minimize the Spectacular - Look for the Meaningful

Most of the events in the heavens in the years surrounding Jesus' birth were not spectacular, however, they have messianic connections. Imagining that the events were absolutely brilliantly spectacular has perhaps been one of the greatest hindrances to actually understanding the famous star or the Magi. Book titles, like Ernest Martin's, *The Star that Astonished the World,* convey a dramatic sense of the spectacular. Despite the numerous problems in his book, Dr. Martin actually broke some new ground which has helped unravel aspects of the story. However, the book title left a false impression. It reflects the expectation of almost everyone that the star had to be exceedingly brilliant and spectacular. However, the "star" actually did not astonish the whole world or even a whole town, a region or a country. The multitudes in Jerusalem, Alexandria, Antioch, Ephesus, Athens and Rome were apparently not talking about a star. If they were, we have no record of it either in the Bible or elsewhere. The star may have been significant and even special, but the starry heavens only got the attention of a relatively small group of wise men from the Middle East. Those men in turn got the attention of the Jews in Jerusalem, but it was not the "star" which troubled and astonished the Jews or King Herod. According to Matthew's text the king did not even notice the star before the wise men arrived. What got Herod's attention was not a star at all, but rather a group of wise men, who were looking for the Jewish Messiah. Herod saw their presence as a political threat, which put in question the continuation of his royal line. The star was apparently not extremely spectacular, although it was certainly significant. Just a small group of wise men from the east was talking about a Messiah, who was unexpectedly linked to a star.

The Meaningful

In what follows a definite effort has been made to avoid esoteric explanations. In general, the simple Jewish astronomical names united with some prophetic passages from the Scriptures and certain specific dates appear to give significant meaning to the events in the heavens from 7 BC to 1 BC. Those events were often relatively discreet, but they did proclaim a definite message.

It is not possible to know or understand everything that the Magi may have seen or thought. We lack large amounts of information.

It is not possible to know or understand everything that the Magi may have seen or thought. We lack large amounts of information. We need to be willing to not understand or interpret everything concerning the heavenly events in the past. In the words of Paul concerning knowledge, we know in part:

> *Love never fails; but if there are gifts of prophecy, they will be done away; if there are tongues, they will cease; if there is knowledge, it will be done away. For we know in part and we prophesy in part; but when the perfect comes, the partial will be done away. When I was a child, I used to speak like a child, think like a child, reason like a child; when I became a man, I did away with childish things. For now we see in a mirror dimly, but then face to face; now I know in part, but then I will know fully just as I also have been fully known. But now faith, hope, love, abide these three; but the greatest of these is love. (I Corinthians 13:8-13)*

Through exploring the celestial events at the end of the 1st century BC it is the author's hope and desire that his readers may be inspired to adore, appreciate and love God the Father and the One whom he has sent. Love is more important and valuable than the accumulation of knowledge or understanding great mysteries.

Precursors ? A Preparation Period ?

Brightess
Righteousness
Sabbatical Rest
King

As one looks at the events leading up to the birth of Jesus, it may be that there was a preparatory period. It is possible that the wise men who eventually went to Bethlehem went through a time of "training" and anticipation. If they were accustomed to thinking in a typical Babylonian or Zoroastrian manner when interpreting the heavens, they would have probably needed to be "retrained" to think in a fashion which could better fit biblical categories. However, if the Magi were already associated with certain Jews or if they had Jewish ethnic origins, they could have seen the links more readily than typical Babylonian or Zoroastrian priests. It may be that any Jewish Magi or Jewish influenced Magi may have received some insights through historic connections with Daniel or through dreams, visions or angelic visitations. If such events happened, we have no information about it.

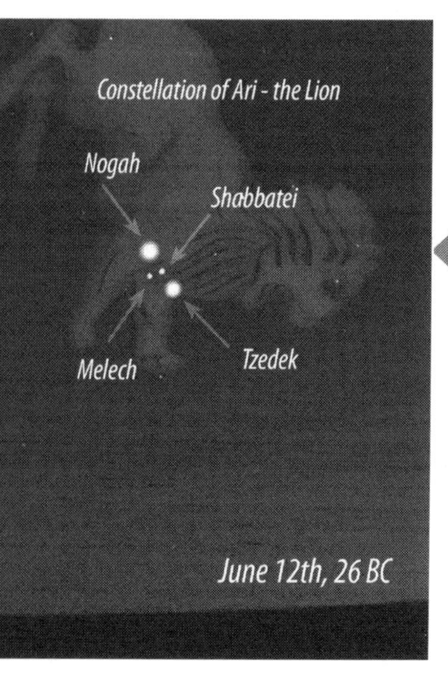

This event was 490 years after the dedication of the second temple in 516 BC.

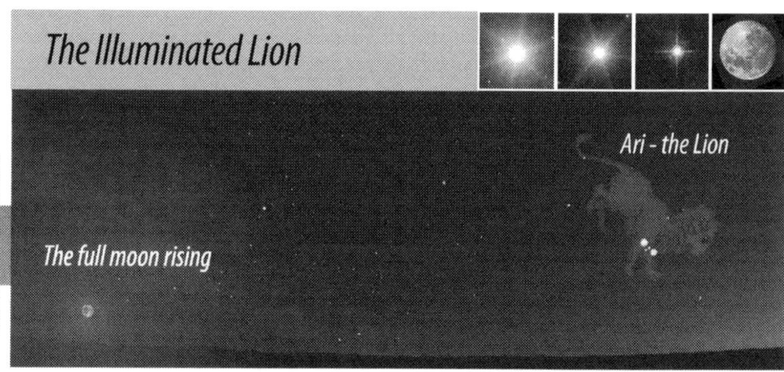

15 Sivan - June 12th, 26 BC

During several months in 27 BC and 26 BC, there was significant astronomical activity in the constellation of Leo. On June 12th in 26 BC, Tzedek (Jupiter / MUL. BABBAR), Nogah (Venus) and Shabbatei (Saturn) were closely gathered together right beside the fixed star Melech (Regulus / LUGAL / Sharru). While this combination illuminated the western sky after sunset, the full moon also rose in the east. Some very similar events happen in 2 BC. In the thousand years before June 12th, 26 BC Tzedek, Nogah and Shabbatei had only been together beside Melech in this manner two other times: (1) In 940 BC, which was a very similar conjunction grouped around Melech (but without the moon) and (2) in 880 BC, but the planets were further east of Melech. It would seem that if someone actually wanted to send a specific message about a king this 26 BC event would certainly qualify either for the Babylonians or the Jews. By itself, it would have been interesting, but hardly enough to cause any Magi to seek Israel's Messiah. We often underestimate the amount of proof which the Magi may have required in order to have confidence that the Messiah had been born.[3]

Shabbatei / Tzedek

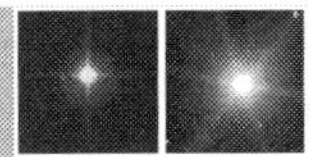

Conjunctions in 7 BC and 6 BC

During the last centuries, many people have thought that a series of conjunctions in 7 BC and 6 BC involving the planets Jupiter, Saturn and Mars (Tzedek, Shabbatei and Ma'adim) may have been at least related to the experience of the Magi. Pope Benedict XVI recently affirmed his own belief that this particular series of events was in all likelihood connected to Jesus' birth.[4]

The three conjunctions of Tzedek (Jupiter) and Shabbatei (Saturn) in 7 BC were unique. In addition the two planets traveled side by side for many months, never being more than 2° or 3° apart for about nine months. Their stopping points and movements corresponded during the whole period. Events such as three successive conjunctions and two corresponding stationary points of Tzedek and Shabbatei had not happened since 861/860 BC.[5] Three periods of significant closeness of about one degree stand out: (1) Pentecost, (2) the Day of Trumpets, the Day of Atonement and the Feast of Tabernacles and (3) December 7 BC. As we shall see, very many of the events in the years 3/2 BC also correspond with Jewish festivals. In many cases this happened in a very explicit and precise manner.

However, were the events of 7 BC enough for the wise men to say that they had seen "his star," the "star of the Messiah"? In reality the two planets never touched in 7 BC. At their closest point they were slightly less than one degree apart, which is about the size of two lunar diameters. How could the wise men say they had seen "the star" of the Messiah when it was evident that there were two stars? This series of conjunctions may not be "the events" that caused the Magi to travel at least 600 miles / 1,000 kilometers to Judea. However, the meeting of Tzedek and Shabbatei in 7 BC does appear to play a role in the experience of the Magi.

As we shall see Shabbatei (Saturn) seems to have connections to events involving the Jewish Sabbath. The name Shabbatei evokes the word Sabbath and sabbatical rest. It is also obvious in our present time that Saturn still has links with the 7th day of the week (Saturday), but that is a different story which goes beyond the subject of this book. However, concerning the conjunctions and events of 7 BC, Tzedek was also involved. Simply aligning the Hebrew names of the two planets Tzedek and Shabbatei evokes the idea of "sabbatical righteousness." The exile and the 70 "sevens" prophecy were linked specifically to Sabbatical years as proclaimed by both Jeremiah and Daniel. In 2 Chronicles 36:20-23 below the association made between the Sabbatical years and the exile is very clear:

> ***Those who had escaped from the sword he carried away to Babylon; and they were servants to him and to his sons until the rule of the kingdom of Persia, to fulfill the word of the LORD by the mouth of Jeremiah, until the land had enjoyed***

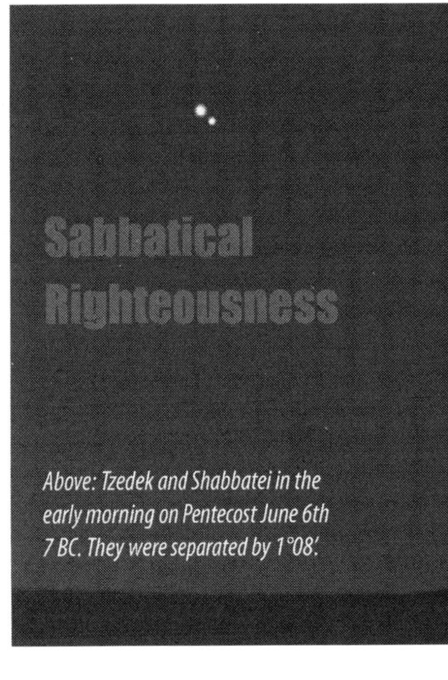

Above: Tzedek and Shabbatei in the early morning on Pentecost June 6th 7 BC. They were separated by 1°08'.

For Zion's sake I will not keep silent, And for Jerusalem's sake I will not keep quiet, Until her righteousness (tzedek) goes forth like brightness (nogah), And her salvation (yeshua) like a torch that is burning.

The nations will see your righteousness (tzedek), And all kings your glory; And you will be called by a new name which the mouth of the LORD will designate.

(Isaiah 61:1-2)

The evening sky
in early December 7 BC

its Sabbaths. All the days of its desolation it kept Sabbath until seventy years were complete. Now in the first year of Cyrus king of Persia--in order to fulfill the word of the LORD by the mouth of Jeremiah--the LORD stirred up the spirit of Cyrus king of Persia, so that he sent a proclamation throughout his kingdom, and also put it in writing, saying, "Thus says Cyrus king of Persia, 'The LORD, the God of heaven, has given me all the kingdoms of the earth, and He has appointed me to build Him a house in Jerusalem, which is in Judah. Whoever there is among you of all His people, may the LORD his God be with him, and let him go up!'" (This decree probably took place in 539 or 538 BC).

Daniel speaks of the 70 years as well:

In the first year of the reign of Darius the Mede (Cyrus' appointed satrap / king named Gobryas or Ugbaru), I, Daniel, observed in the books the number of the years which was revealed as the word of the LORD to Jeremiah the prophet for the completion of the desolations of Jerusalem, namely, seventy years.

7 X 7 = 49 Months

God expanded on the 70 years by saying that in reality *"Seventy 'sevens' have been decreed for your people and your holy city."* It would be normal to think immediately of 70 "sevens" of years. If one uses the logic of counting the years as outlined on pages 96-100, the celestial events in 7 BC were only four years before the important 3/2 BC date which could have been the last year of the 62 "sevens" of years. The events of 7 BC do fall in the general range of years near the date of the Messiah's projected coming. In addition there is a detail, which would have escaped the notice of the wise men at first, but which they may have appreciated later. *There were 49 full lunar months (7 X 7 new moons / months) from the month of the heliacal rising of Shabbatei in Nisan (April) 7 BC to the month of Jesus' conception in the month of Nisan in 3 BC.*[6] Such a correspondence of the dates evokes Daniel's prophecy of the 7 "sevens." All the Jewish festivals and special times in the year 3 BC (Nisan to Kislev) fell exactly 49 lunar months after the 7 BC dates. As we shall see toward the end of the book, 434 (62 X 7) new moons were also important in the story of Jesus' life. The 7 "sevens" of years and the 62 "sevens" of years do indicate a specific time for the arrival of the Messiah in 3/2 BC. However, the prophecy of the 70 "sevens" has several layers. It deals with years, months, weeks, and days. It is both figurative and literal.

The events of 7 BC were 49 lunar months before both Jesus' conception and his birth.

Events in 6 BC

The triple conjunction of Tzedek, Shabbatei and Ma'adim (Mars) in February 2 BC is often evoked in discussions about the star of Bethlehem. However, this conjunction was not visually impressive. The three planets were spread over about 6° of the sky (12 lunar diameters), partly in the evening solar glare. Another event involving a lunar occultation of Tzedek (Jupiter) in April 6 BC may also have had some bearing on the thinking of the wise men. However, the author is not totally convinced, and a full exploration of that event is beyond the scope of this book.[7]

A General Summary of the Celestial Events Near the Date of the Birth of Jesus

There were a variety of heavenly bodies and a significant number of events associated with the Messiah's birth. Many of the events happened on important dates in the Jewish calendar. The events included new moons, full moons, conjunctions, occultations, heliacal risings, heliacal settings, greatest elongations, stationary points of planets and perhaps even an equinox, all involved in announcing the Messiah's birth. One star, Tzedek - often on the left in the illustrations below, can be identified as the principal star which eventually became the "star of Bethlehem." There were some events which may or may not have had a messianic meaning. The events presented below are the most essential ones. Events shaded in light gray in the list were associated with Jewish festivals and appointed times. The event on the 15th of Sivan 2 BC was very special. Readers are encouraged simply to remark the number of events. A close examination of the details will follow.

The Hebrew names and the Sumerian or Akkadian and English names are listed below.

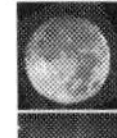

Shemesh (Šamaš / Sun)

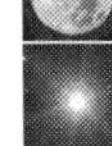

Yareach (^{MUL}GAL / Moon)

Tzedek (MUL.BABBAR / Jupiter)

Nogah (Dilbat / Venus)

Kochav Chammah (^{MUL}Na-bu-u$_2$ / Mercury)

? (SI$_4$ / Antares)

Zerah (SA$_4$ šá ABSIN / Spica)

Melech (LUGAL or Sharru / Regulus)

Shabbatei (Kajjamanu /Saturn)

Three conjunctions of Tzedek and Shabbatei (June, September and December). The two planets were traveling closely together for about 9 months.

The 1st of Nisan in 7 BC was ***seven "sevens" of lunar months (49 months)*** *before the 1st of Nisan in 3 BC. All the Jewish festivals and times set aside for honoring God in 3 BC and possibly early 2 BC were exactly 49 lunar months after the same events in 7 BC. This seven "sevens" of months (49 months) evokes Daniel's prophecy of the 70 "sevens."*

A lunar occultation of Tzedek in April of 6 BC may have had some influence on the thinking of the Magi.

3 BC

Spring

The month of Nisan in 3 BC was a key point in time.
*The last year of the **62 "sevens" of years** began in the month of Nisan in the spring.*

Passover (conjunction)

Pharisaic Pentecost (two conjunctions)

Hypothetical Sadducean Pentecost (heliacal rise)

*Both Pentecost dates make pairs of **7 "sevens" of literal weeks (49 days).***
*Other celestial events followed **62 weeks after the Pentecost dates.***

Summer

28-30 Sivan (conjunction)

1 Tammuz (conjunction at new moon)

*The events above are linked to **70 symbolic days**, which evoke Daniel 9.*

30 Av (close conjunction in Ari - Leo)

This event was the first of four involving Tzedek and Nogah.

Fall

Trumpets (conjunction)

Atonement (conjunction)

Tabernacles (equinox)

The Great Day of Tabernacles (conjunction)

*These events were 49 months after the September - October 7 BC conjunction of Tzedek and Shabbatei. The Day of Trumpets in 3 BC was exactly 1447 days (49 full lunar months or **7 "sevens" of months**) after the Day of Trumpets in 7 BC. It was the same for the other dates of the month of Tishrei, making a link with Daniel 9.*

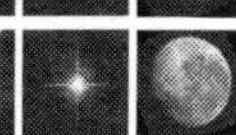

21 Heshvan (conjunction)

17 Kislev (occultation)

Winter

Hanukkah (a conjunction and a heliacal rise)

Hanukkah in 3 BC was 49 full lunar months after Hanukkah in 7 BC.

16 Tevet (conjunction)

2 BC

Winter

13 Shevat (full moon - occultation)

11 Adar I (conjunction)

Purim (conjunction)

Purim in 2 BC was possibly 49 full lunar months after Purim in 7 BC.

Spring

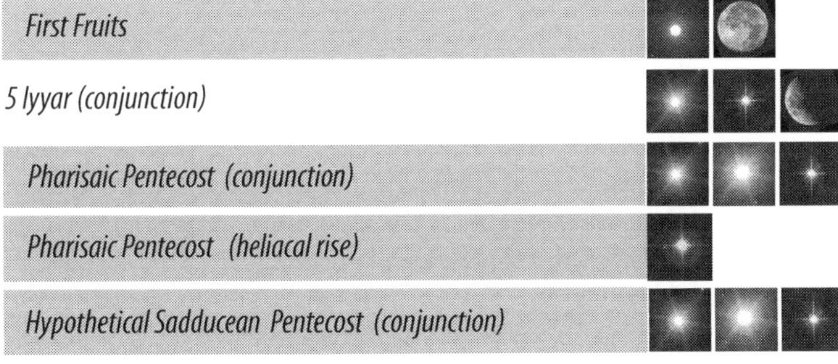

First Fruits

5 Iyyar (conjunction)

Pharisaic Pentecost (conjunction)

Pharisaic Pentecost (heliacal rise)

Summer

Hypothetical Sadducean Pentecost (conjunction)

*The Pentecost dates made pairs of **7 "sevens" of literal weeks (49 days)**.*
*This is followed by other celestial events **62 weeks** after the Pentecost dates.*

The Star *15 Sivan (conjunction in Ari at the full moon)*

The event on the 15th of Sivan (June 17th 2 BC) would have in all likelihood inspired the wise men to say that they had seen "His star." One might even call this a spectacular event.

Sixty-two weeks *after the Pharisaic and Sadducean dates for Pentecost in 3 BC one arrives at other messianic conjunctions.*

Fall

14 Tishrei (conjunction - full moon)
*This was in the **70th week** after another event in 3 BC.*

Winter

The Star of Bethlehem *(Tzedek - 1st stationary point)*

1 BC

January: A total eclipse of the moon preceeding Herod's death

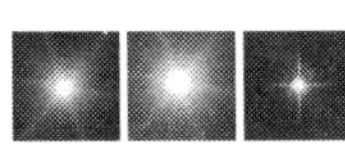

Sixty-two weeks *after the Pharisaic and Sadducean dates for Pentecost in 2 BC one arrives at other messianic stellar events.*

The Calendar in 3 BC

The Jewish calendar used in this book assumes that a second month of Adar was added in the spring of 7 BC, 4 BC and 2 BC.

(Julian dates in the evening - beginning of night)					
1	Nisan	New Moon	March	17	Sun
14	Nisan	Passover	March	30	Sat
1	Iyyar	New Moon	April	16	Tue
1	Sivan	New Moon	May	15	Wed
6	Sivan	Pentecost	May	20	Mon
1	Tammuz	New Moon	June	14	Fri
1	Av	New Moon	July	13	Sat
1	Elul	New Moon	Aug	12	Mon
1	Tishri	New Moon Trumpets	Sept	11	Wed
10	Tishri	Yom Kippur	Sept	20	Fri*
15	Tishri	Tabernacles	Sept	25	Wed
22	Tishri	Tabernacles (Great Day)	Oct	2	Wed
1	Heshvan	New Moon	Oct	11	Fri
1	Kislev	New Moon	Nov	10	Sun
25	Kislev	Hanukkah	Dec	4	Wed
1	Tevet	New Moon	Dec	9	Mon

** Yom Kippur was possibly moved to the day after the Sabbath (Sept. 21st) instead of falling on the Sabbath, Friday Sept. 20th.*

3 BC

Part 9: Events in the Heavens – 1

Spring 3 BC

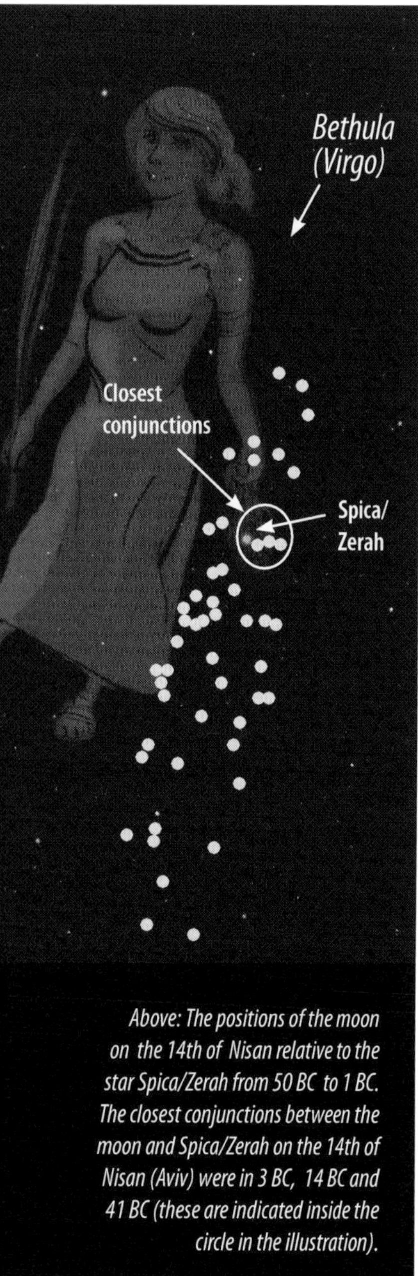

Above: The positions of the moon on the 14th of Nisan relative to the star Spica/Zerah from 50 BC to 1 BC. The closest conjunctions between the moon and Spica/Zerah on the 14th of Nisan (Aviv) were in 3 BC, 14 BC and 41 BC (these are indicated inside the circle in the illustration).

Passover: The Promised Seed

14th Aviv - March 30th

The star named Spica or Zerah (the seed), in the constellation of Virgo, rose with the nearly full moon on the 14th of Nisan in 3 BC.[1] The star traveled with the moon during the whole night of the 14th of Nisan. It should be remembered that the *seed* of the woman in Genesis 3:15 was to crush the serpent's head. We also know that it is through Abraham's *seed* (zerah) that all the nations are to be blessed (Genesis 12:1-3).

This conjunction of Spica/Zerah with the moon would not have been visible to most people. The nearly full moon completely obscures the light of a first magnitude star like Spica/Zerah during a close conjunction. The star may have been briefly visible at the beginning of the evening before the lunar brightness became overpowering, but even that is doubtful. It is necessary to place one's figure in front of the moon to see a star like Spica/Zerah when the moon is nearly full. By making this simple gesture, it is possible to see a first magnitude star, like Spica/Zerah, near the mostly illuminated lunar surface.[2] Most people would have simply gone to bed without having noticed the conjunction.[3]

In the period before the birth of Jesus, we do not know if most Jews thought of the constellation of Bethula (the virgin) in the context of the prophecy of the woman in Genesis. It is possible that some did think in this way concerning the seed of the woman, but it is a supposition. Was Abraham's seed ever linked to Spica/Zerah in the minds of the Jews during the 1st century BC? Again we do not know. A few decades after Jesus' life, death and resurrection, Matthew makes a definite link between Isaiah's prophecy and the birth of the Messiah, just two verses before his account concerning the wise men. He writes: "behold, the virgin shall be with child and shall bear a son, and they shall call his name Immanuel," which translated means, "God with us" (Mt. 1:22-23). Before the event, did anyone understand that a real virgin would have a son who would become the Messiah? It would appear that few people, if any, would have specifically been expecting a virgin birth. Whether anybody made all the connections or not, the conjunction happened at Passover. Spica/Zerah, as the seed of the woman, was being highlighted by the Passover moon on the evening of March 30th in 3 BC. However, Spica/Zerah was not the star of Bethlehem.

If anyone was making calculations about the 70 "sevens" of years in Daniel's prophecy, he may have seen the links between the seed of the woman and the conjunction almost immediately. As we saw, according to one calculation, the end date for the 62 "sevens" of years was in the year 3/2 BC. A "messianic" conjunction

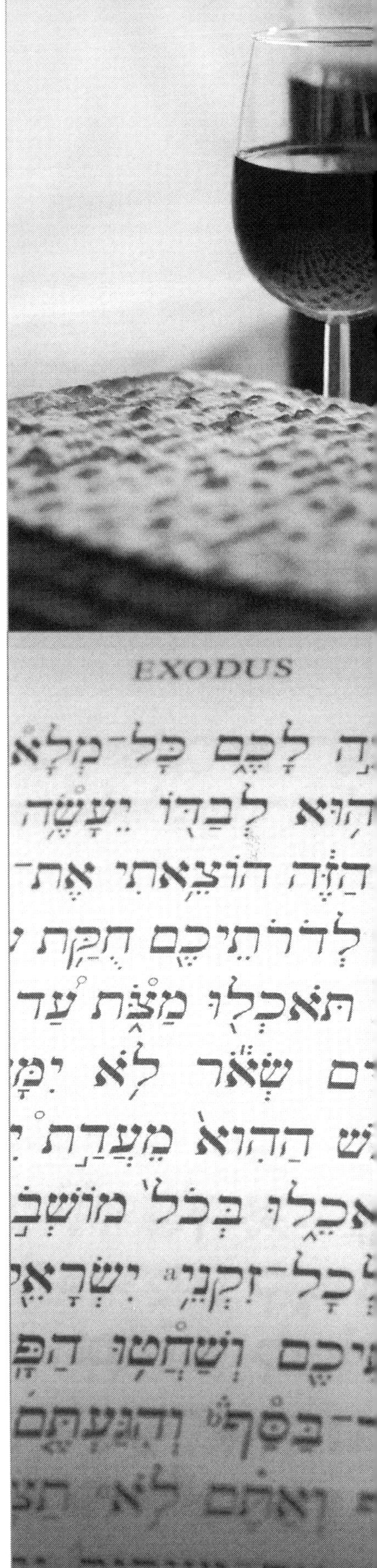

on a major Jewish appointed time could have immediately attracted attention for anyone who had made the correct calculations.

At the time of Christ Spica/Zerah did sometimes rise and travel with the moon on the 14th of Nisan, however, close conjunctions were rare. In the 50 years previous to 3 BC, there were several conjunctions between Spica and the moon. However, the 3 BC conjunction was the closest one on the 14th of Nisan during the whole period. The moon often comes close to Spica even in our day. Sometimes it actually passes in front of the star producing an occultation. However, conjunctions and occultations of Spica on the 14th of Nisan are extremely rare. Today, such conjunctions are even rarer still.[4] The early Church connected Jesus' conception with Passover. This was a heavenly sign that may have linked the Passover in 3 BC with something concerning the Messiah.

Please note:

In some modern messianic Jewish circles, some Bible teachers draw very strong lines between Passover, the Feast of Unleavened Bread and the First Fruits Offering. There are significant differences between each event. However, it would appear that Matthew, Mark and Luke sometimes thought in more general terms by essentially using the terms "Passover" and the "Feast of Unleavened Bread" interchangeably. *"Now the Feast of Unleavened Bread, which is called the Passover, was approaching"* (See Luke 22:1, as well as, Matthew 26:17 and Mark 14:12). It was not necessary to have a specific celestial event for every aspect of the sacrifice of Passover, the Feast of Unleavened Bread and the First Fruits Offering in order to say that God had done something linked to these Jewish appointed times. The entire period was generally referred to, at least by Matthew, Mark and Luke, as the Passover or the Feast of Unleavened Bread.[5]

Spring 3 BC

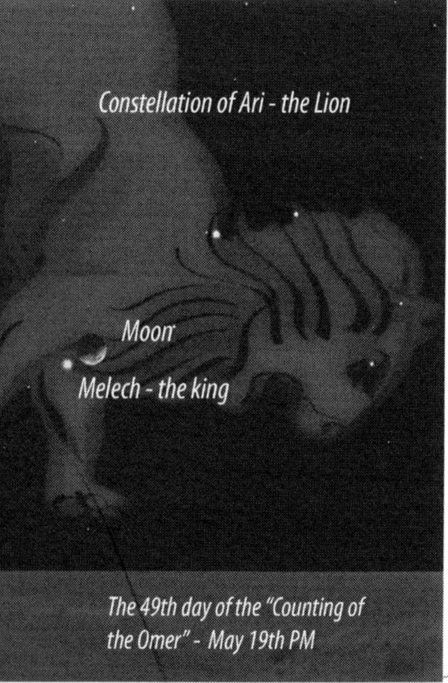

The 49th day of the "Counting of the Omer" - May 19th PM

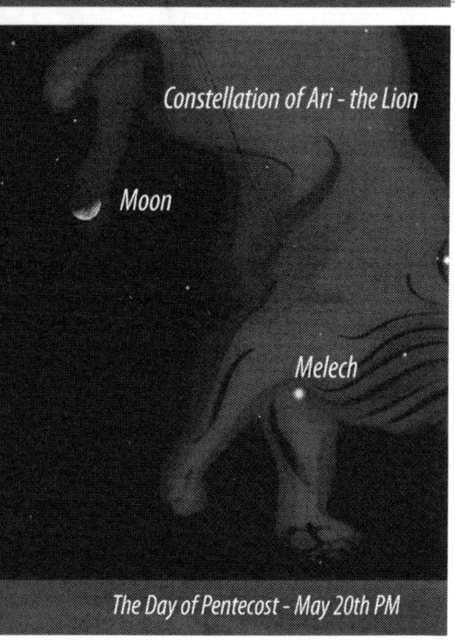

The Day of Pentecost - May 20th PM

Pentecost: Introducing the King

   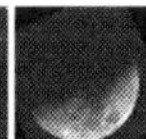

5th and 6th of Sivan - May 19th and 20th

The Feast of Unleavened Bread signaled the beginning of the barley harvest in ancient Israel (Leviticus 23:9-14). In a similar way, the Feast of Pentecost signaled the beginning of the wheat harvest (Exodus 34:22).

> *You shall also count for yourselves ... from the day when you brought in the sheaf of the wave offering ... seven complete Sabbaths. 'You shall count fifty days to the day after the seventh Sabbath; then you shall present a new grain offering to the LORD. You shall bring in from your dwelling places two loaves of bread for a wave offering ... they shall be of a fine flour, baked with leaven as first fruits to the LORD. (Leviticus 23:15-17)*

The Pharisaic date of Pentecost was established by counting seven weeks from the day of the First Fruits sheaf offering (a wave offering of the first harvest of barley), on the 16th of Nisan. Pentecost is called "Shavuot" in Hebrew, which means "weeks." This referred to the seven weeks between the 16th of Nisan and the Pentecost festival. One counts the days to the 49th day, exactly seven weeks after the First Fruits Offering. The next day, the 50th day, is the Pentecost festival. The terminology used for counting the days between the sheaf offering, and Pentecost was called "Counting of the Omer," referring to the counting of a measure of grain (an omer) during the harvest. The Israelites brought loaves of wheat bread as an offering at Pentecost.

On the 5th of Sivan in 3 BC, (the 49th day of the count or the end of the seventh week), the moon was in very close conjunction with the star Melech (the king). This was the first of a series of conjunctions involving the star Melech in 3/2 BC. Melech is in Ari (Leo), the constellation of the lion, which has been historically identified with the tribe of Judah. The Shiloh, the one who has the right to the scepter, in Genesis 49:5-6, could be evoked concerning the events involving Ari and Melech. From time to time, the moon could have been be in conjunction with Melech on the 49th day of the count or on the day of Pentecost. In this case at the end of the evening on May 19th, the two were only separated by about one third of a lunar diameter (0°09'), which would be exceedingly rare exactly on this particular date. Depending on several factors the moon can be placed up to about 11 lunar diameters either above or below Melech on the 5th and 6th of Sivan (up to about 5°30' in either direction). There are significant longitudinal variations as well (See Table 9.1 on the next page). Conjunctions like this one do not happen often on the 5th or 6th of Sivan.

This event in 3 BC involving the moon on the 49th day of counting the omer would have become significant as other events related to the Messiah continued to take place. The wise men could have thought of Psalm 89:34-37 and Psalm 72:5-7ff concerning the promised messianic king.

> *I will not lie to David. His descendants shall endure forever And his throne as the sun before Me. It shall be established forever like the moon, and the witness in the sky is faithful." (Psalm 89:34-37)*

5th of Sivan, May 20th - End of the Night

About eight hours after the conjunction between the moon and the star Melech, another event took place. Just before dawn on the 49th day of the Counting the Omer, the two planets Kochav Chammah and Shabbatei, which one might call the "Sun star" and the "Sabbath star," were in conjunction near the eastern horizon. Even though they were relatively bright, they were not visible because of the solar glare. However, the Babylonians calculated the entire cycle of the planets including their visible and non-visible phases. This was necessary in order to establish the visibility dates in advance. In addition, those who established horoscopes needed to know the positions of the planets relative to the zodiac whether they were visible or not.[7] Someone among the Magi may have been aware that the two planets were in conjunction, even if they were not visible. Within about six days, Shabbatei became visible in the morning sky.

It would seem that the biblical command to count seven Sabbaths (in this case seven complete weeks) after the First Fruits Offering was being underlined because the word Shabbatei means "sabbatical" or "rest" and is related to the word Sabbath. Such a combination of two conjunctions on exactly the 49th day of the seven weeks could have almost certainly attracted the attention of any Jewish or Jewish influenced Magi. Shabbatei was present near this stellar position and time only once every 29-30 years. The conjunction of Kochav Chammah with Shabbatei on exactly the 49th day of the Counting of the Omer would have been exceedingly rare. In the evening and morning conjunctions the biblical "appointed times" seem to be highlighted.[8] Only a limited number of professionals with technical knowledge could have been aware of the second event.

Date	Visual Separation Moon / Melech
2 BC	20°11′
3 BC	0°09′
4 BC	9°07′
5 BC	13°27′
6 BC	4°03′
7 BC	15°56′
8 BC	3°56′
9 BC	7°04′
10 BC	24°50′
11 BC	5°34′
12 BC	5°10′
13 BC	17°26′
14 BC	8°35′
15 BC	7°37′
16 BC	5°56′
17 BC	9°13′
18 BC	29°41′
19 BC	4°27′
20 BC	13°08′
21 BC	8°15′
22 BC	9°25′
23 BC	2°26′
24 BC	8°08′
25 BC	9°55′
26 BC	16°27′
27 BC	3°30
28 BC	12°29′
29 BC	20°25′
30 BC	1°19′
31 BC	8°05′

Table 9.1 As indicated previously, there are many variables in establishing the Hebrew dates. The dates given above are hypothetical. The actual dates varied according to the dates of Passover.[9] The table shows the relative distances from the moon to Melech (Regulus) on the 49th day of the Pharisaic "Counting of the Omer" at about 9:00 PM. One lunar diameter is about half a degree or 30 minutes of arc (0°30′).[9]

You shall bring in from your dwelling places two loaves of bread for a wave offering ...

(Leviticus 23:17)

Pentecost (Shavuot) 3 BC : Part 2

The events surrounding Pentecost did not cease on May 19th / 20th. The Sadducees also had their own method for calculating the date of Pentecost. This would have also been well known to Jews in Babylonia. Both the Pharisees and the Sadducees observed a Sabbath day on the day after Passover, at the beginning of the Feast of Unleavened Bread (Leviticus 23:4-8). This was always on the 15th of Nisan no matter on which day of the week it happened to fall. Sometimes the 15th of Nisan happened on the actual Sabbath day as indicated on page 116.

However, instead of doing the First Fruits Offering on the 16th of Nisan, like the Pharisees, the Sadducees were in favor of doing the offering on the day after the regular weekly Sabbath, which took place during the Feast of Unleavened Bread (See pages 116-117 above). Sometimes this date fell on the same day as the Pharisaic First Fruits Offering; often it did not. It all depended on the calendar, the moon and the date of Passover. To establish the date of Pentecost, the Sadducees counted to the day after the seventh weekly Sabbath following the sheaf offering (49 days + one). The tables below give a precise idea of how the dates would have fallen in 3 BC for both the Pharisaic and the Sadducean interpretations.

For many generations before the 1st century BC, the Sadducean way may have been observed by all the Israelites. However, by the 1st century BC, the Sadducees had to submit to the Pharisaic ideas concerning the sheaf offering and the dates of Pentecost. Even if the Sadducees held the high priesthood, the Pharisees were much more numerous than the Sadducees. The Pharisaic party held the actual power concerning the calendar and the temple services. The Sadducees were bound by an oath to follow the Pharisaic line of thought concerning the festivals and ceremonies. One can be sure that the actual sheaf offering and Pentecost happened at the Pharisaic dates.[10]

3 BC The Probable Dates for : *Passover, Feast of Unleavened Bread / Sheaf Offering*

March 30/31	March 31 / April 1	April 1/2	April 2/3	April 3/4	April 4	April 5/6	April 6/7
Sat/Sun	Sun/Mon	Mon/Tue	Tue/Wed	Wed/Thu	Thu/Friday	Fri/Sat	Sat/Sun
14 Nisan	15 Nisan	16 Nisan	17 Nisan	18 Nisan	19 Nisan	20 Nisan	21 Nisan
Passover	Day of Rest (Leviticus 23:7)	Pharisaic Sheaf Offering				1st Weekly Sabbath	Sadducean Sheaf Offering

Why Does Any of This Matter?

Shabbatei should have been visible in the eastern sky on the morning of May 26th in 3 BC. It was the day of the planet's heliacal rising. Again, Shabbatei is associated with the word Sabbath. Pentecost is the feast of "weeks" which was established by seven "Sabbaths." It is incredibly rare for Shabbatei to become visible in the east on the day of the Pharisaic or the hypothetical Sadducean Pentecost. This can happen only very rarely, possibly once every 29 or 30 years. Even then, the date of the rising would not necessarily match the festival dates. *This 3 BC event was a sign concerning the Sabbath on the date of the Sadducean Pentecost. The timing of the event was extremely important. It was the day after the seventh Sabbath after Passover.*

Two or possibly three celestial events underlining the Sabbath, as outlined above, could have attracted the attention of any Jewish or Jewish influenced Magi. Pentecost is the feast of weeks of seven days each. Exactly seven weeks are involved in the counting. Daniel's prophecy of 70 sevens involves a period of 7 "sevens," 62 "sevens," and one "seven." Each year Pentecost involves counting seven weeks (seven Sabbaths), but 3 BC was different because of the presence of the "Sabbath" star/planet, Shabbatei. The Magi could have thought, "Well, this was interesting, but does it mean anything? They may have responded by saying, "Perhaps, it is certainly very rare." At this point it may have been too early to see a connection with Daniel's prophecy of 70 "sevens," but perhaps not.

There were heavenly events linked to *both* the Pharisaic and Sadducean dates for the end of the Omer Count and the day of Pentecost in 3 BC. These astronomical signs could not have definitively established the "correct date" for the First Fruits Offering or Pentecost (either the Pharisaic or Sadducean). God apparently used both dates to communicate a multi-layered message.

All of this was also important because of something which happened about three weeks after the dates of the Pharisaic and Sadducean Pentecosts.

Spring 3 BC

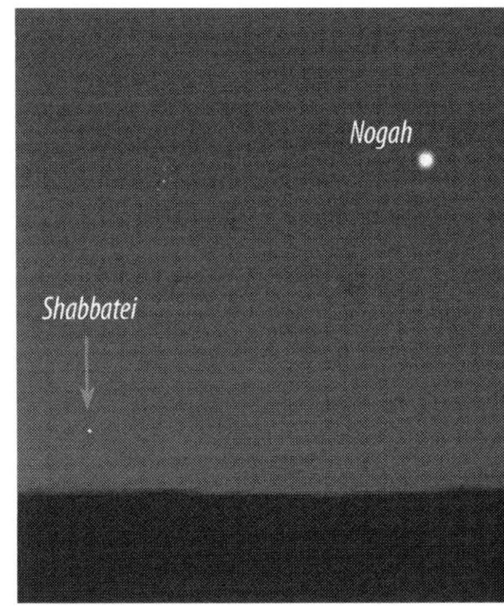

3 BC The Probable Dates for: *The 49th Day of Counting the Omer and Pentecost (Shavuot)*

May 19/20	May 20/21	May 21/22	May 22/23	May 23/24	May 24/25	May 25/26
Sun/Mon	Mon/Tue	Tue/Wed	Wed/Thu	Thu/Fri	Fri/Sat	Sat/Sun
5 Sivan	6 Sivan	7 Sivan	8 Sivan	9 Sivan	10 Sivan	11 Sivan
Pharisaic 49th Day of the Counting the Omer	Pharisaic Pentecost				Sadducean 7th Sabbath 49th Day of the Counting of the Omer	Sadducean Pentecost

All the Jewish dates above start in the evening.

Summer 3 BC

"You are to know and discern that from the issuing of a decree to restore and rebuild Jerusalem until Messiah the Prince there will be seven "sevens" and sixty-two "sevens"; it will be built again, with plaza and moat, even in times of distress. (Daniel 9:25)

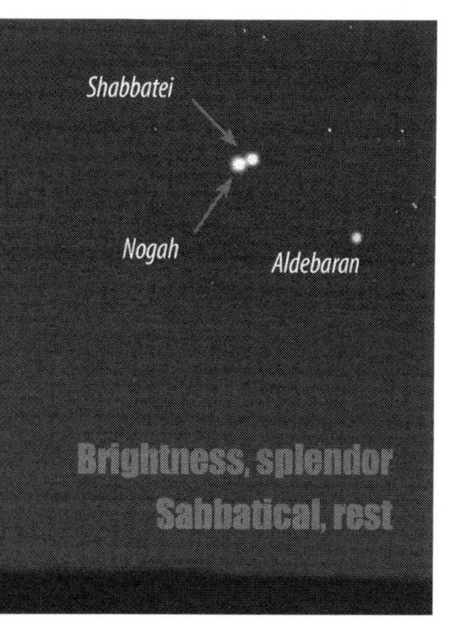

A Bright Sabbath

28th to 30th of Sivan / June 12th - 14th

On the morning of June 13th 3 BC Shabbatei and Nogah (the Sabbath planet and the "bright planet") met in the eastern sky after approaching each other for several weeks. The two planets were actually in conjunction over a period of three days. On June 12th they were relatively close (0°40'), but on the 13th they were even closer still at 0°23,' which is about 2/3 of a lunar diameter. The next morning, on the 14th, as conjunction ended, the separation increased to 1°24.' The closest point of the conjunction was after sundown on June 12th, but this was below the horizon (six hours before becoming visible on the 13th AM). The relative closeness continued through the daylight hours on the 13th (1°05 at sundown).

During the previous 100 years, Nogah had been in about 50 conjunctions of less than 1° with Shabbatei. Most of those conjunctions were difficult or impossible to see because of the solar glare or their timing. The second day of the conjunction, on June 13th 3 BC, was the closest and brightest visible conjunction of the two planets in the previous 56 years. It was also the closest and brightest visible conjunction of Shabbatei and Nogah that the wise men had probably ever seen. Nogah had a magnitude of -4.0 and Shabbatei had a magnitude 0.1.

The day of June 12th / 13th was 73 days after the Pharisaic First Fruits Offering. The number 73 is a key to the planetary cycle of Nogah (Venus). From one heliacal rising of Nogah, to the next one, there are 584 days. (8 X 73 = 584). Seventy three is also one fifth of a solar year (5 X 73 = 365). Numbers like this may have attracted the attention of the Magi.[11]

Having seen how closely incidents concerning the planet Shabbatei had been aligned with Pentecost, the Magi may have also counted the days to the Shabbatei / Nogah conjunction. June 13th in the evening was also the *69th day* from the date of the hypothetical Sadducean First Fruits Offering (the day after the 1st weekly Sabbath of the Feast of Unleavened Bread). It could have appeared that the *69 days* were symbolic of the *69 "sevens" (7 + 62 "sevens")* in Daniel's prophecy, in which 69 "sevens" were linked with the Messiah's appearing.

As we shall see in detail later, there was much more to these events in the spring of 3 BC than one might even dream. The 3 BC Nogah / Shabbatei conjunction was *exactly 23 years <u>after</u> the 26 BC event concerning Melech, Tzedek, Shabbatei and Nogah* (described earlier on page 146). The 3 BC event was also *almost exactly one year <u>before</u>* an event which the Magi probably later referred to as the "star of the Messiah." The following day, the 70th day, was also 70 weeks before another messianic stellar event of some importance.

Righteousness at the New Moon

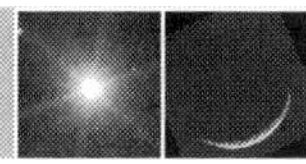

Blow the trumpet at the new moon,
At the full moon, on our feast day.
(Ps. 81:3)

1st Tammuz - June 14th

On the evening of the 14th of June, Tzedek, the "star" of righteousness, was in conjunction with the new moon. This was about three weeks after the Pharisaic and Sadducean Pentecost, and just about 12 hours after the end of the conjunction of Nogah and Shabbatei, the previous night. The name Tzedek evokes the "righteous one," the Messiah. The day of the new moon was not a day of rest, but trumpets were blown and sacrifices were offered at the beginning of each new month.

> *In the day of your gladness and in your appointed feasts, and on the first days of your months, you shall blow the trumpets over your burnt offerings, and over the sacrifices of your peace offerings; and they shall be as a reminder of you before your God. I am the Lord your God." (Numbers 10:10)*

> *'Then at the beginning of each of your months you shall present a burnt offering to the LORD: two bulls and one ram, seven male lambs one year old without defect; and three-tenths of an ephah of fine flour mixed with oil for a grain offering, ... a burnt offering of a soothing aroma, an offering by fire ... And one male goat for a sin offering to the Lord ... (Numbers 28:11-15)*

Tzedek can only possibly be in a conjunction with the new moon on only one day each year. However, the distance between the two can vary considerably. In June 3 BC, Tzedek and the moon were visually close together, separated by about 1°20' at the end of the evening. At Passover, the moon had highlighted the "seed." At Pentecost, the kingship and "Sabbaths" were in the spotlight through the conjunctions of the moon with Melech and the incidents involving Shabbatei. After that a significant conjunction signaled a "bright Sabbath." *Finally the planet of "righteousness" was highlighted at the beginning of the weekly Sabbath, the 70th day following the beginning of the Sadducean "Counting of the Omer."*

69 Days (7 + 62) : There were 69 days from the Sadducean date of the First Fruits Offering in 3 BC to the end of the major conjunction of Nogah and Shabbatei in June 3 BC.

On the 70th day (June 14/15th), Tzedek was in conjunction with the new moon in the evening sky. These events could have been understood by the Magi as being symbolic of the 70 "sevens" in Daniel's prophecy. Much more was to follow. We shall see later that a period of 70 weeks (490 days) was also directly linked to this June 14th date.[12]

70 Days

More about the 70 "Sevens"

7 Weeks

7 weeks (49 days) :
Pharisaic First Fruits Offering and Counting of the Omer / Pentecost:
(See pages 156-157).

A conjunction of Melech and the moon and a conjunction of the Sabbath star, Shabbatei, with Kochav Chammah took place on the 49th day of the "counting of the omer." Both events were rare. One underlines kingship, the other underlines the "7 Sabbaths." Nothing unique happened on the actual day of Pentecost.

7 weeks (49 days) :
Sadducean First Fruits Offering and Counting of the Omer / Pentecost:
There were seven Sabbaths from the hypothetical Sadducean First Fruits Offering date to the Sadducean date for Pentecost (See pages 158-159).

The heliacal rising of Shabbatei took place at the time of Pentecost. This event underlines the Sabbath, and particularly "7 Sabbaths." It could have been relatively easy to make the connection with 7 "sevens" of Daniel's prophecy. Having made the connections with literal weeks it is easy to start making other calculations.

It is difficult to fathom the 70 "sevens" of days, weeks, months and years linked to dates and events! Some "sevens" are repeated. Some overlap.

62 Weeks

Adding 62 weeks (434 days) directly after the dates of the Pharisaic Pentecost and the hypothetical Sadducean date in 3 BC leads one to other messianic stellar events in July and August of 2 BC. (See page 196).

By adding 62 weeks (434 days) to the date of the First Fruits Offering in 3 BC (April 1/2 for the Pharisees or April 5/6 for the Sadducees) one arrives at the Pentecost dates for both groups in for the year 2 BC.

First Fruits 3 BC ⟷ *62 weeks (434 days)* ⟷ *Pentecost 2 BC*

The Star 2 BC

The 62 weeks above ends with Pentecost in 2 BC. The incident which the Magi would have probably referred to as "the Star of the Messiah," was 9 days after the Pharisaic date of Pentecost in 2 BC and within three days of the Sadducean date. Pentecost seems to point to the "star." One could think that the "star" event happened during a symbolic "70th week." This will be explored further in the coming chapters.

Calculating the 70 "Sevens"

It is practically impossible to say exactly when or how the Magi may have understood the significance of the events in the heavens in relation to the 70 "sevens." They were almost certainly not expecting any type of heavenly manifestation concerning the Messiah. However, if they, or someone in their entourage, had done the calculations they would have known that a possible date for the Messiah's appearing was in the Jewish year beginning in the spring of 3 BC.

There seem to be symbolic and literal aspects of the fulfillements of the 70 "sevens."

Some of the heavenly events indicated involve hypothetical Sadducean dates. The Magi may have had links with Jewish aristocratic families in Babylonia. Daniel himself was from such a family. This could have explained why they would have been more aware of, and perhaps even sympathetic towards, the Sadducean dates, because the Sadducees were part of the Jewish aristocracy. Many of the Babylonian Jews saw themselves as being from superior families who had good bloodlines (see pages 52-55). It is certain that the Magi were wealthy, or at least they had access to great wealth. Their gifts and their ability to travel prove this. According to Josephus, Herod's earliest appointment for the high priesthood was a Sadducean Jew from Babylonia who was personally known to the king.

In 605 BC:
Nebuchadnezzar king of Babylon, ordered Ashpenaz, the chief of his officials, to bring in some of the sons of Israel, including some of the royal family and of the nobles, youths in whom was no defect, who were good-looking, showing intelligence in every branch of wisdom, endowed with understanding and discerning knowledge, and who had ability for serving in the king's court; and he ordered him to teach them the literature and language of the Chaldeans. (Daniel 1:3-4)

Witnessing or knowing the date of Shabbatei's heliacal rising through calculation could have been very interesting to the Magi. That would have certainly underlined the 7 "sevens" of weeks (49 days). This may have stimulated other thoughts concerning the 62 "sevens," etc. Later the wise men could have seen the link with the 70 days (10 weeks / 10 Sabbaths) and Tzedek's conjunction with the new moon on the 1st of Tammuz. At some point, someone would have probably understood that there were 62 weeks from the date of the First Fruits Offering in 3 BC until Pentecost in 2 BC. Later there were also 62 weeks from Pentecost in 3 BC to other messianic stellar events in 2 BC. The calculations concerning the events would not have been beyond the ability of the Magi. Symbolic and literal aspects of the fulfillments of the 70 "sevens" took place.

There was much more, even to the point of being bewildering. Focused around Jesus' birth and his life there were 70 symbolic days, one continuous series of 70 weeks, four series of 7 weeks (49 days), six series of 62 weeks (434 days each), a series of 7 "sevens" of months (49 months), a series of 62 "sevens" of months (434 months) and finally 70 "sevens" of years (divided into 7 X 7 years, 62 X 7 years and one set of 7 years). *The entire set of events, dates and figures is mysterious, surprising, dazzling, unexpected and confounding. Some "sevens" are repeated, others overlap.* We will continue to explore this subject, but there are many other events not necessarily related to Daniel's prophecy of 70 "sevens" which also had messianic content.

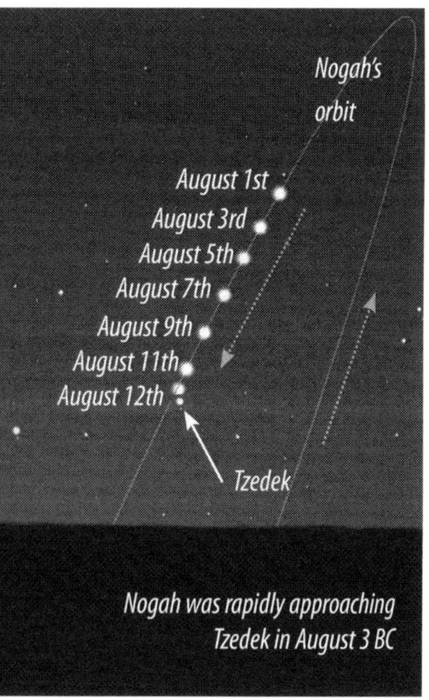

Nogah was rapidly approaching Tzedek in August 3 BC

Within 10 days of meeting the moon in the evening sky on the Sabbath of the 1st of Tammuz Tzedek passed into the solar glare behind the sun. It emirged again from the solar glare in late July 3 BC. Within two weeks it had a rendezvous with Nogah in the morning sky.

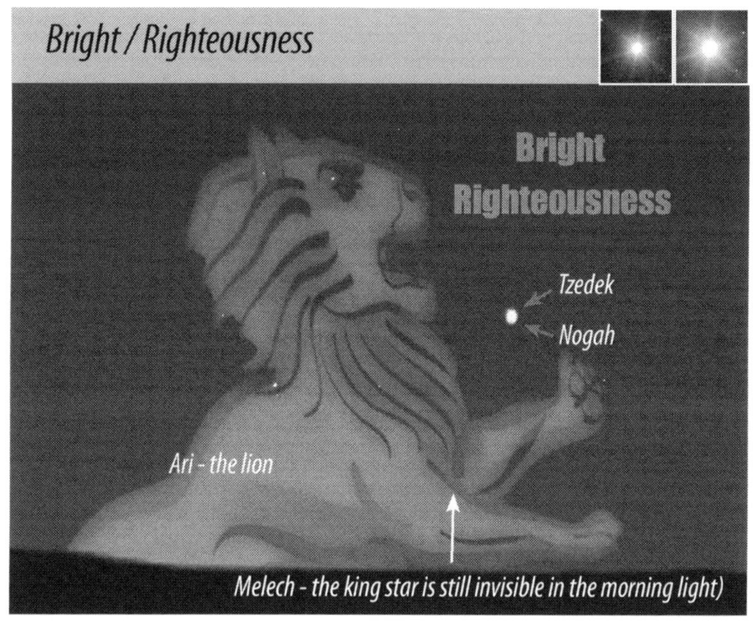

Melech - the king star is still invisible in the morning light)

30th Av - August 12th

Two weeks after meeting the moon in the evening sky, Tzedek passed into the solar glare behind the sun possibly on the day of the full moon. In the morning sky in late July 3 BC, Tzedek emerged again from the solar glare. Within two weeks, it had a rendezvous with Nogah, two months after the Shabbatei / Nogah conjunction.

The conjunction between Tzedek and Nogah on August 12th was remarkable, but it would not have been totally unknown to astronomers in Mesopotamia or Iran or elsewhere. About every two years, Nogah and Tzedek were fairly near each other. They were often involved in conjunctions of one or two degrees of separation. However, they did not always meet in the constellation of Ari (Leo). Nogah passes through the lion constellation once each year, but Tzedek only passes through the lion once every 12 years (11.83 years). The two planets can only possibly meet in Leo about once every 24 years. In the previous 213 years, they were only visible together in Leo in 26 BC, 133 BC, 157 BC and 216 BC. Because of their wide separation, neither the 133 BC, nor the 157 BC conjunctions, were remarkable. However, both the 26 BC and 3 BC conjunctions were very close. As we have seen the 26 BC conjunction was visually remarkable.

At their closest approach in August 3 BC, the distance separating the two planets was only about 0°10' of arc (about one third of the diameter of the moon). It was still possible to distinguish the two planets one from the other, but the conjunction was very close. Besides the 26 BC conjunction, this was the closest visible conjunction of Tzedek and Nogah in Leo for at least 213 years.[13] Outside the exceptional events in 26 BC and 3 BC, no one had seen significant conjunctions between

Tzedek and Nogah in Ari (Leo) for at least 213 years. Both Tzedek and Nogah are bright objects. Again Nogah means brilliance, brightness and splendor. Tzedek means righteousness. That made a combination of "bright righteousness" in the constellation of the lion. Some notes of a messianic composition might be heard in this combination, but other notes would soon sound.

Summer 3 BC

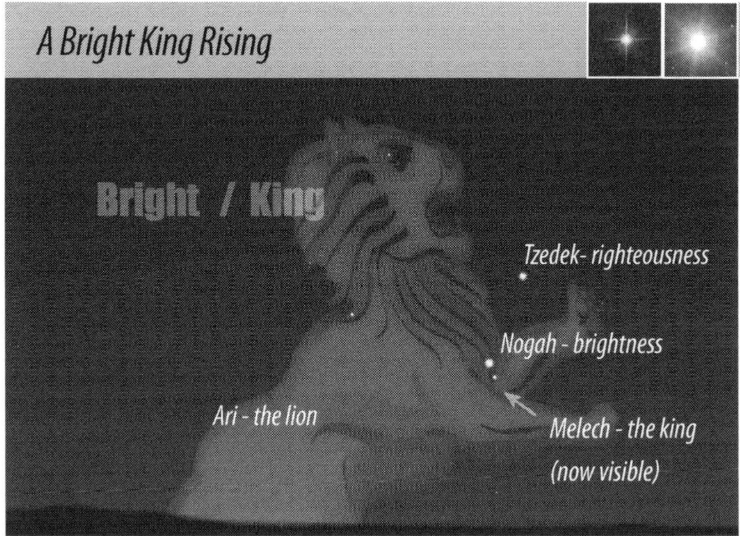

5th Elul - August 17th

Five days after Tzedek's close conjunction with Nogah, the very bright star / planet Nogah moved into conjunction with Melech, "the king." The two were separated by about 0°47' of arc (visually a bit over one and one-half lunar diameters). Melech had just become visible again a few days previously after having been lost in the solar glare since early July. Nogah was in a position to encounter Melech on or near its heliacal rising only once every eight years. This is a cyclical phenomenon, which would have been known to the Babylonians and Zoroastrians. Even so, this event would have underlined the "king" star. However, it may not have been so important for the Magi.

A bright, king of righteousness in the lion

All of this was in Ari, the constellation of the lion, identified with the tribe of Judah. At this point, the nuances were becoming fairly obvious: Tzedek = righteousness; Nogah = brightness, brilliance, splendor; Melech = king.

> *The scepter shall not depart from Judah, nor the ruler's staff from between his feet, until the Shiloh comes, and to him shall be the obedience of the peoples.*
> *Genesis 49:10 (NASB)*

Autumn 3 BC

The words Melech and Tzedek form the roots of the word Melchizedek which means "my king is righteous." Melech and Tzedek together without the possessive "my" simply evokes the idea: "King of Righteousness."

A Group of Three

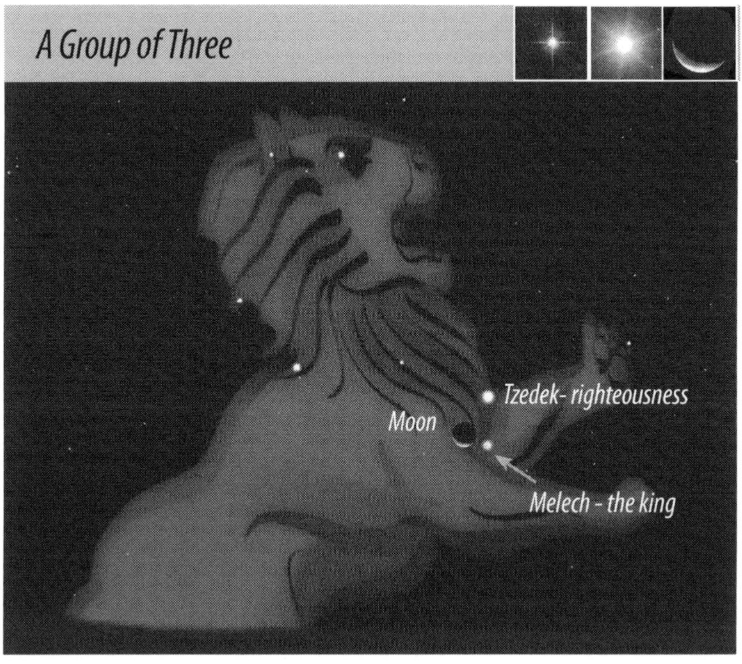

25th Elul - September 6th

Three weeks after the conjunction of Melech with Nogah, the star Melech, the "king," was in a very close conjunction with the moon as they both rise above the horizon early in the morning. At the closest point, the visual distance between the two was only about 20' of arc which is equivalent to about two-thirds of one lunar diameter. Tzedek was then only 1°35' away from Melech (about three lunar diameters away). In the coming months, the moon would play a greater role in the chain of events announcing the Messiah.

Since most believers do not immediately think of David's line or the promised Messiah when we look at the moon, we do not see the implications of the moon having been placed beside Melech and Tzedek; However, the texts of Psalm 89:35-37 and Ps. 72:5-7ff are clear. "The throne of the Messiah will endure forever like the moon, the witness in the sky (the moon) is faithful to testify to it."

In August and September many heavenly bodies moved. The constellation Ari (the lion) became increasingly visible in the morning sky. Nogah, the brightest planet, moved toward the horizon, and Tzedek moved nearer to Melech in the lion. By September 11th, the stage was set for a series of important conjunctions in the constellation of the lion.

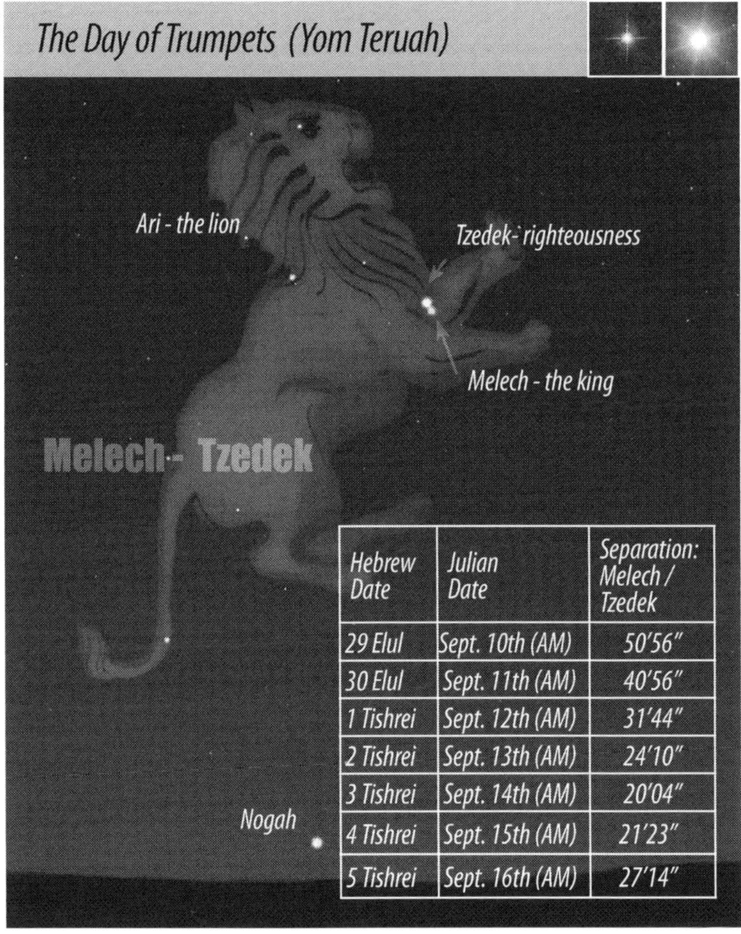

Hebrew Date	Julian Date	Separation: Melech / Tzedek
29 Elul	Sept. 10th (AM)	50'56"
30 Elul	Sept. 11th (AM)	40'56"
1 Tishrei	Sept. 12th (AM)	31'44"
2 Tishrei	Sept. 13th (AM)	24'10"
3 Tishrei	Sept. 14th (AM)	20'04"
4 Tishrei	Sept. 15th (AM)	21'23"
5 Tishrei	Sept. 16th (AM)	27'14"

On the evening of September 11th the new crescent moon should have been sighted in the west signaling the beginning of the month of Tishrei. The next morning (still the same Hebrew day) a significant conjunction took place in the eastern sky.

'In the seventh month, on the first day of the month, you shall have a Sabbath - rest, a memorial of blowing of trumpets (shofars), a holy convocation. 'You shall do no daily work on it; and you shall offer an offering made by fire to the LORD.'" (Leviticus 23:24-25 NKJV)

"Melchizedek" in the lion

1st Tishrei - September 11th / 12th

This event is the one described in the opening story of *The Lion Led the Way.* The 1st day of Tishrei was the Day of Trumpets (shofars), which was celebrated for two days. It is better known today as Rosh Hashanah. In ancient Israel and even today, the Jews blow trumpets, remembering the great trumpet blast at Sinai (Exodus 19) and also the future day of judgment. In 3 BC just six days after the previous conjunction, Melech and Tzedek came together as "Melech - Tzedek" on the Day of Trumpets. The two names make up the roots of the word Melchizedek which has the meaning "My king is righteous." Melchizedek was a messianic figure in the Bible. This conjunction in the constellation of the lion evokes Genesis 49:5-6, Psalm 110 as well as Jeremiah 23:1-6 and 33:14-17. The minimum visual separation between Melech and Tzedek was about 20' of arc which is a distance equal to 2/3 of the visual diameter of the moon. In addition, the 1st of Tishrei in 3 BC was possibly also the beginning of a sabbatical year.[14] This was another major Jewish "appointed time" linked to heavenly events.

Autumn 3 BC

Without the light scattering effects of the earth's atmosphere we would see the sun, stars and planets like the image on the right, even during the "daylight hours."

God's promise to David: "His descendants shall endure forever and his throne as the sun before Me. (Psalm 89:36)

... for you who fear My name, the sun of righteousness (the Messiah) will rise with healing in its wings. (Malachi 4:2)

10th Tishrei - September 20-21st

"The tenth day of this seventh month shall be the Day of Atonement. It shall be a holy convocation for you shall afflict your souls, and offer an offering made by fire to the LORD." (Leviticus 10:27)

Yom Kippur, the Day of Atonement, the 10th day of the month of Tishrei, is the most holy and solemn day of the Hebrew religious calendar. The Jews thought it necessary to respect both the Sabbath and also the Day of Atonement. In 3 BC, the Day of Atonement fell on a Sabbath day and it could have possibly been postponed to the next day. Later, Jewish leaders insisted upon postponing the Day of Atonement if it fell on a Sabbath day. We do not know what was done in 3 BC. On both the 10-11th of Tishrei in 3 BC the star Spica/Zerah, the seed, in the constellation, Bethula, the virgin, was in close conjunction with the sun. It was probably significant that the brightest object in the heavens was in conjunction with a star having messianic significance on the holiest day of the Jewish year. Their closest approach was near sunset on Saturday (at the end of the Sabbath).

Each year the constellation of Bethula (Virgo) spends over a month hidden by the solar glare as the sun passes between the earth and the constellation. The star we now call Porrima (Gamma Virginis) is 14° west of Spica/Zerah, close to the ecliptic, which is the path of the sun. Both Spica, called SA_4 sa ABSIN by the Babylonians, and Porrima (GIR ar ša A) were "normal stars." Such stars were used by the Babylonians to measure the movements of other heavenly bodies near the path of the sun / moon. The sun advances about 1° per day in the sky along the ecliptic and it had passed Porrima about 14 days previously. According to Otto Neugebauer (1899-1990), a former leading expert concerning Babylonian astronomy and mathematics, calculated tables existed in the 1st century BC which gave the longitude of the sun from day to day.[15] Part of a Babylonian astronomer's "toolkit" was a cuneiform tablet, which had the exact positions of the sun calculated for each day in direct reference to the so called "normal stars," such as Spica/Zerah. It was not even necessary to make the calculation concerning the sun's position because the information was already available. Such a document may have been consulted almost daily. The calculations would have been done years previously. We also know that the Babylonians calculated at least some of the invisible phases of Kochav Chammah (Mercury), which also happened to be in conjunction with the sun at that time. All that one had to do in order to "see" that at least two of the objects were in conjunction was to look at the calculated tables on the appropriate cuneiform tablets. No educated guesses, hunches or special calculations would have been necessary.

In 1999, a Rutgers University professor, Michael R. Molnar, published his book, *The Legacy of the Magi,* which explores a possible explanation for the star of Bethlehem from a Western astrological point of view.[20] Professor Molnar's approach to the star of Bethlehem involves an occultation of the planet Jupiter, which would have completely been hidden from view because of the solar glare. The event happened during the middle of the day on April 17th in 6 BC. Professor Molnar quotes a Roman astrologer, who mentions astrological positions similar to the completely *invisible* occultation of Jupiter in 6 BC, as being a portent of great astrological importance. Apparently such an event would have denoted the birth of a royal leader. *By comparison simply claiming that Babylonian astronomers would have known that Spica/Zerah and possibly Kochav Chammah were in conjunction with the sun on the Day of Atonement in 3 BC seems rather minor.*

The wise men may not have understood any messianic significance to the heavenly event on the Day of Atonement in 3 BC until possibly months afterwards. As time passed, the wise men saw numerous other events, which were also taking place during the Jewish festivals in 3/2 BC. They could have eventually asked themselves the question: "What happened on the Day of Atonement?" If events with messianic significance took place on the other dates, it would have been natural to wonder, as well, about the Day of Atonement.[16] By this date, it was also possible that the wise men were already becoming fairly convinced that something was taking place concerning the Messiah. They may have already made the calculation concerning the date of the Messiah's birth based on Daniel's prophecy. By September 12th 3 BC, three messianic stellar events involving biblical feasts and appointed times had already taken place. The events involving Shabbatei and Pentecost were especially striking. Tzedek had been in conjunction with the moon on a Sabbath (the tenth Sabbath in a row since Passover - the 70th day). Someone may have made messianic connections with the Day of Trumpets and the Day of Atonement fairly quickly. Did anyone actually make the link between Spica/Zerah, the Sun, Kochav Chammah and the texts of Psalm 89:36 and Malachi 4:2 cited on the previous page? We may never know, but the star Spica/Zerah, the seed held by the woman, was in close conjunction with the sun on the Day of Atonement in 3 BC.

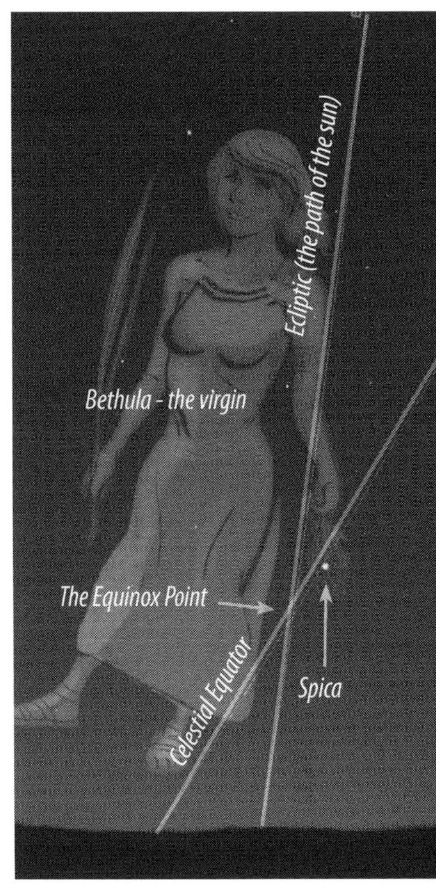

The equinox point is located in the sky where the path of the sun and the celestial equator cross each other. When the sun reaches this point in the sky the length of the day and night are equal, at the spring and autumn equinoxes. In 3 BC the star Spica/Zerah was a bit over 4° from the fall equinox point. The sun moves at about 1° per day in the heavens. Four or five days after the conjunction of the sun with Spica on the Day of Atonement was the date of the autumnal equinox.

Autumn 3 BC

The Festival of Tabernacles (Sukkot) takes its name from the temporary shelters (sukkahs) which were made of palm, myrtle and willow branches.

15th Tishrei - September 25th 3 BC

Each year the Feast of Tabernacles (Sukkot) begins on Tishrei 15 according to the Hebrew calendar, at the time of the full moon. This was exactly six months after Passover and the Feast of Unleavened Bread on the 14/15 of Nisan (Aviv).

The Festival of Tabernacles (Sukkot) takes its name from the temporary shelters (sukkahs) which were made of palm, myrtle and willow branches. These temporary shelters were made to remind the Israelites of their time in the desert during the Exodus. Water was poured out before God in abundance during this festival as the people asked the Lord for an abundance of rain during the following months. Planting was normally done in the weeks following Sukkot. However, according to Zuckerman and Blosser's study of the sabbatical years,[17] this particular year was a sabbatical year so no planting would have been done.

At first, one could think that there is nothing particularly messianic about the beginning of the feast of Tabernacles in 3 BC. However, *the beginning of the Festival of Tabernacles* happened at the same time as the autumnal equinox. At the end of the 1st century BC the equinox happened on September 25th.[18] On this day, the length of the day and the night are equal. The date was astronomically significant. The sun rose at due east and set at due west. The sun and the moon were at center stage because of the equinox. It was not often that the feast would begin specifically on the day of the equinox. This may have also attracted the attention of the Magi. Remember Psalm 89:36-37.

Early on the morning of the *last day of the Festival of Tabernacles* the "Great Day of the Feast," the moon joined Melech and Tzedek. The bright "star" Tzedek had moved slightly farther east away from Melech but the two were still relatively close together. The combination of Melech / Tzedek (the king of righteousness) along with the moon on the great day of the feast was certainly symbolically significant. The Melech / Tzedek conjunction just over three weeks earlier had

'On exactly the fifteenth day of the seventh month, when you have gathered in the crops of the land, you shall celebrate the feast of the LORD for seven days, with a rest on the first day and a rest on the eighth day.'

'Now on the first day you shall take for yourselves the foliage of beautiful trees, palm branches and boughs of leafy trees and willows of the brook, and you shall rejoice before the LORD your God for seven days.'

(Leviticus 23:39-40)

evoked the righteous king, but on the "Great Day" the addition of the moon was also significant (See again Psalm 89:36-37). At this point there have been messianic astronomical events linked to all three of the main pilgrimage festivals of Passover, Pentecost and Tabernacles. In addition righteous kingship was highlighted during the Day of Trumpets. The Great Day happened once per year and varied with the lunar calendar. Tzedek was only in Leo one year out of twelve. The striking coincidence is fairly evident.

Over three decades later during Jesus ministry a significant event took place on the "Great Day of the Feast of Tabernacles."

> *Now on the last day, the great day of the feast, Jesus stood and cried out, saying, "If anyone is thirsty, let him come to Me and drink. He who believes in Me, as the Scripture said, 'From his innermost being will flow rivers of living water.'" But this He spoke of the Spirit, whom those who believed in Him were to receive; for the Spirit was not yet given, because Jesus was not yet glorified. (John 7:37-41a)*

Water was poured out before the Lord in abundance during this festival as the people asked God for an abundance of rain during the following months.

Melchizedek and the Moon

Autumn 3 BC

"David's descendants shall endure forever And his throne as the sun before Me. "David's throne shall be established forever like the moon, And the witness in the sky is faithful."

(Psalm 89:36-37)

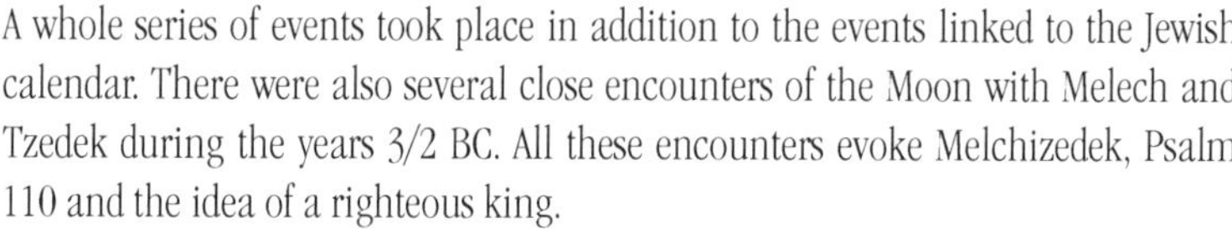

A whole series of events took place in addition to the events linked to the Jewish calendar. There were also several close encounters of the Moon with Melech and Tzedek during the years 3/2 BC. All these encounters evoke Melchizedek, Psalm 110 and the idea of a righteous king.

Each month as it has done for thousands of years, the moon passes through the constellation of Ari (Leo). However, the moon varies in a regular way in its orbit. In the illustration to the right, depending on several factors, the moon can be found anywhere between the two lines above or below the star Melech as it passes through Ari. The moon can also be found almost anywhere between the head and the rear leg of the lion when it passes through the constellation. The moon regularly varies in its orbit up to about 11 lunar diameters above or below the ecliptic line. As indicated earlier, the ecliptic is the path of the sun through the heavens. In 3/2 BC, the moon traveled very near to the ecliptic and close to the fixed star Melech for most of the year. Melech is almost exactly on the ecliptic, on the path of the sun.

In 3/2 BC Tzedek, the planet of righteousness, moved in the heavens near the ecliptic in Ari (Leo). During 10 months Melech and Tzedek were often close together and at three occasions they were in very close conjunction. Twice the Moon, Melech and Tzedek were in conjunction during important dates of the Jewish calendar. Twice the moon occulted (passed in front of Melech). Once this happened during the full moon. Twice the moon made close conjunctions with Tzedek alone. Some of the heavenly rendezvous were not visually impressive, but several of the events could have been symbolically and messianically significant for the wise men.

Conjunction: Tzedek / Moon

  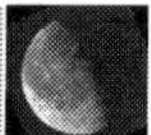

21st Heshvan - October 31st 3 BC

In October, Tzedek was highlighted by the moon in the presence of Melech. In December, a similar type of conjunction happened. Today, the moon, the "faithful witness in the sky," is still proclaiming that the Messiah's throne will last forever.

> *Let them fear You while the sun endures, And as long as the moon, throughout all generations. May he come down like rain upon the mown grass, Like showers that water the earth. In his days may the righteous flourish, and abundance of peace until the moon is no more. (Psalm 72: 5-7)*

Psalm 89, David's Throne, Melech, Tzedek and the Moon

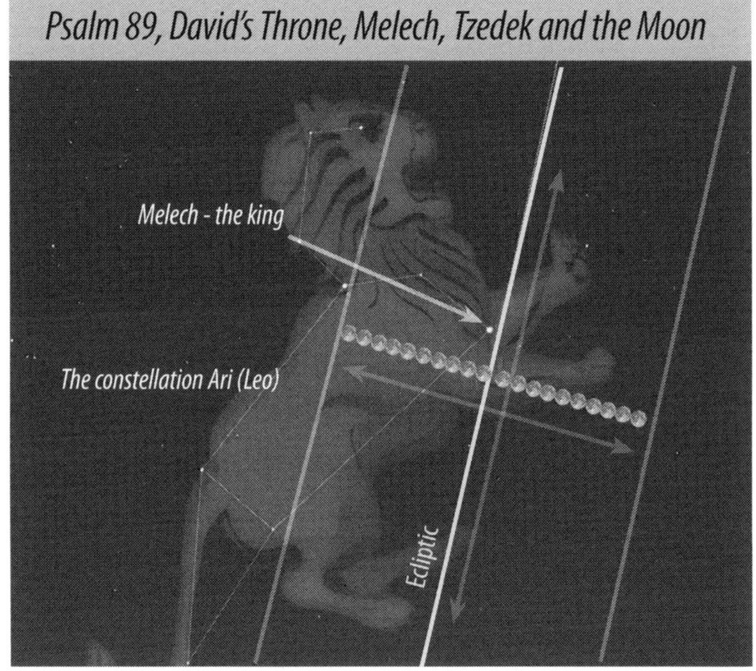

In its orbit the moon can be found about 5.5° (10-11 lunar widths) either above or below the ecliptic. The moon varies in its orbit over a period of about 10 years. Therefore the events of 3 and 2 BC were fairly unusual, even if they were cyclical. The moon was in close proximity with both Melech and Tzedek at the right time.

Occultation: Melech

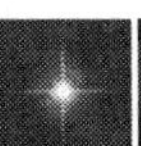

17th Kislev - November 27th

In November 3 BC, when viewed from Babylonia, the moon passed in front of Melech just after the constellation Ari (Leo) had risen above the horizon. Because of the lunar brightness, it may have been necessary for the observers to place their finger or an object over the moon to actually see the star as the moon approached it. Symbolically the occultation of Melech certainly highlighted kingship. The specific association of the moon with the Davidic kingship made this even stronger.

At the time of this occultation Tzedek had moved to the east as far as it would go; this was Tzedek's First Stationary Point, called (Phi) in astronomical terms. It had attained significant brightness (magnitude -2.3). The planet's very slight movements would have been imperceptible to the Magi at this time. Already for about one week Tzedek would have appeared to have stopped, one week later some movement could have again been observed. From an earthly vantage point, some outer planets appear to stop visually twice each year. This was Tzedek's first halt. Being one of the key moments in the planetary cycle, these events were always recorded by the astronomers in Mesopotamia. The Magi were not surprised to see the planets, "wandering stars," stopping from time to time. The Mesopotamians had recorded such things for at least 750 years, and possibly for a much longer period.

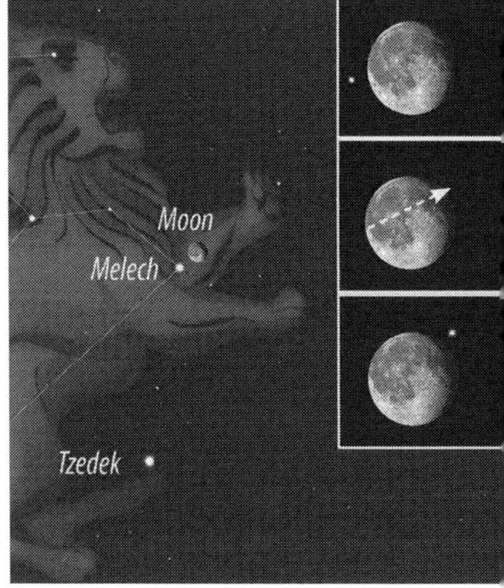

Hanukkah

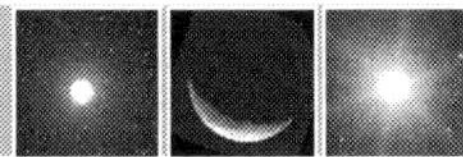

The visual separation of the moon and Antares at the end of the night was about 0° 53' (Slightly less than twice the diameter of the moon).

25th Kislev - December 5th

The Jewish celebration of Hanukkah was a very late innovation in the Jewish religious calendar. It only dates back to 165 BC when the Jews were able to throw off the rule of the Seleucid Empire (This was a Greek empire which had succeeded Alexander). When the Seleucid army was forced out of Jerusalem the temple was purified, and the lamps of the sacred menorah were lit again. However, according to the traditional account there was only one day supply of the holy oil for the lamps, yet the lamps continued to burn for eight days until more oil had been prepared. Although Hanukkah (the Feast of Dedication / Festival of Lights) is not a festival specifically commanded in the Scriptures, Jesus did observe the celebration in Jerusalem during his lifetime (John 10:22).

Jews have historically commemorated the event of the re-dedication of the temple by the Maccabees by lighting a nine lamp menorah. On the first evening of Hanukkah, a special lamp was lit called the "shamash" or "servant lamp." Here, the Aramaic word shamash is exactly the same word used for the sun in Hebrew, but the vowels are different. Also, this is the same word which is used concerning the chief minister (servant) in a synagogue (See Luke 4:20). The "servant" candle (shamash) is usually in the center or on the side of the special nine lamp Hanukkah menorah and it is used to light all the other lamps. The Festival of Hanukkah lasts eight days. Even now on the first evening of Hanukkah the shamash is lit as well as one other lamp. On all the other evenings, an additional lamp is lit until on the eighth evening when all nine lamps are shining (the "servant lamp" and eight others). In our day, the tradition continues but Jewish people usually light candles instead of oil lamps.

The "servant" candle (shamash) is in the center. This is the same word which is used concerning the chief minister (servant) in a synagogue (See Luke 4:20).

During the first night of Hanukkah in 3 BC, the moon was in conjunction with the star Antares. Only five times in the preceding 100 years had the moon been in conjunction with Antares at the beginning of Hanukkah. This time has the closest visual separation was (0°53'). The other closest times were in 4 BC (1°26') and 58 BC (1°26').

We do not know the Hebrew name of Antares in ancient times. This brilliant reddish star is in the constellation of Scorpio (Some apparently also thought this region of the sky represented a great eagle).[19] The conjunction of Antares and the moon could have been significant. Antares has historically been associated with the archangel Uriel, whose name actually means "light of God." In the book of Enoch, which is mentioned in the biblical book of Jude, Uriel gave Enoch understanding concerning the sun, moon and the stars. The conjunction of the moon with a star associated with Uriel at the beginning of Hanukkah (the Festival of Lights) would

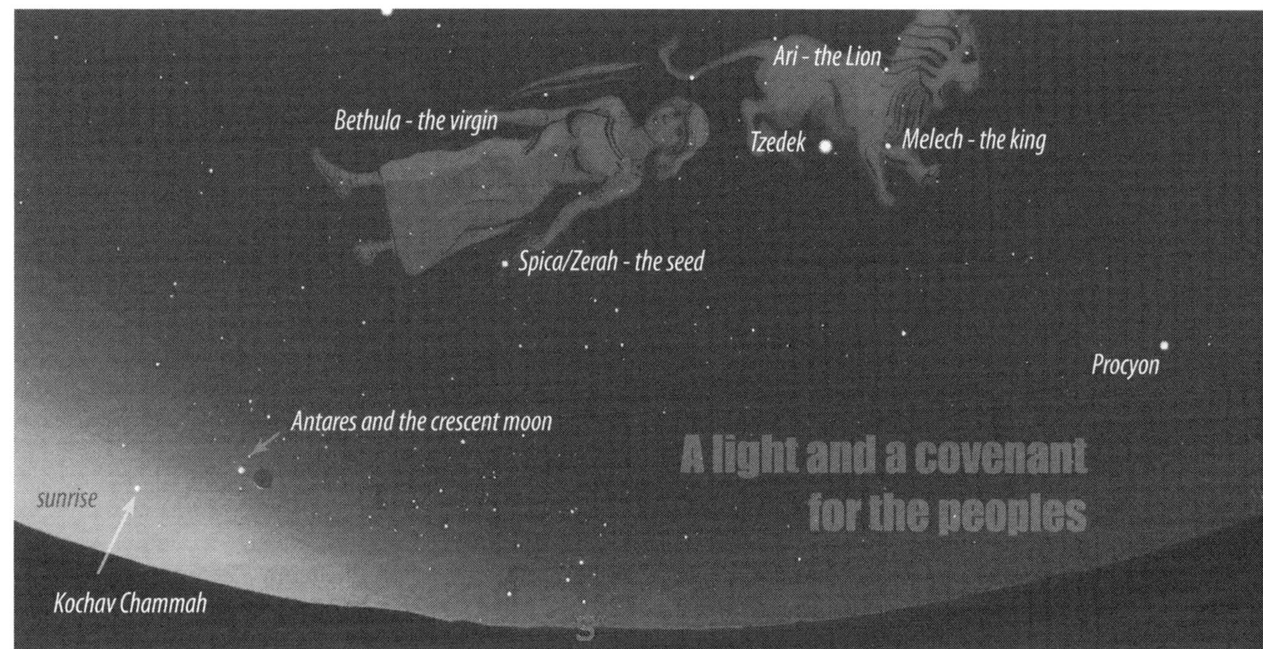

not have been without interest for wise men. They should have been well aware of the book of Enoch, which was popular among some Jews during the century before the Messiah's birth. As we have already seen, the book contains a significant astronomical section which could have interested the Magi, although it did contain many well known errors. Several passages in the book mention the Messiah, the "Righteous One," destined to reign over the whole earth (see pages 107-108). If the wise men were from a Jewish background or if they had been heavily influenced by the Jews, they could have read the book of Enoch in some detail.

"I am the LORD, I have called you in righteousness, I will also hold you by the hand and watch over you, And I will appoint you as a covenant to the people, As a light to the nations." (Isaiah 42:6)

It is likely that at the end of the first day of the "festival of lights" in 3 BC, Nogah, the brightest "star" / planet, made its visible appearance in the evening sky just after sunset. This also could have been significant symbolically.

Hanukkah's Messianic Connection:

The Messiah was supposed to be a light and a covenant for the peoples (see Isaiah 42:6-7, 49:5-6 and 60:1-3). This is a meaningful messianic connection with Hanukkah, the Festival of Lights. The lunar conjunction with Antares, which has historically been linked to Uriel, indicates that God's light was apparently being emphasized. As the brightest "star," Nogah's appearance at the end of the first day was also significant. It is possible that the lighting of the "servant" light could have been symbolic as well. However, different words are used for God's servant: "ebed" in Isaiah and the "shamash" used for the servant candle or lamp (See Isaiah 49:3-7 and 53:11).

I will also make You a light of the nations So that My salvation may reach to the end of the earth." (Isaiah 49:6)

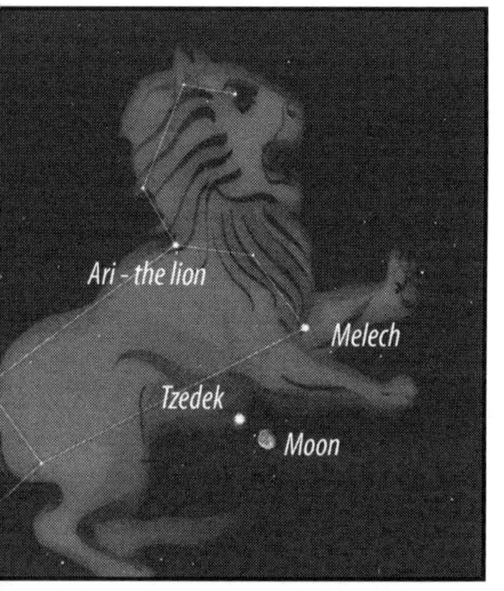

The wise men may have also been interested in the moon's close shave with the Babylonian normal "marker" star now known as Rho Leonis (GIŠ. KUN A) during this particular night. The two were only separated by about 0°9' as the moon passed near Tzedek. This is less than one third of a lunar diameter. However, the brightness of the moon would have almost completely obscured the star. One would have needed to cover the moon with an object in order to see the star.

Conjunction: Tzedek / Moon

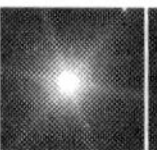 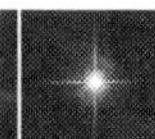 

16th Tevet - December 24th

On the 24th of December in 3 BC, the moon rose in conjunction with Tzedek for the second time just like it had done in October.

We are not absolutely sure of the exact day of Jesus' birth. There may not have been any astronomical event on the day of his birth. None was prophesied; none was needed to usher the Messiah into the world. However, during the night of December 24th and 25th in 3 BC the moon was in close conjunction with Tzedek (visual separation 1°13'). It should be noted that more and more of the lunar surface was being illuminated each month during the moon's encounters with Melech and Tzedek. January would reveal the full glory of the moon.

How Did the Magi Know?

When the wise men arrived in Jerusalem, they asked the question: "Where is he who has been born king of the Jews?" This indicates that they were convinced the had *already been born before their arrival.* How did the Magi know that the Messiah had already been born? One also might ask: "If there was no heavenly sign at Jesus' birth, then how did the Magi know that the Messiah had been born before they arrived? Answer: It was probably a simple matter of deduction and calculation.

In 3 BC there was a sign associated with the "seed of the woman" at Passover. This was also repeated on the Day of Atonement later in the fall of that year. Eventually there was the event which the Magi probably called "the star of the Messiah" in June 2 BC. All these events were well before the probable visit of the wise men to Bethlehem in December or January of 2/1 BC. The first sign at Passover in 3 BC was about one year and eight or nine months before the arrival of the wise men in Jerusalem. The child certainly could have been conceived and could have been born in that time period. The confidence of the wise men upon their arrival in Jerusalem that the Messiah had already been born is understandable. The very first sign linked to a Jewish appointed time / festival was at Passover in the spring of 3 BC. The Passover festival in 3 BC was also important concerning Daniel's prophecy of 70 "sevens." Therefore one could have started counting from Passover in 3 BC by adding nine months. The result would have been obvious.

Part 10: The Birth of the Messiah

The Census Ordered by Augustus

The Emperor Augustus ordered that a census be taken of each province everywhere and that all men be enrolled. At that time, Christ was born and was entered on the Roman census list as soon as he was born. This is the earliest and most famous public acknowledgment which marked Caesar as the first of all men and the Romans as lords of the world ... Since in this one name of Caesar all the peoples of the great nations took an oath (of allegiance), and at the same time, through the participation in the census, were made part of one society. *(This text was explored more thoroughly on page 75).*

The Birth of the Messiah in Bethlehem

Luke's account of the Shepherds

In the same region there were some shepherds staying out in the fields and keeping watch over their flock by night. And an angel of the Lord suddenly stood before them, and the glory of the Lord shone around them; and they were terribly frightened. But the angel said to them, "Do not be afraid; for behold, I bring you good news of great joy which will be for all the people; for today in the city of David there has been born for you a Savior, who is Christ the Lord. "This will be a sign for you: you will find a baby wrapped in cloths and lying in a manger."

And suddenly there appeared with the angel a multitude of the heavenly host praising God and saying, "Glory to God in the highest, And on earth peace among men with whom He is pleased." When the angels had gone away from them into heaven, the shepherds began saying to one another, "Let us go straight to Bethlehem then, and see this thing that has happened which the Lord has made known to us."

So they came in a hurry and found their way to Mary and Joseph, and the baby as He lay in the manger. When they had seen this, they made known the statement which had been told them about this Child. And all who heard it wondered at the things which were told them by the shepherds. But Mary treasured all these things, pondering them in her heart. The shepherds went back, glorifying and praising God for all that they had heard and seen, just as had been told them.
(Luke 2:8-20 - also on pages 28-29 of this book)

One could ask why God decided to reveal the Messiah's birth to anyone in the area around Bethlehem. He could have chosen to keep the birth a complete secret. He could have chosen to announce the Messiah's birth to other people. Why did

Hallelujah

Glory to God in the highest

he not reveal it to people who grew olives, or to carpenters? It is known that the shepherds of the region of Bethlehem supplied lambs for sacrifices at the temple (including the Passover lambs); perhaps that made them special. We may never know all of God's reasoning behind why he chose to reveal the Messiah's birth to a group of shepherds. However, the book of Jeremiah may give us some indications. There are several texts in Jeremiah which speak of leaders, likened to "shepherds," who had displeased the Lord through their abuse and neglect of God's people, his sheep. Jeremiah speaks of judgement against the shepherds which actually came about during his own lifetime (from about 605-587/586 BC). This came about through the capture and the destruction of Jerusalem and the Babylonian exile.[1]

> Jeremiah's text: *"Many shepherds have ruined My vineyard, They have trampled down My field; They have made My pleasant field A desolate wilderness.*
>
> *"The wind will sweep away all your shepherds, And your lovers will go into captivity; Then you will surely be ashamed and humiliated Because of all your wickedness.*
>
> *"Woe to the shepherds who are destroying and scattering the sheep of My pasture!" declares the LORD. Therefore thus says the LORD God of Israel concerning the shepherds who are tending My people: "You have scattered My flock and driven them away, and have not attended to them; behold, I am about to attend to you for the evil of your deeds," declares the LORD.*
>
> *Wail, you shepherds, and cry; And wallow in ashes, you masters of the flock; For the days of your slaughter and your dispersions have come ..." Jeremiah 12:10, 22:22, 23:2. (See also Jeremiah 25:34-36).*

However, judgement does not prevail forever. The Lord promises a new chapter for the shepherds. The cities of Judah and the region around Jerusalem are specifically mentioned. The angel makes the proclamation of God's grace, "Glory to God in the highest, And on earth peace, goodwill toward men!" God expressly sent the angels to the shepherds in a direct prophetic statement concerning his grace which would come to all through the Messiah. This is obvious in the text of Jeremiah 23:1-4 and 33:11-13 (below):

> *"Thus says the LORD of hosts, 'There will again be in this place which is waste, without man or beast, and in all its cities, a habitation of shepherds who rest their flocks. 'In the cities of the hill country, in the cities of the lowland, in the cities of the Negev, in the land of Benjamin, in the environs of Jerusalem and in the cities of Judah, the flocks will again pass under the hands of the one who numbers them,' says the LORD. 'Behold, days are coming,' declares the LORD, 'when I will fulfill the good word which I have spoken concerning the house of Israel and the house of Judah.*

Winter 3 BC - 2 BC

Winter 3 / 2 BC

The passage above is immediately followed by the text about the righteous king, a descendant of David who would reign in justice and righteousness. God manifested his faithfulness in fulfilling his word. The angels appeared to the shepherds to underline God's blessing. The period of judgment had ended.

> *'In those days and at that time I will cause a righteous Branch of David to spring forth; and He shall execute justice and righteousness on the earth. 'In those days Judah will be saved and Jerusalem will dwell in safety; and this is the name by which she will be called: the LORD is our righteousness.' (Jeremiah 33:12-16)*

Timeline: December 3 BC through May 2 BC

Mary and Joseph went to Bethlehem as required by the census. Jesus was born in Bethlehem. Angels and shepherds saw the newborn child. No wise men were present.

About 6,000 Pharisees refused to pledge an oath of allegiance to Augustus and King Herod during the census. They were fined for their refusal. The wife of Pheroras, the tetrarch of Perea and Galilee, who was also Herod's brother, became involved in an effort to pay the fine. The Pharisees were favorable to her husband, even desiring that he replace Herod. This caused a major crisis between Herod and his brother.

In January, Jesus was circumcised eight days after his birth.

Augustus received the title "Pater Patraie" (Father of the Nation) on February 5th from the Roman Senate, the Roman Equestrian Knights and the whole Roman people. The entire empire had taken an oath of allegiance to Augustus and had been registered.

Jesus was presented at the temple in Jerusalem after the 40 days of purification required for Mary (Leviticus 12:2-4 and Luke 2:22). It is possible, but unlikely, that Mary and Joseph visited Nazareth sometime during the year. It would have been difficult to travel with a very small child. They apparently decided to live in Bethlehem. It would have been much easier for some of Mary's family to have visited Bethlehem during one of the festivals, either at Passover, Pentecost or Tabernacles. Luke mentions some events and neglects others which Matthew indicates in his text about the Magi.

Early in the year 2 BC Phraates IV the Parthian emperor was assassinated by his wife Musa and his son Phraataces. The young emperor and his mother held power until AD 4.

On May 12th 2 BC, In Rome the dedication of the Forum of Augustus and the Temple of Mars Ultor (Mars the Avenger) took place. The dedication of the new forum and temple celebrated the achievements of Augustus on the 40th year anniversary of his victory over the murderers of Augustus' father by adoption, Julius Caesar. A summary of the results of the census, called the Breviarium totius imperii, "a summary of all the empire," was perhaps posted in the new Forum of Augustus as part of the celebration.

Presentation of Jesus at the Temple

Mary had to be ceremonially pure in order to access the temple courts. According to Leviticus this would have taken a minimum of 40 days (Leviticus 12:1-8).

> *And when eight days had passed, before His circumcision, His name was then called Jesus, the name given by the angel before He was conceived in the womb. And when the days for their purification according to the law of Moses were completed, they brought Him up to Jerusalem to present Him to the Lord (as it is written in the Law of the Lord, "EVERY firstborn MALE THAT OPENS THE WOMB SHALL BE CALLED HOLY TO THE LORD"), and to offer a sacrifice according to what was said in the Law of the Lord, "A PAIR OF TURTLEDOVES OR TWO YOUNG PIGEONS."*
>
> *And there was a man in Jerusalem whose name was Simeon; and this man was righteous and devout, looking for the consolation of Israel; and the Holy Spirit was upon him. And it had been revealed to him by the Holy Spirit that he would not see death before he had seen the Lord's Christ. And he came in the Spirit into the temple; and when the parents brought in the child Jesus, to carry out for Him the custom of the Law, then he took Him into his arms, and blessed God, and said, "Now Lord, You are releasing Your bond-servant to depart in peace, According to Your word; For my eyes have seen Your salvation, Which You have prepared in the presence of all peoples, A LIGHT OF REVELATION TO THE GENTILES, And the glory of Your people Israel."*
>
> *And His father and mother were amazed at the things which were being said about Him. And Simeon blessed them and said to Mary His mother, "Behold, this Child is appointed for the fall and rise of many in Israel, and for a sign to be opposed-- and a sword will pierce even your own soul--to the end that thoughts from many hearts may be revealed."*
>
> *And there was a prophetess, Anna the daughter of Phanuel, of the tribe of Asher. She was advanced in years and had lived with her husband seven years after her marriage, and then as a widow to the age of eighty-four. She never left the temple, serving night and day with fastings and prayers. At that very moment she came up and began giving thanks to God, and continued to speak of Him to all those who were looking for the redemption of Jerusalem. When they had performed everything according to the Law of the Lord, they returned to Galilee, to their own city of Nazareth. (Luke 2:21-39)*

Luke skips over the incidents with the Magi and the flight into Egypt and instead he begins the next section of his book with Jesus and his family in Nazareth. Luke seems to be underlining that these things were done "according to the law of the Lord." He mentioned the law (the Torah) in Luke 2:22, 23, 24, 27 and 39. He had already indicated in Luke 1:6 that Zachariah and Elisabeth "were both righteous

Miriam is the Aramaic name for Mary. Jesus would have known his mother as Miriam.

in the sight of God, walking blamelessly in all the commandments and requirements of the Lord." This may explain Luke's neglect of the story of the Magi and the star. His way of writing is different from Matthew's, therefore he highlighted some things and not others.

The Calendar in 2 BC

The Jewish calendar used in this book assumes that a second month of Adar was added in the spring of 2 BC. This leap year month was necessary to keep the calendar in line with the seasons. The 1st of Nisan fell on April 5th and Passover fell on April 18th according to this calendar arrangement. The beginning of the month of Nisan established the calendar for the rest of the year.

The Jewish Calendar 2 BC

1	Shevat	New Moon	Jan	7	Tue
1	Adar	New Moon	Feb	6	Thu
13	Adar	Purim	Feb	18	Tue
1	Adar 2	New Moon	March	7	Fri
1	Nisan	New Moon	April	5	Sat
14	Nisan	Passover (Pesach)	April	18	Fri
1	Iyyar	New Moon	May	5	Mon
1	Sivan	New Moon	June	3	Tue
6	Sivan	Pentecost (Shavuot)	June	8	Sun
1	Tammuz	New Moon	July	3	Wed
1	Av	New Moon	Aug	1	Fri
1	Elul	New Moon	Aug	31	Sun
1	Tishrei	New Moon (Yom Teruah)	Sept	30	Tue
10	Tishri	Atonement (Yom Kippur)	Oct	9	Thu
15	Tishri	Tabernacles (Sukkot)	Oct	14	Tue
1	Heshvan	New Moon	Oct	30	Thu
1	Kislev	New Moon	Nov	28	Fri
25	Kislev	Lights (Hanukkah)	Dec	22	Mon
1	Tevet	New Moon	Dec	28	Sun
(Julian dates in the evening - beginning of night)					

2 BC

Part 11 : Events in the Heavens - 2

Thus says the LORD, "Preserve justice and do righteousness,
For My salvation is about to come And My righteousness to be revealed.
(Isaiah 56:1)

Winter through Spring 2 BC

"Melchizedek Events" in 2 BC (Pages 180-183)

In the winter and spring of 2 BC several events involving the Moon, Melech and Tzedek took place. These events seem to underline the Melech Tzedek (the righteous king). Placing the moon with Melech and Tzedek apparently underlines the fact that the righteous king will reign forever. (See Ps. 89:36-37 and Ps. 72: 1-7)

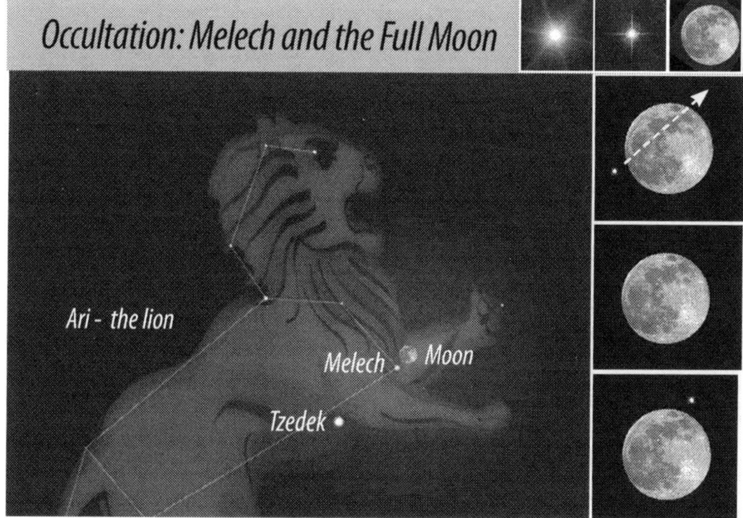

Shebet: rod, staff, branch

Technically Tzedek reached its opposition with the sun and its maximum brightness on Jan. 26th (magnitude -2.5). However, Tzedek had already attained its maximum brightness during the occultation.

15 Shevat - January 20th

In January of 2 BC the full moon passed in front of Melech (the king star) in the presence of Tzedek for the second time. This event happened just after sunset as darkness fell. Melech, Tzedek and the moon rose in the east, as soon as, the sun set in the west. Because of the brightness of the full moon, it would have been necessary for the observers to cover the moon with an object or their finger in order to actually see the 1st magnitude star Melech (Regulus). The moon did pass from time to time in front of Melech in the 1st century BC on this date, however, it was not always visible.

The month of Shevat (Shebat) is linked to the word "shebet" which means a "rod, staff or branch." This is exactly the same word as the word scepter which is found in Genesis 49:10: "The scepter (shebet) shall not depart from Judah, nor the ruler's staff from between his feet, until the Shiloh comes, and to him shall be the obedience of the peoples." By this time the messianic nature of the repeated conjunctions, occultations and other celestial events must have been becoming obvious to the wise men who eventually made the trip to Bethlehem. Many more events were still to follow.

Other Interpretations of the Events

It is very possible that some wise men in the Parthian court may have used the two occultations of Melech (Sharru - 'the king' in the Chaldean language) to indicate or even stimulate a change of government. The choice of the crown prince, Phraataces, and his mother, Musa, to assassinate the Parthian Emperor Phraates IV may have been motivated partly by such an interpretation. Unfortunately, because of the destruction of the royal archives, we do not know the exact date of the assassination. The messianic interpretation flows from the Hebrew names and dates but other interpretations of the heavenly events were possible, using Chaldean or Zoroastrian approaches (omen texts, etc.).

It is very possible that some wise men in the Parthian court may have used the two occultations of Melech to indicate or even stimulate a change of government.

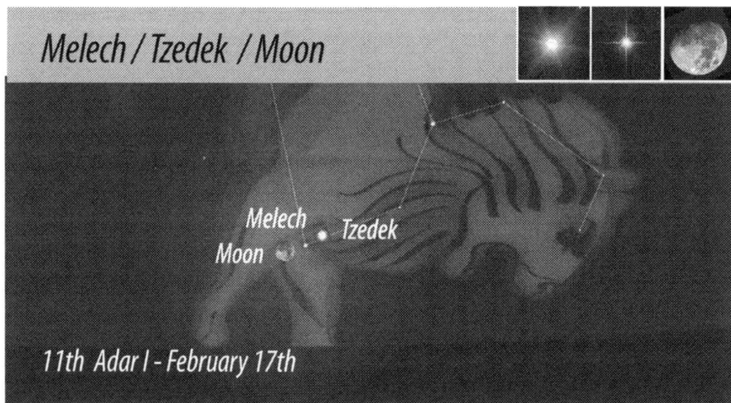

The close conjunction of the moon with Melech and Tzedek on the 11th of Adar I evoked the Messiah. The whole idea of a righteous king was strongly underlined on this date. Here God's promise that David's throne would be established forever is clearly written in the heavens. (See Psalm 89:36-37 and Psalm 72: 1-7)

Melech / Tzedek / Moon

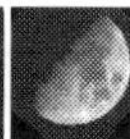

10th Adar 2 - March 16th

In March during the second month of Adar and also on the 7th of the month of Nisan, the Moon, Melech and Tzedek were in two rendezvous. The Adar II conjunction was not particularly impressive. The objects were well separated from each other. However, on the 7th of Nisan, in the early evening, the three were together with Melech in the center. Melech was separated from both Tzedek and the moon by about two degrees. While this particular date did not have a significant meaning for Jews the astronomical combination again evokes: The Melech / Tzedek in the lion with the moon, the righteous king from the tribe of Judah, reigning forever. (See Genesis 49:8-10, Psalm.110, Jeremiah 33:14-17, Psalm 89:37).

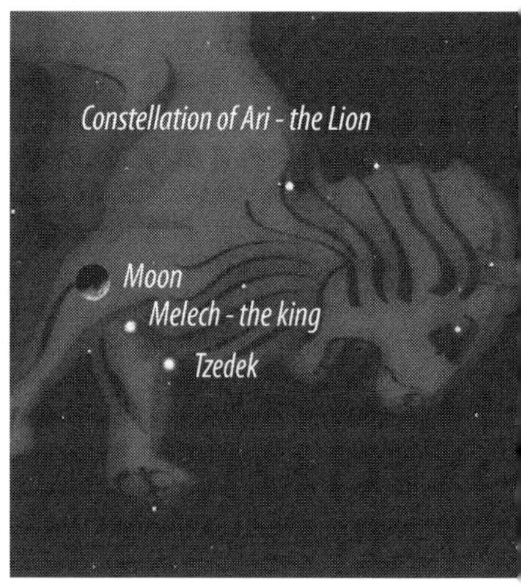

Hebrew Date	Julian Date	Separation:
4th Adar I	Feb 10th (AM)	1°11′36″
10th Adar I	Feb 16th (AM)	51′49″
11th Adar I	Feb 17th (AM)	51′19″
12th Adar I	Feb 18th (AM)	51′36″
13th Adar I	Feb 19th (AM)	52′46″
14th Adar I	Feb 20th (AM)	54′35″
18th Adar I	Feb 24th (AM)	1°06′43″

Table 11:1 This shows the separation of Melech from Tzedek in February 2 BC. Any distance of less than 1′40″ (one minute and forty seconds of arc) is not discernible to the unaided human eye. (Measurements toward 4 AM)

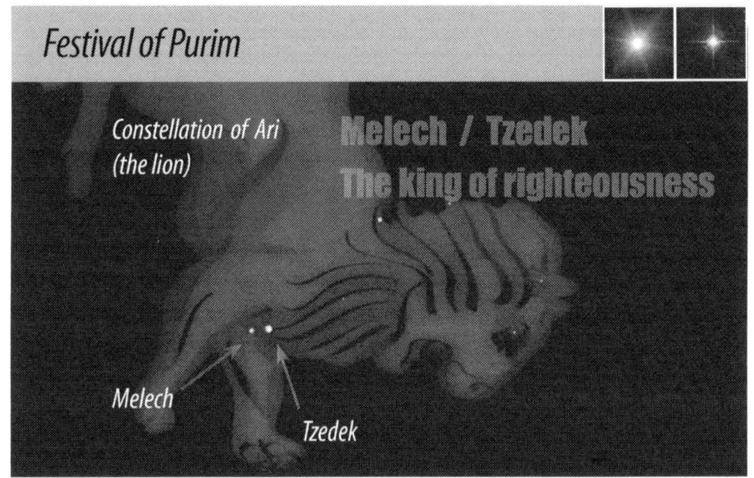

13th -14th Adar I / Feb. 18th -20th or 13th - 14th Adar II / March 19th - 20th

The festival of Purim celebrated the deliverance of the Jewish people from mortal danger during the life of Queen Esther in the 5th century BC. The festival is still celebrated every year on the 13th and 14th of the month of Adar. The Jews in Mesopotamia and Iran in 2 BC would have celebrated Purim at the sites where the events actually happened during the time of Esther. The conjunction of Melech and Tzedek (the righteous king) could have been especially meaningful to Jews in the Parthian dominions where Esther had been queen. The distances of separation between Melech and Tzedek from the 11th to the 14th of Adar I were very small (varying only about 1/15th to 1/10th of a lunar diameter).

In our day during leap years Purim is always celebrated in the second month of Adar. We do not know precisely what happened in 2 BC. If the festival took place in March during Adar II then the moon would have risen with Spica/Zerah during the festival as it had done in 3 BC during Passover. The two celestial objects would have traveled together all night on the second day, the 14th day of Adar II.

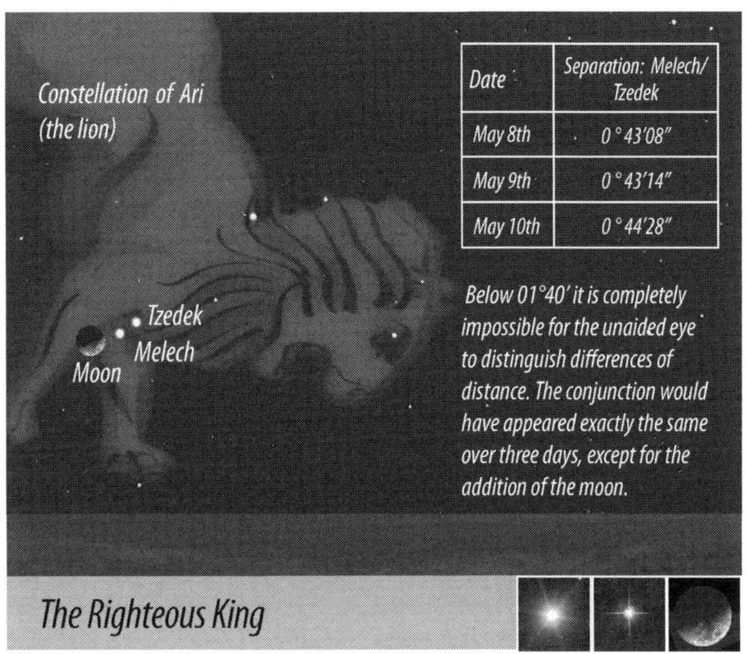

5th Iyyar - May 9th

On this date Tzedek had moved back to make a close conjunction with Melech along with the moon. This was the third major conjunction between Melech and Tzedek during the period of August 3 BC to July 2 BC. The combination seems to point to Melech / Tzedek, the "righteous king" from the tribe of Judah, in the lion constellation. This appointed king will reign forever as indicated by the faithful witness, the moon. See Genesis 49:8-10, Psalm 110, Jeremiah 33:14-17 and Psalm 89:37.

Melech / Tzedek Conjunctions (Table 11.2 - Right)

Once every 12 years Tzedek is in the constellation of Ari (Leo the lion). There is a possibility of conjunctions between Melech and Tzedek during the periods of time when Tzedek is in Leo and these events could have messianic implications according to Genesis 49:8-10. The series of Melech / Tzedek conjunctions repeats itself every 71 and 83 years. From 454 BC to 2 BC there were 55 conjunctions of Melech and Tzedek. None were visible at all during the almost 50 years from 74 BC to 27 BC. A total of eight conjunctions took place in 27-26 BC, 15-14 BC and 3-2 BC (a period of about 25 years). Assuming that the wise men were not over 60 years old in 3/2 BC then these eight conjunctions would have been the only conjunctions of Melech and Tzedek that they had ever seen. However, they would have been aware of the cycles of the conjunctions. While events do repeat themselves they do not always do it at a significant point in time or in a meaningful way. The relatively rare presence of the moon with the conjunctions in 2 BC was messianically significant.

Dates	Melech /Tzedek Conjunctions
3 - 2 BC	Three conjunctions
15 - 14 BC	Three conjunctions
27 - 26 BC	Two conjunctions
38 - 39 BC	No conjunctions
50 - 51 BC	No conjunctions
62 - 61 BC	No conjunctions
74 - 73 BC	One conjunction
86 - 85 BC	Three conjunctions
98 - 97 BC	Three conjunctions
110 - 109 BC	Two conjunctions
122 - 121 BC	No conjunctions
134 - 133 BC	No conjunctions
145 - 146 BC	No conjunctions
157 - 156 BC	No conjunctions
169 - 168 BC	Two conjunctions
181 - 180 BC	Three conjunctions
193 - 192 BC	Three conjunctions
205 - 204 BC	One conjunction
217 - 216 BC	No conjunctions
229 - 228 BC	No conjunctions
241 - 240 BC	One conjunction
252 - 251 BC	Two conjunctions
264 - 263 BC	Three conjunctions
276 - 275 BC	Three conjunctions
288 - 277 BC	One conjunction
300 - 299 BC	No conjunctions
312 - 311 BC	No conjunctions
323 - 322 BC	No conjunctions
335 - 334 BC	Two conjunctions
347 - 346 BC	Three conjunctions
359 - 358 BC	Three conjunctions
371 - 370 BC	Two conjunctions
383 - 382 BC	No conjunctions
395 - 394 BC	No conjunctions
406 - 405 BC	No conjunctions
418 - 417 BC	One conjunction
430 - 429 BC	Three conjunctions
442 - 441 BC	Three conjunctions
454 - 453 BC	Two conjunctions
Total 454 BC to 2 BC	**55 conjunctions**

Passover / Unleavened Bread / First Fruits

14th Nisan - April 18th

On this date the full moon rose as usual on the 14th of Nisan. Nothing particularly noteworthy took place in the sky. There was a sign specifically at Passover in 3 BC, but there was none in 2 BC.

16th Nisan - April 20th

On the day of the First Fruits Offering and the beginning of the Pharisaic "Counting of the Omer" the moon rose with the star Antares. At Hanukkah Antares had underlined God as light, and that the Messiah is a light and a covenant to the nations. It is possible that the Magi may have interpreted the conjunction in the same manner on this day of the First Fruits Offering. However, there were other Babylonian names for Antares which may also have attracted their attention. Antares also had the names *Bilu-sha-ziri* (the Lord of the Seed), *Dar Lugal* (The King), and *Masu Sar* (the Hero and the King).[1] We do not know why these names were attached to the star. However, each of them was perhaps significant from a messianic perspective. Names evoking the "seed" and the "king" certainly could invite Jewish or Jewish influenced individuals to think about the Messiah.

There was not anything particularly remarkable about the day of the hypothetical Sadducean First Fruits Offering and the beginning of their "Counting of the Omer" on April 26th. However, depending on atmospheric conditions Shabbatei may have visually disappeared in the evening sky several days early. If that had happened, it could have been significant when considering the counting of seven Sabbaths and Pentecost. Such an early heliacal setting would not have been unknown. When one compares computed dates with the actual dates of heliacal risings and settings the tendencies are toward late heliacal risings and early dates for heliacal settings. The visual sighting dates often vary by 24 to 48 hours.[2]

***2 BC Dates*:** *Passover, Feast of Unleavened Bread / Sheaf Offering (First Fruits)*

April 18	April 19/20	April 20/21	April 21/22	April 22/23	April 23/24	April 24/25	April 25/26	April 26/27
Fri / Sat	Sat / Sun	Sun / Mon	Mon / Tue	Tue / Wed	Wed / Thu	Thu / Fri	Fri / Sat	Sat/Sun
14 Nisan	15 Nisan	16 Nisan	17 Nisan	18 Nisan	19 Nisan	20 Nisan	21 Nisan	22 Nisan
Passover	Unleavened B. Day of Rest (Leviticus 23:7)	Pharisaic Sheaf Offering					1st Weekly Sabbath	H. Sadducean Sheaf Offering

Omer Count / Pentecost

Sivan 5th - 15th / June 7th - 17th

In June, Shabbatei should have made its first morning appearance, after passing behind the sun, on the Pharisaic date for the end of the "Counting of the Omer" or on the day of Pentecost. The heliacal rising would have been at the beginning of the Sadducean 7th week as well. The "feast of weeks" was again hosting the "Sabbath planet" and underlining the 7 "sevens." The end of the hypothetical Sadducean "Counting of the Omer"and Pentecost was exactly 62 weeks (62 x 7 days) after the First Fruits Offering in 3 BC. The Pharisaic dates were 62 weeks + one day. Tzedek, Nogah and Melech were close to each other during the Pharisaic and hypothetical Sadducean dates in 2 BC (see the next two pages).

Nogah was in conjunction with Melech on June 11th and 12th (the closest approach being 01°10'). Did the Magi see this conjunction as important? At this point such a conjunction would seem like another pearl in a necklace. However, the event is cyclical, it happens every eight years, the event certainly happened at the right moment but it was not unknown at this date. Nogah and Melech together equals "bright king." This was also the moment of Nogah's greatest elongation from the sun, making it visible for about two hours in the evening sky.

While the Babylonians, Jews and the Zoroastrians used mixed lunar / solar calendars, they all knew how to calculate solar years. This Nogah / Melech conjunction was one solar year after the conjunction of Nogah and Shabbatei on June 12-14 in 3 BC. The Magi may have seen a relationship between the "bright Sabbath" conjunction of 3 BC and the "bright king" conjunction of 2 BC. The June 12th, 26 BC conjunction had also involved all the same actors on the same date. We now know that God's bright king of righteousness has established a Sabbath rest filled with light for the people of God. The Magi seemed to have tasted the promise of God's new kingdom in advance.

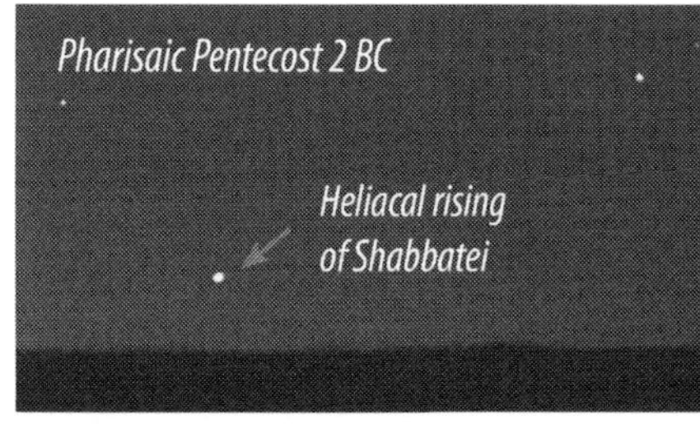

Pentecost (Shavuot) was usually the beginning of the annual wheat harvest. However, this year was apparently a Sabbatical year, therefore there was no regular harvest.

2 BC Dates: *The 49th Day of Counting the Omer and Pentecost (Shavuot)* *(The Jewish dates begin in the evening).*

June 7/8	June 8/9	June 9/10	June 10/11	June 11/12	June 12/13	June 13/14	June 14/15
Sat / Sun	Sun / Mon	Mon / Tue	Tue / Wed	Wed / Thu	Thu / Fri	Fri/Sat	Sat/Sun
5 Sivan	6 Sivan	7 Sivan	8 Sivan	9 Sivan	10 Sivan	11 Sivan	12 Sivan
Pharisaic 49th Day of the Counting the Omer	Pharisaic Pentecost					Hypothetical Sadducean 49th Day of the Counting of the Omer	Hypothetical Sadducean Pentecost

The Evening Sky in the West in the Days Leading up to the "Star"

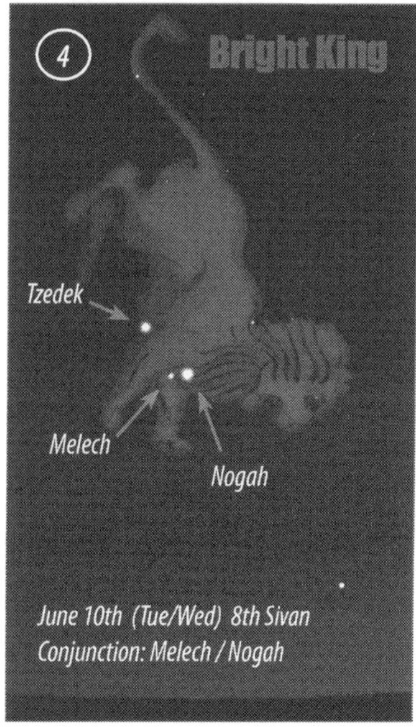

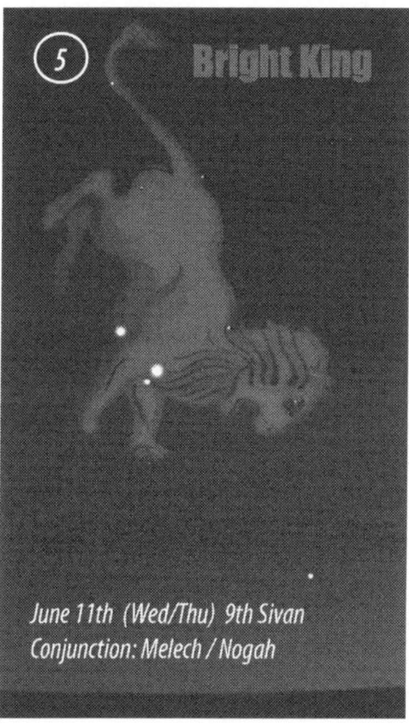

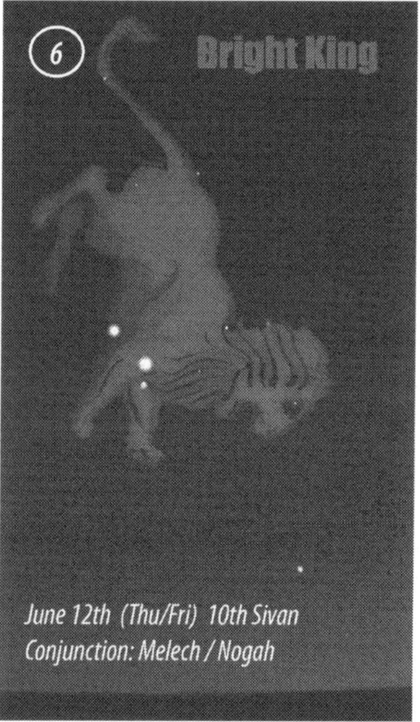

June 2 BC

In this series of events Nogah (Venus) is doing almost all the movement. Nogah begins on the lower right near the lion's mane and moves toward the upper left. Melech (Regulus) is the star between the two front legs of the lion. Tzedek (Jupiter) is on the upper left. Kochav Chammah (Mercury) is the bright star by itself on the lower right in all the images.

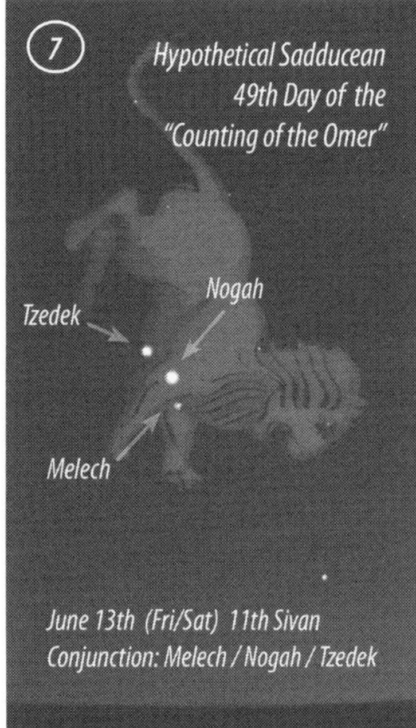

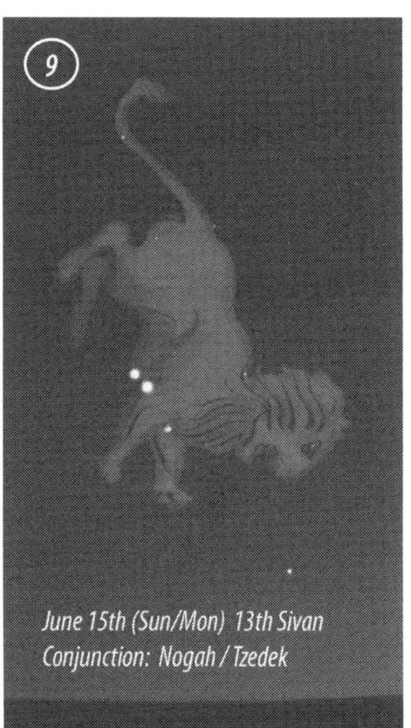

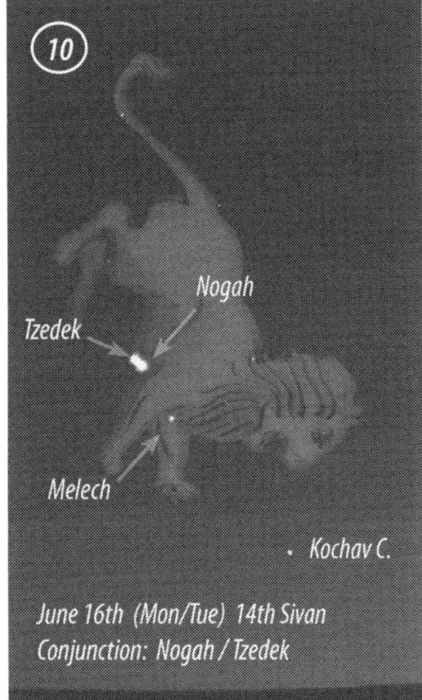

The dates indicated are in the evening at the beginning of each Jewish "day." All the events above lead up to the event, which the Magi most likely called "His Star." The movements took place over a short period of 11 days.

The previous days almost seem to point to this event. As Pentecost came and went, Nogah drew ever closer to Tzedek until the two became one.

A Single Star on June 17th, 2 BC

When the wise men arrived in Judea in December of 2 BC they spoke of seeing "His Star" while they were in the east. It is probable that the wise men were referring to this incident in particular. Tzedek played the principal role over Bethlehem six months later. Both Tzedek and Nogah continue to be visible even today.

The Brightest Righteousness

"We saw his star while we were in the east."

"The Star" seems to be in a 70th symbolic week"

15th Sivan - June 17th

This is one of the more "spectacular" events during the time period near the birth of the Messiah. The two "wandering stars" Nogah and Tzedek visually became "one" during this event, making it possibly the closest such conjunction between Nogah and Tzedek that has ever been seen in all history. The conjunction seems to have highlighted "bright righteousness." The event took place in the constellation of the lion, accompanied by the star Melech, the king. It is not without significance that the full moon rose in the east at the same moment as the conjunction. The "faithful witness" of Psalm 89:37, in its brightest form, again affirmed the establishment of the Messiah's throne forever.[3] The two planets in conjunction, the star Melech and the moon all together seem to herald the "Bright Righteous One, the King, the Son of David whose throne is established forever." Tzedek was the key star. Nogah had a supporting role even though it was brighter.
After more than a year filled with various heavenly events this bright spectacle was like a "crescendo" in a symphony, however, it was not yet the "finale."

During the conjunction it would have been visually impossible to distinguish one planet from the other with the naked eye. A good telescope would have been necessary to discern the two planets individually. The wise men did not have any optical aides which could magnify objects. It is notable that during the one thousand years previous to the Messiah's birth there were only nine conjunctions of Tzedek and Nogah of a somewhat similar closeness. Some of the conjunctions were possibly only visible for a few minutes or not at all due to the solar glare. The closest conjunctions of less than 100 arc seconds (0°01'40"), generally occur too close to the sun to be visible on earth. The smallest distance in the heavens that the unaided human eye can perceive is about 100 arc seconds. Nogah and Tzedek have slightly different orbital inclinations, therefore, their closest, visible conjunctions, when the two objects appear as one, happen over a relatively short time frame of one to two hours. Only a small fraction of timezones on earth would be able to observe such an event near dawn or dusk.[4]

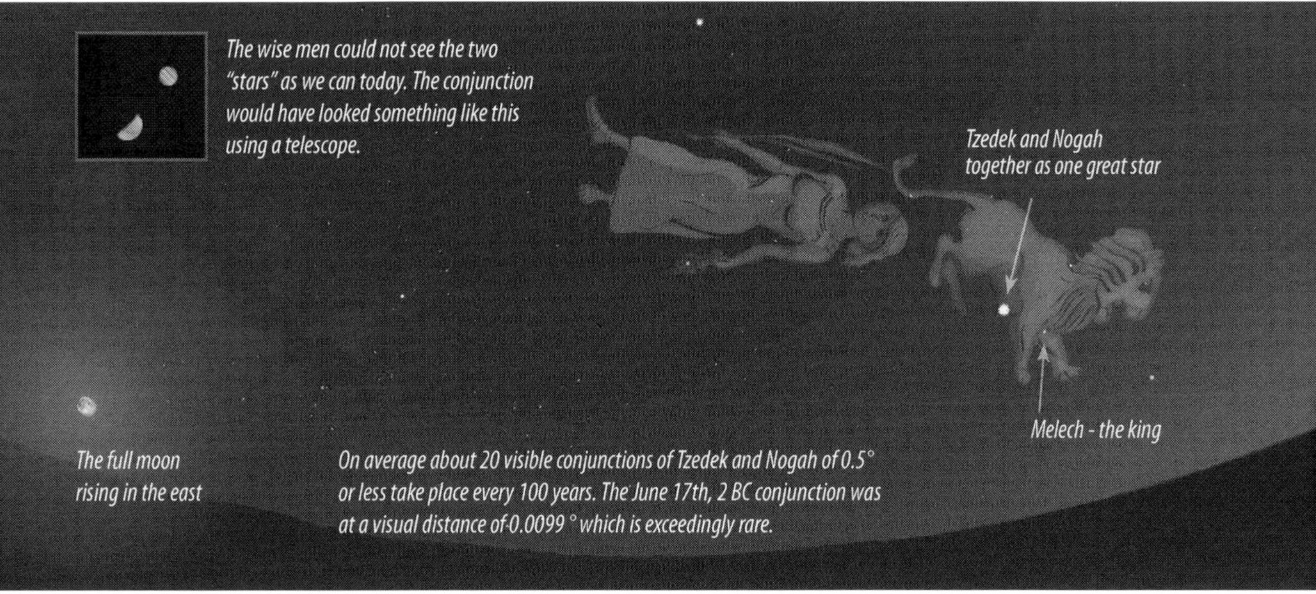

While the conjunction between the two planets almost a year before was significant it would not have been as visually impressive as the June 2 BC event because in 3 BC the two planets were separated by about 13' of arc (a bit over 1/3 of the diameter of the moon). In June 2 BC the two were indistinguishable. The year before neither "star" had been as bright (Nogah had been at magnitude -3.9). Each degree of magnitude is about 2.5 times brighter than the degree below. The brightest objects have the greatest negative value. The sun is at magnitude -26. The full moon is about magnitude -12. Under very good conditions objects which have a magnitude of -4 or greater can sometimes be visible in the daytime.

Contrary to what one could believe calculations show that the two "stars" together would not have been significantly brighter than Nogah alone.[5] Many have made the mistake of thinking that this was one of the brightest stars of all time.[6] It certainly was the brightest known conjunction of all time. However, in some situations Nogah alone can have an apparent magnitude of -4.89. During this event the combined apparent magnitude was -4.4. Please note that an apparent magnitude of -4.89 is about 100% brighter and a magnitude of -4.4.

This June 2 BC event took place just after 62 literal weeks when counting from the dates of the Sadducean and Pharisaic First Fruits Offering in 3 BC. There had been a full series of 7 "sevens" and 62 "sevens." The star shone in the middle of the week following the Sadducean date for Pentecost. Was this also symbolic? One might conclude that this event symbolically announces the 70th "seven" even if it does not fulfill it. The prophecy is complex and simple, partly fulfilled, but not entirely. It has both figurative and literal aspects.

Date 2 BC	Distance between	Nogah / Tzedek	
June 11	04°34'51"	-4.3	-1.8
June 12	03°47'44"	-4.3	-1.8
June 13	03°10'57"	-4.3	-1.8
June 14	02°14'59"	-4.3	-1.8
June 15	01°29'24"	-4.3	-1.8
June 16	00°44'22"	-4.3	-1.8
June 17 15 Sivan (full moon)	00° 00' 37"	- 4.4	
June 18	00°44'03"	-4.3	-1.8
June 19	01°27'22"	-4.3	-1.8
June 20	02'10'06"	-4.3	-1.8

All these measurements were done with using the time of 9:00 PM, at a location near Ctesiphon. This city was the winter capital of the Parthian Empire.

The visual magnitudes of Nogah and Tzedek would have been lower as the "wandering stars" reached the horizon.

Who Will Go to Judea ?

The following text is fictional but it may depict events that may have really happened in a similar way.

Below one of the observatory terraces the tops of several palm trees made a rustling noise as a light breeze moved their branches. The heat of early summer evening was already giving way to the cooler night air as the last hints of light from the sun quickly disappeared in the west. Small lamps illuminated the back of the terrace and a few adjoining rooms where some astronomical instruments were stored. In the faint light of the lamps some scribes were making preliminary notes concerning the night's astronomical observations.

The observatory was on the upper terrace of the Parthian imperial palace in Ctesiphon on the Tigris River about 70 miles (110 kilometers) from Borsippa. It was one the three main capitals of the Parthian Empire. Ctesiphon was on the opposite bank of the Tigris from Seleucia, the greatest city of Mesopotamia with a population of over a half million people. The smaller imperial capital city Ctesiphon was accustomed to the presence of high ranking court officials. This evening was particularly special for the twenty men gathered on the observatory terrace at the request of the Rab Mag, the chief Magus. As foreseen the full moon had risen less than a half hour before. It seemed to be an omen, because of the bright star blazing in the west in the constellation of the Lion. It was an amazing coincidence that the brightest phase of the moon accompanied this brilliant blazing star which was actually a rare close conjunction of the two brightest planets. Tomorrow the spectacle would be over but tonight everyone was impressed.

The same evening the full moon rose in the east adding its light to the spectacle.

The men present at this gathering came from various ethnic, cultural and religious groups of Parthian society. They were gathered on a broad terrace which had an excellent view toward the north, east, south and west. There were three Greeks, descendants of Greeks who had immigrated to Mesopotamia following Alexander's victories over the Persians over three hundred years before. A visiting Latin scholar / astrologer was present as well, speaking in soft tones to the Greeks. On the right side of the terrace four Zoroastrian Magi, including one Parthian, two Medes and a Persian debated about the significance of the heavenly events along with four Chaldean (Babylonian) astronomers. In the center of the terrace beside the balustrade two Babylonians and an ethnic Jew stood with three other Persian Zoroastrians and the Median Rab Mag, the head of the varied assembly of wise men. The two Babylonians and the Jew were present at the special request of the Rab Mag who had summoned them from Babylon. The Rab Mag had been well informed of the activities of the group from Borsippa.

Ekur-zakir, Iqisa and their Jewish friend Zechariah Ben Chokmah, knew that they had won the debate which had gone on in Mesopotamia for much of the last year. For them the remarkable but sometimes discreet heavenly events, involving the sun, moon and several stars carried one great message. This evening looking at the great light in the west, Ekur-zakir, Iqisa and Zechariah were profoundly excited. The Messiah of Israel was certainly arriving. Somewhere off to the west in Judea the Jewish messianic hope of a truly righteous king who would reign in righteousness and justice over all humanity was being fulfilled. Perhaps the young king had already been born.

Only moments before Ekur-zakir's son Iqisa and Zechariah had met the Rab Mag, the official leader of the Magi, for the first time. The old man's massive beard, his probing eyes, his fine clothing and jewelry were intimidating, but he was very hospitable to the 33 year old Iqisa and the 40 year old Zechariah. He greeted them warmly shaking their hands, knowing that Iqisa and Zechariah had greatly helped Ekur-zakir in deciphering the events of the last year.

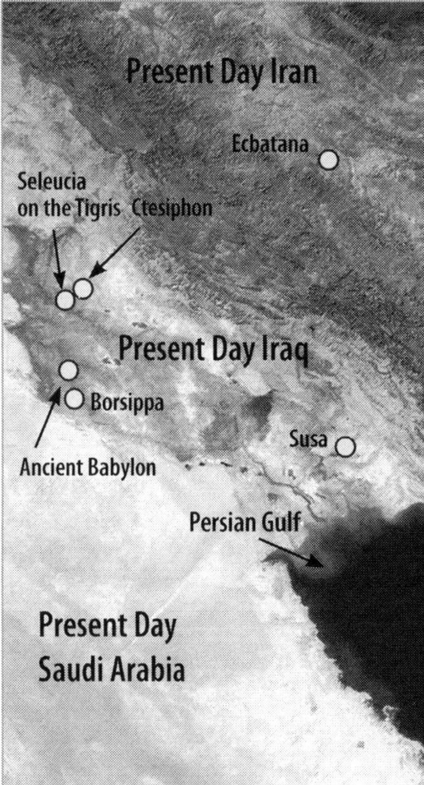

The Rab Mag spoke, "Ekur-zakir, I am convinced. On every major Jewish holiday for over a year there has been a messianic event in the heavens. The timing of the events involving the planet that you call Shabbatei are undeniable. Your son's calculations concerning Daniel's prophecy of the 70 "sevens" seem to be accurate, I am impressed. It seems to me there may be more. You have not yet calculated everything. The God of the Jews, YHWH, has certainly been at work. The ancient planning of these events fills one with awe. Tonight the wandering stars, which the Jews call 'Tzedek' and its accompanying star 'Nogah' along with the moon have again amazed us. Certainly this last event also signals the appearing of the 'bright righteous one' from the tribe of Judah."

"I have decided to send you three, and perhaps some others, to Judea to look for this newly born Messiah. I cannot send you away in the summer heat, but in several months you can go to search for the new-born king. Even though his coming is announced in the stars it would not surprise me that his arrival in Judea may be unnoticed. The God of Abraham knows that Herod the Great is a dangerous man. He has even put two of his own heirs to death, but the great God YHWH knows how to deliver the humble from evil. He demonstrated that repeatedly in the life of the Jewish prophet Daniel. I have also read the texts about this amazing man. I am sure he could teach us all many things if he was still among us. However, his words still speak after five centuries. The God of Abraham will deliver you and the Messiah from Herod and from all evil. He will ensure that the Messiah will accomplish his appointed task and bring in his long-awaited reign of everlasting righteousness. It may well be that there will be other indications of the birth of the righteous king in the coming months. I have not seen anything as interesting as this series of events during my long life; I wish that I could accompany you, but I fear that I am too old for the journey."

62 Weeks after Pentecost in 3 BC

Nogah
Tzedek
Nogah
Ari, the lion (Leo)
July 28th 2 BC
Tzedek
Horizon line
Ma'adim (Mars)
Melech together with the Sun

Above and right: If one could have seen the sky below the horizon without the light scattering effect of the atmosphere, at the right, one would have seen the sun in close conjunction with LUGAL / Melech, the king star. Here it is impossible to tell the two apart.

Below: The positions of the sun, stars and planets are indicated for 62 weeks after the hypothetical Sadducean Pentecost date.

Melech / Sun / Tzedek

"The sun of righteousness will arise with healing in his wings." (Malachi 4:2)

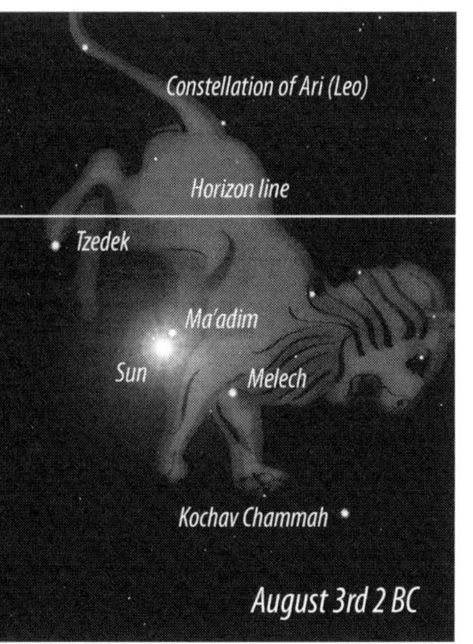

26 Tammuz and 2 Av - July 28th and August 3rd

Exactly 62 weeks (434 days) after the date of the Pharisaic Pentecost in 3 BC was the day of Tzedek's probable heliacal setting in 2 BC, an event which was always noted by Babylonian astronomers. That same day, July 28th 2 BC, the sun was in conjunction with Melech, *which only happens on one day each year.* Mesopotamian astronomers could calculate the positions of the sun, moon, stars and planets for years in advance. An already calculated table on a cuneiform tablet would have shown any Babylonian astronomer the exact longitude of the sun for that particular day. It would have been clear that the sun was passing precisely by the "normal star" called LUGAL (Melech - the king) on July 28th. The symbolism in the constellation of Ari (Leo) was strong. The planet of righteousness, which was also referred to by many as the "king planet," made its last appearance on the same day when the sun was in conjunction with the king star Melech. This again confirmed Daniel's prophecy. The prophecy proclaimed the arrival of the Messiah at the culmination of the 62 "sevens." Tzedek, the Sun and Melech together underlined the righteous king of Malachi 4:2. Sixty-two weeks after the hypothetical Sadducean date of Pentecost in 3 BC, Tzedek, the Sun and Melech were all still together in Leo. The sun had shifted to a position almost exactly between Tzedek and Melech. Ma'adim, "the red, blushing one," was in superior conjunction with the sun. The Magi may or may not have been aware of this conjunction of Ma'adim (Mars) with the sun. If they were aware of it, perhaps it had special meaning for the Magi. On average it only happens once in about every 780 days.[3]

Part 12: Events in the Heavens - 3

Errata:

Tzedek Goes Before

The Magi Travel Westward

Autumn 2 BC

After having disappeared in the west into the solar glare of the setting sun toward the end of July, Tzedek reappeared in the east in the early morning sky at the end of August. Each following night it rose a bit higher in the sky. The wise men would have seen Tzedek rising earlier each night as it was moving from the east toward the west sometime from September 2 BC through mid December 2 BC.

The Magi's journey of over 600 miles (1,000 kilometers) to Judea would have also required planning and possibly approval from the authorities, if the wise men held any responsible positions in the Parthian administration. Several armed men and servants could have accompanied the wise men for their security and comfort. In present day Baghdad the summer temperatures average above 40°C (104°F). Temperatures in winter are generally from 15° to 19°C (59 to 66°F) with lows falling to between 2° and 5°C (35.6 to 41°F).[1] It is obvious that travel to Judea was to be avoided during the summer months. The wise men probably began their two month journey in the fall of 2 BC when it was cooler. They could have begun their journey as late as the middle of October, after having made several arrangements and having waited for the cooler temperatures of the autumn.

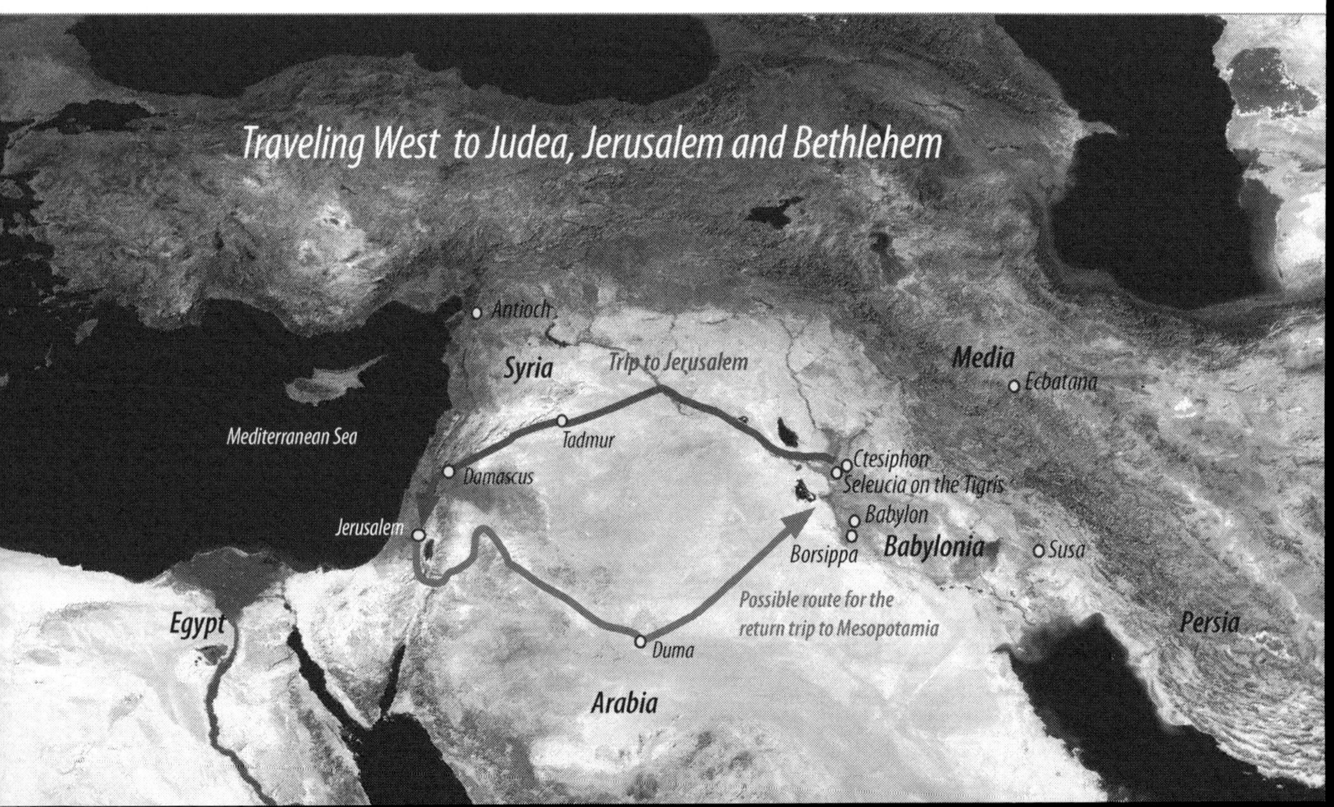

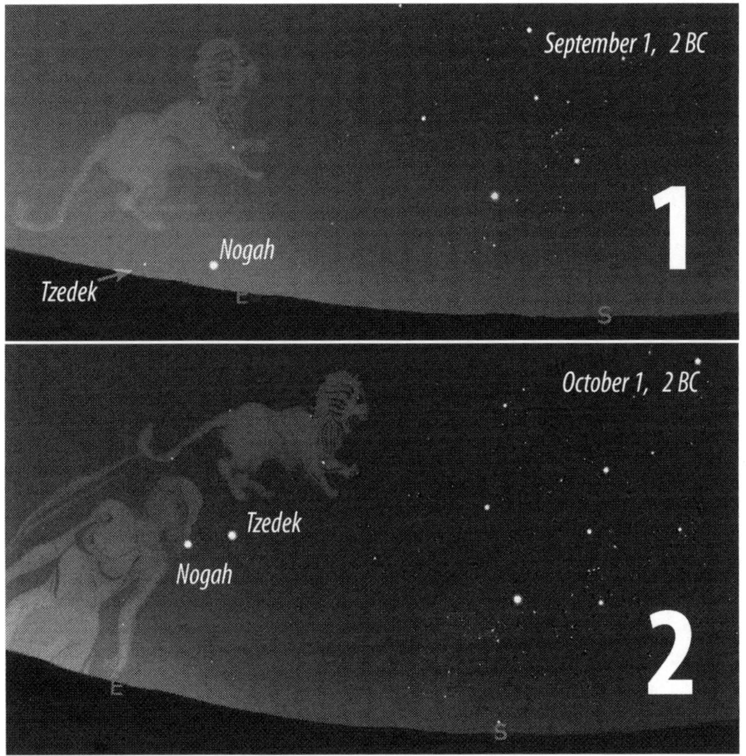

Left: Tzedek moved progressively from the east toward the west from September 2 BC through mid December 2 BC. Here we see the first two months of that progression. On page 201 the following three months are indicated.

The group would have most likely traveled up the Euphrates Valley. Then they would have crossed over the Syrian desert to Tadmur (later called Palmyra). Eventually they could have reached Damascus possibly in late November or early December 2 BC. After at least two months they would have reached Jerusalem from Damascus toward the middle of December.

The wise men probably began their two to three month journey in the fall of 2 BC. They should have arrived in Jerusalem in December.

The wise men would have been well informed about the geography for a trip from the Parthian Empire to Judea. If any of them had a Jewish background perhaps one or more of them had already made the pilgrimage to Jerusalem during one of the festivals like Passover, Pentecost or Tabernacles. Many people traveled this route and it was especially well known to Jewish people living in Babylonia or Media and Persia. The Magi would not have relied upon any specific star to guide them for navigation purposes, despite Christmas carols which indicate that they followed the star in that manner. The men were educated men, well informed about geography. If they were seeking to find the Jewish Messiah, Judea was the logical place to look for him. They would not have leaned on every movement of a star for guidance. The route was well traveled, the way to Jerusalem was well known. They were men with their feet solidly planted on the ground. They were not wild eyed mystics; the "star" did go before them, but it was not their compass.

69 / 70 Weeks After June 14th in 3 BC

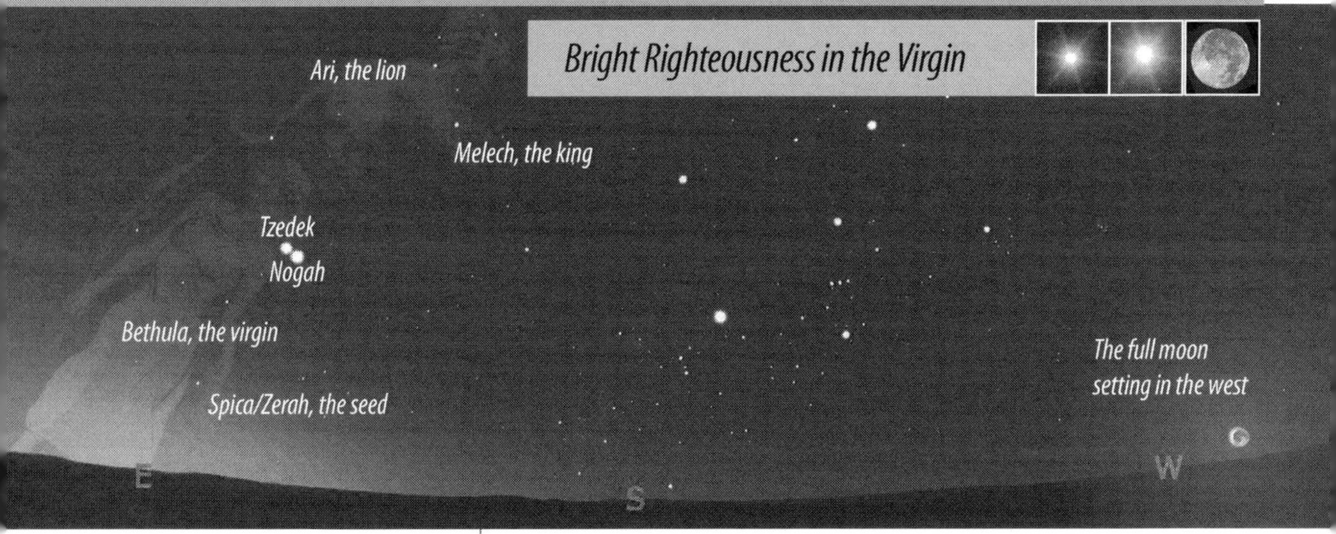

Bright Righteousness in the Virgin

Ari, the lion
Melech, the king
Tzedek
Nogah
Bethula, the virgin
Spica/Zerah, the seed
The full moon setting in the west
E
S
W

Autumn 2 BC

10 Tishrei and 12-15th Tishrei - October 9/10 and 12-15th

In 3 BC, Tzedek had been in conjunction with the new moon on the 10th Sabbath (the 70th day) from the date of the hypothetical Sadducean First Fruits Offering. Counting exactly 69 weeks (7 + 62 weeks) after the June 14th 3 BC date, when Tzedek was in conjunction with the new moon, one arrives at the Day of Atonement in 2 BC. Making atonement for sin was one key aspect of Daniel's prophecy of the 70 "sevens." There was nothing remarkable in the heavens at this moment, but the date was significant. A few days later there was an event in the heavens.

In September Tzedek had moved into the constellation of Bethula, the virgin, and Nogah soon followed. Then exactly four months after their close conjunction on June 17th (15 Sivan), Tzedek and Nogah were again in conjunction in the morning sky in Bethula. Amazingly, the closest conjunction of Tzedek and Nogah took place facing the full moon on October 14th. The Feast of Tabernacles began the next evening on Oct. 14/15th 2 BC. While this fall conjunction was not as visually impressive as the very close June conjunction, it did make an almost mirror image of what had happened four months earlier. This was during the middle of the 70th week from the June 14th 3 BC new moon conjunction involving Tzedek. Did the Magi make the links with the symbolic 69th and 70th weeks counting back from the June 2 BC date? We do not know. However, they would have been well aware of the conjunction which happened at the time of the full moon. This was the last major event in the heavens before the Magi arrived in Jerusalem.

Table 12.1: The distance separating Tzedek from Nogah in October 2 BC.

Date (Hebrew)	Date (Julian)	Separation:
10th Tishrei	Oct 10th (AM)	3°01′
11th Tishrei	Oct 11th (AM)	2°33′
12th Tishrei	Oct 12th (AM)	2°08′
13th Tishrei	Oct 13th (AM)	1°53′
14th Tishrei	Oct 14th (AM)	1°51′
15th Tishrei	Oct 15th (AM)	2°02

Autumn 2 BC

Tzedek Continued to Move Further Toward the West

All during the autumn months of 2 BC Tzedek moved progressively from the east toward the west rising higher in the sky each night. At some point the Magi also started to move west toward Jerusalem. By the end of December 2 BC Tzedek rose about 10:30 PM on the eastern horizon and it advanced each night across over half of the sky till it was positioned toward the south-southwest just before dawn. At the same time Tzedek had also moved among the background stars from the constellation of Ari (the lion) toward Bethula (the virgin). The Magi should have arrived in Jerusalem by mid-December. Soon after their arrival Tzedek stopped moving among the background stars (This was one of its two annual stationary points). The stage was being set for Tzedek's placement over Bethlehem.

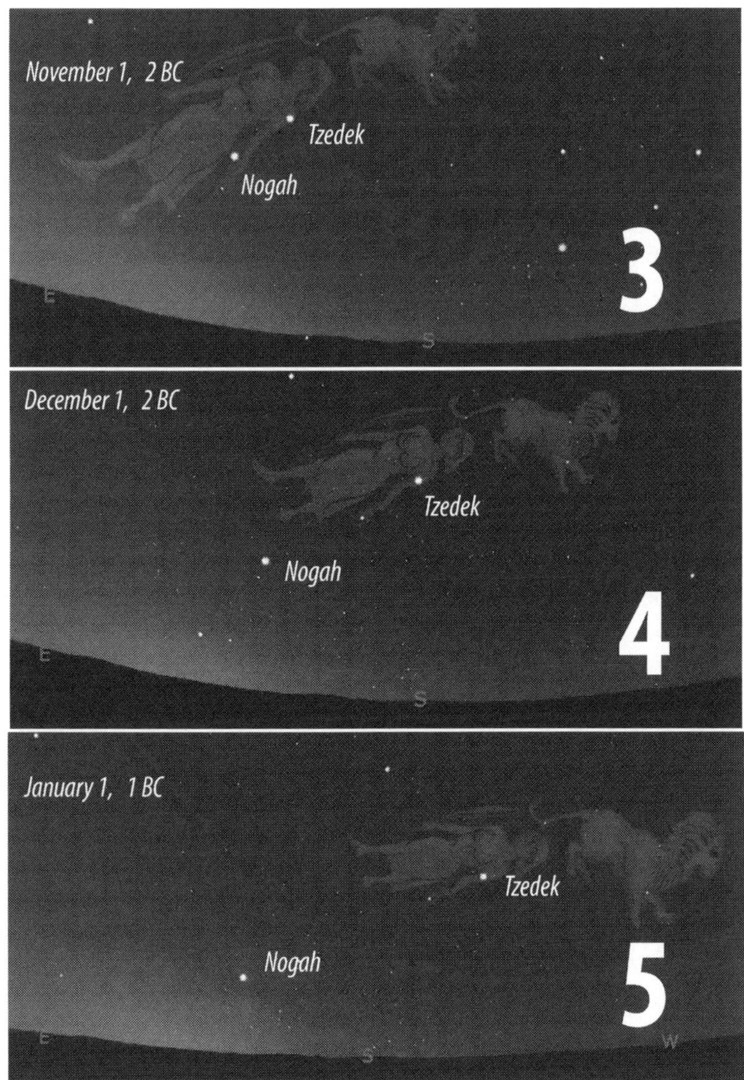

Left: The progression of Tzedek from east to west continued in November and December. Finally the "star" stopped its movement among the background stars at the end of December in 2 BC.

"The star, which they had seen in the east, went on before them until it came and stood over the place where the child was."

Antipater: A Crown Prince in Great Difficulties

The birth of Jesus and the visit of the wise men happened in a context of intrigue, assassinations and betrayal

One aspect of the story of the birth of Jesus which has been seriously neglected in popular accounts concerns King Herod and his offspring. We actually know quite a lot from the historian Josephus concerning the circumstances in Herod's court during the last few years preceding Herod's death. The birth of Jesus and the visit of the wise men happened in a context of intrigue, assassinations and betrayal. Jesus was born in either December of 3 BC or January of 2 BC during the "inventory of the world," the census, ordered by Augustus and carried out by Herod in his dominions. The visit of the wise men happened about one year later, in December of 2 BC or January of 1 BC.

"Where is He who has been born King of the Jews? For we saw His star in the east and have come to worship Him." When Herod the king heard this, he was troubled, and all Jerusalem with him..

Probably toward the beginning of March in 2 BC Herod's son Antipater, the crown prince, went to Rome. He had written to friends in Rome just after the census (end of December 3 BC, beginning of January 2 BC). He had asked to be invited by his friends to the imperial capital. He did this to flee the conflict which was brewing between Herod and his brother Pheroras. This concerned the 6,000 Pharisees who had refused to give their oath of allegiance to Herod and the emperor during the census. Pheroras' wife had offered to pay the fine imposed on the resisting Pharisees. This made some very bad relations between Pheroras and his brother because Herod insisted that Pheroras divorce his wife. Pheroras left Jerusalem for his own territories in Galilee and Perea after the census. Unexpectedly within two or three months Pheroras was poisoned and died. Herod was very grieved by his brother's death and ordered an investigation. Through torturing various slaves and individuals in Pheroras' household it was discovered that Antipater had apparently been in a plot with his uncle to assassinate Herod through poisoning. Herod may have discovered these facts in late March or mid-April of 2 BC. Meanwhile, Antipater spent about seven months in Italy after the discovery of the plot before being recalled by his father (Josephus, The Wars of the Jews, Book 1, Ch. 31, 2).

Herod waited patiently for his son Antipater to return. Antipater did not initially suspect there was a problem. Upon Antipater's arrival in Jerusalem perhaps in November of 2 BC Herod had his son Antipater arrested. He was then tried and found guilty before Herod and the Roman governor of Syria, Publius Quinctilius Varus, who was visiting Jerusalem. Herod wrote to Augustus for instructions because the king did not have the right to execute or exile the crown prince without Augustus' formal approval. Receiving a response from Rome would have taken about two months: (1) a month for Herod's message to arrive in Rome, and (2) a month for a message to come from Augustus in return.

Antipater's betrayal and his trial severely affected the health of the 70 year old king. When the wise men arrived from the east, in mid-December, Herod's health was declining seriously.

Hanukkah 2 BC

25th of Kislev to the 2nd of Tevet (December 22/23 to 29/30)

The wise men probably arrived in Jerusalem several days before the Feast of Hanukkah in 2 BC.

When Herod the king heard this, he was troubled, and all Jerusalem with him. Gathering together all the chief priests and scribes of the people, he inquired of them where the Messiah was to be born. They said to him, "In Bethlehem of Judea; for this is what has been written by the prophet: 'AND YOU, BETHLEHEM, LAND OF JUDAH, ARE BY NO MEANS LEAST AMONG THE LEADERS OF JUDAH; FOR OUT OF YOU SHALL COME FORTH A RULER WHO WILL SHEPHERD MY PEOPLE ISRAEL.'" Then Herod secretly called the magi and determined from them the exact time the star appeared. And he sent them to Bethlehem and said, "Go and search carefully for the Child; and when you have found Him, report to me, so that I too may come and worship Him." (Matthew 2:3-8)

Alerted concerning the presence of the Magi, and alarmed by their questions, Herod summoned his own religious advisors. Being a foreigner himself Herod was not so well versed in the Jewish Scriptures, therefore, he was not well informed about the probable birthplace of the Messiah. After informing himself through his religious advisors, Herod summoned the wise men to his palace in secret. The king asked several questions and eventually he encouraged the Magi to seek the child in Bethlehem six miles (ten kilometers) south-southwest of Jerusalem. Herod probably met with the wise men toward the end of December.

The feast of Hanukkah would have taken place from the 25th of Kislev to the 2nd of Tevet (December 22/23 to 29/30 in 2 BC). We do not know what the Magi may have done during the festival. More details about the festival are on pages 174-175.

We read about Jesus being in the temple courts during the Festival of Hanukkah sometime much later during his years of ministry.

> *At that time the Feast of Dedication (Hanukkah) took place at Jerusalem. It was winter, and Jesus was walking in the temple, in the colonnade of Solomon. So the Jews gathered around him and said to him, "How long will you keep us in suspense? If you are the Christ, tell us plainly." Jesus answered them, "I told you, and you do not believe. The works that I do in my Father's name bear witness about me, but you do not believe because you are not among my sheep. My sheep hear my voice, and I know them, and they follow me. I give them eternal life, and they will never perish, and no one will snatch them out of my hand. My Father, who has given them to me, is greater than all, and no one is able to snatch them out of the Father's hand. I and the Father are one." (John 10:22-29).*

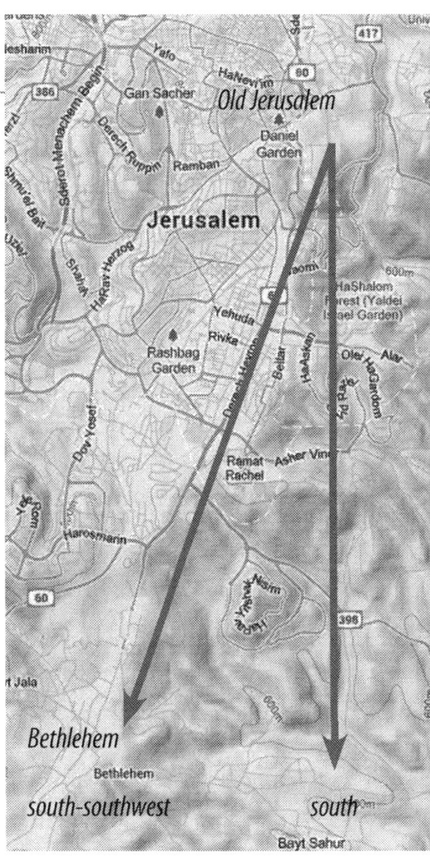

A modern map of the area near Jerusalem.
© Google Maps and Mapa GISrael

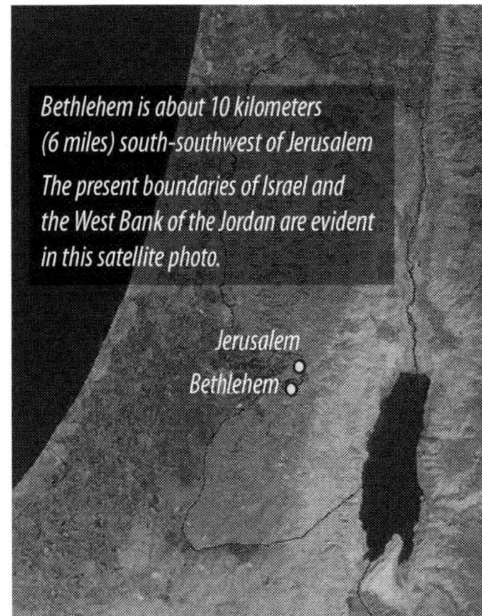

Tzedek Stops Moving "The Star of Bethlehem"

Painting by James Tissot: The Magi with Herod

The visit of the wise men came well after the birth of Jesus, probably about one year after his birth.

The star of Bethlehem was not spectacular. The position of Tzedek over the village of Bethlehem at the end of December 2 BC would not have particularly attracted any attention of masses of people or the authorities. There was almost certainly not any beam of light indicating the way to a specific house. If this had been the case Herod's soldiers and everyone else in the whole region would have found the way to the child Messiah. For the wise men Tzedek's position over the town was a confirmation that they were being rightly guided. When King Herod directed the men toward Bethlehem the star indicated that it was the right direction, but neither the king nor the Magi saw a blazing star with a tail descending to the ground.

Tzedek stopped moving among the stars after having moved from the constellation of Ari (the lion) to the constellation of Bethula (the virgin) during the late summer and fall of 2 BC. Toward the end of December, Tzedek came to its first stationary point after its heliacal rising at the end of August. As indicated previously the outer planets go through two stationary points each year when they visually appear to stop from the perspective of the earth. This also happened concerning Tzedek in November 3 BC and in March 2 BC. After stopping the planet reversed its course (a retrograde motion) until it came to the next stationary point. The earth moves faster than the outer planets like Tzedek so at times the shifting positions of the Earth and Tzedek together causes the planet to appear to stop and to even appear to reverse its course. In December 2 BC Tzedek stopped its visible movement among the stars almost exactly between the stars now called Porrima and Zaniah. Positioned between the two stars, Tzedek's lack of movement would have been easy to discern for trained astronomers. As already indicated (see pages 131-135) the stationary points of the planets were phenomena which had been consistently noted by the astronomers in Babylonia for many hundreds of years. They would not have been surprised that the "star" had stopped.

The stationary position of Tzedek at the end of December 2 BC corresponds well with the traditional date of the Magi's visit in late December or early January. After visiting Herod and having been advised by the king to search for the Messiah in Bethlehem the wise men rejoiced to see the "star" Tzedek placed directly over Bethlehem for several nights just before dawn. For the Magi this was a confirming sign about the presence of the Messiah, the Righteous One. It was most likely in early January that the wise men actually saw the child Messiah in Bethlehem. Each year the Eastern Orthodox churches still celebrate the visit of the wise men on January 6th. This may even be very close to the actual date of their visit.

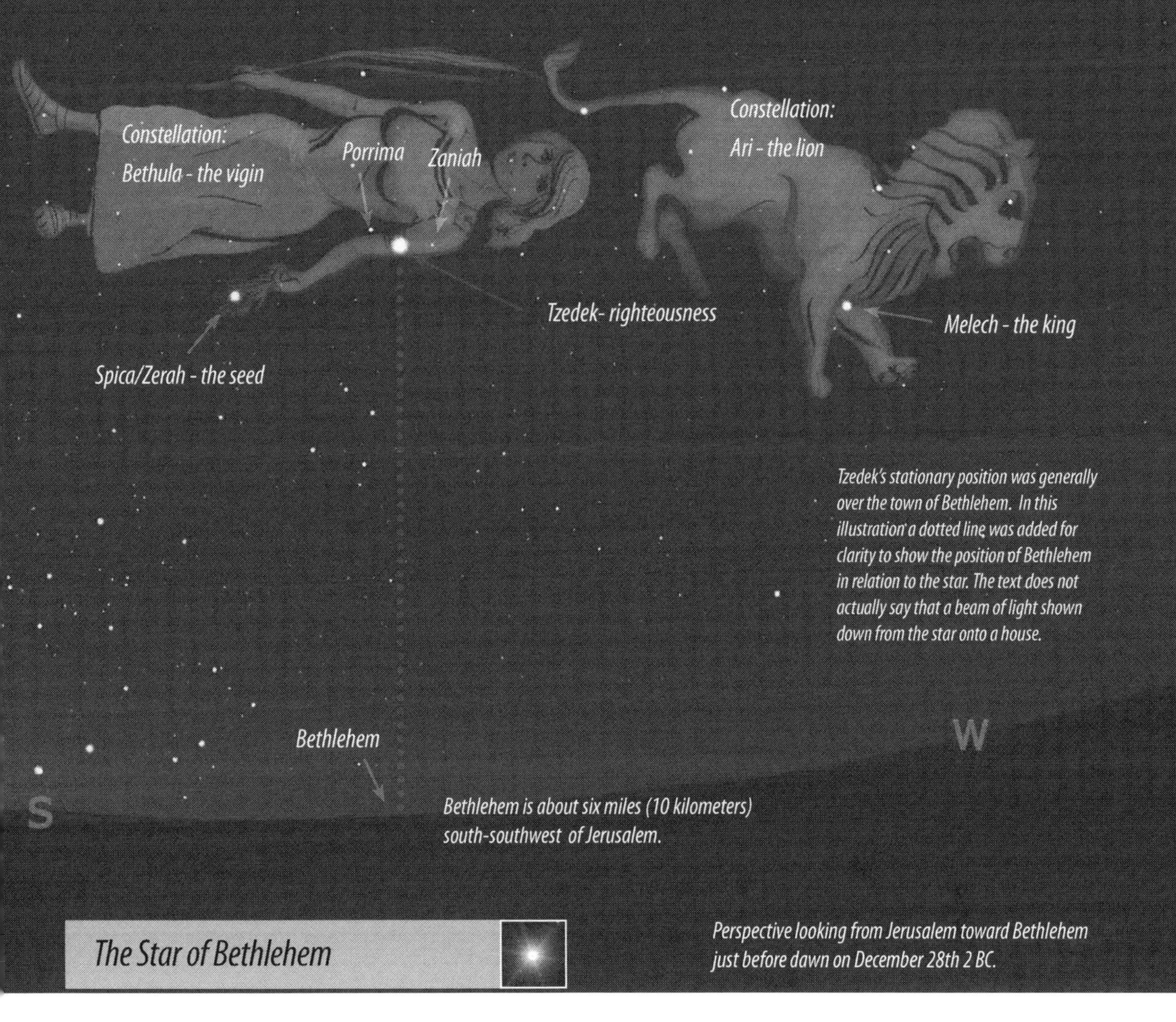

Tzedek's Positions Over Several Weeks [2]

Month	Day	Tzedek distance to Porrima	Tzedek distance to Zaniah	Discernable movement moon = 30′
Nov	13	5°32′02″	0°08′21″	Beside Zaniah
Dec	1	3°44′14″	1°52′54″	2 moons
Dec	5	3°27′17″	2°11′00″	1 & 1/2 moons
Dec	10	3°09′49″	2°29′47″	1 moon
Dec	15	2°56′29″	2°44′09″	1/2 moon
Dec	20	2°47′14″	2°53′57″	1/5 moon
Dec	22	2°44′45″	2°56′43″	not discernable
Dec	24	2°42′50″	2°58′23″	not discernable
Dec	26	2°41′37″	2°59′26″	not discernable

Month	Day	Tzedek distance to Porrima	Tzedek distance to Zaniah	Discernable movement moon = 30′
Dec	27	2°42′16″	2°59′41″	not discernable
Dec	28	2°41′04″	2°59′44″	complete stop
Dec	29	2°41′02″	2°59′36″	complete stop
Dec	30	2°41′11″	2°57′42″	not discernable
Jan	1	3°01′18″	2°56′27″	not discernable
Jan	5	3°05′48″	2°51′40″	1/6 moon
Jan	10	3°14′18″	2°41′27″	1/3 moon
Jan	15	3°27′12″	2°26′41″	1/2 moon
Jan	20	3°44′29″	2°07′32″	2/3 moon

Meeting the King of kings

Above:An early morning view of modern Bethlehem.

How did the wise men actually find Jesus' family and what were the exact circumstances of their time together? We do not know.

It should be remembered that Herod had encouraged the wise men to go to Bethlehem. Herod may have also asked one of the more influential people in the town to host the men and to facilitate the lodging of any servants or guards who may have accompanied them. A small encampment may have been set up on the outskirts of town for some of the servants and guards. The Magi were most likely lodged in the town with some of Herod's contacts. With such an arrangement, Herod would have had relative ease in keeping an eye on the men. But things were more complicated. Herod probably had a whole network of spies and the Magi, being intelligent men, would have realized that their every move was most likely being watched. The wise men may have been suspicious concerning Herod's motives well before their arrival in Judea. Any rendezvous with the young child or his parents would have had to have been very discreet. Even asking for information would have been done in a way so that it would not arouse too much suspicion or interest. Already their presence would have been known to just about everyone in the small town (population of perhaps 500 to 1,000 people). It is possible that the Magi learned about the exact location of the family through someone who knew the family well. Some individuals may have arranged a meeting in the most discreet manner possible, perhaps after dark. It would not have been too hard to arrange to be outside after dark, the men were astronomers. It would have been normal and understandable for them to be outside observing the night sky.

Matthew indicates that the wise men arrived at a house, not at a stable. The visit apparently took place about one year after Jesus' birth. As mentioned previously, according to one ancient tradition Jesus was standing beside his mother during the visit. For a child of one year this would have been entirely possible. He could have been standing, holding onto his mother seated beside him. When the men arrived in the home where Jesus and his parents lived, the Magi were probably in absolute awe. One needs to remember that they thought of this child in terms of scriptural passages like Daniel 7:13-14. For them, he was the ultimate Great King. They may have remembered passages like Psalm 89:26-27 and Psalm 89:36-37.

> *"He will cry to Me, 'You are my Father, My God, and the rock of my salvation. I also shall make him My firstborn, The highest of the kings of the earth."... "Once I have sworn by My holiness; I will not lie to David. His descendants shall endure forever And his throne as the sun before Me. It shall be established forever like the moon, And the witness in the sky is faithful."*

How did the wise men actually find Jesus' family and what were the eaxct circumstances of their time together? We do not know.

No doubt the men would have bowed low to the ground, as one would have done for any of the kings of the east. The Magi had witnessed signs in the heavens over a period of almost two years. They had traveled hundreds of miles across vast deserts and in regions frequented by robbers. They had risked their lives and perhaps part of their personal fortunes to arrive in Judea. They were directed by a ruthless and scheming king to go to Bethlehem and finally they saw the promised Messiah. We can hardly imagine their thoughts or sense their emotions.

The men would have probably bowed low to the ground as one would do for any of the kings of the east.

An even bigger surprise for the wise men may have been to discover the child's God given name and to discover the exact circumstances of his conception and birth. The virgin birth would have amazed them. They may have even thought of Isaiah 7:14. In addition the name Yeshua, which is the name Jesus in Hebrew, means "salvation." The word "yeshua" or forms of it are used 19 times in the book of Isaiah. Passages like the following may have filled their minds:

> *"I bring near My righteousness, it is not far off; And My salvation will not delay. I will grant salvation in Zion, and My glory for Israel. (Isaiah 46:13)* Note that the word righteousness is "tsadaqah" (Tzedek) and salvation is "yeshua."
>
> *... You should be My Servant to raise up the tribes of Jacob and to restore the preserved ones of Israel; I will also make You a light of the nations so that My salvation (yeshua) may reach to the end of the earth." (Isaiah 49:6)*
>
> This text was perhaps also important: *"For Zion's sake I will not keep silent, And for Jerusalem's sake I will not keep quiet, until her righteousness goes forth like brightness, and her salvation like a torch that is burning." Here righteousness is again "tsadaqah," salvation is "yeshua" and brightness is "nogah." (See also Isaiah 49:8, 51:5-8, 52:7 and 10, 56:1, 59:11 and16-17).*

Below: The Magi visiting Mary, Joseph and Jesus. This is from a fresco done in a cave church in Cappadocia (modern Turkey).

Above: Another early morning view of modern Bethlehem.

The wise men presented their gifts. There were without doubt tears of joy. Mary and Joseph must have been astonished by the arrival of such a group of eastern Magi with their important, expensive gifts. Within hours the incident was over. One can imagine the wise men taking one last look at the child king, perhaps with tears in their eyes, then they probably left under the cover of night.

The Magi may have already been warned by God in a dream not to return to Herod even before meeting the Lord's Messiah. Matthew wrote that they returned to their country by another route. It is probable that they went around the southern extremity of the Dead Sea into what is now Jordan. Afterwards they would have crossed the desert into Mesopotamia. This route would have been much more difficult, traveling through a much larger and more dangerous desert. Arriving in Jordan, the wise men may have stopped briefly in Petra, but this is unlikely. Herod would have had agents in the Nabataean capital. The Magi would have probably preferred to avoid such dangers. It is more probable that they would have advanced toward the Wadi Sirhan, taking the route toward Duma, an oasis in the desert of Saudi Arabia. From there, continuing through the desert they would have arrived in the region of the ruined city of Babylon. The return trip may have taken at least two months.

We have no idea what eventually happened to the wise men. Hopefully they lived long lives and prospered. Some Christians have believed that their bones were found in Jerusalem. The remains were transported to Constantinople, then to Milan and later to Cologne, Germany. Today the "Shrine of the Three Kings," in the Cologne cathedral, is a tourist attraction. Any discovery of the bones of the wise men in Jerusalem does not seem realistic. The men would have avoided returning to Judea, where they would have been in mortal danger. Others think the Magi were buried in northern Iran. Marco Polo reported that he visited their tombs in Saveh on the road from present day Tehran to Hamadan (Ecbatana). The Magi remain an enigma. We may only discover their true identity in God's new world of justice and righteousness, which seems to have been so important to them.

Jewish Calendar 1 BC

(Julian dates in the evening - beginning of night)					
14	Tevet	Total Eclipse	Jan	9	Fri
27	Tevet	The Death of Antipater	Jan	22/23	Thu/Fri
1	Shevat	New Moon	Jan	26/27	Mon
2	Shevat	The Death of Herod	Jan	27/28	Tue/Wed
1	Adar	New Moon	Feb	25	Wed
1	Nisan	New Moon	March	25	Thu
14	Nisan	Passover	April	7	Wed

1 BC

Part 13: The Last Events

The paintings above were done by by James Tissot. They show the flight of Joseph, Mary and Jesus to Egypt as well as the slaughtered children in Bethlehem.

The Messiah in Danger

When Herod saw that he had been tricked by the Magi, he became very enraged, and sent and slew all the male children who were in Bethlehem and all its vicinity, from two years old and under, according to the time which he had determined from the magi. Then what had been spoken through Jeremiah the prophet was fulfilled: "A voice was heard in Ramah, weeping and great mourning, Rachel weeping for her children; and she refused to be comforted, because they were no more." (Mt. 2:16-18)

The massacre of the young children in Bethlehem is only recorded in the book of Matthew. The account has been dismissed by some writers and scholars because it is not attested in other sources, yet such skepticism is hardly warranted. In history we only have one account or only one eyewitness for many events. Sometimes historical artifacts are totally missing as well. In France, there are still some lingering doubts about the exact location of the historic battlefield of Alesia, the place where Julius Caesar finally brought the Gauls into submission. No one doubts that the Gauls were conquered by Caesar. However, the archaeological remains of the Alesia battlefield are largely lacking. The massacre of the two or three dozen children was not beyond Herod's ability or outside the limits of his known character. Just days before his own death Herod envisioned having many of the prominent men from his kingdom put to death because of his own bitterness. Herod thought the messianic child to be a threat to himself and to the continuation of his royal line. Would it be so surprising that the murder of a relatively small number of children did not make headlines in Rome or Alexandria? An estimated two million Gauls were reduced to slavery by Julius Caesar. We do not know the actual names of more than perhaps two or three dozen of them.

Events in Jerusalem and Jericho

There were several significant incidents leading up to the death of Herod the Great. It is probable that the Magi were secretly invited to Herod's Palace just before these events. We know that Herod became seriously ill because of the betrayal of his son Antipater. It may be that the visit of the wise men also caused his health to decline. It was apparently in late December of 2 BC or early January of 1 BC that the following events took place. The wise men may have been in Bethlehem at the same moment. The text that follows is a paraphrase of Flavius Josephus' account.

Judas and Matthias, two of the most eloquent men among the Jews, and the most celebrated interpreters of the Jewish laws, were men well beloved by the people, because of their efforts to educate the youth. These men, when they found that the king's sickness was incurable, stirred up a number of young men to pull down all the works which the king had erected contrary to the law of their fathers... For the king had erected over the great gate of the temple a large golden eagle, of great value, and had dedicated it to the temple. However, the law forbids those who wish to live according to it, to erect images or representations of any living creature. So Judas and Matthias persuaded other young men to pull down the golden eagle. They encouraged them to destroy the graven image even if they might be punished. They were all convinced that such an act would be meritorious before God and a good example to all men who sought to follow God's decrees.

In addition to the persuasive words of Judas and Matthias a report came to the group that the king was dead. So, in the very middle of the day, they got up to the emplacement of the statue and they pulled down the eagle, and cut it into pieces with axes. A great number of the people, who were present in the temple courts, witnessed their actions.

One of the king's military leaders, hearing what was happening and assuming that the incident might even be more significant than it was, came upon the group with a large number of soldiers. He caught about 40 men and the leaders in the very act of destroying the eagle, however, some others were able to escape. The prisoners were brought before the king. The men confessed their deed and even added, "We will undergo death, and all sorts of punishments which you can inflict upon us, with pleasure, since we are aware that we shall die, not for any unrighteous actions, but for our love to religion." Their courage was very great in the face of death.

The king ordered them to be bound and he sent them to Jericho, where he called together the principal men from among the Jews. When they arrived many days later Herod made them assemble in the city theater. Because he could not stand, he lay upon a couch, and enumerated the works that he had undertaken on their account, and his building of the temple, and what a vast work and responsibility that was for him. In contrast the Hasmoneans, during the hundred and twenty-five years of their government, had not been able to perform any great work for the honor of God as Herod had done in rebuilding the temple. The king said that he hoped that he had left himself a memorial through this magnificent building, and procured himself a reputation after his death. At that point he then cried out, that the accused men had not waited to insult him, even during his lifetime. In broad daylight, and in the sight of the multitude, they had insulted him by destroying what he had dedicated and had pulled it down to the ground. The Jewish leaders, fearing the king, said that Herod should punish the men for what they had done. Herod removed the high priest from his office and had the leaders of the destructive band burnt alive. That very night there was an eclipse of the moon.

(Antiquities of the Jews Book 17 Chapter 6.1.146 through 6.4.167)

These incidents may have distracted Herod long enough to allow the wise men to make their rendezvous with Joseph, Mary and Jesus. Afterwards the situation also may have given the Magi and Joseph's family enough time to escape.

Above: Herod's golden eagle may have been something like the eagle in the photo above. This is a sculpture at the entrance to the Chateau de Fontainebleau in France.

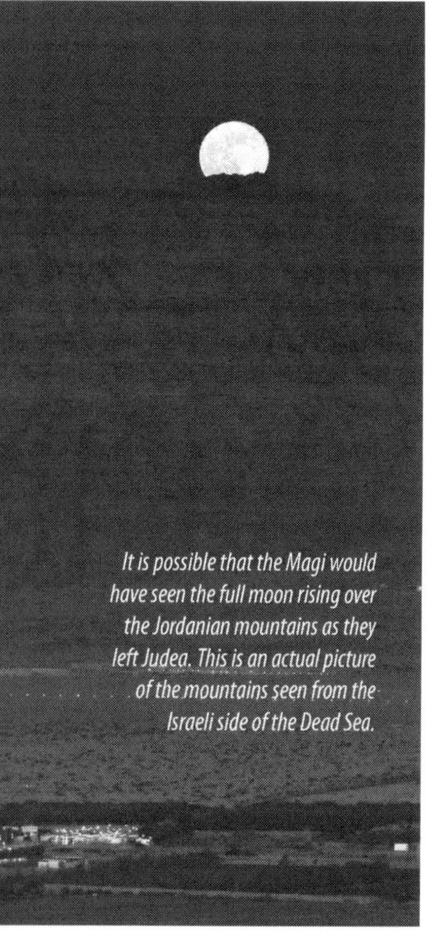
It is possible that the Magi would have seen the full moon rising over the Jordanian mountains as they left Judea. This is an actual picture of the mountains seen from the Israeli side of the Dead Sea.

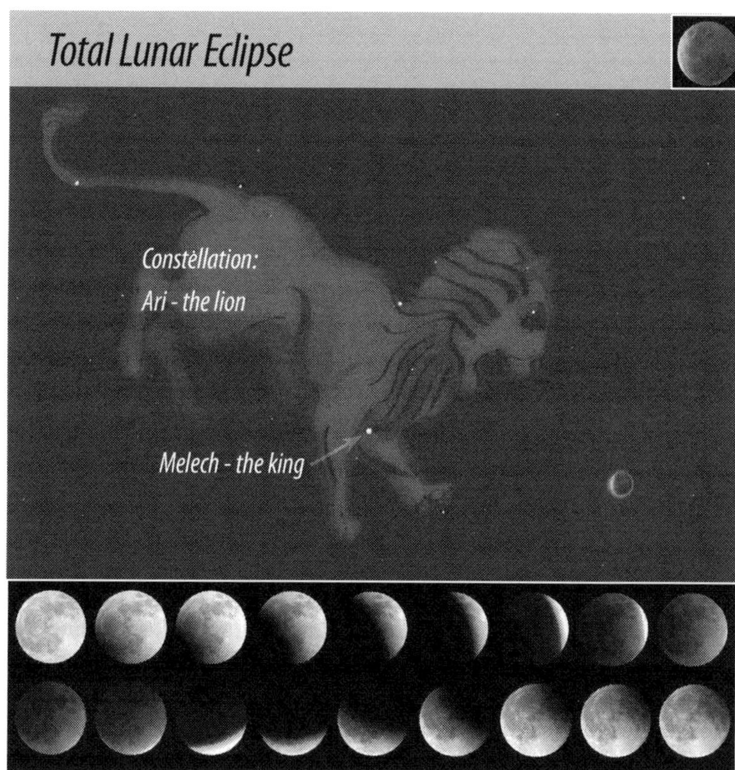

The night of the 15th of Tevet - January 9th - 10th

On January 9th, the two Jewish teachers, who had destroyed the golden eagle, were executed by burning at the command of Herod. That night there was a total eclipse of the moon. Herod the Great died not long after the eclipse of the moon. Two dates are usually proposed for this event: March 13th, 4 BC and January 9-10th, 1 BC. During the 4 BC eclipse less than one-third of the moon's surface was covered by the earth's shadow, however, the January 1 BC eclipse was total.

In a lunar eclipse the earth passes between the moon and the sun. Sometimes the entire lunar surface is darkened but sometimes there is a partial eclipse. In many total and some partial lunar eclipses the moon appears to be somewhat orange or red because some light passing through the earth's atmosphere still illuminates the moon's surface, giving it a reddish aspect. In the January 1 BC eclipse the surface of the moon would have been covered progressively by the earth's shadow. At totality such an eclipse often has a reddish appearance. The entire event would have lasted about four and one-half hours. The moon was positioned in Cancer approaching Leo at the time of the eclipse. During the period from late 5 BC to AD 6 this was the most significant lunar eclipse visible from Judea. It is the only eclipse mentioned in Flavius Josephus' extensive history of the Jewish people. See Appendix 11 on pages 242-243 for further information.

The Death of Herod and Afterwards

Above: Two different photos of the Herodium 12 kilometers south-south-east of Jerusalm and six kilmeters from Bethlehem. Herod the Great was buried at this site. His tomb has only been identified in recent years.

The incidents involving the great eagle and the betrayal of his son Antipater caused Herod to become even more seriously ill. Herod rewrote his will again choosing Archelaus to succeed him as king and his son Antipas was designated to govern Galilee and Perea. Toward the middle of January 1 BC Herod received permission from Augustus to execute or to exile his son Antipater. Herod decided to execute him after having been told by a prison guard that Antipater was glad to know that his father was dying. Five days after Antipater's execution Herod died and Archelaus temporarily became king.

Traditionally Herod's death has been connected to two different dates (7 Kislev and 2 Shevat) in a Jewish document called the Megallit Taanit. The actual text does not mention Herod's death, but some commentary notes added over six centuries later give two different dates for the king's death.[1] It would appear that the 2 Shevat date is correct (January 27/28 in 1 BC). The following is a paraphrase of part of William Whiston's translation of Josephus' text about Herod's painful death:

> *Herod's distemper greatly increased in a severe manner, according to God's judgment upon him for his sins; for a fire glowed in him, which did not so much appear to the touch outwardly, and it augmented his pains inwardly; he had a vehement appetite, and was continually trying to eat, however, his entrails were ulcerated, and the chief violence of his pain lay in his colon; an aqueous and transparent liquid also had settled itself about his feet, and in a similar matter afflicted him at the bottom of his belly. ... When he sat upright, he had a difficulty breathing.*[2]

The king died in great pain. Archelaus, now as Herod's principal heir, presided over the arrangements for Herod's funeral. The funeral was an impressive affair lasting several days. A substantial part of the army and many dignitaries took part. Herod was buried at the Herodium 7.5 miles (12 kilometers) from Jerusalem and 3.5 miles (6 kilometers) from Bethlehem.

Uprising and the War of Governor Varus

Archelaus' new government started very badly. Because of some disturbances in Jerusalem during Passover Archelaus issued orders to his troops which resulted in the massacre of 3,000 Jews in and around the temple courts. Within weeks, this massacre inspired a general revolt. Before the revolt broke out Archelaus and his brothers went to Rome to present themselves before Augustus. Herod's last will was contested by Antipas, who had been destined to receive the kingdom in a previous will. Possibly in May or June Augustus decided to split the kingdom into parts and appointed Herod's son Archelaus as an ethnarch (a type of prince), and Antipas

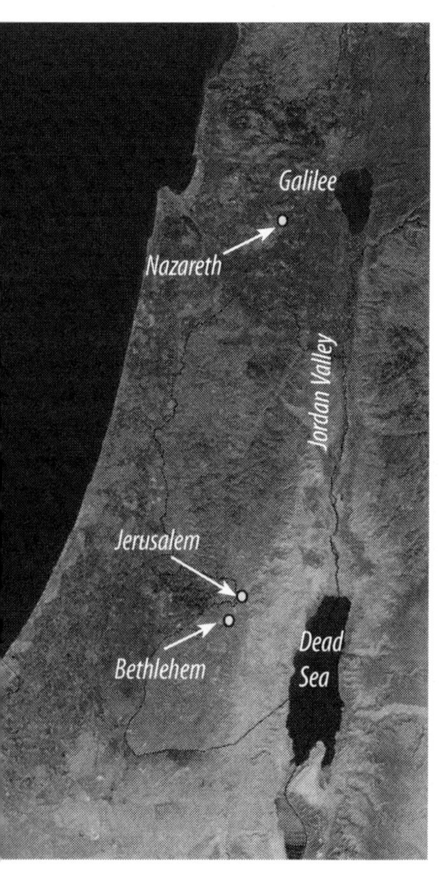

Archelaus was deposed in AD 6. Herod Antipas and Philip were still ruling in their dominions over 30 years later when Jesus was tried, executed and rose from the dead. (Luke 3:1).

and Philip as tetrarchs (perhaps equivalent to a duke) over the each portion of the realm. Augustus promised Archelaus more authority if he conducted himself well. Archelaus received the rulership of about half the kingdom including Idumaea, Judea and Samaria. Herod Antipas was appointed to govern Galilee and Perea, while Philip was appointed over the northeastern portion of the kingdom. In the late spring and early summer a general revolt continued while Herod's sons were in Rome. The Roman governor of Syria, Publius Quinctilius Varus, arrived with three legions to put down the revolt. Many thousands died and two thousand Jews were crucified. The first year of Jesus' life was marked by war.

As the revolt was ending Herod's sons arrived back in their appointed territories. Archelaus reigned over Judea until AD 6. At that point he was deposed by Augustus because of his bad administration. A Roman governor replaced him in Judea. Over 25 years later Pontius Pilate was named the fifth governor of the province. Herod Antipas and Philip were still ruling in their dominions over 30 years later when Jesus was tried, crucified and raised from the dead (Luke 3:1).

Phraataces and Musa reigned over Parthia until they were overthrown in a coup sometime in AD 4. We do not even know how or when they were deposed. Most of the records of the Parthian Empire were destroyed by invading armies during the following centuries. Augustus died on August 19th, AD 14. He was replaced by Tiberius, who was still emperor when Jesus was crucified and raised from the dead. Tiberius remained in power until AD 37.

Joseph and His Family Returned to Judea and Galilee

> ***But when Herod died, behold, an angel of the Lord appeared in a dream to Joseph in Egypt, and said, "Get up, take the Child and His mother, and go into the land of Israel; for those who sought the Child's life are dead." So Joseph got up, took the Child and His mother, and came into the land of Israel. But when he heard that Archelaus was reigning over Judea in place of his father Herod, he was afraid to go there. Then after being warned by God in a dream, he left for the regions of Galilee, and came and lived in a city called Nazareth. This was to fulfill what was spoken through the prophets: "He shall be called a Nazarene." (Matthew 2:16-23)***

According to some traditions Joseph kept his family in Egypt for about two years.[3] We do not know when Joseph received the instructions to return to Judea and Galilee. Matthew's text would make one think that very little time had passed, but it is doubtful that Joseph would have brought his family back from Egypt during the revolt. Finally when Joseph did return to the land of Israel, fearing Archelaus, he took his family to live in Nazareth in Galilee, away from Jerusalem. Perhaps the family stayed in Egypt until Varus had finished putting down the revolt. This could mean that Jesus lived in Egypt for possibly a year or more. The gifts of the Magi would have certainly financed the trip and covered the family's needs in Egypt. They must have been in awe, having seen God's miraculous provision.

62 Weeks after Pentecost in 2 BC

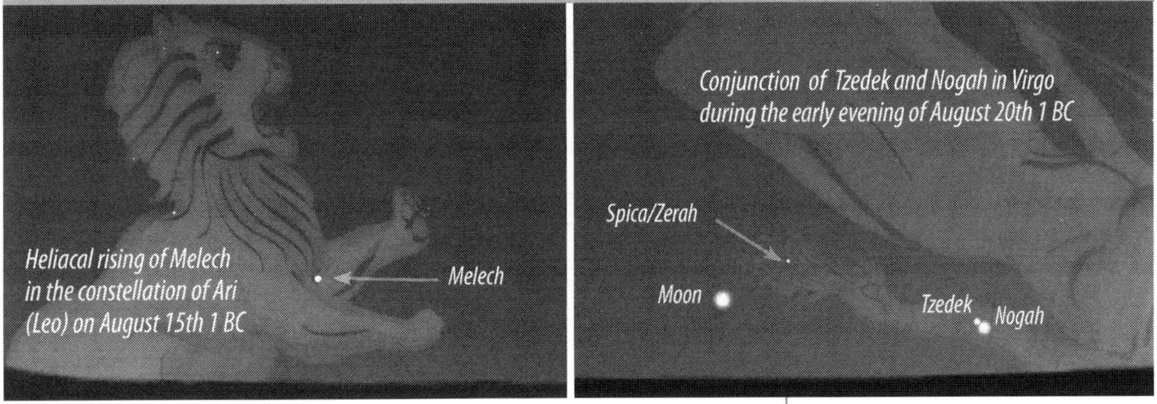

Heliacal rising of Melech in the constellation of Ari (Leo) on August 15th 1 BC

Conjunction of Tzedek and Nogah in Virgo during the early evening of August 20th 1 BC

August 15th and August 20th of 1 BC 25 Av and 2 Elul

The heliacal rising of Shabbatei took place on the Pharisaic date for Pentecost in 2 BC like it had done on the Sadducean date in 3 BC. Then, exactly 62 weeks (434 days) after the Pharisaic date for Pentecost in 2 BC, on 15 August in 1 BC, was a possible date for the visible heliacal rising of Melech. However, the visible heliacal rising may have taken place a day or two earlier.[4] Even so, the date fell within the 62nd week after Pentecost. The projected ideal date and the actual date of the first appearing of stars and planets in the morning sky were always noted by the Babylonians. God is able to arrange visibility factors according to his will. Such an event 62 weeks after the date of Pentecost could have been viewed as a confirming event. But there was more. Exactly 62 weeks (434 days) after the hypothetical Sadducean Pentecost date in 2 BC, Nogah and Tzedek (brightness and righteousness) were in a particularly close conjunction in Bethula (Virgo) at sunset. This happened on the 20th of August in 1 BC. This conjunction could also be viewed as a confirming event. It would have been the fourth "bright righteousness" conjunction of Tzedek and Nogah. The other conjunctions were in August 3 BC, June 2 BC and October 2 BC.

By this time the wise men had already met the young Messiah. There was a literal and symbolic accomplishment of the promise given in Genesis 3:15, the seed of the woman had come. The nation of Israel had symbolically carried the Messiah for many centuries (Revelation 12:1-6). However, a literal virgin of Israel had finished the job. The "seed of the woman" had finally been made manifest in December or January of 3/2 BC. Born in humble circumstances, Jesus was destined to become the greatest man the world had ever seen. As God said, "I shall make him My firstborn, the highest of the kings of the earth." (Psalm 89:27)

Summer 1 BC

The Bright, Righteous One in the Virgin

Jesus was almost certainly in Egypt with Mary and Joseph when this event took place.

Years

Days

Weeks

Months

Lunar Months, New Moons and the 70 "Sevens"

After seeing 70 days, 7 weeks, 62 weeks, 69 weeks, 70 weeks, 7 X 7 months, 7 X 7 years and 62 X 7 years, it would not be surprising that someone among the wise men may have asked the question: "If there were events for days, weeks, 7 X 7 months, 7 X 7 years and 62 X 7 years, the what about the 62 x 7 months?

At some point the wise men apparently made a connection between the "sabbatical righteousness" conjunctions of Shabbatei and Tzedek in 7 BC and the events of 3/2 BC. After their visit to Jerusalem and Bethlehem or possibly before, someone may have seen that the events in 7 BC actually preceded Jesus' conception and birth by 49 lunar months. The 1st of Nisan and the heliacal rising of Shabbatei in early April of 7 BC were 49 lunar months before the beginning of Nisan and Jesus' conception in late March or early April of 3 BC. The two planets, Tzedek and Shabbatei, traveled together for about nine months of the year 7/6 BC. They only began to draw apart from one another in a significant way in late December or early January of 6 BC, which would have been about 49 months before the birth of Jesus in late 3 BC or early 2 BC. Through these well timed events the prophecy of the 70 "sevens" had been partially fulfilled. Some of the fulfillment could be accounted for in the dates surrounding Jesus' conception and birth. But what about the 62 "sevens" of months? How were they fulfilled? *Note: The author considers the last series of "seven" (the one "seven") to be beyond the scope of this book.*

62 x 7 Months

Jesus' conception Passover 3 BC ← 62 "sevens" lunar months (434 months) → ? *How long did Jesus ive?*

Part 14: Reacting to the Messiah

Behold, My Servant, whom I uphold; My chosen one in whom My soul delights. I have put My Spirit upon Him; He will bring forth justice to the nations. He will not cry out or raise His voice, Nor make His voice heard in the street. A bruised reed He will not break And a dimly burning wick He will not extinguish; He will faithfully bring forth justice. He will not be disheartened or crushed Until He has established justice in the earth; And the coastlands will wait expectantly for His law." (Isaiah 42:1-3)

My heart overflows with a good theme; I address my verses to the King; My tongue is the pen of a ready writer. You are fairer than the sons of men; Grace is poured upon Your lips; Therefore God has blessed You forever.

Gird Your sword on Your thigh, O Mighty One, In Your splendor and Your majesty! And in Your majesty ride on victoriously, For the cause of truth and meekness and righteousness; Let Your right hand teach You awesome things Your arrows are sharp; The peoples fall under You; Your arrows are in the heart of the King's enemies.

Your throne, O God, is forever and ever; A scepter of uprightness is the scepter of Your kingdom. You have loved righteousness and hated wickedness; Therefore God, Your God, has anointed You With the oil of joy above Your fellows. (Psalm 45:1-7)

The Suffering King

Despite all the wonderful fulfillments of prophecy which the Magi had witnessed they must have had some questions. Daniel's prophecy itself would have been a major source of continuing questions.

The wise men could have wondered about the meaning of the phrases, "Seventy sevens have been decreed for your people and your holy city, to make an end of sin, to make atonement for iniquity, to bring in everlasting righteousness, to seal up vision and prophecy and to anoint the most holy." What was the real sense of those words? How would these things happen? When would these events take place? But other mysterious lines continue:

> *"After the 62 weeks the Messiah will be cut off and have nothing, and the people of the prince who is to come will destroy the city and the sanctuary. And its end will come with a flood; even to the end there will be war; desolations are determined."*

The restoration and rebuilding of the city had been prophesied and it had been accomplished. The result was visible to all. But there remained this amazing text: The Messiah will be "cut off and have nothing." How could this be? How could the Messiah be "cut off and have nothing"? Why would this happen? What would be the goal? And beyond that, the rebuilt city and sanctuary would be destroyed again? How could this happen? Why would this be necessary? Jesus himself echoed the prophecy concerning the destruction of the city and the temple just days before his own death and resurrection.[1]

Were the wise men pondering these texts concerning Jerusalem as they walked in the temple courts in Jerusalem? We do not know, but it would seem possible. Apparently Daniel's prophecy was part of the Magi's experience in determining the date of the Messiah's appearing. It is more than likely that the entire prophecy demanded their attention. Arriving in Jerusalem and seeing the magnificence of Herod's temple may have filled them with a sense of wonder, but they may have also had a sense of foreboding. All would not go well in Jerusalem, even if the

Jesus is the King of kings !!!
He is the true Shahanshah
(King of kings)
for all of the earth.

7 x 7
62 x 7
Months

49 + 434
Months

7 "sevens" of months (49 months)
From the spring of 7 BC
to the spring of 3 BC

Jesus' conception
Passover 3 BC

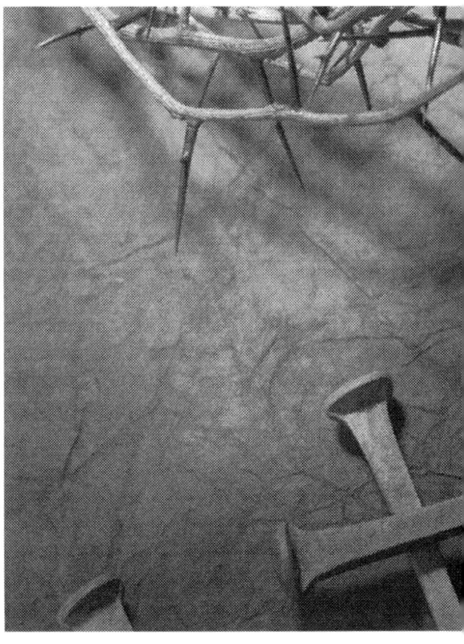

Messiah had arrived. The wise men would have known that the Messiah would be "cut off" and the city and the sanctuary would be destroyed.

"Then after the sixty-two "sevens" the Messiah will be cut off and have nothing ...

Jesus' death and resurrection did come after the 62 "sevens" of years exactly as prophesied. The 483 (49 and 434) years ended in 3/2 BC with the Messiah's conception and birth. Jesus died over 30 years later. But the prophecy was even more complete. Jesus was "cut off" after several series of 7 and 62 literal weeks, in 3 BC to 1 BC. He was also "cut off" after 62 X 7 new moons (434 lunar months).

The wise men may have made the connection between the heliacal risings of Tzedek and Shabbatei in 7 BC and the 49 new moons (7 X 7 lunar months) until the Messiah's conception. They may have also pondered a possible timeline involving 62 X 7 months. Counting (62 X 7) or 434 new moons from the month of Jesus' conception the men may have been aware of another date in the future. Even so, they most likely would not have understood the significance of this date.

Jesus is the "Princeps," the "first citizen" of God's new world.

Jesus is the true Son of God, the king who is to reign in righteousness over all the earth.

The life of Jesus from 3 BC to AD 33 was 62 "sevens" of lunar months (434 months). There were 35 years from his conception to to his death and ressurection.

April 3rd, AD 33 : Death
April 5th, AD 33 : Ressurection

Christ Is Risen!
Truly, He is risen!

Χριστὸς ἀνέστη
ἀληθῶς ἀνέστη

The Magi may have thought that the 434 lunar months might indicate the date of the Messiah's being "cut off." They would not have had any means of knowing this for certain, but the calculation would have been possible. The men may have only done some of the calculations much later, after their visit to Judea. It is also possible that they or their descendants may have only understood this aspect of the prophecy after the events surrounding the end of Jesus' life actually took place. Perhaps they never made an attempt to understand this aspect of the prophecy.

There were 434 new moons from the month of Jesus' conception to the probable month of his death and resurrection in the spring of AD 33. Jesus apparently died and was raised from the dead 35 years after his conception. He would have been 34 years, three months and less than a week old, at his death and resurrection.[2]

Responding to the King

המשיח קם!
באמת קם!

Hameshiach qam!
Be'emet qam!

Christ is risen!
He is risen indeed!
(in Hebrew)

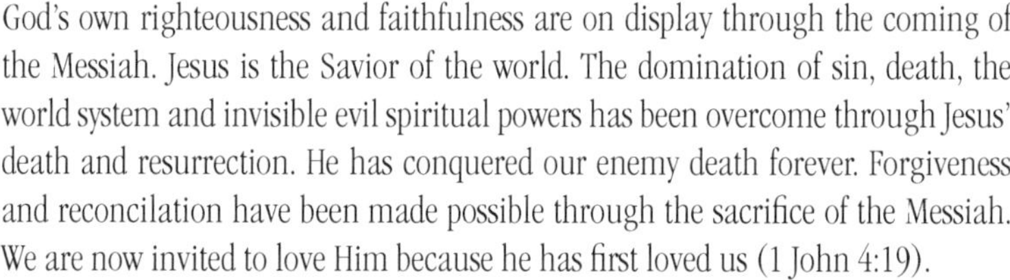

God's own righteousness and faithfulness are on display through the coming of the Messiah. Jesus is the Savior of the world. The domination of sin, death, the world system and invisible evil spiritual powers has been overcome through Jesus' death and resurrection. He has conquered our enemy death forever. Forgiveness and reconcilation have been made possible through the sacrifice of the Messiah. We are now invited to love Him because he has first loved us (1 John 4:19).

Jesus does not leave people indifferent. He has created controversy and he still does. Jesus was conceived, he was born, he lived, died and was raised from the dead. He is still alive. God will faithfully establish his rule in the new heavens and new earth. The Bible tells us:

> *"God has overlooked the times of ignorance, and that He is now declaring to men that all people everywhere should change their way of living, because He has fixed a day in which He will judge the world in righteousness through a Man whom He has appointed, having furnished proof to all men by raising Him from the dead." (Acts 17:30-31)*

While in appearance the Messiah was "cut off and had nothing," in reality he has become the chief authority in the whole universe, even if many refuse his kingship.

> *The Son of God was born of a descendant of David according to his earthly linage, he was declared the Son of God with power by the resurrection from the dead ... (Romans 1:3-4)*

Jesus himself said:

> *"All authority has been given to Me in heaven and on earth." (Mt. 28:18)*

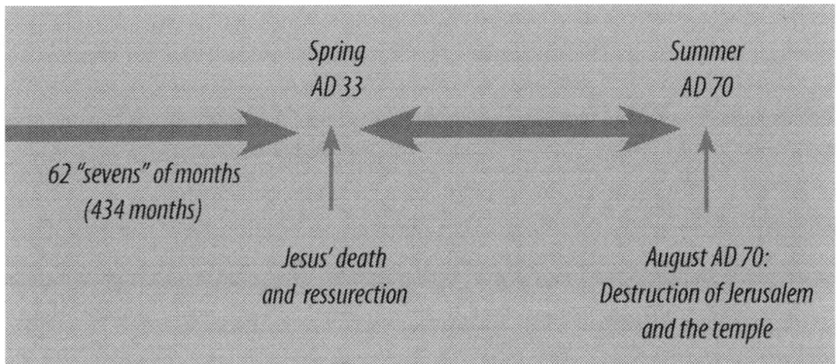

The city of Jerusalem and the temple were destroyed exactly as fortold in Daniel's prophecy.

How do we respond to this man whom God has appointed over all of creation? Will we participate in his reign? Will we receive his very person into our lives? Jesus became King in an unexpected way, through suffering. He defeated sin, death and evil spiritual powers through his cross and resurrection. Most believing Jews were surprised and even shocked by the Messiah's death and resurrection. Many still resist his authority. However, vast numbers of Jews and Gentiles have met the risen Savior. Many have tasted the fullness of life, which is in Jesus the Messiah.

God promised Abraham a large number of descendants who would know and obey the Lord:

> *The Lord took him outside and said, "Now look toward the heavens, and count the stars, if you are able to count them." And He said to him, "So shall your descendants be." Then he believed in the LORD; and He reckoned it to him as righteousness. (Genesis 15:5-6)*

> *Indeed I will greatly bless you, and I will greatly multiply your seed as the stars of the heavens and as the sand which is on the seashore; and your seed shall possess the gate of their enemies. (Genesis 22:17)*

The promise was repeated in a different form through the prophet Jeremiah.:

> *'As the host of heaven cannot be counted and the sand of the sea cannot be measured, so I will multiply the descendants of David My servant and the Levites who minister to Me." (Jeremiah 33:22)*

God is a surprising God. May many more people discover and obey his appointed King. May we all inherit the new heavens and new earth in which righteousness dwells, promised as an inheritance to those who love the Lord.

> *Eye hath not seen, nor ear heard, neither have entered into the heart of man, the things which God hath prepared for them that love him. (1 Corinthians 2:9)*

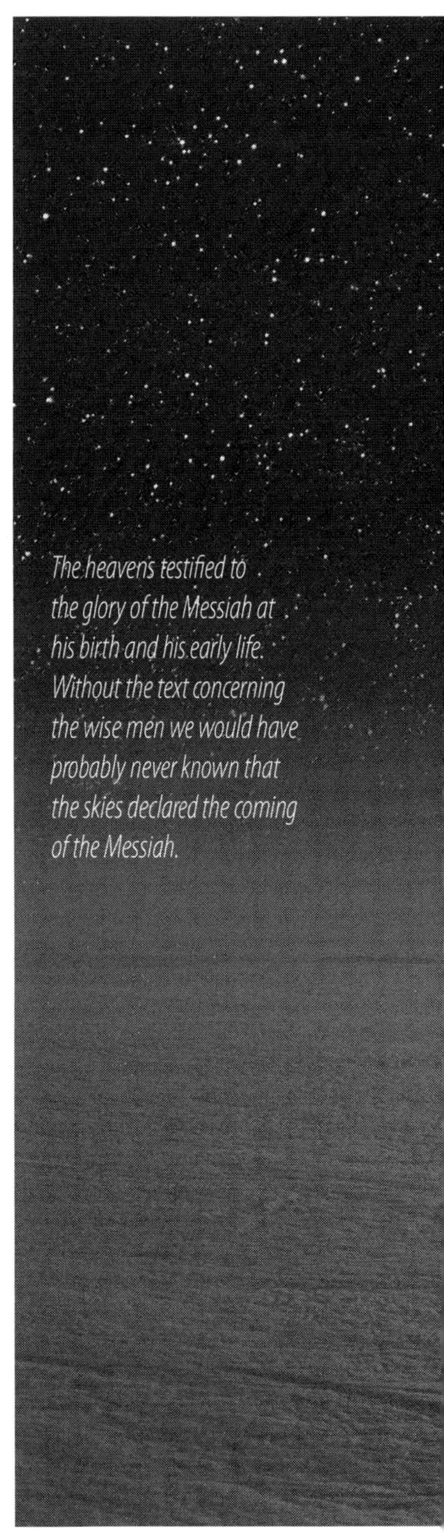

"I am the root and the descendant of David, the bright morning star."

David was referred to in Balaam's prophecy as a "star". Here, Jesus, as David's descendant, uses the words "morning star" concerning himself.

The morning star always signals the coming of a new day. God's new world, his kingdom of light, is overcoming darkness and taking root in the world. A day will come when the full revelation of the kingdon will be manifest for all.

Daniel speaks of a time which is coming.

> *"Many of those who sleep in the dust of the ground will awake, these to everlasting life, but the others to disgrace and everlasting contempt. "Those who have insight will shine brightly like the brightness of the expanse of heaven, and those who lead the many to righteousness, like the stars forever and ever." (Daniel 12:2-3)*

In the Book of Revelation, in practically the last sentences of the Bible, we read the words of Jesus himself:

> *"Behold, I am coming quickly, and My reward is with Me, to render to every man according to what he has done.*
>
> *"I am the Alpha and the Omega, the first and the last, the beginning and the end. Blessed are those who wash their robes, so that they may have the right to the tree of life, and may enter by the gates into the city.*
>
> *Outside are the dogs and the sorcerers and the immoral persons and the murderers and the idolaters, and everyone who loves and practices lying. I, Jesus, have sent My angel to testify to you these things for the churches.*
>
> *I am the root and the descendant of David, the bright morning star." The Spirit and the bride say, "Come." And let the one who hears say, "Come." And let the one who is thirsty come; let the one who wishes take the water of life without cost."*
>
> *(Revelation 22:12-17)*

Part 15: Appendices

Selected Bibliography, Endnotes and Websites

Appendix 1: Heavenly Events in the Present

This book is going to print in November of 2013. The following text was written by the author for a context not related specifically to this book. It concerns imminent astronomical events in November and December 2013, as well as the projected events in 2014 and 2015.

The text:

Right or wrong, a significant number of Christians are discussing upcoming heavenly events as signaling the end of the age. I am more reserved than many concerning this subject, but after having spent 22 months exploring the star of Bethlehem it is possible that I have a bit more perspective than most people concerning heavenly events and the Bible.

The comet ISON:

In November and December of 2013 the comet ISON will pass by the sun. The closest point of the encounter will be at the beginning of Hanukkah and American Thanksgiving on November 28th and 29th. It is very possible that the greatest heavenly spectacle that any of us have ever seen will be manifest in the days before and after ISON's passage near the sun. The comet's tail may cover a significant part of the morning sky. However, it is also possible that very little may actually happen. The exact visual appearance of a new comet is notoriously difficult to predict. We may see something very spectacular or perhaps we will not see very much at all. Comets sometimes leave bright, long tails, but sometimes they do not. It is not at all certain what will happen concerning ISON. Does this event mean anything? Perhaps, one rarely has a major comet reaching the sun on the first day of Hanukkah. A truly great light may be visible on the first day of the "festival of lights." It is also possible that there will be relatively little or nothing of real consequence. If there is no other message, a bright visible comet will proclaim the glory of God (Ps. 19:1). That much is absolutely certain.

The "Blood Moons" in 2014 and 2015:

There is no doubt that the sun shall be turned to darkness and the moon figuratively to blood before the great and terrible day of the Lord (Joel 2 and Acts 2). The crucifixion was accompanied by darkness over the face of the whole earth. The death of Jesus may have been followed by a visibly reddish / orange moon in the evening as a partially eclipsed moon traversed the earth's shadow on April 3rd 33 BC. There will apparently be other such signs in the future.

In 2014 and 2015 four lunar eclipses will take place at two successive Passovers and at the beginning of two successive Feasts of Tabernacles. In addition there will be a solar eclipse visible in some parts of the North Atlantic region. Some people are heralding this as perhaps the beginning of the tribulation period preceding the coming of the Lord. It is exceedingly rare that events like this happen in repetition during biblical festivals. God may be making a statement through the events, yet this is far from certain.

In a lunar eclipse the moon's surface appears red because the only sunlight available is refracted through the earth's atmosphere toward the moon, the red band of light often being the one which is the most prominent. It is important to note that the exact appearance of a "blood" moon is difficult to predict. It is not always possible to know well in advance how an eclipsed moon will appear, it depends on a large number of factors, notably the time of day, the distance separating the earth and the moon and atmospheric dust. Sometimes eclipsed moons are red, sometimes, orange, brownish and in some cases they are gray. I remember seeing one such event in high school which was beautiful but it was not red at all. I saw another one that was orange. It is just about impossible to say exactly how these events will appear. We shall see.

Does this series of "blood moons" signal the soon appearing of the Lord? Perhaps, perhaps not. Jesus will appear when God the Father so desires. Jesus already "appears" daily to everyone who will walk with him in humility. Each day God also resists the proud, but He also gives grace to the humble.

Appendix 2 : The "Gospel in the Stars"

Some Clarifications and Advice from the Author

The scenario presented in this book has little or no connection with the popular theory called "The Gospel in the Stars." I am convinced that a "Gospel in the Stars" approach to astronomy would have definitely hindered my efforts to discover a feasible scenario concerning the Magi and the famous "star."

I can not endorse this so-called "Christan" approach to astronomy / astrology originally developed by Frances Rolleston. Her research and writings have influenced believers for over 150 years. While there are many useful bits of information in Rolleston's book, *The Mazzaroth* (1862), the book is severely flawed at a basic level. Joseph A. Seiss' book, *A Gospel in the Stars* (1882), as well as E. W. Bullinger's work, *The Witness of the Stars* (1893), essentially follow Rolleston's earlier work. These men popularized and expanded upon F. Rolleston's relatively unknown material. In addition to these three main works there are literally hundreds and perhaps even thousands of books, tracts, magazine articles, websites, PowerPoint presentations and blogs which contain some aspect of the "Gospel in the Stars" approach to the heavens. I, myself, tried to use this approach when I began doing my research about the Magi and the famous star. It was not long, however, before I saw that there are definite problems with the theory.

Key Points to Consider Concerning the "Gospel in the Stars" Theory:

A. Our knowledge is limited concerning the ancient names and significance of heavenly bodies including stars, planets and constellations for many ancient peoples and especially for the Hebrews.

Frances Rolleston tried to establish the original names of many celestial objects through etymological word study, seeking to discern the original names from various sources. She assumes that all or most of the names of heavenly objects had an original divine source. While it is true that the Scriptures do say that "God calls all the stars by name," it is not proven that Adam or anyone else ever knew all the names or ever transmitted this knowledge to others. Such knowledge may have existed and its transmission may have happened, but it is not proven or documented. The entire idea that the original "God given names" were known and transmitted to the patriarchs before and after the flood is very questionable. This fundamental concept is far from proven. Anything which is built on the assumption that God gave original names to the stars and constellations, which were then passed on to humanity, may be in error. God probably does have a name for every star that exists. However, it is certain that we do not presently know most of these names, even if a small number of them were transmitted to man.

In the present time we actually have much more understanding of the ancient astronomy of the Sumerians, Assyrians and Babylonians/Chaldeans, Greeks and Egyptians than was even dreamed possible in the 1800s, when Rolleston, Seiss and Bullinger wrote their books. Literally thousands of ancient historical, astronomical and astrological texts have been translated in the last one-hundred years. Some of them have been taken literally from the desert sands in Mesopotamia and Egypt. Several archaeological pioneers led the way in translating vast numbers of cuneiform and hieroglyphic texts. This work continues through new generations of scholars. Our real knowledge of ancient Near Eastern ideas of astronomy was practically non-existent before 1900. It was only in 1929 that the first Babylonian mathematical astronomy texts were translated. Rolleston, Seiss and Bullinger all wrote their books 40-70 years before we actually obtained the more significant translated astronomical texts from Mesopotamia. Some classical Roman and Greek writers mentioned small details concerning the astronomical knowledge of the Babylonians / Chaldeans, but we did not have any first-hand knowledge of their science until this past century.

There was a definite development and evolution of the names of the constellations in ancient Mesopotamia and elsewhere.

The number and types of constellations have changed over time. We know that the Babylonians referred to Virgo as the Furrow (like a furrow for planting seed). The Greeks and Romans associated Virgo with the goddess of grain and agriculture, Demeter / Ceres. The Greeks thought of Aries as a ram but the Babylonians thought of that region of the sky as a "hired man" in their idea of the zodiac.

In this book I do assume that God guided some aspects of the naming of certain constellations, stars and planets for his own purposes. God reigns over the nations. Not everything that happens on the earth is God's will but still his sovereignty does rule over all. He appoints times and seasons, he raises up kings and has "made from one man every nation of mankind and determined their appointed times and the boundaries of their habitation" (Acts 17:26 ff). It is no harder for God to orchestrate the naming of some constellations than it was to engineer the arrival of Mary and Joseph at Bethlehem for the birth of Jesus. God worked in the background through the imperial decree to ensure that the Messiah would be born in Bethlehem according to prophecy. God may very well have been involved in inspiring at least some of the names of certain constellations, stars and planets.

B. Since our knowledge is limited, therefore we do not know in any great detail if there was any original message God-given in the stars and / or the Zodiac.

To say that we know the thoughts of Adam and Eve, Noah, Abraham, Moses, Solomon, Daniel or God, himself, concerning the stars and constellations is simply not provable beyond a few statements from Scripture, bits of archeology and some aspects of etymology. We can speculate about the thoughts of the ancients but such speculations are far from establishing any certain understanding of their perspectives. God does not speak in detail about any heavenly body. He mentions the sun, moon and stars repeatedly but even so we are not given any information about the great majority of the heavenly bodies concerning their original names, functions or their possible symbolism.

C. It is possible that there was an original message that God wanted to express in the stars which symbolically goes well beyond the glory and beauty of God reflected in the heavens.

However, we have no text, research or even astronomical events which definitively prove that God ever wanted to give us a detailed message about the redemption of mankind through the heavens except for possibly some events surrounding the birth of the Messiah. God's glory is eloquently and strongly demonstrated through the beauty of the heavens. This is the main focus of texts like Psalm 19:16, which says that the "heavens declare the glory of God."

D. While Rolleston's, Seiss' and Bullinger's approach speaks of Jesus, his suffering on the cross and his resurrection foretold and illustrated in the stars, their assertions are largely founded on completely subjective, speculative and unproven interpretations of symbolism.

It is true that all of nature can tell us many things about our creator and even give us keys for understanding redemption. One can use many things from daily life to speak of Christian truth including everyday things such as sandwiches, soft drinks, desserts, postage stamps, dynamite or gasoline. However, it is far from obvious or certain that food items, postage stamps, dynamite and gasoline were expressly developed in order to illustrate anything about the death and resurrection of Jesus. In a similar manner no ancient text, prophecy or recorded revelation expressly tells us that the stars, constellations or other heavenly bodies describe anything specific about the death and resurrection of the Messiah. It is not correct to simply suppose meaning which may or may not be accurate.

E. While some of the symbolic figures of the zodiac can be found in Scripture (lion, bull, man, virgin, twins, balance, fish, ram and a scorpion) there are some important exceptions.

The strange constellations of Capricorn (the sea goat) and Sagittarius (the Centaur) do not correspond with any known creature in nature or in the biblical record, either living or dead. It is possible that the original Capricorn was only a normal goat and not a "sea goat." In a similar way perhaps Sagittarius was only an archer which became deformed into a Centaur. But what specific symbolism do we find concerning archers and the Messiah? Do we find any specific Christological significance concerning crabs (Cancer) or twins (Gemini)?

Rolleston and those who follow her try to interpret all the constellations, stars or planets "Christologically." It may be that Rolleston and the others have established interesting and perhaps sometimes spiritually edifying parallels concerning the Gospel message and the constellations. However, this hardly proves that they have found anything approaching any actual message which God may or may not have intended.

Here is one example of an interpretation used by several authors. Mars has been associated with the blood sacrifice of the Messiah. However, we have no proof that the red color of Mars has anything to do with the blood of any sacrifice including that of the Messiah. Mars has been associated in the West with the Roman and Greek god of war (Mars / Aries) so one might think about blood when thinking of Mars. However, even if one often speaks of Mars as being the "red planet" visually Mars is actually more orange than red. The planet Mars is not universally identified either with blood or with war in many cultures. Are Westerners simply predisposed to identify any red / orange star with blood and specifically with the blood of Christ? This is a very sweeping generalization. We do not have any textual or cultural evidence from any time before Christ that the Hebrews identified any star with the blood of sacrifice and certainly not with the blood of the Messiah. There are some negative associations of Mars with violence and war in the Talmud. The actual Hebrew name for Mars, Ma'adim, means "to redden or to blush." This is far from anything remotely linked to sacrifice. Jesus death involved much more than "blushing." The name Edom / Esau has a similar root to Ma'adim. However, we do not identify the "redness" of Edom / Esau with the blood of Christ.

F. The Scriptures make it plain that the mystery of redemption involving Christ's death and resurrection was not made known in any great detail before the actual events of the Messiah's birth, life, death and resurrection.

The ancient prophets, and even the disciples themselves, were not aware of the full significance of the Messiah's role and mission before the actual events took place. It was only afterwards that the disciples understood the significance of many of the words and actions of Jesus, as well as the significance of many prophecies concerning the Messiah. The cross and the resurrection remained a mystery up until the time that the events happened. It is even doubtful that the disciples would have understood most things without the 40 days of instruction that they received from Jesus after his resurrection.

> *Paul writes: "To me, the very least of all saints, this grace was given, to preach to the Gentiles the unfathomable riches of Christ, and to bring to light what is the administration of the mystery which for ages has been hidden in God who created all things; so that the manifold wisdom of God might now be made known through the church to the rulers and the authorities in the heavenly places." (Ephesians 3:8-10)*

The mystery was hidden in God literally for ages. We should appreciate these words. It is only now in this present age that the mystery of the Gospel is being made known. To say that it was always written in the stars and that this knowledge was available to the ancients seems to go well beyond Scripture. The Bible says plainly that the Gospel of the death and resurrection was a mystery hidden in God for ages.

Other Modern Writers - "Christological Star Profiles":

Some teachers, speakers and writers actually go one step further beyond the "Gospel in the Stars" to even talk about individual "Christological Star Profiles" which are essentially types of so-called "Christian" astrological birth chart for individual believers. This is often based on the foundations of the texts written by Rolleston, Bullinger, Seiss and others who follow their lead. This type of reading of one's Christological destiny, gifting and character in the stars is very close to simple astrology baptized in Christian symbols and words. It may not be damning, because it definitely generally points toward Jesus, but it is not far from astrology in many respects. It certainly gives a false impression. The position of the stars, planets, sun and moon at one's birth does not say anything about one's potential destiny in Christ. God, himself, is more than able to give us prophetic and spiritual insight through his body, the Scriptures, prophetic words and prayer concerning our callings, gifts, character and destiny. He does not need for us to understand anything concerning the positions of the planets, the sun, the moon and the stars at our birth or anytime afterwards in order for us to walk with him, to know his will, to be aware of our calling and gifting or to accomplish all of his good pleasure. For centuries believers have discovered their role, gifting, calling and position in Christ without any reference to astrological signs. We should not seek insights into our destiny through the stars even if Christian terms are used. Again the heavens announced the coming of the Messiah. They did not shape his destiny, calling, character, gifting or ministry.

End Times Speculations Linked to the "Gospel in the Stars":

The futuristic sign interpretations which are often associated with "End Times" events and biblical prophecy concerning Israel has also produced a wide variety of Christian, messianic and quasi-biblical interpretations of present and future heavenly events. Some of this type of teaching often has interpretive links to the "Gospel in the Stars" message.

There are some interesting astronomical events which will be happening in 2013-2015. These events involve comets, lunar and solar eclipses and perhaps other phenomena. The Internet is literally being filled with "Christian" interpretations and speculations concerning these events. I cannot endorse, support or encourage speculative efforts to discern the Lord's will and agenda through watching the current events in the heavens. Most everything that is being said about the second coming of Christ and current astronomical events rests in the realm of complete speculation. Few will venture to say "Thus says the Lord" about any of the coming events.

There is no doubt that Jesus indicated to us that there will be signs of his coming in the sun, the moon and the stars. However, several have fallen flat on their face when making predictions based on the "Gospel in the Stars" message and present astronomical events. In my office I have a three volume set of books which details the end times ideas of people from many cultures and civilizations over the last 4,000+ years. Christian end-times approaches take up at least half of the material. Several hundred pages are specifically dedicated to failed Christian end times predictions. We as believers have done this type of speculation for hundreds of years. The result has always been the same. We have failed to accurately predict the second coming of Jesus.

A good principle for all believers to follow would simply be to stop trying to predict the date of the Lord's return. In all likelihood all men will be somewhat surprised by the actual event. However, being people who live during the "day," we know that all will become obvious in its time. The Lord's coming will only be a total surprise for those who are in "darkness." Let us be happy to live with God in the daytime, right now. Jesus is present at all times. He is with us always, "even to the end of the age." Avoid walking in darkness. Live to glorify God and build his kingdom. The rest will all pan out in the end. God will make sure that we are well informed about what He is really doing. As for the rest it really does not matter. We are not to let ourselves be completely distracted from God's real agenda by filling our minds with last days scenarios.

Recommended Reading:

An article by the Christian astronomer, Danny Faulkner is very helpful: "A Further Examination of the Gospel in the Stars"

Answers Research Journal 6 (2013): 35-62.
www.answersingenesis.org/articles/arj/v6/n1/gospel-in-stars-further-examination

Appendix 3: Was Jesus Born During the Fall Feasts?

The Approach Taken by Some Modern Messianic Jews Concerning Jesus' Birth

A very large number of messianic Jews think that Jesus was certainly born in September or October of either 3 BC or 2 BC, during the Jewish month of Tishrei, possibly at the moment of the Day of Trumpets or during the Feast of Tabernacles. I also entertained these ideas for some time. The English scholar John Lightfoot was apparently also interested in such ideas in the 1600s. However, these comparatively modern ideas linking dates of the Jewish calendar to the date of Jesus' birth do not stand up well under close examination.

Calculations of the Births of John and Jesus Based on the Priestly Cycles:

Messianic Jews, and others who hold the September / October 3 BC or 2 BC date for Jesus' birth, almost always base this on certain astronomical events and calculations concerning the dates when John the Baptist's father Zacharias could have possibly done his service in the temple. There are several competing theories concerning the dates when Zachariah's priestly division, Abijah, would have served in the temple. According to two of the theories Zacharias' division would have served in the temple at dates appropriate for John to have been born in the summer of 3 BC. This would have made it possible for Jesus to have been born either in December 3 BC or in January of the year 2 BC. It may also be the case that Zacharias actually entered the temple and ministered at the altar of incense during a major Jewish festival. All the priests were normally present in Jerusalem during Passover, Pentecost and Tabernacles. One early Church Father says that Zacharias was offering incense on the Day of Atonement as the high priest, but this was almost certainly an error. If Zachariah was ministering in the fall, Elisabeth could have been in her sixth month in the spring placing John's birth in the summer and Jesus' birth in the following December or January. As mentioned in the principal text it is entirely possible that Zacharias heard from God, but his wife may have become pregnant months later rather than immediately. We have no exact idea of when Elisabeth became pregnant.

The Traditions Concerning Elijah' Coming:

It is good that Jewish people invoke the memory of Elijah and his promised coming before the "great and terrible Day of the Lord" in the Passover Seder. Indeed John the Baptist fulfills the prophecy that Elijah would come, preceding the Messiah. However, this cannot be used to establish the date of John's birth at Passover or at any other time during the year. We simply do not know the exact date of John's conception or his birth.

The Practical and Religious Difficulties:

Those who propose a Tishrei birth date for Jesus have seldom profoundly thought about the religious and practical difficulties which such a date would certainly impose on a census. Mary and Joseph were in Bethlehem because of a government-sponsored census / registration. Certainly God was sovereignly arranging things behind the scenes and Jesus was born at God's appointed time. However, the census was carried out through Herod's administration under orders from the Emperor Augustus. Most of the Jewish month of Tishrei (September / October) would not have been a good moment for governments to ask Jewish men to return to the "home of their ancestors" for any type of census. According to the Torah all Jewish men were supposed to be in Jerusalem for the Feast of Tabernacles from the 15th to the 22nd of the month. Some would have had to make the journey from Jerusalem to northern Israel to return to the "land of their ancestors." That would have been impossible during Tabernacles if all the men were supposed to have been in Jerusalem. While the Bible does say that Jesus "tabernacled" among us as a human being (John 1:14), it does not say that this word indicates that he was born in a temporary shelter during the Jewish festival. It simply means that he lived among us as a human being.

The last part of the general harvest was taking place in the month of Tishrei. Agricultural societies function based on the rhythm of planting and harvest so disrupting such activities would not be a wise manner of conducting a census which involved a pledge of allegiance to the emperor and to the king. Logically, Herod would not have attempted a census during the month of Tishrei simply to avoid practical difficulties and religious insurrection. There would have been many other possible dates for a government sponsored census. The authorities would probably have reasoned: "Why disrupt agricultural activities and create a religious riot if it can be avoided?" The Day of Trumpets (shofars) is on the first day of the month of Tishrei. It would have been possible to organize a census before that date if one disregarded some agricultural activities, however, afterwards things would have gotten complicated. The Day of Atonement on the 10th day of Tishrei was the holiest day of the year. It was preceded by many days of serious personal examination.

Following the month of Tishrei the fall rains began and a time of preparing the ground for planting of crops and the actual sowing and planting lasted till about the time of Hanukkah (70 days after Tabernacles). After Hanukkah, the rains continued and there were small harvests of figs and lemons. As indicated in the main text, the weather is usually mild during the winter in the land of Israel. The temperatures average about 12°to 6° C (54 to 43° F) in January in Jerusalem. Such temperatures would not halt censuses. We know that Abraham and many others lived in tents all their lives. Their livestock largely lived outside even during the cooler rainy winter months. Shepherds actually were with their flocks all during the year in Judea. In reality the period following Hanukkah may have been more appropriate for a census / registration because it would not have interrupted most of the agricultural cycle. It should be remembered that agriculture was the main employment and source of revenue and provision for the vast majority of Jews in the land of Israel in the 1st century BC. To interrupt farming activities to conduct censuses would not have been good economic or political policy. Even so, it seems likely that the year from Tishrei 3 BC to Elul 2 BC (Sept 11th, 3 BC through the end of September 2 BC) was a sabbatical year. Normally, there would not have been any planting during that year. Again, we do not know in any kind of definitive way when Augustus issued his order for the census. Neither do we know exactly when the census was carried out in Judea and Galilee.

Was it Necessary for Jesus to be Born on a Jewish Holiday?

The Bible does not actually say that the Messiah had to be born on any particular holy or special day. It might be symbolically desirable for Jesus to have been born on the Day of Trumpets or during Tabernacles but it may not have been absolutely necessary. The circumstances of Jesus' birth could call into question some of our values concerning what we might call significant, important, necessary or meaningful.

In the film *The Nativity* there is an especially moving segment when someone says, "The greatest of kings, born in the most humble of places." God's values do not always reflect common ideas of what would be appropriate or desirable. Did God really want trumpets to be sounding on the day of Jesus birth (the Day of Trumpets)? God informed shepherds about the birth of Jesus, but he did not inform the chief priests. One of the themes of this book is that the Jewish calendar is a key to understanding the wise men. However, it is far from certain that Jesus was born on any particular holy day. Often God does not meet our expectations. He will always act in a loving manner but sometimes our idea of what is loving is actually warped.

Jesus came to serve and give his life as a ransom for many. We do know that Jesus died and he was raised from the dead at a special moment, during the Passover festival, which was and is an exceedingly important date for the whole Jewish nation. Perhaps the old tradition mentioned earlier is true. If Jesus was conceived at Passover and died on the same day over three decades later, then in his very conception his Jewish roots, heritage and culture were much more important than many of us had suspected. The early Church Fathers thought that the date of his conception was more important than the date of his birth. We could learn from them.

Jesus' Birth and Astronomical Events in 3 and 2 BC

Sometimes messianic Jews seeking to encourage a 3 BC or a 2 BC date for Jesus' birth do so because they try to make a astronomical correspondence between the woman clothed with the sun in Revelation 12:1-2 and the constellation of Virgo (the virgin). The sun was in the constellation of Virgo during the month of Tishrei (Sept - October of 3 BC and also

2 BC). On the Day of Trumpets in 3 BC the moon was at the feet of the woman, but this would not have been visible. The setting sun would have hidden the stars and the entire constellation of Virgo. Here is the text of the book of Revelation 12:1-2:

> *A great sign appeared in heaven: a woman clothed with the sun, and the moon under her feet, and on her head a crown of twelve stars; and she was with child; and she cried out, being in labor and in pain to give birth.*

This text was not meant to identify a moment when the woman actually gave birth. It is most naturally linked with Joseph's dream in Genesis 37:9-11. In the dream there were 11 stars, representing Joseph's brothers, who were bowing down to him. In Revelation the 12 stars represent the twelve tribes of Israel. In Joseph's dream the sun and the moon referred to Joseph's parents who were also bowing down to him. This was the interpretation which Jacob / Israel gave concerning the dream.

> *He related it to his father and to his brothers; and his father rebuked him and said to him, "What is this dream that you have had? Shall I and your mother and your brothers actually come to bow ourselves down before you to the ground?" (Genesis 37:10).*

It would seem that the woman in Revelation also represents the nation of Israel and the male child is the seed of the virgin daughter of Israel, the expected Messiah. The woman was clothed with the sun, who is Jacob / Israel, the patriarch. The moon represents the submissive mothers of the twelve tribes (Rachel, Leah, Bilhah and Zilpah). The vision figuratively speaks of a male child as a descendant of Jacob / Israel. Ps. 89:36-37 may also be important for the interpretation.

Some have suggested that the 12 stars near the woman's head can also be identified with physical stars (Pi, Nu, ecliptic Beta, Sigma, Chi, Iota, Theta, Star 60, Delta, Star 93, 2nd Magnitude Beta and Omicron). However, the stars supposedly linked to the "crown" of the woman are exceedingly dim in the constellation of Virgo. In addition, they really do not form a true crown. It would seem doubtful that these stars could have possibly been the 12 stars indicated in the text, especially when the text says that the woman was "clothed with the sun." Dim stars are not at all visible in the presence of the sun. This would mean that the stars would have needed a very significant boosting in luminescence to even be visible near the sun. While one could certainly argue that the position of the constellation of Virgo with the sun is interesting on the Day of Trumpets in 3 BC, few have ever tried to thoroughly identify the dragon in the next verses with the heavenly constellations (Revelation 12:3-9).

> *Then another sign appeared in heaven: and behold, a great red dragon having seven heads and ten horns, and on his heads were seven diadems...*

The text says "another sign appeared in heaven." The text does not say that the sign was there all along. One should also ask, "What constellation has the seven heads and the ten horns?" At the present time no constellation looks like a dragon with seven heads and ten horns. While both the signs of the woman and the dragon "appeared in heaven" this does not necessarily mean that the figures in the vision were constellations which were normally visible. The text says that they appeared in heaven. This may simply mean that they appeared in the vision and nothing more. Why insist on interpreting the text as referring to known constellations?

It would seem that placing Jesus' birth at the moment of the Day of Trumpets on the basis of a few verses in Revelation may be a mistake. Every year the sun passes through Virgo and at some point the moon is positioned toward the feet of the woman. There is nothing particularly striking in this combination which makes it necessary to conclude that Jesus was born on the Day of Trumpets in either 3 BC or 2 BC. It would appear that the text of Revelation is relating facts about a vision which John saw. It was not designed to designate specific constellations or dates.

Many people have sought an alternative to the supposedly pagan roots of Christmas. There are some pagan roots of Christmas, but the most significant root is Hebraic. In the scenario outlined in this book the Passover conception date of Jesus in the spring of 3 BC was at the origin of the December and January birth dates.

Appendix 4: Christmas: Pagan Festival or Christian Celebration?

Written by Dr Anthony McRoy

This article was first published in the Church of England Newspaper of 14th December 2007, placed on pages 12 and 21. It is reproduced here with the permission of the author.

Dr. McRoy uses the following sources:

Joseph F. Kelly, The Origins of Christmas, (Collegeville: Liturgical Press, 2004)

J. Neil Alexander, Waiting for the Coming: The Liturgical Meaning of Advent, Christmas, Epiphany, (Washington DC: Pastoral Press, 1993)

Susan K. Roll, Toward the Origins of Christmas, (Kampen: Kok Pharos, 1995)

Maxwell E. Johnson (Ed.), Between Memory and Hope: Readings on the Liturgical Year, (Collegeville: Pueblo/Liturgical Press, 2000)

John F. White, Restorer of the World: The Roman Emperor Aurelian, (Stroud: Spellmount 2007)

The article:

Atheist and Muslim polemicists – and some Protestants – often claim that Christmas derives from a previous pagan festival. The books above help answer this accusation. Those by Kelly and Alexander are brief, readable and informative (though it must be cautioned that none of the liturgical studies books here have a conservative approach to the Bible). Johnson's book is a collection of liturgist articles; those by Thomas Talley, 'Constantine and Christmas', and Susan Roll, 'The Origins of Christmas', being particularly interesting and pertinent.

Polemicists (and The Da Vinci Code) frequently state that 25 December was Mithras' birthday, yet the renowned Mithraic scholar, Dr Richard Gordon has corresponded to me that he is unaware of 'a single date on a Mithraic inscription that falls in the winter, let alone late in December… We know NOTHING about the cycle of rituals in the cult...' So, Christmas owes nothing to Mithraism. This is one area where Kelly (p. 65) and Roll (p.111) are inadequate.

Roll's book presents two theories for the origins of Christmas: the 'History of Religions' school, and the 'Computation' thesis. The first only goes back to the eighteenth century, proposed by Paul Ernst Jablonski, an Egyptologist who claimed that 'Constantine exercised a personal influence on the establishment of Christmas', p. 130. However, the main figures responsible for the claim were Hermann Usener in 1889 and Bernard Botte in 1932. Usener's thesis was that the Church adapted certain pagan customs to keep the converts happy, such as the Natalis Sol Invicti – birthday of the Unconquered Sun, pp. 132-133. Botte similarly held that the Church '"christianized" certain non-Christian practices, Christmas being intended as 'a counterfeast in regard to the pre-Christian feast', p. 141.

The argument on 'Christianisation' usually rests on one or both of two foundations: the Roman Feast of the Saturnalia, which ran 17-23 December, characterised by carousing, merry-making, gifts and candles, and the Sol Invictus event on 25 December. One can immediately dismiss the supposed link with the Saturnalia: it did not stretch to 25 December, was not inclusive of any Solstice commemoration, and ended on 23 December when another event began – the Larentalia, a feast of the dead!

The evidence suggests that Christian festivals in the fourth century were accompanied by worship and fasting, not dissipation, cf. p. 203. As Kelly notes: 'early Christian leaders found the Saturnalian practices offensive', p. 69. Alexander observes (p. 9ff) that the 380 Saragossa synod obliged daily church worship for 17 December-6 January. All the indications are that fasting, rather than secular 'feasting' was prescribed, as demonstrated by the writings of Bishop Filastrius of Brescia (d. 397), pp. 14-15.

Gregory Nazianzen, Bishop of Constantinople c. 379, in his sermon On the Theophany indicates that proper practice for celebrating the Nativity differed from pagan Saturnalia practices – not least riotous conduct: '…let us not strive to outdo each other in intemperance... Let us leave all these to ... the ...festivals of the Greeks... But we, the Object of whose adoration is the Word... seek it ['luxury']...in the Divine Law ...' There are no patristic references to a conscious decision to copy or usurp the Saturnalia.

Secondly, all polemicists – and unfortunately, all the books reviewed here – make the mistake of over-emphasising the Solstice and especially Aurelian's contribution. Emperor Aurelian, as White's excellent, informative and lucid book demonstrates, was a remarkable man, who in a short five-year reign re-united and strengthened the Roman Empire. The book is also superb for presenting the cultural/historical background for church history during this era, and White pays special attention to Christianity, e.g. p. 168. Most pertinently, regarding claims that White notes (p. 136) that Aurelian dedicated a temple to Sol Invictus in 274 'perhaps on 25 December'; note the caution here – the dating is not secure. Apparently, Aurelian did institute Games in honour of Sol on October 19-22 – but not 25 December.

A prominent Roman Studies specialist, Dr Steven Hijmans, has demonstrated that contrary to claims (unfortunately, repeated in the liturgical studies books here) that Aurelian borrowed from a Syrian cult brought to Rome by the degenerate Emperor Elagabolus some decades earlier, Aurelian's religion was a development of the existing Roman cult. Moreover, in Hijmans' article, Sol Invictus, the Winter Solstice and the Origins of Christmas, we read: '...December 25 was neither a longstanding nor an especially important feast day of Sol... the suggestion that it was established by Aurelian cannot be proven. In fact, there is no firm evidence that this feast of Sol on December 25 antedates the feast of Christmas at all.' He continues: 'The traditional feast days of Sol... were August 8, August 9, August 28, and December 11. Of these, only August 28 is still mentioned in the Calendar of 354, along with October 19 and October 22, the latter being the most important, judging by the 36 chariot races with which it was celebrated.'

He also emphasises that we must distinguish between the Sun-god - the cult of Sol - and the Sun - i.e. the astronomical body. Hijmans states that the failure to differentiate 'between astronomy and cult' touches upon the 'fatal flaw in the contention that Christmas was instituted on December 25 to counteract a pagan feast.' The winter solstice in December was an astronomical event: the major feast of Sol, the Sun-god, was October 22. Christians could deal with the astronomical symbolism of the Sun, without engaging the deity Sol. Thus Natalis Solis Invicti i.e. the winter solstice, observed on December 25, was recognised as the 'birthday' of the astronomical entity, not necessarily the solar deity! This allowed the Christians to utilise the imagery of Malachi 4:2 - that Christ was the 'Sun of Righteousness'.

The essential point is this: if Aurelian did not initiate any festival on 25 December, and there was no major festival before that, it follows that the Christian feast of the Nativity – Christmas – cannot be construed as deriving from a pagan festival! This is where so many accusations of 'paganism' against Christmas fall down. As for claims that Constantine was responsible for the December 25 Nativity feast, there is no hard evidence for this. The first recorded celebration occurred in Rome in 336, a city Constantine left for the last time in 326 and never returned, (Talley, Between Memory and Hope, p. 267). By this time Constantine was in Constantinople, but he ordered no such Nativity festival on December 25 there. It seems likely that the Constantinople December Nativity only began with Gregory Nazianzus c. 380.

The second theory is 'Computation', based on the Rabbinic concept of the 'integral age' of prophets, that they died on the same date they were born, or with Jesus, on the date of his conception (Roll, pp. 95-96). Since Rome and North Africa held that Jesus died on March 25, and the East that He died on April 6, He must have been conceived on either of those dates. Add nine months and you get His birth on January 6 (when Armenians still celebrate the Nativity) or 25 December, Alexander, p. 52.

There is evidence from North Africa from the third and fourth centuries that the date of the nativity had been computed to 25 December (Roll, p. 87). We know from Clement of Alexandria (c. 159-215) in Stromateis 1:21 that in Egypt people were computing the date of Christ's birth, and that the Basilidian Gnostics even celebrated the event of His baptism (believing that the heavenly Power endued the man Jesus at this point). On the basis of Luke 3:23: 'And Jesus was himself beginning about thirty years' many believed that Jesus was baptised on His birthday. Hence the earliest Nativity celebrations – which occurred on January 6 (Alexander, p. 72) commemorated both the Baptism and the Birth (again, Armenians still celebrate both).

It appears that the earliest Easter celebration was 'a unitive feast which included the incarnation' (Roll, 'The Origins of Christmas', p. 287), as demonstrated in the Paschal homily of Melito of Sardis c. 165. However, by the time of Origen (c. 185-254), in Against Celsus VIII:XXI, it had fragmented into Preparation-Day, Passover and Pentecost. The emergence of the Nativity feast was simply an extension of this fragmentation (p. 212). It is also possible that Christological controversies which questioned the true deity or humanity of Jesus spurred the practice. Certainly, we find people like Gregory Nazianzus, Leo, Ambrose and John Chrysostom using the Nativity feast as an occasion to attack Christological heresies (ch.4). Perhaps the process of festal fragmentation and the need to emphasise the true simultaneous deity and humanity of Jesus came together to encourage the Nativity festival.

What about the candles and lights? We know that the January 6 Nativity feast was sometimes called 'the Festival of Lights' (Ta Phota), and Chanukah, the Jewish 'Festival of Lights' was characterised 'by lighting lamps and kindling fires' (p. 121). How about the 'pagan' Christmas tree? The earliest record of Christmas trees comes from 16th century Germany, when one was decorated with apples, nuts, dates, pretzels and paper flowers. Later, Martin Luther, impressed by the stars shining through the evergreen trees, decorated his Christmas tree with candles to reproduce the majesty of Creation. In Britain, the Christmas tree was introduced by King George III''s German-born Queen Charlotte, and popularised by Queen Victoria's German husband, Prince Albert.

The pagan Germans revered an Oak, not a Fir tree! The centre of their worship was the Oak of Geismar, dedicated to Thor (Donar). It was felled by the British/Saxon 'Apostle of Germany', Boniface in 723. Falling, it crushed every tree around except a small fir tree. Boniface declared the fir tree's survival a miracle: 'Let this be called the tree of the Christ Child.' Boniface used the triangular shape of the fir to illustrate the Trinity.

Regarding holly and ivy, all ancient cultures used greenery/flora as decorations, and in winter evergreens were used. There was nothing specifically religious in this, and in Medieval and Tudor times, no 'arcane' properties were ascribed to either plant (Ronald Hutton, Stations of the Sun, p. 35). Tertullian in On Idolatry XIV-XVI is concerned that Christians do not participate in pagan festivals, and on that basis attacks Christians who use evergreens during such. Holly became associated with the Crown of Thorns and the red berries with Christ's blood.

As an Irishman working in Wales, I am always amused by 'Celtic' traditions like the Welsh hat which actually date no earlier than the 18th century. The same is true of the supposed Druid 'fertility' link with kissing under the mistletoe. Although mistletoe was used with other evergreens, kissing under it only began in the 18th century (Susan Drury, 'Customs and Beliefs Associated with Christmas Evergreens: A Preliminary Survey' [Folklore 98.2 1987, p. 194]) – long after the demise of Druidism! The so-called Druid association is found in Pliny the Elder, The Natural History, Book XVI, where he claims (based on reports) that Druids believe 'that the mistletoe, taken in drink, will impart fecundity to all animals that are barren…' Nothing about kissing.

The other fantasy is that in Norse mythology, the evil god Loki used mistletoe to kill Baldur, but that his mother Freya caused him to be restored to life and then changed the plant to a symbol of love, blessing any who kissed under it. In fact, the Norse Eddas, whilst confirming that Baldur was killed by mistletoe, say nothing about a resurrection, still less about kissing under the plant!

This 25 December, enjoy your Christmas, celebrating the Nativity of Our Saviour: the festival is truly Christian, not pagan.

A related article by Dr. McRoy on the origin of Easter was published by Christianity Today: Was Easter Borrowed from a Pagan Holiday?

Appendix 5: Understanding "We Saw His Star in the East"

Many Christian teachers, preachers and authors have made the mistake of claiming that Matthew was using technical astronomical language for a heliacal rising when he wrote, "For we saw His star in the east and have come to worship Him." Some have thought that this text means that the wise men saw the "star" rising in the eastern sky in the morning. Actually it simply means that the wise men saw the star while they were in the east.

Courtney Roberts, in her book *The Star of the Magi,* quotes a translator Robert Schmidt about Matthew's text and informs us about his qualifications:

> *"Robert Schmidt is perhaps the premier translator of ancient Greek astrology into contemporary English. The many translations to his credit include the works of Vettius Valens, Hephaistio of Thebes, Ptolemy, Antiochus of Athens, Paulus Alexandrinus." According to Mr. Schmidt the phrase written in Matthew's Gospel,* εν τη ανατολη, *means that the Magi observed the star while they were in the East. It has nothing to do with watching the star come up in the East before dawn (a heliacal rising).*[1]

Schmidt continues:

> *"My conjecture is that someone with very little Greek looked up the anatole in the Greek lexicon, found the cross-reference to epitole, which defines it as the rising of a star "as the sun rises or sets," and then misinterpreted this definition. He certainly could not have studied this word in the context of astrological or astronomical texts in Greek and come up with such a notion."*[2]

A translator of Greek astrological texts, Dorian Gieseler Greenbaum, says:

> *"Schmidt is correct in saying that en anatole is not consistent with the usual phraseology in Greek astrological texts. A heliacal rising phase would more likely be described as heoia anatole, and an acronycal one a hesperia anatole (this can also be used of the first visibility of the moon in the west after conjunction with the sun)."*[3]

Anatolia was the name of the eastern portions of modern Turkey during the Byzantine era. The name referred to the "East" as viewed from Constantinople. Many generations previously Matthew was simply referring to the "East" by the phrase εν τη ανατολη. He was not using any technical astronomical or astrological term for a heliacal rising. The Magi saw the star while they were in the East. They were not referring to its heliacal rising.

1 Courtney Roberts, *The Star of the Magi* (Franklin Lakes, New Jersey, Career press, 2007), 120.

2 Roberts, 121.

3 Roberts, 121.

Appendix 6: The "Royal Stars of the Persians"

Reading almost anything about the Magi and Persian astronomy one will find the phrase "the royal stars of the Persians." Many people, including myself, have thought that the concept of "royal stars" must have been linked to the star of Bethlehem. In popular literature and on the internet the phrase "the royal stars of the Persians" usually refers to the stars Regulus, Antares, Aldebaran and Fomalhaut. It seems that a Frenchman, named Jean Bailley, speculated in his book on astronomy in 1775 that the Persians must have identified these four stars as the "Persian chief stars." Those stars were near the equinox and solstice points about 3200 BC, giving them some astronomical significance. The stars were already important in Christian circles because of their association with four angels and Bailly actually attached new meaning to them by naming them the "Persian Royal Stars." Jean Bailley was a very famous man and had a very wide influence. He was the first President of the French National Assembly and also Mayor of Paris. Unfortunately he died in the Reign of Terror in 1793. Charles François Dupuis followed Bailley in writing about the four stars and was apparently the first one to call them the "Persian royal stars" in 1794. While Zoroastrian documents do speak of certain "chief stars" (leading or principle stars) they are not referred to as "royal stars." Other Frenchmen repeated the error in the 1800s and the phrase "Persian Royal Stars" began to appear in English just after 1900.

The designation "royal stars" does not have a long history. It is no where present in the ancient Zoroastrian texts. The concept and phrase "royal stars" appears to be a complete invention from the late 1700s based on a bit of speculation. Now a simple internet search yields literally millions of references to the "Royal Stars of the Persians." However, no one actually knows even if the Persians were doing anything at all with astronomy in 3200 BC. There are no records, no artifacts and no specifically Persian monuments from that period at all. Anything which is affirmed about Persian astronomy in 3200 BC is complete speculation.

On deeper examination it becomes clear that the "Persian chief stars" were actually refering mainly to constellations. It is clear that Sirius (the "Dog star" in Canis Major) was called "Taschter" by the Persians (also spelled: Tascheter, Tishtar, Tishtrya). This star, which is the brightest star in the night sky, and its constellation, was called the chief of all the fixed stars. Plutarch gives us some information about Magian beliefs at about AD 100. He clearly identifies the main Persian "chief star" as Sirius. This star was said to have dominated the eastern sky and was associated with the coming of rain.

Haftorang is another of the chieftains. We know Haftorang today as the constellation Ursula Major (the Big Dipper) which dominates the northern skies. Its seven brilliant stars are even reflected in its Persian name which actually means "seven thrones." This is the only "royal" aspect of the name. But it is important to note that like Sirius, Haftorang (Ursula Major) is not one of the modern so called "royal stars" (Regulus, Antares, Aldebaran and Fomalhaut).

The constellations of Aquarius (called Satevaesa / Satevis), and Scorpio (called Vanant / Venant) were also chieftains among the constellations for the Persians. Satevaesa means "the 100 dwellings" and their are about 100 readily visible stars in Aquarius and Piscis Australis (where one finds Fomalhaut). Satevaesa dominated the southern skies. Vanant with its star Antares dominated the western sky.

The Persian "chief stars" were actually Sirius and the constellations Ursula Major, Acquarius and Scorpio, but they were never called "royal stars" by the ancient Persians. In reality the Persian chief stars were composed of a significant number of stars in four constellations. Their royal status developed from the minds of the Frenchmen Jean Bailley and Charles François Dupuis in the 1700s.

Recommended text: Davis Jr, George A. "The so-called royal stars of Persia." Popular Astronomy 53 (1945): 149. This appendix was largely based on this article.

Appendix 7: The Course of World History in Zoroastrian Thought

Ancient Past	*1st period of 3,000 years*	*2nd period of 3,000 years*
The great uncreated, omniscient and omnipotent God, Ahura Mazda, created the world and various spirits called the Amesha Spentas and Yazatas. An evil spirit called Angra Mainyu also existed.	*Creation of the world. Mankind came from the sperm of one primeval man. The good creation grew to completion.*	*There was a great conflict of light and darkness. Evil entered the world and mixed with the good creation.*

3rd period of 3,000 years			
1st part of final 3,000 years	*2nd part of final 3,000 years* *Beginning of the 2nd Millenia*	*3rd part of final 3,000 years* *Begininning of the 3rd Millenia*	*The End of the 3rd Millenia*
Age of Zoroaster	*1st messianic figure, the Usedar, born of a virgin*	*2nd messianic figure, the Usedarmah, born of a virgin*	*The long awaited one, the 3rd messianic figure, the Saoshyant, will be born of a virgin as were his two predecessors.*
1,000 year period	*1,000 year period*	*1,000 year period*	*Finally with the arrival of the Saoshyant, the Great God, Ahura Mazda will be victorious. The Saoshyant will win the final victory over evil and bring about its destruction, This will bring the renewal of the world and the resurrection of the dead. The world will be completely transformed through the 3rd messianic figure.*
This period began with the appearing of Zoroaster sometime in the past, probably sometime between 5,000 BC and 600 BC.	*A first messianic figure was supposed to arrive 1,000 years after Zoroaster. With his coming the world slowly begins to change for the better.*	*The change for the better in the world continues with the arrival of the 2nd messianic figure.*	

Appendix 8: Dating the 1st of Nisan by Various Programs - 27 BC to 1 BC

In the table dates are listed for the first of Nisan in the years leading up to the birth of Jesus. The table was prepared using dates from Parker and Dubberstein's work on the Babylonian calendar, the www.torahcalendar.com website, the astronomy program Voyager 4.5 and the website www.abdicate.net. All the dates were corrected using the www.torachcalendar.com website which reflects the actual visibility of the cresent moon.

The "LY" in the table indicates the "Leap Years". The leap year with the symbol X^U is referring to a second month of Elul (Ulūlu), which was used once during each cycle of 19 years by the Babylonians. The Voyager and Abdicate programs do not take into account the late date of the equinox in the 1st century BC (March 25th). All four calendars match 11 times, three match 13 times and in three cases two sets of calendars match.

	Parker & Dubberstein			Torahcalendar.com			Voyager 4.5			Abdicate.net		
Year	Month	LY	Day	Month	LY	Day	Month	LY	Day	Month	LY	Day
27 BC	April		13	March		13	March		13	March		13
26 BC	April		1	April	X	1	April	X	1	April	X	1
25 BC	April	X	19	March		20	March		20	March		20
24 BC	April		8	March		9	March		9	March		9
23 BC	March		28	March	X	28	March	X	28	March	X	28
22 BC	April	X	16	March		17	March		17	March		17
21 BC	April		4	April	X	4	March		6	March		6
20 BC	March		25	March		25	March	X	25	March	X	25
19 BC	April	X	13	March		15	March		15	March		15
18 BC	April		3	April	X	3	April	X	3	April	X	3
17 BC	April	X	21	March		22	March		22	March		22
16 BC	April		10	March		11	March		11	March		11
15 BC	March		30	March	X	30	March	X	30	March	X	30
14 BC	April	X	18	March		19	March		19	March		19
13 BC	April		6	April	X	6	March		7	March		7
12 BC	March		26	March		26	March	X	26	March	X	26
11 BC	April	X	15	March		16	March		16	March		16
10 BC	April		4	April	X	4	April	X	4	April	X	4
09 BC	March		24	March		24	March		24	March		24
08 BC	April	X^U	13	March		13	March		13	March		13
07 BC	April		1	April	X	1	April	X	1	April	X	1
06 BC	April	X	21	March		21	March		21	March		21
05 BC	April		9	March		9	March		9	March		9
04 BC	March		28	March	X	28	March	X	28	March	X	28
03 BC	April	X	17	March		17	March		17	March		17
02 BC	April		5	April	X	5	March		7	March		7
01 BC	March		25	March		25	March	X	25	March	X	25

Appendix 9: The Visibility of Heliacal Risings and Settings

Visible heliacal rising and settings are notoriously difficult to predict well in advance. The following quotes illustrate this fact.

> *As anyone who has tried to observe such phenomena knows, the idea of a fixed date for heliacal rising or setting is something of an illusion, even though observations over several years would lead to a meaningful number. It is certainly true that historical records of these phenomena cannot be expected to fall on the precise computer-generated date; they are greatly affected by rather subtle atmospheric conditions: haze, fog, suspended dust, presence of the moon, and so on. Even visual acuity plays an important role. Furthermore, while the altitude difference at sunrise or sunset may change as much as 1°.75 per day for Mercury, and 1°.5 for Venus, the values may be much less, affecting the precision with which the heliacal date will be determined. For stellar objects the rate of change of the difference in altitude is essentially constant, but a function of the observer's latitude. Nonetheless, experience has shown that under ideal conditions the difference between a 'theoretical' or computed date and the real date may be no more than a day or two, one way or the other (usually late for rising at sunrise and early for setting at sunset).*

Taken from pages 12-13, Purrington, R.D., "Heliacal rising and setting: quantitative aspects," Archeoastronomy (JHA), no. 12, S72-85 (1988)

Determining the exact dates for visible heliacal risings and settings is still difficult even though the computer technology for doing the calculations has advanced a lot in the time since Roger Purrington wrote his article in 1988. In a doctoral dissertation published in 2009 we find more recent comments:

> *... calculating the date on which a planet or star is visible for the first or last time depends on what values have been assumed for several variables, such as the quality of atmospheric viewing conditions at the horizon, or the distance below the horizon the sun must be for a particular planet to be visible. Obviously, it is impossible to find a method of calculation which would perfectly replicate the recorded Babylonian dates of planetary phenomena, because the day-to-day observing conditions could never be reproduced exactly. Therefore, one must not use these computer programs expecting exact Babylonian dates of phenomena but rather approximate dates on which the phenomena could have been viewed in Babylon, perhaps assuming slightly better viewing conditions than were available at the time.*

GRAY, JENNIFER,MARY,KNIGHTLEY (2009) A Study of Babylonian Goal-Year Planetary Astronomy, Durham theses, Durham University. Available at Durham E-Theses Online: http://etheses.dur.ac.uk/101/

Since the Babylonians seem to have had some success in predicting the risings and settings of planets and stars it would not be surprising that they placed most of their confidence in their calculated dates. Statements about the ideal dates for risings and settings are present in the Babylonian Astronomical Diaries. The ideal date, when the star or planet should have been visible for the first time after passing behind the sun, are listed with the actual dates of the visible sightings. Whether the Babylonian astronomers visibly saw the rising or setting or not they were entirely aware of when the events should have happened. Having hundreds of years of records greatly facilitated having accurate dates for such cyclic phenomena.

Below are calculations for the planet Shabbatei (Saturn) for the years 3/2 BC calculated by a program, which is often used in archeoastronomy (Alcyone software at www.alcyone.de).

Heliacal setting and rising dates for Saturn in 3 BC and 2 BC
location: Babylon (Iraq) 32° 33' 00" N 44° 25' 00" E
*heliacal: arcvis[°] = 10.5 + 1.4 * magnitude*
critical altitude: 0.50°

3 BC	*2 BC*
Last visible (setting): April 16	*Last visible (setting): April 30*
First visible (rising): May 26	*First visible (rising): June 8*

Appendix 10: Diodorus Siculus Concerning the Chaldean Astronomers

Bibliotheca historica ("Historical Library")

This text was written by Diodorus Siculus, who lived from about 90 to 30 BC. it was possibly published in the year 49 BC. It gives the perspective of a Greek historian concerning the Chaldean astronomers. Diodorus was born in Sicily. He may have died there as well. *It should be noted that Diodorus refers to the planets as stars repeatedly in imitation of the Babylonians (Chaldeans).*

The text was reproduced from: The Library of History of Diodorus Siculus published in Vol. I of the Loeb Classical Library edition, 1933. Downloaded from http://penelope.uchicago.edu/Thayer/E/Roman/Texts/Diodorus_Siculus/ The notes at the end of the text are also from the listed source. (The text is public domain).

Book 2, Chapters 30-31

30:1 Now, as the Chaldeans say, the world is by its nature eternal, and neither had a first beginning nor will at a later time suffer destruction; furthermore, both the disposition and the orderly arrangement of the universe have come about by virtue of a divine providence, and today whatever takes place in the heavens is in every instance brought to pass, not at haphazard nor by virtue of any spontaneous action, but by some fixed and firmly determined divine decision.

2. And since they have observed the stars over a long period of time and have noted both the movements and the influences of each of them with greater precision than any other men, they foretell to mankind many things that will take place in the future.

3. But above all in importance, they say, is the study of the influence of the five stars known as planets, which they call "Interpreters"[57] when speaking of them as a group, but if referring to them singly, the one named Cronus[58] by the Greeks, which is the most conspicuous and presages more events and such as are of greater importance than the others, as they call the star of Helius, whereas the other four they designate as the stars of Ares, Aphrodite, Hermes, and Zeus,[59] as do our astrologers.

4. The reason why they call them "Interpreters" is that whereas all the other stars are fixed and follow a singular circuit in a regular course, these alone, by virtue of following each its own course, point out future events, thus interpreting to mankind the design of the gods. For sometimes by their risings, sometimes by their settings, and again by their color, the Chaldeans say, they give signs of coming events to such as are willing to observe them closely;

5. For at one time they show forth mighty storms of winds, at another excessive rains or heat, at times the appearance of comets, also eclipses of both sun and moon, and earthquakes, and in a word all the conditions which owe their origin to the atmosphere and work both benefits and harm, not only to whole peoples or regions, but also to kings and to persons of private station.

6. Under the course in which these planets move are situated, according to them, thirty stars,[60] which they designate as "counseling gods"; of these one half oversee the regions above the earth and the other half those beneath the earth, having under their purview the affairs of mankind and likewise those of the heavens; and every ten days one of the stars above is sent as a messenger, so to speak, to the stars below, and again in like manner one of the stars below the earth to those above, and this movement of theirs is fixed and determined by means of an orbit which is unchanging forever.

7. Twelve of these gods, they say, hold chief authority, and to each of these the Chaldeans assign a month and one of the signs of the zodiac, as they are called. And through the midst of these signs, they say, both the sun and moon and the five planets make their course, the sun completing his cycle in a year and the moon traversing her circuit in a month.

Chapter 31:1 Each of the planets, according to them, has its own particular course, and its velocities and periods of time are subject to change and variation. These stars exert the greatest influence for both good and evil upon the nativity of men; and it is chiefly from the nature of these planets and the study of them that they know what is in store for mankind.

2. And they have made predictions, they say, not only to numerous other kings, but also to Alexander, who defeated Darius, and to Antigonus and Seleucus Nicator who afterwards became kings, and in all their prophecies they are thought to have hit the truth. But of these things we shall write in detail on a more appropriate occasion.[61]

3. Moreover, they also foretell to men in private station what will befall them, and with such accuracy that those who have made trial of them marvel at the feat and believe that it transcends the power of man.

Beyond the circle of the zodiac they designate twenty-four other stars, of which one half, they say, are situated in the northern parts and one half in the southern, and of these those which are visible they assign to the world of the living, allow those which are invisible they regard as being adjacent to the dead, and so they call them "Judges of the Universe."

And under all the stars hitherto mentioned the moon, according to them, takes her way, being nearest the earth because of her weight and completing her course in a very brief period of time, not by reason of her great velocity, but because her orbit is so short. They also agree with the Greeks in saying that her light is reflected and that her eclipses are due to the shadow of the earth. Regarding the eclipse of the sun, however, they offer the weakest kind of explanation, and do not presume to predict it or to define the times of its occurrence with any precision.

Again, in connection with the earth they make assertions entirely peculiar to themselves, saying that it is shaped like a boat and hollow, and they offer many plausible arguments about both the earth and all other bodies in the firmament, a full discussion of which we feel would be alien to our history. This point, however, a man may fittingly maintain, that the Chaldeans have of all men the greatest grasp of astrology, and that they bestowed the greatest diligence upon the study of it. But as to the number of years which, according to their statements, the order of the Chaldeans has spent on the study of the bodies of the universe, a man can scarcely believe them; for they reckon that, down to Alexander's crossing over into Asia, it has been four hundred and seventy-three thousand years, since they began in early times to make their observations of the stars.

Notes

[57] i.e. to mankind of the will of the gods, as explained below.

[58] Saturn.

[59] Mars, Venus, Mercury, Jupiter.

[60] According to Bouché-Leclercq, L'Astrologie Grecque, p43, n4, Diodorus has confused here two distinct systems, that of the thirty-six stars known as decans, which Babylonian astrology designated as rulers of ten degrees in each zodiac,° and that of the thirty stars which the Egyptians believed to be gods, each of whom presided over one of the thirty days of the month.

[61] For prophecies to Alexander cp. Book 17.112, and to Antigonus, Book 19.55.

Appendix 11: Dating The Death of Herod

An eclipse recorded in Josephus' writings has been used as a marker for the death of Herod. The king died not long after an eclipse of the moon, which in recent times has been commonly dated in 4 BC. However, the March 12/13, 4 BC event was an unremarkable partial lunar eclipse. Herod's death was sometime between the lunar eclipse and the date of Passover. The eclipse date was important because it was linked to the execution of two Jewish leaders who were burnt alive on the orders of Herod. Those men had been involved in destroying a great golden eagle above the temple gate, which they considered to be idolatrous. During the night following their execution there was an eclipse of the moon.

Jewish tradition largely affirms the death of Herod during the month of Shevat (January/February). There was a remarkable total lunar eclipse on the night of January 9-10, 1 BC (Tevet 15). This eclipse followed a minor fasting day on the 10th of Tevet, which may be the one indicated by Josephus in *The Antiquities of the Jews* 17.164-167. According to Jewish tradition Herod died on the 2nd day of Shevat. In 1 BC that would have been on January 27/28th (17 or 18 days after burning the two Jewish leaders). This book follows a January 1 BC date for the death of Herod the Great.

Jack Finegan, E. Martin and A. Steinmann (see Bibliography) have all pointed out how many things happened in the period between the eclipse and the Passover following Herod's death. See Josephus (Antiquities of the Jews. 17.146-218).

- *The two Jewish leaders were executed by burning.*
- *The eclipse took place the following night.*
- *Herod went to Jericho from Jerusalem.*
- *Herod went from Jericho to Callirrhoe.*
- *Herod returned to Jericho.*
- *Herod grew even more ill.*
- *Herod called together the main Jewish leaders of the country.*
- *Herod rewrote his will.*
- *Herod ordered the execution of his son Antipater.*
- *Herod died five days after the execution of Antipater.*
- *Archelaus became the reigning successor to Herod.*
- *The funeral arrangements were made.*
- *The army was assembled.*
- *The funeral took place at the Herodium involving the army.*
- *Archelaus continued mourning for seven days.*
- *Archelaus offered sacrifice at the temple and was acclaimed by the people after the period of mourning. Archelaus celebrated his new status with friends.*
- *Archelaus received various groups who had requests.*
- *A group arose which had religiously based claims.*
- *The people began to gather for the Feast of Passover.*
- *Passover. There was the beginning of an insurrection and thousands died even in the temple courts.*

A 4 BC date gives a total of 29 days for all these things to take place. A 1 BC date allows a period of three months. The time is very limited and even crapped if the 4 BC date is correct. Another aspect of the chronology which is frequently ignored involves the 4 BC date for the execution by burning of the two Jewish leaders. If that date is accepted the burning of the two men would have taken place during the festival of Purim, which would have been highly unlikely. This is mentioned by E. Martin and others. The execution was highly unpopular and doing it during a festival would have been exceedingly unwise. Herod's counselors would have certainly tried to dissuade the king from such an action.

The texts on the facing page are from pages 300 and 301 of *The Handbook Of Biblical Chronology* written by Jack Finegan. Some portions of the passages have been omitted because of length. J. Finegan explains various aspects of the dating problems concerning Herod and his sons. The text is divided into sections, indicated by numbers, i.e. § 516, etc.. The manuscripts examined by Beyer (§ 518) effectively establish 1 BC as the year of Herod's death.

Jack Finegan, *Handbook of Biblical Chronology Principles of Time Reckoning in the Ancient World and Problems of Chronology in the Bible, Rev. ed.* (Peabody, Mass: Hendrickson, 1999), 300-301.

§ 516. The matter of the reigns of Herod's three sons and successors is also relevant to the question of the date of Herod's death, and has usually been taken as the major reason for accepting 4 B.C. as the correct date, on which basis the three rulers are usually listed as Archelaus, 4 B.C.-A.D. 6; Antipas, 4 B.C.-A.D. 39; Philip,4 B.C.-A.D. 34.[62] *As for the end point of each reign, the references or evidences seem plain: Herod Archelaus, ruler of Judea, Samaria, and Idumea, was banished in A.D. 6 in the tenth year of his reign (Dio 55, 27, 6; Ant. 17.342). Herod Antipas, tetrarch of Galilee and Perea, lost his tetrarchy during the second year of the emperor Gaius (38/39) and had reigned according to the evidence of coins for forty-three years (Ant. 18.252). Herod Philip, tetrarch of Gaulanitis and related regions, died in the twentieth year of Tiberius, A.D. 33/34, after a reign of thirty-seven years (Ant. 18.106). Calculating backward from these points, all seem to have begun to reign in 5 or 4 B.C.*

§ 517. Filmer however, considers that this kind of evidence can be misleading because co-regency and antedating were common.[63] *As he points out, in the case of the kings of Israel and Judah there were several occasions when a king appointed a son as co-regent and the son's reign overlapped the father's by several years, thus the reign could appear longer than it actually was. In the time after Alexander the Great we have seen specific examples of the antedating ... and there were other examples in the Hellenistic and early Roman period.*[64] *On an occasion when Herod was testifying to the Roman general and governor of Syria, Quintilius Varus, about his son Antipater, he spoke of him "to whom I have in a manner yielded up my royal authority while I am alive," and in his reply Antipater said that he had no reason to conspire against his father since "I was a king already ... you proclaimed me king in your lifetime" (War 1.624, 625, 631-632). See below (§654) for antedating in the reign of Herod Agrippa II. Similar antedating could, therefore, easily have been practiced in the reigns of Herod Archelaus and Herod Antipas. In regard to Herod Philip there is now specific evidence (§518).*

§518. As cited just above (§516), the currently known text of Josephus's Ant. 18.106 states that Philip died in the twentieth year of Tiberius (A.D. 33/34) ... after ruling for thirty-seven years. This points to Philip's accession at the death of Herod in 4 B.C. (4 years B.C. + 33 years A.D. =37 years). But Filmer suspected that a figure had dropped out and that the text should probably read the twenty-second, rather than the twentieth, year of Tiberius (A.D. 35/36). Barnes rejected this reading as "comparatively ill-attested," although he agreed with Filmer that it was a pivotal point of the debate. In fact, however, already in the nineteenth century Florian Riess reported that the Franciscan monk Molkenbuhr claimed to have seen a 1517 Parisian copy of Josephus and an 1841 Venetian copy in each of which the text read "the twenty-second year of Tiberius." The antiquity of this reading has now been abundantly confirmed. In 1995 David W. Beyer reported to the Society for Biblical Literature his personal examination in the British Museum of forty-six editions of Josephus's Antiquities published before 1700 among which twenty-seven texts, all but three published before 1544, read "twenty-second year of Tiberius," while not a single edition published prior to 1544 read "twentieth year of Tiberius."[65] *Likewise in the Library of Congress five more editions read the "twenty-second year," while none prior to 1544 records the "twentieth year." It was also found that the oldest versions of the text give variant lengths of reign for Philip 32 and 36 years. But if we still allow for a full thirty-seven-year reign, then "the twenty-second year of Tiberius" (A.D. 35/36) points to 1 B.C. (1 year B.C. + 36 years A.D. = 37 years) as the year of death of Herod.*[66] *This is therefore the date which is accepted in the present book. Accordingly, if the birth of Jesus was two years or less before the death of Herod in 1 B.C., the date of the birth was in 3 or 2 B.C. presumably precisely in the period 3/2 B.C., so consistently attested by the most credible early church fathers... Furthermore, we have seen evidence for a time of Jesus' birth in the mid-winter (Beckwith, our §473), therefore mid-winter in 3/2 B.C. appears the likely date of the birth of Jesus.*

---

[60] Bao-Lin Liu and Fiala, Canon of Lunar Eclipses, 89.

[61] Goldstine, New and Full Moons, 84 (April 7).

[62] E.g., Perowne,Later Herods.

[63] Filmer,JTS17 (1966): 296-298.

[64] Bickerman, in Berytus 8 (1943-44): 75, 77.

[65] Filmer,JTS 17 (1966): 298; Barnes,JTS 19 (1968): 205; Riess, Das Geburtsjahr Christi(Freiburg: Herder, 18 8 0); Beyer, "Josephus Reexamined."

[66] Beyer, "Josephus Reexamined," 4.

Selected Bibliography

Some of the material in this bibliography could easily be in two or more categories. An effort has been made to only place each item in one category.

Mesopotamian and Persian Astronomy / Astrology :

George A. Davis, Jr., "The So-Called Royal Stars of Persia," Popular Astronomy Vol 53, number 4, April 1945, 149-159.

Evans, James. The History and Practice of Ancient Astronomy. New York: Oxford University Press, 1998. Print.

Ferrari D'Occhieppo, Konradin, "The Star of the Magi and Babylonian Astrology," in Yamauchi, Edwin and Vardaman, Jerry. Chronos, Kairos, Christos: Nativity and Chronological Studies Presented to Jack Finegan. Winona Lake, IN: Eisenbrauns, 1989. Print.

Hunger, Hermann, and David Edwin Pingree. Astral Sciences in Mesopotamia. Leiden: Brill, 1999. Print.

Gray, Jennifer,Mary,Knightley (2009) A Study of Babylonian Goal-Year Planetary Astronomy, Durham theses, Durham University. Available at Durham E-Theses Online: http://etheses.dur.ac.uk/101/

Kasak, Enn and Veede, Raul, Understanding Planets in Ancient Mesopotamia, Electronic Journal of Folklore ISSN 1406-0949 is available from http://haldjas.folklore.ee/folklore/vol16/planets.pdf

Kasak, Enn, and Veede, Raul. Understanding Planets In Ancient Mesopotamia. (Folklore Vol. 16 ISSN 1406-0957, electronic edition, published by the Folk Belief and Media Group of ELM). http://haldjas.fo7lklore.ee/folklore/vol16/planets.pdf

Kelley, David H., and E. F. Milone. Exploring Ancient Skies an Encyclopedic Survey of Archaeoastronomy. New York: Springer, 2005. Print.

Koch-Westenholz, Ulla. Mesopotamian Astrology An Introduction To Babylonian And Assyrian Celestial Divination. The Carsten Niebuhr Institute Of Near Eastern Studies, Copenhagen: Museum Tusculanum Press, 1995. Electronic Version from Academia.com

Neugebauer, Otto. The Exact Sciences in Antiquity. 2d ed. New York: Dover Publications, 1969. Print.

Neugebauer, Otto. A History of Ancient Mathematical Astronomy. Berlin: Springer-Verlag, 1975. Print.

Ossendrijver, Mathieu. Babylonian Mathematical Astronomy Procedure Texts. New York, NY: Springer, 2012. Print.

Parker, Richard A., and Waldo H. Dubberstein. Babylonian Chronology 626 B.C.-A.D. 75. Providence, R.I.: Brown University Press, 1956. Print.

Reiner, Erica, and David Pingree. Babylonian Planetary Omens. Groningen: Styx, 1998. Print.

Roberts, Courtney. The Star of the Magi. Franklin Lakes, New Jersey: Career press, 2007.

Rochberg, Francesca. Babylonian Horoscopes. Philadelphia: American Philosophical Society, 1998. Print.

Rochberg, Francesca. In The Path Of The Moon Babylonian Celestial Divination And Its Legacy. Leiden: Brill, 2010. Print.

Rochberg, Francesca. The Heavenly Writing: Divination, Horoscopy, And Astronomy in Mesopotamian Culture. Cambridge: Cambridge University Press, 2004. Print.

Sachs, Abraham, and Hermann Hunger. Astronomical Diaries and Related Texts from Babylonia. Wien: Verlag der Österreichischen Akademie der Wissenschaften, 1988. Print.

Sachs, Abraham Joseph & Walker, Christopher B.F., "Kepler's View of the Star of Bethlehem and the Babylonian Almanac for 7/6 B.C.", Iraq, 46 (1984), 43-55.

Steele, John M.. A Brief Introduction To Astronomy in The Middle East. London: Saqi, 2008.

Steele, John. "Astronomy and Culture in Late Babylonian Uruk." "Oxford IX" International Symposium on Archaeoastronomy. International Astronomical Union 2011. Symposium S278, Lima, Peru. 9 Jan. 2011. Lecture.

Swerdlow, N. M.. The Babylonian Theory of the Planets. Princeton, N.J.: Princeton University Press, 1998. Print.

Swerdlow, N. M.. Ancient Astronomy and Celestial Divination. Cambridge, MA : MIT Press,1999. Print.

Astronomy in General / Star Names :

Allen, Richard Hinckley. Star names and their meanings. Glastonbury: Lost Library, 2010. Print.

Kunitzsch, Paul, and Tim Smart. A Dictionary of Modern Star Names: A Short Guide to 254 Star Names and Their Derivations. Cambridge, Mass.: Sky Pub. Corp., 2006. Print.

Purrington, Robert D. Heliacal Rising and Setting: Quantitative Aspects. Archeoastronomy, no. 12 (JHA, xix 1988)

Mesopotamia / Iran:

Bidmead, Julye. The Akitu festival: religious continuity and royal legitimation in Mesopotamia. Piscataway, N.J.: Gorgias Press, 2002. Print.

Delorme, Paul. Musa: Esclave, reine et déesse. Paris: Harmattan, 2005. Print.

McIntosh, Jane. Ancient Mesopotamia: New Perspectives. Santa Barbara, Calif.: ABC-CLIO, 2005. Print.

Rawlinson, George. Parthia. Originally published in 1893 ed. New York, NY: Cosimo Classics, 2007. Print.

Magi: Babylonian, Zoroastrian and Other

Collins, John Joseph. The Encyclopedia of Apocalypticism, Vol. 1. New York: Continuum, 1998. Print.

Maalouf, Tony. Arabs in the Shadow of Israel: the Unfolding of God's Prophetic Plan for Ishmael's Line. Grand Rapids, MI: Kregel Publications, 2003. Print.

McIntosh, Jane. Ancient Mesopotamia: New Perspectives. Santa Barbara, Calif.: ABC-CLIO, 2005. Print.

Pearse, Roger. "Mithras and Christianity." The Tertullian Project. N.p., n.d. Web. 5 Aug. 2013. http://www.tertullian.org/rpearse/mithras/display.php?page=mithras_and_christianity.

Pingree, David. ASTRONOMY AND ASTROLOGY IN INDIA AND IRAN Isis Vol. 54 No. 2 (June 1963), pp229-246.

http://penelope.uchicago.edu/Thayer/E/Journals/ISIS/54/2/Astronomy_and_Astrology_in_India_and_Iran*.html

Yamauchi, Edwin M.. Persia and the Bible. Grand Rapids, Mich.: Baker Book House, 1990. Print.

Chronology / Calendars:

Anderson, Robert. The Coming Prince: The Marvellous Prophecy of Daniel's Seventy Weeks Concerning the Antichrist. 19th ed. Grand Rapids: Kregel, 1975. Print.

Beckwith, Roger T.. Calendar and Chronology, Jewish and Christian: Biblical, Intertestamental and Patristic Studies. Leiden: E.J. Brill, 1996. Print.

David W. Beyer, "Josephus Reexamined: Unraveling the Twenty-Second Year of Tiberius," Chronos, Kairos, Christos II, edited by E. Jerry Vardaman. Macon: Mercer University Press, 1998. Print.

Finegan, Jack. Handbook of Biblical Chronology Principles of Time Reckoning in the Ancient World and Problems of Chronology in the Bible. Rev. ed. Peabody, Mass: Hendrickson, 1999. Print.

Hoehner, Harold W.. Chronological Aspects of the Life of Christ. Grand Rapids: Zondervan Pub. House, 1978. Print.

Michael A. Lombardi. Why is a minute divided into 60 seconds, an hour into 60 minutes, yet there are only 24 hours in a day? Scientific American, Monday, March 5, 2007. www.scientificamerican.com/article.cfm?id=experts-time-division-days-hours-minutes

Parker, Richard A., and Waldo H. Dubberstein. Babylonian chronology 626 B.C.-A.D. 75. Providence, R.I.: Brown University Press, 1956. Print.

Steinmann, Andrew. From Abraham to Paul: a Biblical Chronology. St. Louis, MO: Concordia Pub. House, 2011. Print.

Yamauchi, Edwin and Vardaman, Jerry. Chronos, Kairos, Christos: Nativity and Chronological Studies Presented to Jack Finegan. Winona Lake, IN: Eisenbrauns, 1989. Print.

Judaism :

Amaral, Joe. Understanding Jesus: Cultural Insights into the Words and Deeds of Christ. New York: FaithWords, 2011. Print.

Charlesworth, James H.. The Old Testament Pseudepigrapha. Peabody, Mass.: Hendrickson ; 2010. Print.

Collins, John Joseph. The Scepter and the Star: Messianism in Light of the Dead Sea Scrolls. 2nd ed. Grand Rapids, Mich.: W.B. Eerdmans Pub., 2010. Print.

Edersheim, Alfred. Sketches of Jewish Social Life: in the Time of Christ. West Valley City, UT: Waking Lion Press, 2006. Print.

Grenier, Denis. L'évangile dans le calendrier: Marc révélé par la liturgie juive. Sherbrooke, Québec: Pictogram, 2004. Print.

Johnson, Paul. A History of the Jews. London: Weidenfeld and Nicholson, 1987. Print.

Young, Brad. Meet The Rabbis: Rabbinic Thought and the Teachings of Jesus. Peabody, Mass.: Hendrickson Publishers, 2007. Print.

Mordechai, Avi. Signs in the Heavens: A Jewish Messianic Perspective of the Last Days and Coming Millennium. 3rd ed. Millennium 7000 Communications International, 1996. Print.

Neusner, Jacob. A History of the Jews in Babylonia, Part I, The Parthian Period. Wipf and Stock Publishers, Eugene, Oregon 1999. Print.

Noam, Vered. "Megillat Taanit - The Scroll of Fasting." The Literature of the Sages. Assen: Royal Van Gorcum ;, 2006. 339-361. Print.

Rapaport, Samuel. Tales and maxims from the Midrash. London: Routledge ; 1907. Print.

Thobois, Jean-Marc. Les Fetes de l'Eternel. Montmeyran, France: Emeth Editions, 2010. Print.

Sasson, Haim Hillel, and Abraham Malamat. A history of the Jewish people. Cambridge: Harvard University Press, 1985. Print.

Dates of Christmas :

Beckwith, Roger T.. Calendar and Chronology, Jewish and Christian: biblical, intertestamental and patristic studies. Leiden: E.J. Brill, 1996. Print.

Bokenkotter, Thomas S.. A Concise History of the Catholic Church. Rev. and expanded ed. New York: Doubleday, 2004. Print.

Brunt, P. A., and J. M. Moore. Res Gestae Divi Augusti = The Achievements of the Divine Augustus. Reprinted ed. Oxford [u.a.: Oxford Univ. Press, 1991. Print.

"Sol Invictus and Christmas." N.p., n.d. Web. 5 Aug. 2013. http://penelope.uchicago.edu/~grout/encyclopaedia_romana/calendar/invictus.html.

Duchesne, Louis. Origines du culte chrétien ... Cinquième édition, revue et augmentée. Paris, France: Ernest Thorin, 1889. Print.

Finegan, Jack. Handbook of Biblical Chronology: Principles of Time Reckoning in the Ancient World and Problems of Chronology in the Bible. Rev. ed. Peabody, Mass.: Hendrickson Publishers, 1998. Print.

Hijmans, Steven. "Sol Invictus, the Winter Solstice and the Origins of Christmas." Mouseion Calgary 3.3: 377–398, 2003. ISSN 1496-9343, OCLC 202535001

Hijmans, Steven E. Sol : the Sun in the Art and Religions of Rome (Thesis/dissertation), 2009 ISBN 90-367-3931-4

Johnson, Maxwell E.. Between Memory and Hope: Readings on the Liturgical Year. Collegeville, Minn.: Liturgical Press, 2000. Print.

Josephus, Flavius, and William Whiston. Josephus: the Complete Works. Nashville, TN: Thomas Nelson Publishers, 1998. Print.

Kelly, Joseph F.. The Origins of Christmas. Collegeville, Minn.: Liturgical Press, 2004. Print.

McRoy, Anthony. "Christmas: Pagan Festival or Christian Celebration?." Answering Islam, A Christian-Muslim Dialog and Apologetic. N.p., 14 Dec. 2007. Web. 5 Aug. 2013. http://www.answering-islam.org/pagan/christmas.html.

Pope Benedict XVI. Jesus of Nazareth The Infancy Narratives. London: Bloomsbury Publishing, 2012. Print.

Roll, Susan K.. Toward the Origins of Christmas. Kampen, The Netherlands: Kok Pharos Pub. House, 1995. Print.

Steinmann, Andrew. From Abraham to Paul: a Biblical Chronology. St. Louis, MO: Concordia Pub. House, 2011. Print.

Talley, Thomas J. . Origins of the Liturgical Year, 2nd ed. Collegeville, MN: Liturgical Press, 1991. Print.

White, John F.. Restorer of the World: the Roman Emperor Aurelian. Staplehurst: Spellmount, 2005. Print.

Star of Bethlehem

Hughes, David W.. The Star of Bethlehem Mystery: An Astronomer's Confirmation. London: J.M. Dent & Sons, 1979. Print.

Kidger, Mark R.. The Star Of Bethlehem: An Astronomer's View. Princeton, N.J.: Princeton University Press, 1999. Print.

Martin, Ernest L.. The Star that Astonished the World. Second Edition; Portland, Oregon: ASK Publications, 1996. Print.

Molnar, Michael R.. The Star of Bethlehem: the Legacy of the Magi. New Brunswick, N.J.: Rutgers University Press, 1999. Print.

Gregg, Daniel. The Ressurrection Day of the Messiah Yeshuah, © Daniel Gregg. Second Edition, www.torahtimes.com.

Sinnott, R.W., "Computing the Star of Bethlehem", Sky & Telescope, 72 (1986), 632-635.

Humphreys, Colin J., "The Star of Bethlehem: A Comet in 5 BC and the Date of the Birth of Christ", Quarterly Journal of the Royal Astronomical Society, 32 (1991), 389-407.

Roman Civilization :

Bénabou, Marcel. Suétone, Vies des douze Césars. Paris: Gallimard, 1975. Print.

Fox, Robin. The classical world: an epic history from Homer to Hadrian. New York: Basic Books, 2006. Print.

Lewis, Naphtali, and Meyer Reinhold. Roman Civilization Sourcebooks.Ed.with an Introd.and Notes by N.Lewis and M.Reinhold.. New York: Harper & Row, 1966. Print.

Néraudau, Jean. Auguste: la brique et le marbre. Paris: Belles Lettres, 1996. Print.

Endnotes

Most of the quotations from the Bible came from the New American Standard Version.

Part 1: Introduction

Pages: 9-32

1 In the 1st Century BC the system of astronomy developed and used by the Babylonians for hundreds of years was in decline. The last surviving Babylonian astronomical almanac written in cuneiform dates from AD 74. There are only four other surviving astronomical almanac documents from the 1st century AD. In contrast there are literally hundreds of surviving astronomical documents from the 5th through the 1st Century BC.

We do not know when the use of ziggurats and the temples of Marduk, Ishtar, Sîn and Nabu actually ceased. Pliny the Elder indicated that the temple of Marduk in Babylon was still functioning in AD 77.

The inclusion of apprentice Zoroastrians in this fictional text does illustrate the transfer of Babylonian knowledge to the Zoroastrians, however, we do not know exactly how or when this was done. It is possible that this fictional account is not at all accurate in that respect.

The astronomical events did happen exactly as described on September 11/12, 3 BC. Some individuals were certainly aware of these events. However, it is very possible that their circumstances of observation were different from those described in the text.

The names of the two main characters in this story were adapted from Babylonian names. The Ekur-zakir family was a family of priest / scribes that lived in ancient Uruk in Babylonia. These names were taken from the following article:

John Steele, "Astronomy and Culture in Late Babylonian Uruk," ("Oxford IX," International Symposium on Archaeoastronomy. International Astronomical Union 2011. Symposium S278, Lima, Peru. 9 Jan. 2011), Lecture.

2 The word "ziggurat" was the Babylonian name for the man made pyramids which were built in several Mesopotamian cites. They had a religious function and they were apparently used for astronomical observations as well.

3 Several members of the royal House of Adiabene (the region around Arbela, which has become present day Erbil, Iraq) were converted to Judaism in the years that followed the death and resurrection of Jesus. The account of these incidents is told in Josephus, *Antiquities of the Jews,* Book 20, 17-95: The Conversion of the House of Adiabene.

4 See Book of Acts. In Chapter 2, Jews and proselytes were present at the day of Pentecost. Many of them came from the Parthian domains.

5 Targum was the name given to the Aramaic oral translations of the Hebrew Bible.

6 The cuneiform illustrations and some of my information about the Mesopotamian names of the planets were taken from the following article: Enn Kasak, and Raul Veede, "Understanding Planets In Ancient Mesopotamia," (Folklore Vol. 16 ISSN 1406-0957, electronic edition, published by the Folk Belief and Media Group of ELM).

7 Jeremiah 23:5-6. See also the larger context which mentions shepherds and as well Jeremiah 33:12-22.

8 Psalm 89:35-37. The context of this entire Psalm is important because it speaks of God's covenant with king David.

9 Astronomy, Dictionary.com. The American Heritage® New Dictionary of Cultural Literacy, Third Edition. Houghton Mifflin Company, 2005. http://dictionary.reference.com/browse/astronomy (accessed: February 18, 2013).

10 Astrology, Dictionary.com. Dictionary.com Unabridged. Random House, Inc. http://dictionary.reference.com/browse/Astrology (accessed: February 18, 2013).

11 Epiphanius, *Panarion, electronic edition, Book 1, Section 1, Part 16, Epiphanius Against the Pharisees,* Located at: www.masseiana.org/panarion_bk1.htm

12 www.en.wikipedia.org/wiki/We_Three_Kings

At the beginning of the article we read: "We Three Kings", also known as "We Three Kings of Orient Are" or "The Quest of the Magi", is a Christmas carol written by the Reverend John Henry Hopkins, Jr., who wrote both the lyrics and the music. It is suggested to have been written in 1857 but did not appear in print until his Carols, Hymns and Song in 1863. John Henry Hopkins, Jr., then an ordained deacon in the Episcopal Church, was instrumental in organizing an elaborate holiday pageant (which featured this hymn) for the students of the General Theological Seminary in New York City in 1857 while serving as the seminary's music director.

13 See pages 198-199 and 208 of this book.

14 Rick Larson, in his DVD and web site http://www.bethlehemstar.net/ helped me understand that Herod was not actually aware of the star before the arrival of the wise men. Larson's observations concerning the men and events proved invaluable to me in my research. Unfortunately, his effort to make June 17th 2 BC correspond to the birth date of Jesus is completely untenable. There is no historical tradition linked to this date. It also has significant chronological difficulties.

15 Jack Finegan, *Handbook of Biblical Chronology,* (Peabody, Mass.: Hendrickson Publishers, Inc.) page 319, § 548. Quote: According to the papyrus codex Boder V, attributed to the third century A.D., when the Magi came they saw the child Jesus "standing by his mother Mary's side."

16 I am indebted to Daniel Gregg for this insight which clarifies the meanings of the two words brephos and paidion. Daniel Gregg, *The Resurrection Day of the Messiah Yeshuah,* electronic edition, (© Daniel Gregg. Second Edition, www.torahtimes.com), p. 237

17 Konradin Ferrari D'Occhieppo, "The Star of the Magi and Babylonian Astrology," in Edwin Yamauchi, and Jerry Vardaman, *Chronos, Kairos, Christos: Nativity and Chronological Studies Presented to Jack Finegan,* (Winona Lake, IN: Eisenbrauns, 1989), 41-53.

Part 2: When was Jesus Born? Pages: 33-42

1 Jack Finegan, *Handbook of Biblical Chronology,* (Peabody, Mass.: Hendrickson Publishers, Inc.) page 291, Table 139.

Please note: As in Finegan's chart this book takes into account the fact that Jewish years are split between two years. Hebrew years begin and end about the time of the spring equinox. Therefore, their years, including the Sabbatical years, always sit astride two years. That is why in this book so many dates are indicated by two numbers.

2 See the references in notes 3 and 17 below (See also Appendix 11).

The main source of our information about the end of Herod's reign comes from Josephus. While in general Josephus' writings are reliable, unfortunately they are not totally without errors. Josephus sometimes contradicts himself, which can lead one to make chronological mistakes. Sometimes it is not clear how Josephus calculates his dates since differnt methods are possible.

The partial eclipse of the moon which supposedly dates Herod's death in 4 BC was not at all remarkable. The time between the eclipse, Herod's funeral and the following Passover was very short. It seems impossible that all the events described in Josephus could have taken place during the time period. However, the 1 BC eclipse of the moon is several months before the following Passover and the eclipse itself was total and it was probably quite remarkable.

One important piece of evidence concerning the dating of Herod's reign was unknown till 1995. In that year a researcher conclusively proved that Herod's son Philip, the tetrarch, died in the 22nd year of Tiberius' reign (AD 35/36), Philip having reigned 37 years. It has been assumed for many generations that Philip died in the 20th year of Tiberius' reign (AD 33/34) having reigned 37 years. The older written manuscripts indicate that the later printed versions of Josephus' text were in error, all the manuscript versions of Josephus before AD 1544 read that Philip died in the 22nd year of Tiberius' reign. Whereas the printed texts after AD 1544 read Tiberius' 20th year. There was apparently a mistake in printing which altered the number. Philip came to power in 1 BC. See Jack Finegan, *Handbook of Biblical Chronology (1998),* pages 300-301, Sections 516-518.

See Andrew Steinmann, When Did Herod the Great Reign? in Novum Testamentum, Volume 51, Number 1.

3 Jack Finegan, *Handbook of Biblical Chronology,* Sections 474-569.

Paul Keresztes, *Imperial Rome and the Christians: From Herod the Great to About 200 AD* (Lanham, Maryland: University Press of America, 1989), pp.1–43.

Ormond Edwards, "Herodian Chronology," Palestine Exploration Quarterly 114 (1982) 29-42.

E.W. Filmer, "Chronology of the Reign of Herod the Great", Journal of Theological Studies ns 17 (1966), pp. 283–298.

Andrew E. Steinmann, *From Abraham to Paul: a Biblical Chronology* (St. Louis, MO: Concordia Pub. House, 2011) 219-256.

Andrew E. Steinmann,"When Did Herod the Great Reign?", Novum Testamentum, Volume 51, Number 1, 2009, pp. 1–29.

4 http://penelope.uchicago.edu/~grout/encyclopaedia_romana/calendar/saturnalia.html

5 Steven Hijmans, "Sol Invictus, the Winter Solstice, and the Origins of Christmas", Mouseion Calgary 3.3: 377-398. See also the following page: http://penelope.uchicago.edu/~grout/encyclopaedia_romana/calendar/invictus.html

6 Steven E. Hijmans, *Sol : the Sun in the Art and Religions of Rome* (Thesis/dissertation, 2009 ISBN 90-367-3931-4), 588.

7 T.C.Schmidt, "Sol Invictus Evidently not a Precursor to Christmas" http://chronicon.net/blog/christmas/sol-invictus-evidently-not-a-precursor-to-christmas/

8 Thomas Bokenkotter, *A Concise History of the Catholic Church*, (New York: Doubleday, 2004) 39.

9 http://www.answering-islam.org/pagan/christmas.html

10 Thomas Bokenkotter, *A Concise History of the Catholic Church*, 39.

11 Constantine's actual decree went as follows: *On the venerable day of the sun let the magistrates and people residing in cities rest, and let all workshops be closed. In the country however persons engaged in agriculture may freely and lawfully continue their pursuits because it often happens that another day is not suitable for grain-sowing or vine planting; lest by neglecting the proper moment for such operations the bounty of heaven should be lost.*

12 (Justin Martyr, First Apology 67)
See also: www.christian-history.org/sabbath-to-sunday.html

13 See a short comment on a 12th century manuscript of Dionysius Bar Salibi, in Thomas J. Talley, *Origins of the Liturgical Year, 2nd ed.* (Collegeville, MN: Liturgical Press, 1991), 101-102.

14 In his book concerning biblical chronology Jack Finegan writes: "While replacement of pagan festivals may have been a factor, historical tradition about the actual time of year of the birth of Jesus may have been more important. The winter solstice and the beginning of the increase of light may also have seemed an appropriate time to remember the coming into the world of the 'sun of righteousness' " (Mal 4:2). Jack Finegan, *Handbook of Biblical Chronology*, (Peabody, Mass.: Hendrickson Publishers, Inc.) p. 231, § 552

15 Origen, Homilies on Leviticus (VIII.3.2)

16 Sol Invictus and its relation to Christmas: http://penelope.uchicago.edu/~grout/encyclopaedia_romana/calendar/invictus.html

See also: http://chronicon.net/blog/christmas/sol-invictus-evidently-not-a-precursor-to-christmas/

17 See the following works:

Jack Finegan, *Handbook of Biblical Chronology*, page 320-328, § 552-569.

Andrew McGowan, "How December 25 Became Christmas" Biblical Archaeology Society, Web.12/07/2012: www.biblicalarchaeology.org/daily/biblical-topics/new-testament/how-december-25-became-christmas.

Louis Duchesne, *Origines du culte Chrétien, 5th ed.* (Paris: Thorin et Fontemoing, 1925), 275–279.

Thomas J. Talley, *Origins of the Liturgical Year, 2nd ed.* (Collegeville, MN: Liturgical Press, 1991), 85-140.

Maxwell E. Johnson, *Between Memory and Hope: Readings on the Liturgical Year,* (Collegeville, Minn.: Liturgical Press, 2000), 265-347.

18 Some of the historic denominations which celebrate Gabriel's announcement and the incarnation of Jesus at his conception are the following: Catholic Church, Anglican, Lutheran, Eastern Orthodox, Oriental and Eastern Catholic.

19 Jack Finegan, *Handbook of Biblical Chronology,* Table 179, page 363. The possible dates for a Nisan 14 crucifixion given by Finegan are the following, with the most likely dates being in AD 30 and AD 33:

AD 27 : April 10 (Thursday)
AD 28 : March 30 (Tuesday)
AD 29 : April 18 (Monday)
AD 30 : April 7 (Friday)
AD 31 : March 27th (Tuesday)
AD 32 : April 14 (Monday)
AD 33 : April 3 (Friday)
AD 34 : March 24 (Wednesday)

The probable dates for Passover from 7 BC to 1 BC are listed below (counting from the evening and continuing to the next evening). The dates correspond to the approximate date of the first full moon after the spring equinox. The precise date of the full moon varies from the 14th to the15th of the lunar month.

The dates of Passover 7 BC through 1 BC :

7 BC : April 14/15
6 BC : April 3/4
5 BC : April 22/23
4 BC : April 9/10
3 BC : March 30/31
2 BC : April 18/19
1 BC : April 7/8

20 Clement of Alexandria, Stromata 1.21.145-1462:

From the birth of Christ, therefore, to the death of Commodus are, in all, 194 years, 1 month, 13 days. And there are those who have determined not only the year of our Savior's genesis, but even the day, which they say took place in the twenty-eighth year of Augustus on the 25th of Pachon... And treating of his passion, with very great accuracy, some say that it took place in the sixteenth year of Tiberius, on the 25th of Phamenoth, but others the 25th of Pharmuthi and others say that on the 19th of Pharmuthi the Savior suffered. Indeed, others say that he came to be on the 24th or 25th of Pharmuthi."

Hippolytus of Rome Commentary on Daniel 4.23 :

> *The first coming of our Lord, that in the flesh, in which he was born at Bethlehem, took place eight days before the kaldens of January, a Wednesday, in the 42nd year of the reign of Augustus ...*

21 "We found that the length of the pregnancies varied by as much as 37 days." Oxford University Press (OUP). "Length of human pregnancies can vary naturally by as much as five weeks." ScienceDaily, 6 Aug. 2013. Web. 7 Oct. 2013.

22 Roger T. Beckwith, *Calendar and Chronology, Jewish and Christian: Biblical, Intertestamental and Patristic Studies*: (Leiden: E.J. Brill, 1996), 79-92. *See also:*

Jack Finegan, Handbook of Biblical Chronology, 130-134, § 237-243.

And: Kurt Simmons, "Priestly Courses for the years A.D. 70-B.C. 23" www.dec25th.info (Listed under Priestly Courses).

23 I am indebted to the chart produced by Kurt Simmons for this insight. "Priestly Courses for the years A.D. 70-B.C. 23," http://www.dec25th.info/ (Listed under Priestly Courses).

24 The author recognizes that these festivals and appointed times are the Lord's Festivals and appointed times. The words "Jewish festivals" are simply used for communication purposes. Please note as well that Hanukkah and Purim were not specifically feasts which were ordained in the same way as the feasts and appointed times in Leviticus chapters 23 and 25. There should be enough freedom among messianic believers to refer to the feasts and appointed times in various ways. To insist that one say continually "The Lord's Feasts and appointed times" is not necessary.

The Apostle John has no problem using the words "feast of the Jews" :

> *John 5:1 After these things there was a feast of the Jews, and Jesus went up to Jerusalem.*
> *John 6:4 Now the Passover, the feast of the Jews, was near.*
> *John 7:2 Now the feast of the Jews, the Feast of Booths, was near.*

One should certainly recognize that the feasts and special days were appointed by God. Although later Jewish traditions have significantly changed some of the important celebrations and dates of the religious calendar.

25 See Josephus, *Antiquities of the Jews* Book 17 Chapter 4 section 82 concerning the seven months. In addition, after the census two months were necessary for Antipater to send a message to Rome and then to receive an invitation. After Antipater's arrest at the end of his seven months away from Judea another period of two months was necessary to send a message to Augustus and to allow time for the emperor's message to return to Judea.

Part 3: Wise Men from the East Pages: 43-72

1 Jane McIntosh, *Ancient Mesopotamia New Perspectives,* (Santa Barbara, Calif.: ABC-CLIO, 2005), 118-122.

2 Jacob Neusner, *A History of the Jews in Babylonia, Part I, The Parthian Period,* (Wipf and Stock Publishers, Eugene, Oregon 1999), 94-99.

3 Julye Bidmead, *The Akitu festival: religious continuity and royal legitimation in Mesopotamia,* (Piscataway, N.J.: Gorgias Press, 2002), 143.

4 Tony Maalouf, *Arabs in the Shaw of Israel,* (Kregel Publications, a division on Kregel, Inc. P.O. Box 2607, Grand rapids, MI. 2003), 196-197. The author is very much indebted to Tony Maalouf for most of this paragraph. Tony Maalouf's insights liberate the term Magi from a singular definition uniquely centered on Median Magi.

5 David Pingree, "Astronomy And Astrology In India And Iran," Isis Vol. 54 No. 2 (June 1963), 241.

6 George A. Davis, Jr., "The So-Called Royal Stars of Persia," Popular Astronomy Vol 53, number 4, April 1945, 149-159.

6 Romulus, Remus and Perseus supposedly had virgin mothers. Alexander the Great was said to have been conceived through sexual relations involving a god.

7 The "History of Religions School" of thought usually assumes that Zoroastrian thought influenced Judaism and Christianity. However, the actual verifiable Zoroastrian texts only came into their final form well after both Rabbinical Judaism and Christianity were well established.

8 Denis Grenier, *L'évangile dans le calendrier: Marc révélé par la liturgie juive,* (Sherbrooke, Québec: Pictogram, 2004), 221.

Jacob Neusner, *A History of the Jews in Babylonia*, 123.

9 Ben-Sasson, Haim H., Editor, *A History of the Jewish People, English translation 1976,* (George Weidenfeld and Nicholson Ltd, 1969 by Dvir Publishing House, Tel Aviv), 373.

10 Brad Young, *Meet the Rabbis: Rabbinic Thought and the Teachings of Jesus,* (Hendrickson Publishers, Inc. Peabody, Mass. 2007), 190-194.

11 Pliny the Elder, *Pliny's Natural History in Thirty-Seven Books,* (S.l.: Nabu Press, 2010), 31.

12 The official Vatican web site: www.vatican.com/articles/info/urbi_et_orbi-a74

13 John Steele, *A Brief Introduction to Astronomy in the Middle East,* (Saqi books, London, 2008), Kindle edition.

14 Gray, Jennifer, Mary, Knightley (2009) *A Study of Babylonian Goal-Year Planetary Astronomy,* Durham theses, Durham University. Available at Durham E-Theses Online: http://etheses.dur.ac.uk/101/ p. 46-47. This information was compiled and altered based on information obtained from Gray's material.

15 Michael A. Lombardi, "Why is a minute divided into 60 seconds, an hour into 60minutes, yet there are only 24 hours in a day?" (Scientific American, March 2007) http://www.scientificamerican.com/article.cfm?id=experts-time-division-days-hours-minutes

16 The caves at Lascaux and in other places in France may contain the marks of early conceptions of constellations.

17 Review of a book by Francesca Rochberg, *The Heavenly Writing: Divination, Horoscopy, and Astronomy in Mesopotamian Culture* by Eleanor Robson, Department of History and Philosophy of Science, University of Cambridge Eleanor Robson http://bmcr.brynmawr.edu/2005/2005-06-29.html

18 Gray, *A Study of Babylonian Goal-Year Planetary Astronomy,* 46-47

19 Adapted from raw data found in Gray - pages 65, 174, 224, 292. The Seleucid Era dates are taken from Parker and Dubberstein dates calculated through: Robert Gent's Babylonian calendar web page: www.staff.science.uu.nl/~gent0113/babylon/babycal.htm.

Also: A. J. Sachs and C. B. F. Walker, Kepler's View of the Star of Bethlehem and the Babylonian Almanac for 7/6 B.C., Iraq (journal), Vol. 46, No. 1 (Spring, 1984), pp. 43-55

The "Phenomena" column was done by the author.

20 Gray, *A Study of Babylonian Goal-Year Planetary Astronomy,* 26-27.

21 Hamid M.K. Al-Naimiy, "Astronomy At Mesopotamian Region (3000 BC-1400 AD," International Symposium on Solar Physics and Solar Eclipses (SPSE) 2006, page 6.

22 Hermann Hunger and Abraham J. Sachs, *Introduction of Volume 1 Astronomical Diaries And Related Texts From Babylonia, (*Wien: Verl. der Österr. Akad. der Wiss., 1988), adapted from the Introductory page 11.

23 Gray, *A Study of Babylonian Goal-Year Planetary Astronomy,* 27 and 49.

24 Gray, *A Study of Babylonian Goal-Year Planetary Astronomy,* 49.

25 Gray, *A Study of Babylonian Goal-Year Planetary Astronomy,* 49.

26 Hermann Hunger and Abraham J. Sachs, *Introduction of Volume 1 Astronomical Diaries And Related Texts From Babylonia,* adapted from the Introduction pages 6-7).

27 Yohanna Sultan R'Bido, "Mesopotamia: Ils ont quadrillé le ciel," Cahiers Science et Vie, N° 129, May 2012), 46.

28 Review of a book by Francesca Rochberg, *The Heavenly Writing: Divination, Horoscopy, and Astronomy in Mesopotamian Culture* by Eleanor Robson, Department of History and Philosophy of Science, University of Cambridge Eleanor Robson http://bmcr.brynmawr.edu/2005/2005-06-29.html

29 Francesca Rochberg, *Babylonian Horoscopes,* (Transactions of the American Philosophical Society, New Series, Vol. 88, No. 1, 1998), page 3.

30 John Steele, *A Brief Introduction to Astronomy in the Middle East, Kindle edition,* (London: Saqi, 2008).

31 John Steele, *A Brief Introduction to Astronomy in the Middle East, Kindle edition, (*London, Saqi, 2008).

32 Michael R Molnar, *The Star of Bethlehem: the Legacy of the Magi,* Kindle Edition, *(*New Brunswick, N.J.: Rutgers University Press, 1999), Chapter 3, section "Wise Men from the East."

33 Francesca Rochberg, *Babylonian Horoscopes,* Volume 88, Part 1, (Philadelphia: American Philosophical Society, 1998). page 2.

> F. Rochberg's text reads: *Despite the evidence of transmission and borrowing from Mesopotamia found in specific elements of Greek astrology, and that the basic idea of predicting the life of a person on the basis of astronomical phenomena associated with the birth date was originally Babylonian, Babylonian and Greek horoscopes reflect substantially different genethialogical systems. There is neither chronological overlap between the two corpora, nor any similarity between their underlying cosmologies or their philosophic/religious underpinnings.*

34 Pliny the Elder indicates that the temple of Bel was still functioning when he wrote his book *A Natural History* in the late AD 70s. He does affirm that most of the city had been reduced to desert although many of the walls were standing. (Pliny. *Natural History,* Book 6 Chapter 30) http://www.perseus.tufts.edu

35 Francesca Rochberg, *In the Path of the Moon: Babylonian Celestial Divination and Its Legacy,* (Leiden: Brill, 2010) 250.

36 Ulla Koch-Westenholz, *Mesopotamian Astrology An Introduction To Babylonian And Assyrian Celestial Divination,* Electronic Version from Academia.com, (The Carsten Niebuhr Institute Of Near Eastern Studies, Copenhagen: Museum Tusculanum Press, 1995) Chapter 8, p. 162.

Part 4: The Kings of the Earth

Pages: 73-82

1 Claude Nicolet calls his book about Roman censuses and political geography *L'INVENTAIRE DU MONDE. - Géographie et politique aux origines de L'Empire romain.*

2 Gerard Gertoux, "Dating The Death Of Herod," page 27. See Tacitus, Annals I:11,4. The reference cites Tacitus' description of the documents used to prepare the Res Gestae of Augustus. The census of 3/2 BC was part of the documentation was used for Augustus' text.

3 The publication of a summary of the results of the census / registration in 3/2 BC may have happened on May 12th, 2 BC as part of the ceremonies surrounding the dedication of the Forum of Augustus and the Temple of Mars Ultor.

4 Josephus, *The Wars of the Jews*, Book 2 Chapter 16; Many aspects of Augustus' text, the *Res Gestae Divi Augusti,* were probably shaped by the census / registration in 3/2 BC.

5 A similar although different oath of allegiance was sworn by the inhabitants of the province of Paphlagonia in the spring of 3 BC. It is possible that the oath sworn by Joseph would have been similar. There were doubtless several adjustments, which took into account the Jewish religious sensibilities. We know that Augustus was well aware of the Jewish sensitivities and even tried to protect the Jews from theft and abuse, see Josephus, *Antiquities of the Jews* Book 16 chapter 6 part 2. Josephus says that the oath mentioned in the *Antiquities of the Jews* Book 17 was sworn both to both the emperor and to Herod.

The text of the Paphlagonian oath is reproduced below:

In the third year from the twelfth consulship of the Emperor Caesar Augustus, son of a god, March 6, in the ... at Gangra, the following oath was taken by the inhabitants of Paphlagonia and the Roman businessmen dwelling among them:

> *"I swear by Jupiter, earth, sun, by all the gods and goddesses, and by Augustus himself, that I will be loyal to Caesar Augustus and to his children and descendants all my life in word, in deed, and in thought, regarding as friends whomever they so regard, and considering as enemies whomever they so adjudge; that in defense of their interests I will spare neither body, soul, life, not children, but will in every way undergo every danger in defense of their interests; that whenever I perceive or hear anything being said or planned or done against them I will lodge information about this and will be an enemy to whoever says or plans or does any such thing; and that whomever they adjudge to be enemies I will by land and sea, with weapons and sword, pursue and punish. But if I do anything contrary to this oath, or not in conformity with what I swore, I myself call down upon myself, my body, my soul, my life, my children, and all my family and property, utter ruin and utter destruction unto all my issue and all my descendants, and may neither earth nor sea receive the bodies of my family or my descendants, or yield fruits to them."*
>
> *The same oath was sworn by all the people in the land at altars of Augustus in the temples of Augustus in the various districts. In this manner did the people of Phazimon, who inhabit the city now called Neapolis, all together swear the oath in the temple of Augustus at the altar of Augustus.*

This text is from: N. Lewis and M. Reinhold, Roman Civilization, Sourcebook II: The Empire (New York, New York: Harper & Row, 1966) 34-35.

6 Jack Finegan, *Handbook of Biblical Chronology*, page 302-306, § 519-526.

7 Paulus Orosius, *Historiae Adversus Paganos,* VI.22.7 and VII.2.16

8 Josephus, *Antiquities of the Jews,* Book 17, Chapter 2

9 http://en.wikipedia.org/wiki/Jerusalem (under climate).

10 Photo used with permission: www.parscoins.com.

11 Much of this paragraph is explored in the book by Paul Delorme, *Musa: Esclave, reine et déesse,* (Paris: Harmattan, 2005). Print.

12 http://en.wikipedia.org/wiki/File:Coin_of_Phraataces_and_Musa.jpg

13 See also Josephus, Wars of the Jews, Book 1.625 and Book 1. 631-632.

Part 5: God's Chosen King

Pages: 83-108

1 The author is indebted to Kurt Simmons and his site www.dec25th.info for this insight.

2 Sir Robert Anderson, *The Coming Prince: the Marvellous Prophecy of Daniel's Seventy Weeks Concerning the Antichrist 19th ed.* (Grand Rapids: Kregel, 1975)

3 PDF copies of a portion of Dr. Hoehner's book can be found online using the title: Chronological Aspects of the Life of Christ, Part VI: Daniel's Seventy Weeks and New Testament Chronology.

4 Personal note: Insights concerning the sequence of years in Daniel's prophecy came toward the very end of the author's period of research, shortly after other discoveries about the literal days and weeks. Discoveries about the seven "sevens" of months and 62 "sevens" of months followed within hours of the insights about the years. Communications with Allan Johnson, an independent researcher, were important in gaining understanding into the prophecy. Allan Johnson's initial research into the Sabbatical and Jubilee years opened up a new door of interpretation to the author. Later Mr. Johnson's simple suggestion that it might be worthwhile to investigate the Sadducean dates for the First Fruits Offering and Pentecost actually turned the switch in my thinking which eventually put flood lights on the prophecy. I have since come to see that the *Seder Olam* contained ideas about Sabbatical years and Daniel's prophecy in the 2nd century AD. Some other people have also proposed a similar approach to the years but using different sets of Sabbatical years.

5 Roger T. Beckwith, *Calendar and Chronology, Jewish and Christian: Biblical, Intertestamental and Patristic Studies*: (Leiden: E.J. Brill, 1996), 232, 239 and 248.

6 Beckwith, *Calendar and Chronology,* 249.

7 Unfortunately many Christians only think of God's righteousness uniquely in terms of judgement. The Lord's righteousness also has to do with his role as a savior for his people. The following quote from the Holman Bible Dictionary makes these things plain:

The Old Testament is the starting point is the Hebrew notion of God's "righteousness." The Hebrew mind did not understand righteousness to be an attribute of the divine, that is a characteristic of God's nature. Rather, God's righteousness is what God does in fulfillment of the terms of the covenant that God established with the chosen people, Israel (2 Chronicles 12:6 ; Psalm 7:9 ; Jeremiah 9:24 ; Daniel 9:14). God's righteousness was not a metaphysical property but that dimension of the divine experienced by those within the covenantal community. (Author: They experienced God's righteous behavior. The cross and Jesus' resurrection demonstrate God's righteousness).

... God's righteousness was understood in relation to the image of God as the Judge of created order (Psalm 96:13). God's judgments are consistently redemptive in nature, God's judgments protected, delivered, and restored Israel (Isaiah 11:4-5). At times God's righteousness was experienced in God's delivering Israel from enemies and oppressors (Psalm 71:1); at other times, in God's delivering Israel from the nation's own sinfulness (Psalm 51:19). Such deliverance involved God's righteousness of wrath against the persecutor and the wicked (Psalm 106:1). Salvation and condemnation exist together as the two sides of God's righteousness; the leading side is always deliverance: God condemns only because He also saves (Psalm 97:1).

Holman Bible Dictionary Online, under the theme of righteousness, taken from www.studylight.org.

Part 6: God's Appointed Time Pages: 109-118

1 It was not unusual to think of the beginning of the day as starting in the evening. This was also true of the Assyrians and Babylonians.

2 Samuel Rapaport, *Tales and Maxims from the Midrash, Section on the Genesis (Bereshith) Rabba* (George Routledge and Sons Limited, London and E.P. Dutton and Company, New York, 1907), 75.

3 Beckwith, *Calendar and Chronology,* 283.

4 Beckwith, *Calendar and Chronology,* 283.

5 Beckwith, *Calendar and Chronology,* 285.

6 The author has not yet discovered a complete computerized astronomy program which simulates the visibility factor correctly. Perhaps such a program exists however, he is not aware of it.

7 Robert Harry van Gent, University of Utrecht, http://www.staff.science.uu.nl/~gent0113/ (See Babylonian Calendar).

8 Parker, Richard Anthony & Dubberstein, Waldo Herman. *Babylonian Chronology 626 B.C. – A.D. 45* (Providence, Rhode Island. Brown University Press 1956), tables on pages 25-47.

9 The author is not in agreement about every idea presented on the www.torahcalendar.com site. He does greatly appreciate the page on sighting the new moon which contains a very helpful application for determining the visibility of the new moon.

10 The author recognizes that the Sadducean perspective may have some merit concerning the timing of the Fruit Fruits wave offering. It may have been the older practice.

11 Many Christians do not realize that there was a Feast of Pentecost every year. The events at Pentecost several weeks after the death and resurrection of Jesus were certainly unique. However, the actual festival of Pentecost had taken place each year for over 1400 years before the outpouring of the Holy Spirit at Pentecost in AD 33.

12 Alfred Edersheim, *Sketches of Jewish Social Life, Electronic edition,* Chapter 15.

Part 7: Looking to the Heavens Pages: 119-142

1 Epiphanius, *The Panarion of Epiphanius of Salamis,* (Online edition at: http://www.masseiana.org/panarion_bk1.htm), Book 1, Section 1, Part 16.

2 I have taken the information concerning the Greek names of planets in Part 7 from: Steele, John M., *A Brief Introduction To Astronomy in The Middle East*, (Kindle Edition, London: Saqi, 2008).

3 Nogah / Venus has two names in Epiphanius' list. One is basically positive and descriptive (Zerouah / Zerva - see above) and the other Lilith / Loueth and sometimes Dilibath (Dilbat) which have much more negative connotations. Lilith was the name of a particularly seductive woman in Jewish mythology who lead men astray and who was aligned with evil spirits.

4 Other Babylonian names for MUL.BABBAR, were listed on page 14.

5 Tzedek is the name used by Abba Arikka (AD 175–247), also called Rav or Rab. This clearly shows that the name was common by about AD 200. See Babylonian Talmud, Tractate Shabbath, Online edition: www.come-and-hear.com/shabbath/shabbath_156.html#PARTb

6 Finegan, Vardaman, and Yamauchi. *Chronos, Kairos, Christos*, (Winona Lake, Indiana: Eisenbrauns, 1989), 45.

7 Noel Swerdlow, *Ancient Astronomy and Celestial Divination*, (Cambridge, Ma: MIT Press, 1999), 75.

8 I owe these insights to personal discussions with an Arab writer about the meanings of the names Al Zimach or Al-Simak al-A'zal and Al Zimach or Al-Simak Ramih.

9 Richard Hinckley Allen, *Star Names. Their Lore and Meaning*, (New York, 1963: Dover Publications, Inc. Reprint of Allen's 1899), p. 365, 366.

10 http://penelope.uchicago.edu/Thayer/E/Gazetteer/Topics/astronomy/_Texts/secondary/ALLSTA/Virgo*.html

11 Herodotus, *History*, book 2, chap. 109, in Loeb Classical Library, Herodotus, Vol. 1, p. 399.

12 It may be that here we have an explanation of the origin of the twenty-four-hour division of the day. The assignment of planetary stations, two to each sign, over the twelve constellations of the zodiac may have given rise to the substitution of the twenty-four-hour day for the twelve-hour one.

13 Ossendrijver, Mathieu. "Babylonian computational astronomy." Altorientalisches Seminar . Univ. Tubingen. Max Planck Institute, Katlenburg-Lindau. 1 Nov. 2006. Lecture. Notes from this lecture helped me construct the synodic cycle of Jupiter in the details presented on page 132.

14 See Ernest Martin, *The Star that Astonished the World* (online at www.askelm.com/star/), Chapter 4 paragraph six (Chapter About the Real Star of Bethlehem):

> *Jupiter was known astrologically as the Father of the Gods. The planet Jupiter symbolized this deity. And in early August 2 B.C.E. Jupiter had just left its vicinity near the Sun and conjoined with Venus. This could have been an indication of a coming birth. "Jupiter often was associated with the birth of kings and therefore called the King planet."[5] And here was the King planet in conjunction with Venus. To the Chaldeans and the Magi, Venus was Ishtar, the Mother, the Goddess of Fertility. Thus Jupiter (the Father) was now in conjunction with Venus (the Mother). Could this have signified to astrologers that the birth of a new king was imminent?*

Later in the same chapter:

> *Venus (now in its double role as a Mother because the planet was now an evening star) had just extended itself as far east as possible to encounter Jupiter (the King planet) which was moving west in a direct path to meet her. What occurred was a splendid planetary conjunction visible west of Babylon. Besides that, this beautiful conjunction again happened while the planets were in the constellation of Leo (Judah) and at the exact time of the full moon. So close were the two planets that they would have appeared very much like one gigantic star in a "marriage union" with each other.*

If he were still living Ernest Martin would no doubt reject the implications of all these statements. He would probably say that it was a mistake to express things in this way. However, a significant part of his interpretation of the June 17, 2 BC event is founded precisely on such ideas. The "implication" is clear. He might even want to say "I really did not mean that" and he most likely did not. In his interpretation the new king was at least symbolically announced through a coming together of a father and a mother. Martin is groping for understanding and suggesting possible interpretations. The words, "Could this have signified?" is in his text. This is understandable. He is breaking new ground. He does not entirely understand the event nor how to interpret it. Apparently Martin did not know about the traditional Hebrew names otherwise he would have approached the event differently.

Fredrick Larson copies Martin's concept in his DVD (See minute 44 of the DVD). Larson says Venus is the "mother planet" and then he adds "The king star Jupiter came into close conjunction." Then he says "That seems rather pregnant does it not." This is joking, but the real implication is clear. Unintentionally the pagan gods end up being crucial to the interpretation process. Venus is mentioned as the "mother planet" on the web site at: www.bethlehemstar.net/starry-dance/westward-leading/ (1st paragraph).

To clarify:
Venus was not primarily a "mother planet." She was a sex / fertility goddess. Jupiter was not a respectable "father" figure. He was a mar-

ried adulterer god who was sexually involved with very many goddesses and human women in ways that included rape.

Many others have used the same thoughts following Martin's and Lawson's lead. We do not need to continue this type of interpretive method. There is a better way.

15 Enn Kasak, and Raul Veede, "Understanding Planets In Ancient Mesopotamia," (Folklore Vol. 16 ISSN 1406-0957, electronic edition, published by the Folk Belief and Media Group of ELM), page 22.

16 Reiner, Erica, and David Pingree, *Babylonian Planetary Omens,* Groningen: Styx, 1998. p.45

17 N T Wright, *What St Paul Really Said, Was Paul of Tarsus the Real Founder of Christianity?,* (Grand Rapids: Eerdmanns, 1997), 58.

18 Gray, *A Study of Babylonian Goal-Year Planetary Astronomy,* 82.

Part 8: Intro: Events in the Heavens P: 143-152

1 For example the simple exchange of wedding rings and saying vows before a justice of the peace in 1957 signaled and sealed the start of my parents' family. It was an exceedingly simple ceremony but the implications for my own existence and the future of my parents were significant.

2 See page 106.

3 It may only be a coincidence but 26 BC is 490 years after the reconstruction of the Jerusalem temple which was finished in 516 BC. Some Magi could have evoked Daniel's prophecy of the 70 "sevens" at this point, but we have no evidence that this did take place. If someone did evoke the prophecy this may have been the first time anyone would have tied the fulfillment of Daniel's prophecy to an event in the heavens.

4 Pope Benedict XVI, *Jesus of Nazareth The Infancy Narratives,* (London: Bloomsbury Publishing, 2012), 99-100.

5 A series of three conjunctions did take place in 146/145 BC. However, the stopping points were not similar and there was substantial separation between the two planets at various moments.

6 Shabbatei's heliacal rise should have taken place on the 3rd of Nisan according to the Babylonian calendar (April 3rd in the Julian calendar). The 49 lunar months (29.53 days x 49) equal 1447 days. This was from April 1, 7 BC (1 Nisan) to March 17th 3 BC (1 Nisan).

7 Michael R. Molnar, *The Star of Bethlehem: The Legacy of the Magi,* (New Brunswick, N.J.: Rutgers University Press, 1999). This book proposes that the occultation of Jupiter on April 17th, 6 BC was an event which could have signaled the Messiah's birth, the "star" of Bethlehem being Jupiter. The approach taken by Professor Molnar is interesting however, it uses a largely "Western" astrological approach. This perspective does not reflect the ideas presented in *The Lion Led the Way.* It may very well be that biblically informed Magi may have made a connection between the occultation of Jupiter and the promise of a Messiah, but the April 17, 6 BC sign would not have been as strong as some of the indicators in the years (7 BC and 3/2 BC), which were certainly linked to Daniel's prophecy of the 70 "sevens."

Part 9: Events in the Heavens - 1 P: 153-176

1 The author is aware that the new moon sighting on the 1st of Nisan 3 BC (March 17th) could have been somewhat difficult. However, the sighting was very far from being impossible. Normally the date for the beginning of Nisan and Passover would have been fixed from the first day of the visible crescent moon. The date for the 1st of Adar in 3 BC was much more certain and in non-leap years Adar would normally have had 29 days, so even if there were clouds, it is probable that the new moon would have been declared despite the lack of a sighting. God could have easily arranged either clear skies or clouds to be sure that the month of Nisan (Aviv) would start on March 17th 3 BC, thus establishing March 30th as the date of Passover.

2 On April 25th 2013 the author had the personal experience of seeing the nearly full moon in conjunction with Spica/Zerah.

3 In the overall story it may be significant as well that: Nogah (Venus) became visible as a morning star on January 20th about 1/5th of a year before Passover. Nogah / Venus, as a morning star arrived at its greatest elongation from the sun on the 29th of March (at Passover). Visually there would have been no difference the next day on the 30th. Seventy-five days (1/5th of a solar year) later Nogah was in a morning conjunction with Shabbatei (this was 73 days after the First Fruits Offering). This event happened one solar year before the conjunction of Nogah and Melech on June 12th 2 BC.

4 Because of the precession of the equinoxes, Spica/Zerah now rises about three weeks after the dates in the 1st century BC.

5 John was probably doing something similar in John 19:14 were he writes "Now it was the day of preparation for the Passover ... And Pilate said to the Jews, "Behold, your King!" Jesus and his disciples had eaten the Passover meal the night before. However here John uses the term Passover referring to the Feast of Unleavened Bread.

6 <u>*Author's testimony:*</u> When I first understood that Melech was with the moon on the day before Pentecost I thought to myself that it is really too bad that it was not on the day of Pentecost itself (the 50th day). However, later I saw that the 49th day is actually the key moment. It is the last day of the "counting of the omer" which is the signal for Pentecost. The counting is done to the <u>49th</u> day, the seventh Sabbath. Then the 50th day was the festival.

7 It was well known that Kochav Chammah was not visible during this period of time, but even so its position was calculated. See Otto Neugebauer, "Problems and Methods in Babylonian Mathematical Astronomy," Henry Norris Russell Lecture, 1967. The Astronomical Journal, Volume 72, Number 8, October 1947. page 970 .

8 This event concerning Kochav Chammah and Shabbatei most likely indicates that professional astronomers were involved in interpreting the events surrounding Jesus' birth. The fact that this event falls on the 49th day of the counting of the omer is remarkable. Only professional astronomers influenced by Judaism would see the symbolism of this event falling on the 49th day of the omer count (the seventh Sabbath in the Pharisaic manner of counting).

9 The distances were calculated using the astronomy program Voyayer 4.5 by Carinasoft.

10 Alfred Edersheim, *Sketches of Jewish Social Life, Electronic edition,* Chapter 15.

11 The numbers attracted the author's attention. He first concentrated on the Venus cycle because there are a series of conjunctions, etc. related to the number 73. Later it became evident that something was happening with Shabbatei, Pentecost and Daniel's prophecy.

12 It was this set of 70 days which provided a key which opened up Daniel's prophecy of 70 "sevens" for the author.

13 These calculations were done with the astronomy programs Voyager 4.5 and SkySafari. Much of the searching for other conjunctions of Jupiter and Venus in Leo was done manually, year by year.

14 Jack Finegan, *Handbook of Biblical Chronology*, pages 116-126, § 224-231.

15 Otto Neugebauer, *The Exact Sciences in Antiquity,* 2d ed. (New York: Dover Publications, 1969), 121.

16 This question also arose in the author's mind.

17 See note 14.

18 According to the author's calculations concerning the solstices and equinoxes dates listed in the book *Babylonian Horoscopes,* the Babylonian dates seem to fall at the correct moment. However, The Babylonian dates for the solstices and equinoxes in an almanac for 7/6 BC fall about two days after the correct dates. These calculated dates were not accurate. Did anyone correct the errors for the year 3/2 BC. We do not know. See: Francesca Rochberg, *Babylonian Horoscopes,* Philadelphia: American Philosophical Society, 1998), 44.

20 Michael R. Molnar, *The Star of Bethlehem: The Legacy of the Magi,* whole book (See note 7 in Part 8).

21 Occasionally a website or a book mentions that the constellation of Scorpio was sometimes thought of as a great eagle, but the author was not able to find definitive evidence for this. It is definitely associated with an eagle as part of the tetramorph.

Part 10: The Birth of the Messiah P: 177-182

1 Anecdote: The insights into the passages in Jeremiah happened in the fall of 2012 while the author was reading the Book of Jeremiah, while flying over the Sahara Desert on the way to Togo in West Africa.

Part 11: Events in the Heavens - 2 P: 183-196

1 Richard Hinckley Allen, *Star Names. Their Lore and Meaning,* (New York, 1963: Dover Publications, Inc. Reprint of Allen's 1899), p. 365, 366.

2 Robert D. Purrington, "Heliacal Rising and setting: Quantitative Aspects." Archeoastronomy, no. 12 (JHA, xix 1988) 12-13.

3 The moon had also risen in a similar way on June 12th in 26 BC. The two incidents in 26 BC and 2 BC would have been extremely rare.

4 The discussion on the following web page inspired much of this paragraph. http://newswatch.nationalgeographic.com/2011/12/26/searching-for-the-star-of-bethlehem/

5 Below are the calculations of the apparent magnitude of the two planets together. These figures were done by an astronomer and a cosmologist:

In general, a magnitude, m, is expressed as:

$m = -2.5 \log (I/I0)$,

Where I is the intensity and I0 is the intensity of a reference intensity where m = 0. Let m1 and I1 be the magnitude and intensity of Venus, and let m2 and I2 be the magnitude and intensity of Jupiter. Thus,

$m1 = -2.5 \log (I1/I0)$,

and $m2 = -2.5 \log (I2/I0)$.

These can be rearranged as:

I1 = I0 10-0.4m1 and
I2 = I0 10-0.4m2.
The combined intensity is:
I = I1 + I2 = I0 (10-0.4m1 + 10-0.4m2),
And the combined magnitude is:
m = -2.5 log (I/I0) = -2.5 log (10-0.4m1 + 10-0.4m2).
Taking m1 = -4.3 and m2 -1.8, m = -4.4.
The apparent magnitude of the combines stars was -4.4

6 This was apparently the brightest conjunction of two planets which was ever seen. It was not the brightest star ever seen.

Part 12: Events in the Heavens - 3 P: 197-208

1 Baghdad temperatures: http://en.wikipedia.org/wiki/Baghdad

2 These calculations / measurements were done with the Voyager 4.5 astronomy application.

3 It is a truly amazing coincidence that by adding 62 weeks to the date of the hypothetical Sadducean Pentecost in 3 BC brings one exactly to this event, which has the sun in conjunction with Ma'adim (Mars). Would the Magi have been aware of the conjunction? The wise men were certainly aware that Ma'adim was in Leo at that moment. They were capable of at least making an approximate calculation of its position. But did they know? it is not certain. The interpretation of the conjunction of the "blushing, red planet" with the sun is not obvious. The author does not believe that the Creator planned and desired for Ma'adim (Mars) to be associated with war or be known as a negative, malefic planet. The odds of the conjunction happening just at this moment by chance are very small. Perhaps even smaller than the odds concerning the conjunction of Melech (Regulus) with the sun several days earlier. One time each year the sun is in conjunction with Melech (one day out of 365), however, with Ma'adim it only happens once in every 780 days on average (it is somewhat variable). The sun is located in the lion constellation with the king star (Melech) and the king planet (Tzedek) on either side. The words, "sun of righteousness will arise" come to mind (Malachi 4.2), as well as Genesis 49:8-10. But, if there is meaning to the presence of Ma'adim, it is not clear.

Part 13: The Last Events Pages 209-216

1 Noam, Vered, http://www.verednoam.com/html/Publications.html "Megillat Taanit: The Scroll of Fasting", Chapter eight of The Literature of the Sages, Second Part, ed. Shmuel Safrai et al., 339-62.

Page 355 of Vered Noam's text shows how the Megillat Taanit has gone through many changes in the hands of copyists, etc (The Scholions O and P are the Oxford and Parma copies of commentaries on the document which are very different one from the other). Even so combining the Megillat Taanit with known astronomical events seems to indicate that Herod died on the 2nd day of Shevat, January 27/ 28, in 1 BC. The dates for Kislev are too early and the Shevat date fits the incidents well.

2 Antiquities of the Jews Book 17 Chapter 7

3 Jack Finegan, Handbook of Biblical Chronology, p. 297, Section 510.

4 The visible rising could have taken place on the 13th or the 14th. The calculated date done by Alcyone software was on the 13th.

Part 14: Reacting to the Messiah P: 217-222

1 It is amazing to think that the Daniel 9 passage was always in plain view of all who could read the passage. It is said explicitly in the text that the city and the sanctuary would be rebuilt and destroyed again. Why people did not take this to heart in the years leading up to the destruction of Jerusalem and the temple in AD 70 is really difficult to explain.

2 A lunar month is equal to 29.53 days. Calculation: 62 x7 = 434 lunar months. 434 lunar months: 434 X 29.53 days = 12,816 days. The 12816 days start with the month of Jesus conception on the 1st of Nisan 3 BC (March 17th) and they end with the end of the month of Nisan in AD 33 (April 17th). The number of days is too long by two weeks. Such an "anomaly" can be expected over such a long period, especially when one considers that lunar months have 29.53 days (fractions of days). However, there were 434 new moons from the month of Jesus conception to the month of his death (inclusive). The new moon was always the signal for a new month.

Some Recommended Websites

Please note: The author does not necessarily agree with all the attitudes and opinions expressed, or all the information on any of these websites. However, they do all contain useful information. Some websites are much more professionally done than others. The websites are not presented in any particular order. It is very possible that this list does not contain the best sites available. If anyone has suggestions, the author would like to improve the list. You can write to : contact@tzedek.info

The Lion Led the Way Website:
www.tzedek.info (under construction)

Astronomy:

www.alcyone.de
www.calsky.com
www.culturediff.org
www.staff.science.uu.nl/~gent0113/ (Site of Robert Gent)
www.nakedeyeplanets.com
www.imcce.fr

Babylonian Astronomy:

www.caeno.org
www.astronomy.pomona.edu/archeo/outside/aneastro.html
http://members.westnet.com.au/gary-david-thompson/
(Site of Gary D. Thompson)

History of the Period around Jesus' Birth:

www.parthia.com
www.iranicaonline.org
www.forumromanum.org
www.roman-empire.net
www.livius.org/babylonia.html
www.virtualmuseumiraq.cnr.it/homeENG.htm
www.ted.com (Search for "Cyrus Cylinder")
www.iranchamber.com

The Star of Bethlehem:

www.bethlehemstar.net
www.eclipse.net/~molnar/
www.whychristmas.com/customs/star-of-bethlehem.shtml
(There are hundreds of articles about the star of Bethlehem on line, but few full sites).

Dates for Christmas:

www.dec25th.info
www.chronicon.net/blog/category/christmas/
www.christian-history.org
www.biblicalarchaeology.org (How December 25 Became Christmas)

Calendar / Chronology sites:

www.livius.org/caa-can/calendar/calendar_babylonian.html
Babylonian Calendar: www.staff.science.uu.nl/~gent0113/babylon/babycal.htm.
http://en.wikipedia.org/wiki/Babylonian_calendar
www.torahcalendar.com/
www.abdicate.net/cal.aspx
www.webexhibits.org/calendars/calendar-jewish.html
www.jewfaq.org/calendar.htm
www.friesian.com/calendar.htm
www.ortelius.de/kalender/idx_en.php
www.rcyoung.org
www.chronosynchro.net

Judaism / Messianic Judaism:

www.jewfaq.org/
www.chabad.org/
hwww.karaite-korner.org/
www.firstcenturyfoundations.com
www.levitt.com/
www.hebroots.com
www.hebrew4christians.com
http://en.wikipedia.org/wiki/Messianic_Judaism

Online Bibliographies:

Robert Gent: www.staff.science.uu.nl/~gent0113/stellamagorum/stellamagorum_bibl.htm

Made in the USA
Charleston, SC
30 November 2013